CANADA AND
THE UNITED STATES

KENNIKAT PRESS SCHOLARLY REPRINTS

Dr. Ralph Adams Brown, Senior Editor

Series in
**AMERICAN HISTORY AND CULTURE
IN THE TWENTIETH CENTURY**
Under the General Editorial Supervision of
Dr. Donald R. McCoy
Professor of History, University of Kansas

Political Map of the United States and Canada

CANADA AND THE UNITED STATES

Some Aspects of
The History of the Republic and the Dominion

BY

HUGH Ll. KEENLEYSIDE, M.A., Ph.D.

FORMERLY AMERICAN ANTIQUARIAN SOCIETY FELLOW IN AMERI-
CAN HISTORY AT CLARK UNIVERSITY; INSTRUCTOR IN BROWN
UNIVERSITY; SPECIAL LECTURER IN HISTORY AT THE
UNIVERSITY OF BRITISH COLUMBIA

WITH AN INTRODUCTION BY

W. P. M. KENNEDY, M.A., Litt.D.

PROFESSOR OF LAW AND POLITICAL INSTITUTIONS
IN THE UNIVERSITY OF TORONTO

KENNIKAT PRESS
Port Washington, N. Y./London

CANADA AND THE UNITED STATES

First published in 1929
Reissued in 1971 by Kennikat Press
Library of Congress Catalog Card No: 73-137971
ISBN 0-8046-1429-6

Manufactured by Taylor Publishing Company   Dallas, Texas

KENNIKAT SERIES ON AMERICAN HISTORY AND
CULTURE IN THE TWENTIETH CENTURY

TO

MARGARET LOUISE KEENLEYSIDE
ELLIS WILLIAM KEENLEYSIDE

MOST DELIGHTFUL
OF
PARENTS

CONTENTS

MAPS

CHARTS

ix

PREFACE

Geographically the United States and Canada form a single unit; politically and to some extent socially they are divided and unique. The international boundary, cutting laterally through the continent, has in physiographic terms no logical or rational explanation; it is a thoroughly human product. Invisible and illogical as that boundary is, however, it has in certain ways acted as a barrier more effective than a mountain range; marked divisions more radical than an ocean need produce.

Due to causes that have been both political and geographic, the United States has expanded and developed much more rapidly than its northern neighbor, until today the forty-eight States contain a population of 115,000,000 as compared with a meager 10,-000,000 to be found in the provinces and territories of the Dominion of Canada. The United States, moreover, has been managing its own destiny since 1783, while self-determination is a comparatively recent phenomenon in the Dominion.

The proximity of the United States forms a constant and a serious problem to Canadians. Comparatively weak in numbers, limited in present wealth, of secondary importance in world affairs, Canada cannot escape the inevitable comparison with her colossal, wealthy, and potent neighbor. Americans, on the other hand, are seldom reminded of the existence of their northern kinsmen, in spite of the fact that the Dominion ranks first among the customers of the United States, that it sells more to the Republic than does any other state, that it is the *locus* of more than one-fourth of all American foreign investments, and that the total trade between the two countries far exceeds that of any other trading communities.

Canadians can neither forget nor ignore the United States; the influence of the Republic may be seen in every aspect of their lives. In literature and in education, in science and in art, in social standards and in religious concepts, in legislation and above all in economics, the enormous pressure of American custom impinges upon those who reside north of the forty-ninth parallel. Perhaps the clearest evidence of American influence is to be found in the daily and weekly press of the Canadian cities and towns. It is an unusual edition of a Canadian newspaper that does not devote at least one-third of its front page to dispatches originating in the United States; and it is even more unusual to find an issue of a metropolitan journal that does not devote editorial space to American affairs. In the United States, on the other hand, news of Canada—although more common now than ever before—is still extremely rare. The explanation of this condition is perfectly obvious and is not a matter for praise or blame; it is the inevitable result of the juxtaposition of the two countries, their comparative size, and their relative importance.

In studying the history of American-Canadian relations, therefore, it is not surprising to find that the Canadian people have generally known a great deal more about American conditions and have been far more interested in American actions, than Americans have known or cared to know about the situation in the Dominion. The United States is the only foreign country in which Canadians are vitally interested, as it is the only country in a position seriously to influence the course of Canadian history. To Americans, on the other hand, Canada is only one of many foreign states in which they are about equally interested, or perhaps it would be more accurate to say, concerning which they have an equal lack of interest. The Republic is itself so large and so varied that it has little opportunity or incentive to be concerned about foreign affairs. In Canada, however, public opinion is extremely sensitive to American conditions. This situation is not a recent development; it was even more true in the early history of the republic and of British North America. The present book, therefore, will present much more about Canadian opinions and Canadian conditions than about the conditions and opinions of the United States.

The situation is now changing, however, and the American people are slowly but surely turning their attention to the expanding

Dominion. This is probably due, in large part, to the increased economic importance of Canada, but Canadian artists, educators, and even athletes have also played a part in rousing this new interest. The vogue of Canada as a holiday resort has also done something to stimulate American curiosity. But it is, after all, the economic aspect that is most important. "For where your treasure is, there will your heart be also," and Americans have invested three billion dollars in the industries of Canada.

It may be argued, furthermore, that Canadians are less sensitive now than they were during the nineteenth century. The growth of nationalism, the ending of the old colonial subordination to Great Britain, and the extraordinary progress made by the Dominion since 1900 have done much to eliminate the old sense of inferiority and consequent touchiness, but Canadians are still alive to American developments and still vitally interested in the relations of the two states.

In preparing this study of some aspects of the history of North American relations, the author is well aware that he is treading on highly débatable ground. Every incident here discussed has been the center of a more or less serious conflict—a conflict that has enlisted historians as well as politicians or soldiers. Differences of opinion still exist, even among those who cannot be accused of tempering their historical technique to gratify their nationalistic impulses. Under such circumstances the most that any writer can do is to examine the material available, write what he conceives to be the truth,—and concede the same liberty to his critics.

Another difficulty that has had to be faced is that resulting from the innumerable ramifications of the subject. Each chapter could easily have been expanded into a book, each sentence to a chapter. Greater difficulties of selection and elimination could hardly be imagined: the very plenitude of the materials has been a source of difficulty and of trial.

No attempt has been made here to live up to the implications of the remark of Hardy's Spirit Sinister, whose "argument was that War makes rattling good history; but Peace is poor reading." War and threats of war must be recorded in relating the history of Canada and the United States, but of much greater importance are the accomplishments and intercourse of peace. Yet there has been no effort made to prove that the two countries are the unique possessors of the virtues of pacifism. The author is not a chauvinist, but neither is he a professional "ambassador of goodwill."

Much has been written in celebration of the century of peace that has recently been completed, and it is indeed an achievement worthy of all praise—the more so because there have been so many temptations to resort to the code of the barbarian. Indeed without these temptations peace could hardly be looked upon as a virtue. It may also be pointed out that Canada and the United States were not the only nations involved in the century of peace— Great Britain may also well claim a share of the praise, for during a great part of the century it was London that had the final decision on the British side of the controversies.

In bringing together this material in what he hopes will prove to be a convenient form, the author has endeavored to make a small contribution to rational thinking on the subject of international relations. It is only on a sound knowledge of the past that a genuine plan for future decency in the relations of the two states can be based. If this book serves in any degree to aid in the attainment of that knowledge, the hopes of the author will be realized.

Ottawa, Ont.,
January, 1929.

ACKNOWLEDGMENTS

The number of persons who have, in one way or another, assisted in the preparation of this book is so large that it is quite impossible adequately to acknowledge their aid, deeply and sincerely as it is appreciated.

I should be truly ungrateful, however, if I failed to take this opportunity to express my thanks to Dr. George H. Blakeslee of Clark University, and Professor Harry Elmer Barnes of Smith College. It was on the suggestion of Dr. Blakeslee that the work was originally undertaken, and his kindly encouragement and invaluable critical assistance have been a constant support and an unfailing corrective. The encyclopedic range of knowledge and the stimulating friendship of Dr. Barnes have been of the utmost assistance from the beginning to the end of the whole undertaking. No trouble has been too great, no detail too small for his never-failing kindness.

Special mention must also be made of the aid rendered in the final stages of preparation by Dr. George W. Brown of the University of Toronto, assistant editor of *The Canadian Historical Review*. At a considerable personal sacrifice Dr. Brown went over the whole manuscript and gave me the benefit of his exceptional knowledge of Canadian history and his unusual powers of critical discrimination. I must also acknowledge the assistance of Prof. Frederick H. Soward of the University of British Columbia, who examined the first three chapters in detail, and whose friendship and criticism were equally appreciated.

Certain sections of the manuscript were read and annotated by the following gentlemen, whose special knowledge was united to my great benefit—with unusual kindness; Prof. W. Stewart Wallace read the chapter on the Loyalists; Prof. W. N. Sage read the sections on the Oregon Boundary and the Annexation Movement in British Columbia; Mr. William A. Found, Director of Fisheries for the Dominion of Canada, read the chapter on the Fisheries Dispute; Prof. George M. Jones read the sections on the Rebellions of 1837–38 and the Annexation Movement of 1849; Prof. D. A. McArthur and Prof. Kenneth W. Taylor read the chapter on Commercial Intercourse; Prof. Edwin P. Tanner read the whole manuscript but devoted particular attention to Chapters I and III; and Prof. George M. Smith read Chapter X. Mr. Charles A. Magrath, Chairman of the Canadian section of the International Joint Commission, and Mr. Laurence J. Burpee, secretary of that organization, read the pages dealing with the organization and work of the commission. These gentlemen are not, of course, to be held responsible for any mis-statement of fact or failure in interpretation; these are the exclusive responsibility of the author.

Prof. Carl Wittke of Ohio State University, whose *History of Canada* has recently been published, was good enough to read the original manuscript—an almost impossible task—and his suggestions were of the highest value. The same is true of Prof. A. E. Martin of Pennsylvania State College. I am also deeply indebted to Dr. Mack Eastman of the International Labour Office, Geneva, under whose inspiration I first caught a glimpse of the fascination of historical study; to Dr. O. D. Skelton, Under-Secretary of State for External Affairs, Ottawa; to Prof. Walter C. Barnes of the University of Oregon; to Dr. Verner W. Crane of Brown University; to Prof. Ross W. Collins of Syracuse University; to Dr. Julius Klein of the Department of Commerce, Washington; to Mr. R. H. Coats, Dominion Statistician, Ottawa, and to many others who have given of their time and their knowledge to assist one who had no just claim upon either.

Mr. Hugh S. Eayrs, President of the Macmillan Company of Canada, has assisted most generously in the surmounting of obstacles having to do both with the text itself and with its preparation for the printer.

Mention should also be made of the kindness of the members of the staff of the Widener Library at Harvard University; of the Congressional Library, Washington, D. C.; of the American

Antiquarian Society Library, Worcester; of the Dominion Archives, Ottawa; and of the Provincial Libraries at Toronto, Winnipeg, Regina and Victoria.

I must also express my deep gratitude for the highly efficient, painstaking, and generous assistance of Miss Alison Ewart of the University of Toronto. It would be very difficult indeed to find a more competent research assistant.

Above all I must acknowledge the invaluable contributions of my wife, Katherine Hall Keenleyside. At every stage in the preparation of the manuscript her critical advice has been of the greatest value, while without her practical assistance and constant encouragement the task might never have been completed.

Finally, I would acknowledge my indebtedness to Miss Isabel Abercrombie for willing and careful assistance with the typing.

H. L. K.

INTRODUCTION

That knowledge and intelligent study of international affairs constitute important elements in the peaceful progress of the world is a political and social commonplace. A fact, however, of this nature is none the less valuable for being a commonplace; and it is extremely important that it should be emphasized with sincerity and honesty during a period such as this, with a cataclysm in the immediate background, with fears and with failings of hearts making wise decisions more than ever difficult and tending to obscure future international understandings. Too frequently in the past the commonplace has in truth degenerated into intellectual vulgarity, in that superficiality has passed for learning, acquaintanceship for intimacy, and platform and after-dinner affability for that critical insight which ought to guide men of different nations if they would follow the paths of ordered peace and mutual progress. In relation to the United States and Canada all this has been far too prominent. A common language, a common sharing in the economic development of a continent, a common tradition in public and private law and in democratic government and such like have been over-emphasized at the expense of that deeper and more profound knowledge which in reality constitutes international understanding. Indeed, it is not too much to say that the very width of those things which the United States and Canada have in common has been influential in befogging the past, in charging the present with friction, and in loading the future with apprehension. In addition, it is quite evident that the relations between the two nations have been studied and discussed as though they were solely and exclusively Anglo-American. In other words, scholars, statesmen, and public writers and speakers have tended to lay stress on the European or imperial aspect in them at the expense of the ever-developing point of view of British North America. The Canadian community, with its peculiar social, economic, and political values, while not being neglected, has suffered through being viewed too much from London. There was necessary then a study in which a great commonplace should be dignified, and in which the emphasis would be rightly placed. I venture to think, without indeed committing myself either to Dr. Keenleyside's facts or to his interpretations, that this book in its conception and form will fill a long felt want.

Dr. Keenleyside moves along sound lines. First of all, he realizes that the present and future relations between the two nations lie deep in the past. He is, I need hardly say, too fine a scholar to believe in historical determinism; but he does recognize that a national "personality" cannot be divorced from its origins and evolution if understanding of it is to emerge, any more than would be the case in that of a natural person. Thus then, he sets his whole work in a frame of history to which he has brought sound original research and not a little insight, which ought to do valiant service in ridding the whole subject of cant. Secondly, he is not afraid of critical interpretation. I may not, many of his readers may not, agree with him in detail. Be that as it may, Canadian-American relations cannot be explained, much less understood, when governed by a polite and conventional smugness which only covers the inevitable rivalries with a thin veneer of international hypocrisy. Thirdly, he is not afraid to treat the present, to see it in such reality as the spirit within him allows, and to interpret it with such objectivity as human frailty will permit.

No one, then, can read Dr. Keenleyside's study without being convinced of the soundness of his methods and of his general success in accomplishment. I believe that he has set down nought in malice. Little good—indeed great harm—is done when such phrases as "the unguarded line," "blood is thicker than water," "kindred peoples" and so on, do duty for that patient search for truth, that sincerity of knowledge, and that spirit of criticism which wise men ordinarily give to their own affairs. Such search, such sincerity, and such spirit are emphatically necessary amid those vaster activities which we call international; and they are of the very essence of wisdom where our common heritages are so liable to obscure our vast differences. Dr. Keenleyside has done valuable work for civilized progress; for this cannot be without truth, frankness, and insight. It is on these that the real security of Canadian-American relations must be based, and this book will perform an international service of immense importance.

In its æonian processes nature has endowed the United States and Canada with vast economic resources, thus making possible the development side by side of two cultural groups separated politically by the processes of human history. On the other hand, we have daily before our eyes the evidence that forces of interdependence are at work which in the pedestrian affairs of life may tend to cloud realities. It is the function of the scholar and the thinker to see all the forces—to see municipal law and international law, cultural idiosyncrasies and cultural likenesses, the foundations and superstructures of separate political integrity and the foundations and superstructures of moral unity in the things that are more excellent. In a word his quest is philosophical: to relate the many to the one. That quest must be pursued with all the honesty of purpose available if reality of aim is to be realized. I believe that Dr. Keenleyside's book will do much to lift the relationships of the United States and Canada to a plane of sane dignity, removing them from empty verbiage, uninformed deductions, and doctrinaire theories. Insofar as it accomplishes such an end it will have contributed to that future of mutual understanding and peaceful self-respect, each country secure in its independence, which are essential if the facts of interdependence are to bring forth the fruits of a world-wide civilization parallel with the domestic civilization of each state. "A nation is the workshop of the world."

W. P. M. KENNEDY

Baldwin House,
University of Toronto,
February 2, 1929.

CANADA AND
THE UNITED STATES

CHAPTER I

Canada and the American Revolution

I. THE BACKGROUND OF THE REVOLUTION

THE American Revolution divided the English-speaking peoples into two distinct and competing nations. On the continent of North America this division has taken little cognizance of geographical factors, and a territory essentially homogeneous has been bisected by arbitrary political and economic barriers. One result of this condition has been a continuous succession of geographic, economic, and political problems—problems which have frequently led the countries to the verge of war, and which on one occasion did result in armed conflict. The genesis of these international difficulties is to be found in the civil war which disrupted the British Empire in 1783.

To appreciate the national viewpoint of Canada, or of the United States, and to understand the principles upon which these nations were founded, a knowledge of the causes and issues of the American Revolution is essential.

On September 18, 1759, the fortress of Quebec surrendered to Great Britain. Less than four years later France finally renounced all claim to Canada, and the Treaty of Paris [1] marked the termination of one of the most momentous epochs in the political and military history of the world. The Seven Years' War resulted, in its immediate effect, in the relegation of France to the position of a second-rate colonial power, and presaged the world dominance of the so-called Anglo-Saxons—a dominance which apparently will continue at least until the industrial awakening of the Orient brings new factors into world relations. In its immediate effect on the continent of North America, the war resulted in the expulsion of the French government from Quebec, and the establishment in its stead of British rule.

[1] Signed February 10, 1763.

3

Terminating the struggle between two world empires, the Treaty of Paris raised the curtain on civil war. Before 1763 the imminence of French aggressive power had made vitally necessary the protection which the British army and fleet alone could afford the American colonies;[2] but with the foreign foe defeated and peace attained, the ministers of the King found opportunity to institute those internal reforms which the satisfaction of the imperial ideal and the financial embarrassments incurred through the recent war alike demanded.

Imperial reorganization was rendered imperative by the burdens contracted during the lengthy struggle—burdens of administration and of finance, involving a vast territory and varied nationalities. The public debt of Great Britain had risen, by 1763, to the sum of £130,000,000 and this debt was due in large part to the war in the American colonies.[3]

In an attempt to insure at least the partial payment of this debt by those in whose behalf it had been chiefly incurred, the government of George III decided upon the strict enforcement of the Regulatory Laws. Many of these laws had been on the statute book since the days of Cromwell and Charles II, but had never been seriously enforced. They were, as was natural, based upon the mercantilist theory—an economic doctrine that was accepted without argument by the statesmen and economists of the

[2] This was recognized at the time by some of the more clear-sighted observers. Peter Kalm, the distinguished explorer, wrote in the middle of the eighteenth century: "The English Government has sufficient reason to consider the French in North America as the best means of keeping the Colonies in their due subjection." *Travels* (English translation), London, 1770–1771, vol. I, pp. 264–265. See also Vergennes, quoted in Bancroft, *History of the United States,* New York, 1885, vol. I, p. 525: "England will soon regret having removed the only check that will keep her colonies in awe." Lecky, in *The American Revolution,* New York, 1905, p. 3, declares that William Burke and others favored returning Canada to France for this reason.

[3] *Journals of the House of Commons,* XXIX, p. 760, where the funded debt is stated to be £129,586,789. Chalmers, in his *Estimate of the Strength of Great Britain,* states that the debt due to the Seven Years' War was £72,111,000.

day.[4] Restrictive laws were, therefore, supplemented in number and made effective in practice.

Inter-colonial feuds [5]—for even during the French war the colonies had never united in any lasting community of purpose [6] —and, what was even more important, the addition of Canada and the Mississippi Valley to the British holdings in North America, made *administrative* reform essential.[7] The demands of this reorganization required the presence in America of British civil and military officials. Thus, not only did the new regulations react unfavorably upon the business interests of the colonies, but a bureaucratic social caste was strengthened. The philosophy of this class inevitably conflicted with the doctrines of individualism and equality which were inherent in a society characterized by frontier conditions.[8]

The background of the American opposition to the new laws is to be discovered in the considerable period during which the colonies had been almost completely free from external regulation. Between 1660 and 1763 the American colonies had enjoyed an economic freedom unknown in any other colonial system of the period.[9] Legally, the Regulatory Laws of 1660 were operative

[4] Great Britain was, in reality, the only colonial power that had not fully applied, or attempted to apply, the principles of this doctrine. See G. L. Beer, *The Commercial Policy of England toward the American Colonies,* New York, 1893, pp. 8–9; C. M. Andrews, *Colonial Self-Government,* New York, 1904, chap. 1; Haney, *History of Economic Thought,* New York, 1911, pp. 87–112.

[5] To this may be added colonial disagreements between the colonies and the mother country. See McCormack, *Colonial Opposition to the British Empire During the French and Indian War* (University of California Publications in History).

[6] Beer, *British Colonial Policy,* New York, 1907, pp. 228–316; Becker, *The Beginnings of the American People,* Boston, 1915, pp. 203–213, 236.

[7] This is the thesis of Alvord's very able work, *The Mississippi Valley in British Politics,* Cleveland, 1917.

[8] See Turner, *The Frontier in American History.* New York, 1920.

[9] Woodburn, *The Causes of the American Revolution,* Baltimore, 1892, pp. 56–57; S. G. Fisher, *The True History of the American Revolution,* Philadelphia, 1912, pp. 26–27; Adams, *Revolutionary New England, 1691–1776,* Boston, 1923; Schlesinger, *New Viewpoints in American History,* New York, 1922, chap. 7.

during this period, but in fact they were consistently ignored. Thus, the colonists had become accustomed to a status of self-government, and representative institutions had developed to a stage far beyond that attained in England itself.[10] They had controlled their executive through the "bargain and sale" procedure,[11] and had enjoyed an economic and legislative freedom which was an exact reversal of the practice in French and Spanish colonies.[12] It was, therefore, logically impossible to expect that the colonists would peacefully agree to accept the restrictions which enforcement of the existing laws would entail. Habit and interest were both opposed. "Great Britain had given the colonies free rein for too long a period to make it safe or practicable to attempt the enforcement of any important and extensive restrictive regulations, however legally or morally just they may have been." [13]

Thus every action of the British government was obnoxious to the long unrestricted colonists and, judged by the standards of today, these actions were unduly repressive and altogether unjustified. Given the economic theory of the time, however, they were the just and unavoidable result of the new problems forced upon imperial Britain after 1763. It was not a matter for censure or praise; it was the logical result of the existing conditions. Or again, as one of America's foremost historians has well expressed it, "after a century of great laxity towards the Colonies,—a century in which the colonists were favored by political privileges shared by no other people of that age; after environment had established new social conditions, and remoteness and isolation had created a local and individual hatred of restraint; after the absence of traditions had made possible the institution of representation by population, and self-government had taken on a new meaning in the world; after a great gulf had been fixed between

10 Van Tyne, *The American Revolution*, New York, 1905, pp. 12–14; H. E. Barnes, *Anglo-American Relations Reconsidered*, Clark University, 1921; Goldwyn Smith, *The United States*, London, 1907, pp. 68 ff.

11 E. B. Greene, *The Provincial Governor*, New York, 1898, pp. 204 ff.

12 Van Tyne, *op. cit.*, pp. 45–46; see also Bruce, *Institutional History of Virginia in the Seventeenth Century*, New York, 1910.

13 Barnes, *op. cit.*

the social, political and economic institutions of the British Empire—only then did the British government enter upon a policy intended to make the empire a unity." [14]

Psychologically, the colonists had long been independent; it required only an overt act on the part of Great Britain to arouse a demand for legal freedom. The reorganization of 1763 to 1775 provided the needed impetus.

From this background, hastened and provoked by the personal ambitions and antipathies of the leaders,[15] arose the American Revolution. Colonist turned against Englishman, and the empire so recently acquired was rent apart by civil strife.[16] In the American Revolution, Americans and Canadians—as such—for the first time came face to face in conflict.[17]

2. CANADA AFTER THE BRITISH CONQUEST

When Quebec surrendered to the British in 1759, Canada had a French population of approximately 70,000. The vast majority of this total were the habitants—simple peasant farmers, kindly in spirit, industrious and devout. They were, primarily, tillers of the soil, and, in a small way, trappers; yet, when occasion demanded, they had been ready to exchange the hoe for a musket, and, under the leadership of their semi-feudal overlords, to go forth to battle against the hated foreigner. "A strong healthy race," wrote Governor Murray, "plain in their dress, virtuous in their morals; temperate in their living." [18] Nominally occupying a political and social status comparable with that of the medieval peasant of Europe, the French-Canadian habitant [19] enjoyed in fact a more worthy position. It is true that he was unlearned and

[14] Van Tyne, *op. cit.*, p. 45
[15] See Schlesinger, *New Viewpoints in American History,* New York, 1922, pp. 166–167.
[16] McIlwain, *The American Revolution: A Constitutional Interpretation,* New York, 1923.
[17] Fisher, *The Struggle for American Independence,* Philadelphia, 1908, vol. I, pp. 206–213.
[18] "Murray's Report, June 5th, 1762," *Canadian Archives,* B. 7, p. 55.
[19] He even objected to the use of the term "peasant."

credulous; but it is also true that he was very largely free from feudal dues and services. He had a simple, firm, and direct belief in a personal Devil, a literal Hell, and the innate wickedness of man, but in this he was not unique. His economic situation was, on the whole, satisfactory, and if he was at times dragged away to unwelcome military service or oppressed by a petty tyrant among the nobles, his general lot was infinitely superior to that of his European cousin. His land was protected by legal agreements, his services to seigneur and priest were clearly understood and might not be lightly altered either to his detriment or to his benefit. He was neither educated nor free, but he was busy and, on the whole, content.[20]

The nobility of New France was a miscellaneous class.[21] From the military and executive officials of Quebec to the simple seigneur of the Yamaska River was a far longer descent than that from the latter to the lowly habitant. Many of the seigneurs worked as hard and lived almost as humbly as did their legal inferiors. It was an honor to be a seigneur, but hardly a privilege. To be an official of the Crown was, however, another matter. This class, accustomed to the old world prerogatives of their order, did not lose the feudal spirit in their new surroundings. Rulers in peace and leaders in war, they did not suffer defeat gladly, and many of them returned to France in 1763.[22]

Occupying a position more powerful than either habitants or *noblesse* were the clergy of the Roman Catholic church. The secular and regular clergy combined to control not only the conscience, but, to a lesser degree, even the person and possessions

[20] On the habitant, see: Garneau, *Histoire du Canada,* Paris, 1913, vol. IV, chap. 1; Munro, *The Seigneurs of Old Canada,* Toronto, 1915 (an excellent study); Parkman, *The Old Régime in Canada,* Boston, 1901. It should be noted that religious unity was maintained and economic and social progress retarded by the laws prohibiting entry of Huguenots and other heretics as settlers in New France.

[21] Munro, *op. cit.,* chaps. 1–4; *Canadian Archives,* B. 7, p. 55; Parkman, *op. cit.,* pp. 232, 294, 305.

[22] For the extensive privileges of the leading seigneurs, see *Report on Canadian Archives, 1899,* pp. 122–123; also *Seigneurial Tenure, Titles and Documents,* Legislative Assembly, Quebec, 1851, pp. 37–39.

of their ignorant communicants. All education and much of the local government was directly in the hands of the clergy. Living, in many instances, brave, self-sacrificing, and adventurous lives, they were acquainted also with the sources of power, the paths of wealth. The influence of the clergy was so great that few, even the most exalted administrators or nobles, cared to offend the priest in holy orders. The absence of the printing-press was no inconsiderable factor in the maintenance of their control.[23] With the coming of the British, their power was weakened, but was not annulled.

For the greater part of the history of New France trade had been a governmental or a private monopoly, and in consequence no strong commercial middle class had developed. The few important merchants domiciled in the colony were closely allied with the political and military leaders. For many years before the coming of the British, graft, jobbery, and corruption were not uncommon in Canadian life. The habitant was oppressed by every method of political and commercial chicanery, with the result that moral degenerates, such as Bigot, and fools, such as Vaudreuil, were enabled to live in luxury and lascivious extravagance. Against these conditions the honorable and able Montcalm had fought in vain, and on the Governor and the Intendant rests, and should rest, a large part of the immediate blame for the success of British arms in the capture of New France.[24]

This, then, was the colonial organism against which the British fought, and in its political and economic aspects it was overthrown by the invaders.[25] A military government was at once established under General Murray, the most unusual of all rulers—a tolerant militarist. Under his reasonable and kindly control, the habitants enjoyed a freedom from military burdens and a security against unjust taxation to which they had long been strangers. Strict financial probity was demanded of the British officials; feudal dues were abolished; freedom of worship, including the abolition of compulsory tithes, was assured; and many French-Cana-

[23] Garneau, *op. cit.*, vol. III, chap. 4.
[24] Parkman, *Montcalm and Wolfe*, Boston, 1901, chap. 23.
[25] Eastman, *Church and State in Early Canada*, New York, 1910.

dians were employed in the legal and political administration.[26]

Following the estabishment of the British rule, traders, both from the homeland and from the American colonies, began to appear in Canada. Almost immediately, in an effort to exploit the one and thwart the other, this new element entered into conflict with both the French people and the British military officials. In their striving for wealth they were violently impatient of all obstacles. General Murray characterized the traders of Montreal as "the most immoral collection of men I ever knew." [27] Later on, Governor Carleton, who was of a similar opinion, added to the bitterness of the new arrivals by depriving the Justices of the Peace of their civil jurisdiction—a power which he believed them to be using to the detriment of the habitants.[28] Making full allowance for the differences which were bound to arise between the military and the commercial interests in the colony, for the exasperation which colored the reports of Murray and Carleton, and in spite of the proof which is available regarding the integrity of some individual merchants, it still may be admitted that the Governor was probably exaggerating very little when he wrote that these traders "all have their fortunes to make, and are little solicitous about the means." [29] It is not an unusual attitude. They were, and it is not peculiar to their day or occupation, more concerned with results than with methods.

In August, 1764, the military regime was ended, and a civil administration substituted. By the terms of the proclamation marking this change, the supreme executive powers were placed in the hands of a Governor-in-Chief, appointed by the Crown, and supported by a council with whose "advice and consent" he was expected to act. The proclamation established English civil as well as military law; required an oath of loyalty and a declaration against transubstantiation of all who would seek office or exercise the franchise; and it professed to hope for the establishment of a

[26] Lareau, *Histoire du droit canadien,* Montreal, 1888–1889, vol. II, p. 87; *Canadian Archives,* Q. 2, p. 87; Trevelyan, *The American Revolution,* London, 1903, vol. I, p. 70.

[27] *Canadian Archives,* B. 8, p. 1.

[28] *Idem,* Q. 5, p. 260.

[29] *Idem,* Q. 2, p. 233.

representative form of government "as soon as the state and circumstances of the said colonies will admit." [30] The execution of this last suggestion was obviously impracticable so long as the civil disabilities remained to disqualify Roman Catholics. In 1764 a representative system of government in Canada would have meant that a few hundred English Protestants would have elected representatives to legislate for more than seventy thousand Catholic Canadians.[31] Impossible as such a condition would have been, the British traders of Montreal and Quebec continually demanded the fulfilment of this "promise," and kept the colony in a state of turmoil for many years.[32]

In spite of the best efforts of Governor Murray,[33] and later of Sir Guy Carleton, to administer justice to all classes in the community, conditions grew steadily worse during the decade following 1764. The clergy were displeased by the abolition of compulsory tithing; the power of the nobles was shattered by English civil law; the British citizens clamored for representative government; and the habitants, disturbed by the general unrest, felt a logical dislike for the foreign conquerors, and disapproved such radical innovations as trial by jury.[34] So unsatisfactory was the whole situation that Carleton finally returned to London, and by persistent and powerful lobbying succeeded in securing the passage of a new legal instrument for the government of Canada. The principles of the famous Quebec Act of 1774 were very largely the product of his mind, and its passage was primarily due to his efforts.[35]

[30] *Canadian Archives,* Q. 62, p. 114.

[31] Coffin, *The Province of Quebec and the Early American Revolution,* University of Wisconsin, June, 1896, pp. 444 ff. See also a review of Coffin by Adam Shortt in *Review of Historical Publications Relating to Canada,* University of Toronto, 1897, vol. I; also Bolton and Marshall, *The Colonization of North America, 1492–1920,* New York, 1920, p. 419.

[32] *Canadian Archives,* Q. 10, p. 56.

[33] For details of Murray's incumbency, see Mahon, *Life of General The Hon. James Murray,* London, 1921, chaps. XIII–XVI.

[34] *Annual Register, 1774,* p. 75.

[35] It should not be overlooked, however, that the situation in the thirteen colonies also influenced the British government in drafting the terms of the act. This influence is most clearly shown in the clauses extending the bound-

The Quebec Act extended the boundaries of Canada to include "all the lands beyond the Alleghanies coveted and claimed by the old English Colonies." [36] Executive and legislative powers were placed in the hands of the Governor and a legislative council appointed by the Crown; English criminal law was retained, but the civil law of France was reëstablished, thus doing away with trial by jury and *habeas corpus*. The Roman Catholic religion was recognized subject to "the King's supremacy, declared and established," and the forbidding of "all appeals to, or correspondence with, any foreign ecclesiastical jurisdiction." The oath of allegiance was so altered as to allow Roman Catholics to sit on the Council—a condition not paralleled in England until 1829. Compulsory tithing was again introduced for all who professed the Roman Catholic faith.[37]

The Quebec Act inaugurated a new form of control, and one more efficient than any hitherto evolved in British Canada. That the Mississippi valley should be placed under the control of the new administration at Quebec was due to two important factors: the unstable conditions existing in the thirteen colonies, and the fact that throughout the period of French domination this territory had been ruled from Canada. In the latter respect, the Quebec Act did not inaugurate a new policy: it merely reëstablished a tradition. To what extent the idea of "hemming in" the rebellious Atlantic colonies was present in the minds of those who framed the Quebec Act, is still a matter of conjecture and dispute.[38] No doubts on this subject, however, were expressed by

aries of Canada to include the Ohio and Mississippi valleys. As Professor McArthur has said, the British government had "one eye on Boston, the other on Quebec." For the terms of the Quebec Act, see Kennedy, *Documents of the Canadian Constitution, 1759-1915*, Ottawa, 1918; the latest monograph on the subject is Coupland, *The Quebec Act*, Oxford University Press, 1925, reviewed by Adam Shortt in *The Canadian Historical Review*, December, 1925, pp. 357–360. See also Cavendish, *Debates on the Canada Bill in 1774*, London, 1839.

[36] Bourinot, *op. cit.*, p. 46.

[37] Egerton and Grant, *Canadian Constitutional Development*, pp. 3–97; Egerton, *A Short History of British Colonial Policy*, London, 1913, Book II, chap. 9.

[38] Opposing views may be found in J. Winsor, "Virginia and the Quebec

the citizens of Boston and New York. The act formed the basis for one of the major grievances advanced against the Crown by the Revolutionary leaders in the colonies.[39] Among others, Alexander Hamilton analyzed it at some length and proved, at least to his own satisfaction, that its real object was to encircle the thirteen colonies in a ring of British steel.[40] The concessions to the Roman Catholic church were also assailed by the non-conformists of New England in terms more violent than sagacious.[41]

The results of few legislative enactments have been more widely discussed, or more variously interpreted, than those which followed the promulgation of the Quebec Act in 1774. It is a subject upon which no historian can be dogmatic. The influence of the act was most injurious on the attitude of the thirteen colonies toward the mother country. But the older and more conventional idea that it succeeded in attaching all classes of Canadian society to the British Crown, and thereby saved that colony for the empire when America revolted, has now been generally discarded. It is true that the Roman Catholic clergy were gratified by the legal assurance of their tithes, for during the first decade of English rule they had encountered no little difficulty in this connection.[42] It is also true that the nobles were grateful, for the

Bill," *American Historical Review,* April, 1896, vol. I, p. 436, and M. Farrand, *The Development of the United States,* Boston, 1918, p. 42. More recent studies, in addition to Coupland, may be referred to: E. P. Hamilton Smith, *The Quebec Act,* unpublished, University of Toronto, 1921; F. H. Soward, *The Purpose and Immediate Operation of the Canada Act of 1791,* unpublished but summarized in "The Struggle over the Laws of Canada, 1783–1791," *Canadian Historical Review,* Dec., 1924; Kennedy, *The Constitution of Canada,* Oxford, 1923; William Smith, "The Struggle over the Laws of Canada, 1763–1783," *Canadian Historical Review,* June, 1920.

[39] Wrong, *Washington and His Comrades,* Yale, 1921, pp. 38–39. See also the reference to the Quebec Act in the Declaration of Independence, and Brymner, *Report on Canadian Archives, 1890,* p. 20.

[40] Henry Cabot Lodge (editor), *The Works of Alexander Hamilton,* London, 1885, vol. I, pp. 173–188.

[41] Farrand, *op. cit.,* p. 42. One New England pastor declared that the Quebec Act must have caused a "jubilee in Hell." See Smith, *op. cit.,* vol. I, pp. 32 ff.

[42] *Canadian Archives,* B. 8, p. 1 ff.

tendency of the new law was to return to them the honors and prerogatives which they had enjoyed under the old regime.[43]

The English traders in the larger towns, however, were vigorously opposed to the Quebec Act, and they carried on a constant propaganda against it among the ignorant peasantry. Needless to say, these merchants were not interested in protecting the habitants; the latter were merely the most convenient tools for use against the Governor.[44] These attacks were very similar to those being made against the British policy by the mercantile classes of Massachusetts and Virginia. The privileges and the restrictions of the law were alike denounced, and in time many of the peasantry began to understand the implications of "that damned word, Liberty." [45] On the whole, however, the habitants appear to have been indifferent rather than opposed, although the revival of the compulsory tithe, so pleasing to the priesthood, was a matter of dissatisfaction to the peasants. Of some of the latter it can probably be justly said that this act "which was supposed to comprise all they either wished or wanted, had become the first object of their discontent and dislike." [46] This, however, was true only of a minority; but the number steadily increased as a result of the ceaseless propaganda carried on by the British traders—a propaganda which did much to make the soil receptive to the argument of the emissaries of the Continental Congress, and, later, of the American soldiery.[47]

[43] Smith, *op. cit.*, vol. I, p. 67; Chapais, *Cours d'Histoire du Canada,* Quebec, 1919, vol. I, pp. 135ff; Groulx, *Vers l'émancipation,* Montreal, 1921, pp. 167 ff.

[44] Carleton of course, had the typical aristocratic attitude toward the trading class. Moreover he felt that Canada would, and should, remain entirely French in population. He not only wanted no more English settlers, but desired to get rid of those already there. Adam Shortt, *Canadian Historical Review,* Dec., 1925, p. 538; Soward, *op. cit.,* p. 7.

[45] *Colonial Correspondence,* Public Records Office, Quebec, Vol. II, p. 14.

[46] Hey to Chancellor, Aug. 28, 1775. *Canadian Archives,* Q. 12, p. 203.

[47] Bradley, *The Making of Canada,* New York, 1908, pp. 74 ff. "Supplemented as it was by the misrepresentation of its opponents, and still more by the most ill-advised attempt to establish through it the old military position of the noblesse, it drove the people into the arms of the revolutionists." Coffin, *The Province of Quebec and the Early American Revolution*

In spite of the criticisms of the Quebec Act, it did improve the immediate conditions in Canada. Whether or not the policy of conciliation toward French-Canadian culture here adopted has been advantageous to Canada, viewing her history as a whole, and particularly the present divisions in the Dominion, is a question yet unanswered.

3. CANADA AND THE COMMITTEES OF CORRESPONDENCE

This, then, was the situation in Canada when, on September 5, 1774, the first Continental Congress met in Philadelphia.

Inasmuch as Canadian conditions had formed the subject of many and vigorous complaints on the part of American radical leaders from 1763 down to the date of the Congress, it was logical that the position of Canada should be seriously discussed in that famous gathering. Nor was the subject forgotten by the press and platform of the day. Throughout the thirteen colonies there was a real desire for the inclusion of Canada in any scheme of opposition to Great Britain.[48] American leaders and people alike were convinced that Canada should be included if federation and rebellion were resolved upon.[49] The Congress took immediate action to fulfil this popular desire. On October 26th an address was ordered to be printed for distribution in Canada. This document spoke largely of the "transcendent nature of freedom" which was to overcome all differences of language and religion. It went on to invite assistance in united opposition to the arbitrary actions of Great Britain. In closing, it even went so far as to suggest that punishment would follow in the event of a

(University of Wisconsin Bulletins, Economic and Historical, no. 1.), Madison, 1896, p. 506.

[48] Franklin in particular was insistent upon the subject; see letter of March 17, 1775, of Franklin to his son in Sparks (editor), *Franklin's Works*, Boston, 1837, vol. V, pp. 4, 65. See also Samuel F. Bemis (editor), *The American Secretaries of States and Their Diplomacy*, New York, 1927, vol. I, pp. 11–13.

[49] Riddell, *The International Relations Between the United States and Canada—An Historical Sketch*, Maryland Peace Society, 1911, no. 5, p. 5.

refusal to coöperate.[50] It is estimated that over two thousand copies of this document were circulating in Canada by the following March.[51] Its effect was strengthened by American emissaries who went among the Canadians, playing on their fears with tales of the Inquisition which the British were about to establish; of oppressive taxes to be imposed; and of foreign wars in which the manhood of New France would be sacrificed.[52]

During October, 1774, the British residents of Canada gave a practical demonstration of their sympathy for the revolutionary leaders. Aroused by reports of royal oppression in Boston, many of the merchants of Montreal and Quebec combined to collect and ship a contribution of grain and of money to the New England port.[53]

Early in February, 1775, the leaders of the American patriots decided to issue a more formal invitation to Canada to join in the struggle against Great Britain. Congress referred the matter to the Boston Committee of Correspondence. This committee met on February 20th and Samuel Adams was instructed to draw up a letter to the merchants of Montreal.[54] The letter as finally drawn contained a statement of the economic and political grievances of New England; a denunciation of the Quebec Act as a despotic imposition against which all loyal Canadians should revolt; an invitation to send delegates to the second session of the Congress, which was to meet in Philadelphia on May 10th; and a request "for the return of this message with your own sentiments."[55]

The reply from Montreal was sympathetic but hopeless. Canada was depicted as being in a worse condition than New England, and the administration as too strongly entrenched for attack.[56] Interpreted in the light of modern knowledge, this meant that Walker

[50] Bradley, *op. cit.,* p. 66; Smith, *op. cit.,* p. 101.

[51] *Canadian Archives,* Q. 11, p. 129.

[52] Bradley, *op. cit.,* pp. 66 ff.

[53] Smith, *Our Struggle for the Fourteenth Colony: Canada and the American Revolution,* New York, 1907.

[54] John Adams, *Works,* Boston, 1856, vol. X, p. 251.

[55] Quoted in Smith, *op. cit.,* vol. I, pp. 92–93.

[56] Codman, *Arnold's Expedition to Canada,* New York, 1901, p. 7.

and the other merchants of Montreal, though sympathetic with the cause of revolt, knew that such a solution was impossible in Canada at that time, and that the only result would be the loss of a very lucrative fur trade.

A third letter, following the same lines as its predecessors, was written by John Jay on May 29, 1775, and forwarded to the "oppressed inhabitants of Canada." [57]

When it had become apparent that no real assistance could be expected from Canada, and when the appeal to arms had finally been made, the patriot leaders began to look with apprehension toward the northern boundary of the colonies. Knowing by reputation something of the ability and energy of Sir Guy Carleton, the fear of an invasion from the north was a constantly growing anxiety.[58] In reality, Carleton was in no position to wage an offensive war, as his forces had been reduced to the danger point in favor of General Gage, who was campaigning in New England. Moreover, the habitants in many districts were demonstrating a decided disinclination to obey orders.[59] The failure of the British leaders to recognize the situation in Canada is clearly evidenced by the instructions sent to Carleton in 1775, inviting him to enroll six thousand French-Canadians for immediate service. Sixty willing recruits would have surprised him at the time.[60] But the American Congress, failing to recognize the impotence of the Canadian Governor, came to agree with Arnold in his declaration that an invasion of Canada was made necessary by "a due regard to our defense." [61] Congress hoped by one

[57] Johnson (editor), *Correspondence and Public Letters of John Jay,* London, 1890, vol. I, pp. 32–36.

[58] Fiske, *The War of Independence,* Boston, 1889, p. 93. In common with many other American historians, Fiske overlooks the inherent impossibility of such an attack, and accepts as fully justified the fears of Adams and Arnold.

[59] In May, 1775, many of the French-Canadians refused to enroll, at Carleton's order, to repel the attacks of Ethan Allen and Benedict Arnold on Crown Point and Ticonderoga. Both places were captured. *Canadian Archives,* Q. 12, p. 203.

[60] W. Wood, *The Father of British Canada,* Toronto, 1916, p. 73.

[61] Arnold's message to the second Continental Congress, in 4 *American Archives* II, p. 976.

strong action to defeat an enemy, conquer a country, remove the fear of a flank attack, gain recruits, and liberate a people.

4. THE AMERICAN INVASION OF CANADA

An invasion having been determined upon, General Schuyler was appointed to relieve Arnold of his command at Ticonderoga, which became the rendezvous of the American forces.[62] The plan of campaign provided for simultaneous attacks upon Montreal and Quebec.[63] It was hoped that Quebec could be stormed while Carleton was defending Montreal, a development which would inevitably result in his subsequent surrender and a complete conquest of Canada. The fatal weakness in this plan lay in discounting British sea control, which made a real blockade of Quebec impossible.[64]

The first care of General Schuyler was to send emissaries into Canada to observe the temper of the inhabitants, and to report on the military situation. The information obtained by General Schuyler,[65] together with the letters of Carleton, Cramahe and other British officials give a vivid, if overdrawn, picture of Canadian feeling. John Brown, Schuyler's personal representative, reported that everywhere he was received with the greatest kindness, and that the inhabitants appeared unitedly favorable to the American cause.[66] Schuyler wrote to Washington that "accounts from all quarters agree that the Canadians are friendly to us," [67] and a little later he reported to the New York Congress that "they

[62] Smith, *op. cit.*, vol. I, p. 241.

[63] No plans were made to attack Nova Scotia, as it was felt by the Americans that this territory would inevitably join the revolting colonies if the latter gave evidence of success in their struggle. In regard to Nova Scotia, see 4 *American Archives* III, pp. 90, 619, 1127, 1184; *idem,* V, pp. 522–524, 936–939.

[64] 4 *American Archives* III, pp. 926, 927, 945, 947.

[65] *Idem,* II, pp. 1676, 1702, 1704, 1808, 1892, etc.

[66] *Idem,* III, p. 135; Almon, *Remembrancer,* London, 1775.

[67] Schuyler and Washington, July 18, 1775. 4 *American Archives* II, p. 1685.

are friendly to us and join us in great numbers," [68] On September
21, 1775, Cramahe wrote to Carleton that many Canadians were
actually serving with the Americans. "No means have been left
untried," he said, "to bring the Canadian peasantry to a sense
of their duty, and engage them to take up arms in defense of
the Province, but all to no purpose." [69] On the same day Carleton himself reported that "the Americans have been more successful with them and have assembled them in great numbers." [70]

Reassured by the reports of their agents, the American forces
moved forward into Canada. Over a thousand men under Arnold
started from Cambridge to attack Quebec, while the main force
under Schuyler followed the old French route along Lake Champlain, the Richelieu, and the St. Lawrence rivers in the direction
of Montreal. The British made their first defense at Fort St.
John's, some twenty-five miles southeast of Montreal, and a
protracted siege ensued. Here General Schuyler, lacking the
physical energy demanded by winter campaigning, and suffering
from a disease that gave him little respite, was forced to give up
his command, and was succeeded by the brilliant and impetuous
Montgomery. On November 1st St. John's fell and with it the
Americans captured about two-thirds of all the regular troops
in Canada.[71]

The way was now open to Montreal, and Montgomery entered
the city on November 13th, capturing stores and ammunition that
had been collected for the use of Carleton's troops. Carleton himself had left the city during the night, taking all of the boats
that were in condition to sail. The ships, however, were becalmed
a few miles below the city, and Montgomery sent troops and
guns to stop them at the point near Sorel where the river nar-

[68] Schuyler to New York Congress, September 29, 1775. 4 *American Archives* III, p. 841.
[69] Cramahe to Carleton, September 21, 1775, *Canadian Archives*, Q. 11, p. 249.
[70] *Canadian Archives*, Q. 11, p. 261.
[71] 4 *American Archives*, III, pp. 1374, 1395. Montgomery here took 41 cannon, 11 boats, 688 prisoners, and stores and ammunition. Wood, *op. cit.*, p. 80. *Canadian Archives*, Q. 11, pp. 278, 282, 284; Jones, *New York in the Revolution*, vol. I, p. 58.

rowed. But Carleton outwitted his enemies, escaping during the
night in a small boat that drifted past the American patrols, and
was rowed with muffled oars, silently, in the shadows of the
bank.

The American successes at St. John's and Montreal still further
influenced the wavering Canadians. In spite of the influence and
vigorous loyalty of the Roman Catholic priesthood, who even
went so far as to refuse absolution to all traitors,[72] the American
battalions daily increased as the Canadian militia melted away.[73]
In his report from Montreal on November 24th, Montgomery
wrote that he "could have as many Canadians as I know how to
maintain"; then wisely added, "at least I think so, while affairs
wear so promising a prospect." [74] Montgomery's difficulty was
financial: he could "maintain" very few. Had he been strongly
supported with "hard" money, so that he could have taken full
advantage of the favorable conditions, the whole history of the
continent might have been vitally affected. Carleton, as he wrote
to Lord Dartmouth, could do little to offset the drawing power
of American success, as he lacked both financial and military
strength.[75]

On November 19th Carleton arrived in Quebec, after an adventurous journey from Montreal, and his appearance was hailed
with "unspeakable joy" by "the friends of the government," and
with "the utter dismay of the abettors of sedition and rebellion." [76] But a third greeting also awaited him—a greeting from
the muskets of an investing army of some five hundred and
fifty Americans under the resolute leadership of Benedict Arnold.

Much has been written upon the strategic importance of the
city of Quebec. As well as being the only post in Canada which
"had the least claim to be called a fortified place," [77] it was the

[72] *Canadian Archives,* B. 27, p. 398; Jones, *Expedition to Canada,* p. 33;
Journal of the Principal Occurrences During the Siege of Quebec, London, 1804.

[73] *Canadian Archives,* Q. 12, p. 274.

[74] 4 *American Archives* IV, pp. 220, 1392; *idem,* III, pp. 1012, 1098.

[75] *Canadian Archives,* Q. 11, p. 261.

[76] 4 *American Archives* III, p. 1696.

[77] Carleton to Shelbourne, quoted in Shortt and Doughty, *Canada and
its Provinces,* Edinburgh, 1914–1917, vol. III, p. 96.

key to the defenses of the colony, and, until it was captured, Canada was unconquered. The taking of Quebec was, then, the fundamental object of American strategy. To this end Washington had dispatched Arnold, with eleven hundred picked men from Massachusetts, overland to the St. Lawrence. At Quebec he was to join forces with Montgomery, descending from Montreal, and together they were to possess themselves of the key to continental power.

In spite of the lurid exaggerations so commonly employed in describing Arnold's march, the event does deserve a high place in the annals of military achievement. Leaving Cambridge with more than one thousand sturdy men, he struggled for three hundred miles through the autumnal wilderness, by swift streams and long portages, through the pathless forest and over windswept hills, soaked by day and freezing by night, harassed by accident and desertion, ever menaced by hostile Indians,[78] and with a diminishing supply of food. Finally exhausted, their clothing torn and their shoes in shreds, weak with hunger and disease, and leaving one-third of their number dead upon the way, he and his men accomplished their journey and sighted their objective.

After a short stay among the friendly habitants, in order to recuperate strength and repair equipment, the Americans then advanced to the river and on November 8th prepared to cross. But for three days they were delayed by inclement weather—a delay that was to spell the doom of their hopes, for during that brief respite Colonel MacLean, the picturesque and energetic military defender of Quebec, was organizing his defenses and collecting necessary supplies. When Arnold finally succeeded in crossing the river he was confronted by an opponent who, in spite of the positive disloyalty of many of his troops, and the covert hostility of some of the citizens of the city, was prepared

[78] Influenced by the Six Nations, most of the northern Indians were loyal to Great Britain during the War of Independence. Special mention should be made of the Mohawks under the able but ruthless leadership of Joseph Brant. See Wood, *The War Chief of the Six Nations* (*Chronicles of Canada* Series).

to offer a resolute defense. Facing these conditions, and lacking a naval force to make a blockade fully effective, Arnold could only await the coming of Montgomery.[79]

On the same day that word was first received in Quebec of the coming of Arnold, Cramahe, the commandant, had received a letter from General Howe in Boston. This lazy and incompetent commander declared that no aid could possibly be sent to Canada until spring. In his reply Cramahe declared: "There is too much reason to apprehend the affair will soon be over." [80] It was at this depressing moment that Colonel MacLean appeared in Quebec with a force of two hundred Highlanders. These recruits had been obtained as the result of a daring and adventurous trip not only in Canada, but in several revolting colonies as well.[81] The impetuous Scot, taking control from the weaker hands of Cramahe, began to organize a systematic defense. "Those vagabonds," he had earlier told the burghers, "come with no other view than that of plunder and pillage." [82] Such statements as this, combined with the ragged appearance of the American troops, very shortly had an appreciable effect on the attitude of the more wealthy citizens. The admission to the city of six hundred half-starved and desperate men was not lightly to be connived at, even by those who were politically sympathetic to the republican cause.

On November 14th Arnold wrote to Cramahe demanding the evacuation of Quebec, stating that "on the surrender of the ctiy the property of every individual shall be secured to him; but if I am obliged to carry the town by storm, you may expect every severity practised on such occasions." [83] Under the influence of

[79] On Arnold's march information can be found in many journals, either printed or in manuscript, of participants. Readily accessible are: Smith, *Arnold's March from Cambridge to Quebec*, New York, 1903; Codman, *Arnold's Expedition to Canada*, New York, 1901. Both make extensive use of the journals mentioned.

[80] Cramahe to Howe, November 8, 1775, quoted in Smith, *Our Struggle for the Fourteenth Colony*, vol. II, p. 16.

[81] 4 *American Archives* III, p. 67; *idem*, IV, p. 290.

[82] Quebec *Gazette*, October 5, 1775.

[83] Arnold to Cramahe, November 14, 1775. 4 *American Archives*, III, p. 1685.

Colonel MacLean, Cramahe answered this demand from the mouth of a cannon. The American leaders thereupon undertook to blockade the city.

Despite the unhesitating rejection of the American offer, all was not well in Quebec. Of the six thousand inhabitants, many openly favored the American cause; the militia was half-hearted or openly insubordinate; the defenses were old and in many places insecure; and the troops, though well armed, were few in number. Chaos reigned and no one knew what each succeeding day might bring forth. In the midst of this confusion, and to the great joy of the loyalists, Governor Carleton arrived from Montreal.[84] Three days later he issued a proclamation stating that "in order to rid the town of all useless, disloyal, and treacherous persons," those who refused to serve in arms "must quit the town in four days." [85]

The city having been thus purged, Carleton and MacLean set their forces to work on the defenses, hoping to get them into condition to withstand an attack. In order to gain time, a rumor was circulated to the effect that the British were preparing for a sortie against Arnold's lines. The Americans, with ammunition reduced to five rounds for each man, and still suffering from the effects of their long march, determined to retreat up the river to Point aux Trembles, there to recuperate their strength and await the arrival of Montgomery.[86] This withdrawal made Carleton's task more simple, and he worked steadily to collect supplies and to strengthen the ramparts of the city. By the enlistment of every able-bodied citizen he succeeded in marshaling a body of over eighteen hundred men. Five hundred and thirty-one of these, however, were French-Canadian militia of very doubtful loyalty.[87]

[84] November 19, 1775.

[85] 4 *American Archives* III, p. 1639. See also Wurtele, *The Blockade of Quebec in 1775–1776 by the American Revolutionists,* Quebec, 1905–1906.

[86] Smith, *op. cit.,* vol. II, p. 31.

[87] *Canadian Archives,* Q. 12, p. 35. *Ainslie's Journal* for November 30, 1775, gives the following muster roll: 543 militiamen; 400 British seamen; 330 British militiamen and burghers; 230 MacLean's Royal Immigrants; 120 artificers, 70 fusiliers, 50 naval officers; 35 marines; 22 artillerymen. Total: 1800.

Meanwhile General Montgomery had been having troubles of his own at Montreal. Having followed the usual American custom of enlisting recruits for certain definite periods, the General was faced, shortly after the capture of that city, by the prospect of losing the greater part of his forces. Fatigued by a strenuous campaign, unpaid and poorly equipped, their immediate object accomplished, and the term of their enlistment expiring, the American soldiery viewed with rapidly vanishing enthusiasm the prospects of a winter campaign against Quebec. Nor did the true sons of Massachusetts and New Hampshire respond with alacrity and pleasure to the commands of a general from New York.[88] Refusal of duty was a daily problem among officers as among the men, and "sick parades" were well attended by those whose only desire was to escape further campaigning.[89] It was not until a Congressional committee had arrived in Montreal and had promised increased pay, bonuses, and new equipment, that Montgomery was in a position to advance with three hundred men to reinforce Benedict Arnold,[90] an advance that was made the more desirable by reason of the growing friction between the citizens of Montreal and the occupying forces. Montgomery and Arnold joined forces on December 2nd and three days later they encamped before Quebec.[91] The city was now completely blockaded,[92] and Montgomery, in command of approximately one thousand Americans and about five hundred Canadian volunteers, prepared for the final clash.[93]

5. THE ASSAULT ON QUEBEC

Another tragic drama was now to be staged under the grim walls of old Quebec. It was rapidly enacted. On the day following his arrival Montgomery wrote to Carleton demanding an

[88] 4 *American Archives* III, p. 1688.

[89] *Idem*, p. 796.

[90] *Idem*, p. 1065; *Journal of Congress*, October 16, November 11, 1775.

[91] *Canadian Archives*, Q. 12, p. 11.

[92] British naval power was of little value during the winter when navigation on the St. Lawrence was impossible.

[93] 4 *American Archives* IV, pp. 190, 309.

immediate capitulation. "You have," he said, "a great extent of works from their nature incapable of defense, manned by a motley crew of sailors, the greatest part our friends, or of citizens who wish to see us within their walls, and a few of the worst troops who ever styled themselves soldiers."[94] The Governor refused even to receive communications from a former British officer, once his friend, now a traitor. Attempts to arouse the citizens to make a demonstration favorable to the Americans met with no success. Carleton's control was complete. As the siege continued the situation of the republican troops, improperly housed, suffering severely from the cold, poorly supplied with food, and inadequately protected by artillery, became more and more desperate. The New York troops, moreover, had given warning that they would not remain after the end of the year—when their period of enlistment expired.[95] Montgomery attempted to encourage his soldiers with promises of plunder after the conquest of the city.[96] This, however, afforded little immediate comfort. On December 20th the supreme disaster occurred—smallpox was reported in the American camp.[97]

Action, immediate and final, was now imperative. A hurried consultation among the American leaders resulted in plans for a surprise attack. Scaling ladders were prepared, ammunition was collected, and the men were organized for the great adventure. After many delays and much indecision the attack was finally launched under the protecting cover of a turbulent snowstorm on the last night of the year.

Arnold, with the major portion of the troops, attired for the most part in British uniforms captured at St. John's,[98] attacked where the defenses of the Lower Town dropped to the St. Charles; Montgomery led a smaller party against the southwest corner of the Lower Town, below Cape Diamond.[99] They were to join within the city and carry the citadel from below.

[94] *Canadian Archives,* Q. 12, pp. 16–18.
[95] Wood, *op. cit.,* p. 107.
[96] *Canadian Archives,* Q. 12, p. 20.
[97] Fisher, *op. cit.,* vol. I, p. 411.
[98] Wood, *op. cit.,* p. 109.
[99] J. J. Henry, *The Siege of Quebec, 1775–1776, etc.,* Lancaster, 1812.

Through the darkness, under a storm-wracked sky, the two detachments struggled toward their objectives. Between four-thirty and five o'clock a rocket shot up from Cape Diamond—the attack had been launched. Quebec became an inferno of noise. Between the storm-gusts could be heard the clangor of bells from church and convent; the rattle of musketry; the cries of wounded men; while deep and resonant came the sound of firing cannon. Montgomery and his little force dashed for the barricade which stretched across their way—a barricade the position of which they knew, but which they could not see. But success lay not that way. The burly skipper whose duty it was to guard this path had trained his largest gun upon the clear approach. Warned that the Americans were approaching, he fired into the murk and darkness of the storm. His effort was crowned with amazing success; the gallant Montgomery and many of his men were killed by the first discharge; the remainder had no choice but to retreat. The following day the body of the American leader was recovered from its shroud of ice and snow, to receive honorable burial at the hands of his foes.[100]

Arnold's plight was but little better. Wounded himself at the first barricade, he handed over the command to Captain Morgan, who, taking the place of his fallen leader, drove the British to their second rampart. Here the defenders stood their ground until, a circling movement having been accomplished, the Americans found themselves attacked from the rear. Their ammunition exhausted, and now with no hope of success, four hundred and thirty-one of Arnold's men surrendered. The attack was over, Quebec and Canada were saved, and the British loss was thirty killed and wounded.[101]

[100] By Carleton's special order. See Henry, *Account of Arnold's Campaign Against Quebec*, Albany, 1877, p. 134.

[101] For the assault on Quebec, see: Ms. description by one of the defenders, published in *New York Historical Society Collections*, 1880, p. 173; W. Smith, *History of Canada*, Quebec, 1815, vol. II, p. 31; Codman, *op. cit.*, p. 182; 4 *American Archives* IV, pp. 480–481, 589, 656, 670, 336; Paul Leicester Ford (editor) *Writings of Washington*, vol. VIII, p. 504; Moore, *Diary of the American Revolution*, New York, 1860, p. 186; Wood, *op. cit.*, pp. 109–121.

6. THE CHANGING ATTITUDE OF THE CANADIANS

The American defeat at Quebec was indeed the crucial event in the struggle for possession of Canada. Larger bodies of troops were placed in the field in 1776, but never again did the danger to Quebec appear imminent. Never again did the habitants, disillusioned by this defeat, risk their lives and property, in comparable numbers, on behalf of a losing cause. British authority was here established, to remain unquestioned for more than three decades.

Despite his wound and the clouded aspect of American fortunes, General Arnold and the remnants of his force attempted to maintain the siege. Washington urged him on and sent what troops he could spare, though not the five thousand requested by Arnold.[102] Carleton, realizing that the elements were fighting for the British, made no attempt to break the blockade.

Arnold's position was indeed precarious. Suffering from scurvy and smallpox, with food supplies rapidly dwindling, the mutinous spirit of his troops became dangerous, and this condition was gravely aggravated by his inability to pay their allowances.[103] An even more fundamental misfortune was the rapidly changing attitude of the Canadian populace. The military mind is never conducive to good relations between soldier and civilian. When to this professional attribute is added a distinct consciousness of racial superiority, such as the Americans felt toward the unenlightened French-Canadians,[104] pleasant intercourse cannot long be maintained. After the American defeat at Quebec the Canadians had little need to refrain from the expression of their sentiments, and the weary, undisciplined, ragged Continentals were

[102] 4 *American Archives* IV, p. 1513. During January, 1776, 530 men joined Arnold. *Canadian Archives,* Q. 12, p. 100.

[103] Desertions at this time were very common. *Secret Journal of Congress,* July 30, 1776.

[104] General Wooster wrote to Schuyler that the Canadians were "but little removed from savages." This letter was intercepted and copies of it spread throughout Canada by the British. 4 *American Archives* IV, p. 668.

no longer objects of respect.[105] American offenses, which had previously been glossed over or condoned, were now bitterly resented.
As the resentment of the Canadians grew, so increased the causes
for complaint. "The licentiousness of our troops," wrote Schuyler,
"is not easily to be described, nor have all my efforts been able
to put a stop to these scandalous excesses." [106] Another American
General subsequently stated that "few of the inhabitants have
escaped abuse, either in their persons or their property. . . .
Court martials are vain when officers connive at the depredations
of the men." [107] Not only personal abuse, but the regulations rendered essential by the military occupation weighed heavily upon
the Canadians, and when Arnold was forced, on March 4, 1776,
to declare all who refused continental money to be "enemies," [108]
their indignation was violently expressed. A final cause of animosity was the attitude of the American soldiery toward the
Roman Catholic church. Flamboyant in his zealous Protestantism,
the recruit from New England or New York found no little
difficulty in obeying the order to treat all religious persons and
buildings with punctilious respect. Thus resentment spread, and
the American leaders found it ever more difficult to maintain
friendly relations with the "oppressed" people whom they had
come to free. A Congressional committee including the arch-
diplomat Franklin, and a Jesuit priest, John Carroll, was sent to
Montreal to smooth out the existing difficulties. Even the abilities of
these commissioners, however, were insufficient, and they returned
to the United States discouraged and unsuccessful.[109]

[105] Arnold to Wooster, January 4, 1776. 4 *American Archives* IV, p.
854; *Secret Journal of Congress,* January 24, 1776; Coffin, *op. cit.,* p.
523.

[106] *American Archives* V, p. 1098.

[107] Sullivan to Washington, April 27, 1776. 4 *American Archives* VI,
p. 413.

[108] 4 *American Archives* IV, p. 1470. In many cases receipts were given
for goods; these were later repudiated. 4 *American Archives* V, pp. 1166,
1237. See also Bancroft, *History of the United States from the Discovery
of the Continent,* New York, 1883–1885, vol. IV p. 376.

[109] 4 *American Archives* VI, pp. 590, 592; 4 *American Archives* V, pp.
1166–1167, 1237, 1643–1645.

7. THE FINAL DEFEAT

Faced by constantly increasing difficulties, Arnold remained at his post throughout the winter. Reinforcements arrived in the spring, but such was the condition of the American forces that no offensive measures could be immediately initiated. On May 1st General Thomas reached Arnold's camp with eight regiments; but five days later Quebec was relieved by the arrival of British ships. The first ship to reach the city was commanded by Sir Charles Douglass, and it was but the forerunner of a fleet with ten thousand men.[110] Carleton, however, availing himself of the assistance of two hundred men from Sir Charles' ship, waited for no further aid, but placing himself at the head of his forces issued forth to give battle.[111]

In the American camp all was confusion: a condition aggravated by the pretensions and inexperience of General Thomas. With the approach of the British troops under the leader whose ability the Americans had come to know only too well, all thought of defense was abandoned, and each soldier, for himself, sought safety in flight.[112] In this situation Sir Guy Carleton displayed another facet of his many-sided character. Showing a humanity that gave a luster to his name that military achievement alone could never confer, he recalled his troops from the pursuit, and sent word to all the farmers between Quebec and Montreal, ordering them to treat the Americans with every kindness. Search parties were organized to bring in the sick and exhausted, and not only did he care for his enemies in their weakness, but, having cured their diseases and healed their wounds, he set them at liberty to return

---

[110] 4 *American Archives* VI, p. 456.

[111] 4 *American Archives* I, p. 129; Fisher, *The Struggle for American Independence*, Philadelphia, 1908, vol. I, p. 445.

[112] 4 *American Archives* VI, p. 129; *Canadian Archives*, Q. 12, pp. 69, 75–79; Sloane, *The French War and the Revolution*, New York, 1902, p. 204.

to their homes.[113] Such acts of mercy fittingly crowned the first British defense of Canada.

At the same time that he himself was defeating the Americans in the east, Governor Carleton arranged for an attack on American power in the west. This blow was struck by Captain Foster against the invaders' post at The Cedars, forty-five miles southwest of Montreal, and was entirely successful.[114]

The scattered American troops found a rendezvous at Three Rivers, and there their leaders planned to make a stand against the advancing British. Here General Thomas died of smallpox and was succeeded in command, first by General Thompson, and then by General Sullivan. Hardly had the latter organized his command and made tentative but hopeful plans for the future, when the British attacked.[115] On June 14th the Americans began a second retreat—a movement that did not make a lasting stop until Crown Point was reached.[116] By July 25th the only American soldiers left in Canada were prisoners in the citadel, and patients in the hospitals of Quebec.

More slowly Carleton followed his retreating foe. The British advance ended at the northern end of Lake Champlain, and on that inland sea a curious conflict took place. Arnold at one end of the lake and officers of the Royal Navy at the other undertook to carve ships of war from the forests bordering the shore.[117] By October the fleets were ready and on the eleventh day of that month a naval battle commenced, in which the Americans, outnumbered and more lightly armed, were completely defeated after a prolonged and vigorous engagement.[118] In the larger view,

[113] 4 *American Archives* VI, pp. 398, 418; *Diary and Letters of Thomas Hutchinson,* vol. II, p. 115; Bancroft, *op. cit.,* vol. VII, p. 186; Melvin, *A Journal of the Expedition to Quebec* (the diary of a prisoner), New York, 1857.

[114] 4 *American Archives* VI, pp. 458, 469, 479, 480 ff.; 5 *American Archives* I, pp. 158, 169.

[115] *Idem,* pp. 640, 684, 826 ff.

[116] *Idem,* pp. 925–930, 937–948; *Digby's Journal,* Albany, 1887, pp. 107–109.

[117] *Digby's Journal,* pp. 139 ff.

[118] Fonblanque, *Life of Burgoyne,* London, 1876, pp. 217 ff.; *Digby's Journal,* pp. 160–163.

however, Arnold's tactics were successful. His brilliant defense had so delayed the progress of the British forces that winter was now at hand, and a further advance was impossible. Having reconnoitred the surrounding districts, General Carleton led his troops back to Canada.[119]

8. THE DENOUEMENT

Thus ended the first American invasion of British Canada. In seeking the causes of defeat, due importance must be given to the natural difficulties of the undertaking; to the unstable quality of the American troops; and to the military genius of General Carleton. More significant than any of these causes, however, was the fundamental error of the American leaders. Had Schuyler and Montgomery prepared and executed comprehensive plans for the utilization of the potential strength of the friendly Canadians; had this force been enlisted and trained for even a short period; and had Congress given Montgomery the financial support necessary to carry out these plans; the conquest of Canada might well have been assured. As it was, however, as soon as disaster overtook the invading forces, the few Canadian auxiliaries deserted and the general populace, with no apparent stake in American success, either lost interest or became actively hostile. In June, 1776, General Washington wrote that many of the American misfortunes "can be attributed to a want of discipline and a proper regard to the conduct of our soldiery." [120] Had he written with full cognizance of all of the factors involved, he must have placed the primary condemnation on those generals and politicians who neither succeeded in nor strongly attempted capitalizing the friendly attitude of the Canadian population.

The victories of 1776 ended the direct connection of Canada with the American Revolutionary War. Subsequent interest in

[119] Palmer, *History of Lake Champlain,* chap. VII; 5 *American Archives* II, p. 1038; Mahan, "The Naval Campaign on Lake Champlain, *Scribner's Magazine,* February, 1898.

[120] 4 *American Archives* V, p. 927.

the struggle was only incidental. An attempt was made in 1777
to organize a winter campaign against Canada. General Gates,
president of the American Board of War, appointed Lafayette
to command this expedition, but gave no further support. The
movement never progressed beyond its American base. There
now seems good reason to believe that the whole plan was simply
an attempt on the part of General Gates to lower the brilliant
Frenchman in the esteem of George Washington. The opposition
of the latter to such a scheme was widely known.[121] In the following year an abortive attempt was made to enlist a brigade of
Canadians under French officers. According to the general plan
of which this was a part, France was to equip an expedition
against Halifax and Quebec, while American troops were to advance on Detroit, Niagara, Oswego, and Montreal. This plan was
endorsed by Congress, but was subsequently vetoed by the strong
commonsense of General Washington.[122]

A few of the habitants who had enlisted under Arnold and
Montgomery remained with the American forces until the end
of the war;[123] but at no time did the vital interests or ultimate
safety of Canada become seriously involved. Apart from the
military difficulties to be faced by an invading army in Canada,
the American leaders would have been faced by another problem had they attempted such a movement. This difficulty was
tersely described by Franklin as the "want of a sufficient quantity
of hard money." "The Canadians," he wrote, "are afraid of paper
and would never take the Congress money. To enter a country
that you mean to make a friend of with an army that must have
occasion every day for fresh provisions, horses, carriage labor
of every kind, having no acceptable money to pay those that serve
you, and to be obliged therefore from the necessity of the case

[121] *Harper's Encyclopaedia of United States History,* New York, 1902,
vol. II, p. 44. For the French policy in the Revolution, see *French Policy
and the American Alliance of 1787,* Princeton, 1916; also Tower, *LaFayette
in the American Revolution,* Philadelphia, 1895.

[122] *Harper's Encyclopaedia of United States History,* vol. II, p. 45;
American Diplomatic Correspondence, vol. I, pp. 336–337, 346–349.

[123] 5 *American Archives* I, p. 656.

to take that service by force, is the sure way to disgust, offend, and by degrees make enemies of the whole people, after which all your operations will be more difficult, all your motions discovered and every endeavor used to have you driven back out of the country." [124]

The formal entrance of France into the Anglo-American struggle ended all real prospect of a second American invasion of Canada. Immunity was now assured, for the American leaders feared that, should the allies succeed in conquering Canada, France would demand the return of her former colony. Against such a demand Congress would have protested in vain. The King of France categorically denied that his ministers had any such intentions,[125] but when Lafayette in 1778 suggested a new attack on Canada, Washington refused his consent.[126]

Among some sections of the Canadian population disaffection continued to smoulder throughout the war, and, in consequence, Governor Haldemand was frequently to be found reporting in a pessimistic vein.[127] But on the whole conditions steadily improved. The clergy gradually regained their ascendency through the use of pulpit and school; and the imperative demands of personal duties, together with the reasonably just rule of British officials, gradually bred forgetfulness—the dream of republican liberty was slowly forgotten in the press of concrete facts.

American interest in Canada did not, however, end with military defeat. Force having proved ineffective, the subtler methods of diplomacy were brought into action. For this purpose few more competent agents could have been found than John Jay, John Adams, and Benjamin Franklin, the American commissioners at Paris in 1783. Congress had instructed these diplomats to per-

[124] Franklin to Jay, June 9, 1779. Wharton, *Diplomatic Correspondence of the American Revolution*, Washington, 1889, vol. III, pp. 215–216.

[125] See section 6 of the Franco-American treaty signed Februrary 6, 1778; see also Curwen, *Journal and Letters*, New York, 1842.

[126] Wharton, *op. cit*, vol. III, p. 321; *Memoirs and Correspondence of Lafayette*, London, 1837, vol. I, pp. 38-44; Paul Leicester Ford (editor), *Writings of Washington*, vol. VI, p. 298, 432–437.

[127] Haldemand Collection. By dates: July 28, 1778, June 7, 1779, June 18, 1779, October 18, 1779, etc. Haldemand was General Carleton's successor.

suade the British representatives to incorporate the cession of Canada to the United States in the treaty of peace.[128] This was "a difficult errand in diplomacy . . . demanding wariness and adroitness if not even craft and dissimulation." [129]

It appeared at first as though the American diplomats would be successful as Oswald, the head of one group of British commissioners, was a weakling, unversed in such negotiations, and lacking in detailed knowledge of North American conditions—in spite of extensive possessions in the new world.[130] When Mr. Strachey—a new commissioner—arrived in Paris, however, conditions changed, and at the same time the British government emphatically reiterated its earlier orders against any such surrender.[131] The United States had demanded the cession of Canada as part of the reparations for losses during the war; to prevent future wars; and as compensation for indemnifying the Tories or Loyalists.[132] In reply, Great Britain refused to pay any reparations; stated that there were other ways of preventing war; and declared that the Loyalists must be provided for in any case, if a treaty was to be made.[133]

The strategic position of Canada, as well as the value of the fisheries, the fur trade, and the lumber resources of the colony, made it a particularly valuable possession, and all Franklin's logic and suave manipulation proved unavailing.[134] The statesmen

[128] *Continental Congress Papers. Reports of Committees,* vol. I, p. 35.

[129] Morse, *John Adams,* Boston, 1890, p. 165.

[130] Franklin imparted the American viewpoint to Oswald in his "Canadian Paper," and the latter was ready to accede. See Sparks (editor), *Franklin's Works,* vol. IX, pp. 250, 269; J. Q. and C. F. Adams, *The Life of John Adams,* Philadelphia, 1871, vol. II, p. 13; Lewis, *Administrations of Great Britain, 1783–1830,* p. 81; Bemis, *op. cit.,* pp. 12, 13, 38, 51–52, 54, 66.

[131] John Adams, *Works,* vol. I, p. 360; Winsor, *Narrative and Critical History,* London, 1889, vol. III, pp. 101, 109, 175–182.

[132] Fitzmaurice, *Life of Lord Shelbourne,* London, 1875–1876, vol. III, pp. 175–182, 188 ff. Franklin's proposal that Canada be ceded is quoted in Colquhoun, "The First Lord Landsdowne," *Canadian Magazine,* November, 1918.

[133] Wharton, *op. cit.,* vol. III, p. 281.

[134] *Idem,* vol. V, pp. 476, 484–485, 497–498, 540–549.

of Great Britain recognized some truth in Washington's statement that the loss of Canada "would be a deadly blow to her trade and empire." [135] The refusal of France to support the American demands was an interesting commentary on the relations of the erstwhile allies.[136] Congress, realizing that American independence was not yet assured, had wisely refrained from making the cession of Canada a *sine qua non*. The American representatives turned to more promising discussions.[137]

One of the most important decisions of this conference was the legal definition of the boundary between the British colonies and the revolted states—a boundary that was later to be the cause of bitter and extended discord.

With the signing of the Treaty of Paris the first Anglo-American struggle for the "Fourteenth Colony" was over, and the formation of the two nations was assured.

[135] Paul Leicester Ford (editor), *Writings of Washington,* vol. VII, p. 239.

[136] Winsor, *op. cit.,* vol. VII, p. 140. The United States shortly made a separate treaty of peace contrary to the terms of her treaty of alliance with France.

[137] Sparks, *Diplomatic Correspondence,* vol. III, p. 286; Wharton, *op. cit.,* vol. III, p. 295.

CHAPTER II

The Influence of the United Empire Loyalists

I. THE LOYALISTS

THE American Revolution won independence for the thirteen colonies; and, in a very real sense, it created British Canada.

The migration to Canada of thousands of colonials who had opposed the Revolution gave to the northern colony a solid basis of British stock which was of fundamental importance in guaranteeing the existence and persistence of Anglo-Saxon civilization in what had been, before this time, simply a conquered French province. Yet it has been only within the past thirty-five years that the importance of this movement has been recognized.[1] Among the indictments that may be charged against the American historians of the nineteenth century few are more important, or more fully justified, than the accusation that they have almost totally disregarded the lives and influence of the group known as United Empire Loyalists—the Tories of the Revolution who migrated during or after that conflict.

Second only to the American Revolution itself, in its effect upon the history of the continent, was the formation and persistence of the Canadian nation; and in both the establishment and the preservation of this political and cultural entity the Loyalists played a conspicuous role. Until recent years, however, the nationalistic historian of the United States was content to anathematize the Tory as a traitor,[2] while the Canadian textbook

---

[1] There are two exceptions to this statement: Sabine's *Loyalists of the American Revolution* was published in Boston in 1864. Ryerson's *The Loyalists of America and Their Times* was published in Toronto in 1880, and may be included despite its many obvious faults.

[2] See M. C. Tyler, "The Loyalists in the American Revolution," *American Historical Review,* vol. I (1895–1896), pp. 25 ff., for a discussion of

Herbert Lang & Cie AG
Buchhandlung
Münzgraben 2

CH-3000 Bern
Schweiz

WILHELM FINK VERLAG

8 MÜNCHEN 40

Nikolaistraße 2

paid him passing tribute as a martyr and a hero; but neither American nor Canadian has recognized in the Loyalist a force which has played a vital part in molding and directing the history of a continent. Yet had it not been for the Loyalist pioneers, imbued as they were with a bitter hatred for things American, it is altogether probable that Canada would have fallen before the republican assaults in 1812, and that it would be today a political division of the United States. The indignities which they had suffered had burned into the souls of the Loyalists a hatred of Americans which, bequeathed to succeeding generations, has not been negligible in its influence upon modern Canadian history. In the early and critical days it was a determining force.[3]

Few movements in history have been more distorted in the popular mind than the American Revolution. It is not to be supposed—as has been done so often—that the response of the American colonists to the arbitrary actions of a harried and stupid imperial government was spontaneous, spectacular, and unanimous.[4] Society in the colonies was divided gradually, and by the interaction of many influences, into two groups; but within each group was to be found a wide diversity of sentiment. It was only after years of conflict, economic, political, and military, that a majority of the people came to favor independence. The greater number were, at first, opposed to separation, and many retained such sentiments even after July 4, 1776.[5] At least one

the difficulties facing any American historian who would discuss the Loyalists with fairness. Fortunately, this condition no longer exists—except perhaps in Chicago or among the members of the D. A. R.

[3] See any of the more recent histories, particularly: Van Tyne, *The Loyalists in the American Revolution,* New York, 1902; Wallace, *The United Empire Loyalists,* Toronto, 1914 (brief but excellent); Winsor, *op. cit.,* vol. VII, pp. 185–214; Denison, "The Influence of the United Empire Loyalists," *Proceedings of the Royal Society of Canada,* vol. X. See also articles by W. H. Siebert in *Transactions of the Royal Society of Canada,* Third Series, vols. VI and VII; Howard, *Preliminaries of the American Revolution (The American Nation* Series), chap. 18.

[4] This is well shown in Schlesinger, *New Viewpoints in American History,* New York, 1922, chap. 7.

[5] See the summary of opinions on the compartive number of Loyalists and patriots in Fisher, *The Struggle for American Independence,* Phila-

hundred thousand residents of the various states maintained their opposition so clearly that they were forced by the zeal of the Patriots to leave the colonies. These individuals who, through their support of the imperial cause, lost their homes and possessions, later became known, by decree of their sovereign, as the United Empire Loyalists. The causes leading to their extraordinary display of fealty were as varied as the individuals themselves, and as the facts with which they were confronted.

In every society are to be found two classes: those who fear change more than they dislike the faults of the existing order, and those whose emotional or rational hostility toward contemporary conditions leads them to a desire for radical alteration. In the early days of the revolutionary agitation the conservatives of American society were altogether opposed to any plan of separation from the empire. Many of them were willing to take part in non-importation agreements, and other forms of economic and political argument, but they thoroughly condemned physical force and the agitation for independence.[6] They recognized, with some truth, that the British colonial system tended to stabilize business conditions, to strengthen the moral code, to introduce social refinements, and to add to the amenities of life. Thus the conservative tendency was altogether in the direction of loyalism, many going so far as to oppose all criticism of imperial measures. Gradually, however, as British regulations widened their scope and increased in severity, many of these conservatives, feeling the pinch themselves, becoming accustomed to conflict, and fearing classification as Loyalists, tended to condone and finally to join in active support of the Patriot policies.[7] Large numbers of this class, nevertheless, maintained their opposition to the Revolution, and oppression served only to inflame their hostility to the "rebels."

delphia, 1908, vol. I, pp. 241 ff.; see also Van Tyne, *op. cit.,* and Siebert, "The Dispersion of the American Tories," *Mississippi Valley Historical Review,* September, 1914.

[6] Jones, *New York in the Revolution,* vol. I, p. 34; *New York Historical Society Collection, 1877,* p. 35; James Truslow Adams, *Revolutionary New England,* New York, 1925.

[7] *Idem.*

In addition to these "natural conservatives," there were many other classes whose loyalty to the empire was a product of the immediate social and economic conditions:[8] office holders under the Crown; clergymen of the established church;[9] the more prominent and successful of the professional classes; and those, in general, whose economic prosperity and social prestige depended upon the continuation of the existing order. There were many colonists, moreover, who objected to rebellion on religious grounds: who believed with Dr. Myles Cooper that "the principles of submission and obedience to lawful authority are as inseparable from a sound, genuine member of the Church . . . as any religious principles."[10] Religious authority was not a negligible force in eighteenth-century America. Finally, the sentimental attachment which characterizes the Canadian or Australian of today in his attitude toward the mother country was no small factor in adding members to the Loyalist party in 1776.[11]

The Loyalists, in large part, were "the prosperous and contented men, the men without a grievance. Conservatism was the only policy that one could expect from them; men do not rebel to rid themselves of prosperity. The Loyalist obeyed his nature as truly as the patriot, but, as events proved, chose the ill-fated side."[12] Yet this is not altogether true. The Loyalist party contained men and women from all classes in society, from governor to cobbler, and from priest to tavern keeper. It contained, again, men of varied nationality—Dutch, Irish, Indian, German and

[8] For a discussion of the types of Loyalists see Alexander C. Flick, *Loyalism in New York During the American Revolution,* New York, 1901, chaps. 1, 2; Van Tyne, *op. cit.,* chaps. 1, 3; Ellis, "The Loyalists and Their Fortunes," in Winsor, *Narrative and Critical History of America,* vol. VII, pp. 185 ff.

[9] 4 *American Archives* I, p. 301.

[10] Cooper, *A Friendly Address to All Reasonable Americans,* 1774; W. S. Wallace, *op. cit.,* chapter 2.

[11] Moore, *Diary of the American Revolution,* New York, 1860, vol. II, pp. 143 ff; Lossing, *Field Book of the American Revolution,* New York, 1860, vol. II, p. 667; Stark, *The Loyalists of Massachusetts,* Boston, 1907, chaps. 5, 6.

[12] Van Tyne, *op. cit.,* p. 307.

Scotch—who had joined for even more varied reasons.[13] It is true that habit, fear of change, local jealousies, sentiment, and hope of profit all contributed their quota, yet social, political, and economic vested interests really explain the strength of the Loyalist cause. The Loyalists were not men of peculiar virtue, nor of excessive vice; they were ordinary human beings seeking to protect their own interests.

Had the Crown triumphed in its struggle with the thirteen colonies, the almost universal condemnation which has been visited upon the Tories would have fallen instead upon the patriots; the victors have enjoyed the spoils of approbation. *Ut mos est hominum!*

2. THE TREATMENT OF THE LOYALISTS

It was not until after the signing of the Declaration of Independence that the cleavage between Patriot and Loyalist became pronounced. Prior to that time there was much shifting from one side to the other, and the majority of the people were definitely and finally committed to neither party. As the struggle between the colonies and the Crown became intensified, however, the Revolutionary leaders labored under the imperative necessity of assuring to themselves the coöperation and support of the people. Adherence to the Crown could not be tolerated in the newly-formed state, and expediency demanded a policy both harsh and effective. By legislative enactment, social pressure, and mob compulsion, the ideal of uniformity was sought.

One of the first important actions of the Revolutionary Congress and the local state committees was the passage of a series of Test Laws designed to reveal the political complexion of those whose loyalty was in doubt. The justice or injustice of these laws is still a matter of dispute, and, as is usual in such matters, logical arguments can be advanced on either side. To the Patriot, King George III was no longer the supreme authority in the free states, and those who still paid him homage were

[13] 4 *American Archives* VI, p. 1157; Tyler, *op. cit.,* pp. 27–45.

traitors to the newly-formed and independent republic. The Loyalist, on the other hand, denied that the Crown had lost its power and denounced as rebels those who signed the Declaration of Independence. To the Patriot leaders, Test Laws appeared necessary for the preservation of the new freedom; to the Tory, they were unauthorized measures of oppression, enforced by extra-legal organizations. Granting its premise, each argument was sound; but, just or unjust, such laws were inevitable.

Supplementing the Test Laws were hundreds of regulatory enactments designed to eliminate loyalism, or at worst, to weaken the Tory cause.

Varying slightly from colony to colony, the Regulatory and Test Laws contained, in essence, the same provisions. Loyalists were barred from all civil rights;[14] they could neither collect debts, nor claim legal protection from slander, assault, or blackmail. They could not hold land, make a will, or present a gift. The professions were closed to them and military service in the Whig ranks was frequently demanded. Freedom of speech, press, and travel were rigidly curtailed, and, on the charge of treason, Loyalists were hanged, exiled, or imprisoned.[15] On the same charge property was confiscated. Heavy fines and forced donations were levied, and in many districts those suspected of Tory sympathies were herded together in concentration camps—camps which in some cases compared unfavorably with the worst of British prison ships.[16] The extent to which these laws were enforced depended upon local political and military conditions. Their incidence varied directly as the strength of the Patriot cause.[17]

Administered with justice, and with judicial care, many of these

14 Greenleaf, *Laws of New York,* vol. I, p. 127.

15 In some instances, women as well as men were attainted of high treason, a most unusual procedure. Rives (editor), *Correspondence of Thomas Barclay,* New York, 1894, p. 137.

16 *Rivington's Gazette,* May 29, 1779; Van Tyne, *op. cit.,* pp. 213 ff.

17 For the laws concerning the Loyalists see: Paltsits (editor), *Ministries of the Commissioners for Detecting and Defeating Conspiracies in the State of New York,* Albany, 1909; Van Tyne, *op. cit.,* Appendix B, C; Flick, *op. cit.,* chaps 3, 4, 9; Sabine, *op. cit.,* vol. I, chapter 9.

laws could not fairly be criticized, in view of the conditions of
the time; but enforced as they were by local Committees of Public
Safety composed, for the most part, of the most violent members
of their respective communities, they were intolerably oppressive.
Thousands of Loyalists were driven from their homes to seek
asylum in such Tory strongholds as New York and Philadelphia.

The intensity of the feeling against the Loyalists can with
difficulty be exaggerated.[18] They were accused, and often quite
justly, of acting as spies for the British army, of supplying it
with food and munitions, of counterfeiting American currency,
and of enlisting bands to attack patriot strongholds.[19] General
Washington declared them to be "abominable pests of society,"
and advised against their execution only from fear of retaliation
on Patriot prisoners. He urged all Tories to commit suicide.[20]
John Adams "strenuously recommended" hanging all those who
were inimical to the progress of the Revolution.[21] Even the philosophic Franklin became vigorous in denunciation, although he himself had long opposed the idea of independence.[22] To the rabble
of town and city the plight of wealthy Loyalists was an invitation to pillage and destruction. Espionage, informing, slander,
and robbery were praised as virtues and as evidence of patriotic
zeal.[23]

Persecution of the Loyalists was not confined to the legal enactment of the various Revolutionary bodies. The factors most
important in giving rise to the bitter hatred with which the Loyal-

[18] Nevins, *The American States During and After the Revolution,*
New York, 1924, pp. 66, 112, 268–274, 250–278, 276–278, 384–389, etc.:
Rivington's Gazette, November 17, 1774.

[19] 4 *American Archives* VI, p. 1072; *idem,* V, p. 821; *Original Papers of
the American Antiquarian Society,* vol. I, p. 102.

[20] Sparks (editor), *Writings of Washington,* New York, 1848, vol. III,
pp. 396, 441; Paul Leicester Ford (editor), *Washington's Writings,* March
31, 1776; Van Tyne, *op. cit.,* pp. 57, 125, 223.

[21] Adams to Cushing. See *Annual Register,* 1781, pp. 259–261.

[22] Oswald correspondence in *Sparks Manuscripts,* no. 40, p. 179.

[23] For a statement of the famous James case see *Original Papers of the
American Antiquarian Society,* vol. I, p. 101.

ists came to regard the United States were the indignities which many of them suffered at the hands of Whig mobs. On suspicion of loyalty to the Crown the homes of reputable citizens were broken open, hoodlums from the worst elements of the community ransacked the rooms, closets, desks, even women's clothing, and frequently such raids culminated in the destruction of the house by fire. Property was destroyed, women were insulted, and men were subjected to every conceivable brutality. Against these excesses such leaders as John Jay, General Greene, and Alexander Hamilton protested in vain, for such acts received the enthusiastic applause and approbation of the great majority of the war-intoxicated Whigs.[24]

But the evil was not all on one side. When opportunity offered, the Loyalists, in their turn, were responsible for brutal and mischievous actions.[25] The failure of the British leaders to utilize the potential strength of their Loyalist supporters led to the organization of independent and irresponsible bands such as that headed by the fanatic Fanning.[26] The Loyalists, moreover, were confident of ultimate victory and they despised and derided their opponents. They could not conceive that the power of the British Empire would ever be defeated by "rascally mobs" drawn from

[24] On mob action see: *Canadian Archives Report, 1880,* pp. 840, 841, 843; *Rivington's Gazette,* July 28, September 8, September 15, 1774, etc.; Wallace, *op. cit.,* chap. 3; 4 *American Archives* I, pp. 715–718, 731–732, 762–763, etc.; *Idem,* II, pp. 34, 46, 131, 174–176, 340, 1419, etc.; *Idem,* III, pp. 125–129, 145, 151, 170, etc.; *Idem,* IV, pp. 247, 288, 884–887, etc.; *Idem,* VI, p. 1273; 5 *American Archives* I, pp. 361–381; Trevelyan, *The American Revolution,* New York, 1907, vol. III, pp. 32, 368 ff.

[25] 4 *American Archives* VI, p. 808; 5 *American Archives* I, p. 9.

[26] This failure on the part of the British was one of the supreme blunders of the war. There was a tendency among some of the royal leaders to despise Whig and Tory alike as colonials, and to refuse the aid of the latter as they underestimated the strength of the former. At no time were more than 9000 Loyalists actually under arms, although many times that number might readily have been obtained. See *Diary and Letters of Thomas Hutchinson,* Boston, 1886, vol. II, p. 259; 4 *American Archives* VI, pp. 1054, 1116 ff.; *Rivington's Gazette,* August 25, September 17, November 10, 1779, February 28, 1781, etc.; Sparks (editor), *Writings of Washington,* vol. V, p. 544; Wallace, *op. cit.,* chapter 4.

the lower classes of colonial society. This social snobbery added to the fury of the Whigs.[27] The Loyalists have long been accused of cruelty and excess because of their employment of Indian allies, and this criticism is not without foundation. In this, however, they were not unique. As Professor Channing has pointed out, the Patriots also employed the redskins and throughout the war every effort was made by each side to enlist the Indian tribes.[28] It was sheer hypocrisy for either Whig or Tory to inveigh against such employment, for the colonies had long been using Indians in their wars against the French.

The methods used by both parties in this civil war were far from justifiable, but, owing to the greater possibilities which were presented to them, the Patriots far excelled the Loyalists in the amount and degree of suffering which they caused. As the war continued and the revolutionary party increased in strength, the attacks upon the Loyalists increased in severity.

3. THE EMIGRATION OF THE LOYALISTS

The American Revolution was ended by the signing of the Treaty of Paris on September 3, 1783. The pressure of British public opinion had forced the King's delegates at Paris to insist upon the inclusion in the treaty of some clause protecting the Loyalists. Thus Article V was evolved. In it the American negotiators agreed that Congress would "recommend" to the various states that all persecution of the Loyalists should cease; that the property of those who had not actually taken up arms should be restored; and that all Loyalists should be allowed to return to their homes for the period of one year in order to settle their affairs.[29]

It soon became apparent, however, that the state, county, and civic bodies in America would pay little attention to the Congres-

---

[27] Trevelyan, *op. cit.,* vol. I, p. 377.

[28] Channing, *History of the United States,* vol. III, pp. 216–217.

[29] Treaty of 1783, Article 5. Malloy, *Treaties, Conventions, International Acts, Protocols and Agreements Between the United States of America and Other Powers, 1776–1909,* Washington, 1910, vol. I.

sional recommendation.[30] With the exception of South Carolina, no state made any real effort to carry out the recommendations of the commissioners.[31] When, relying on the treaty, many of the Tories attempted to return to their homes, they were met with indignant, organized, and virulent opposition.[32] The Whigs made little attempt to discriminate; the name "Tory" sufficed to arouse the popular frenzy. The indignities suffered by the Loyalists *after the signing of the treaty of peace* were even more brutal and degrading than their miseries during the war itself. Referring to these excesses of the Whig mobs, John Adams wrote, "profaneness, intemperance, thefts, robberies, murders and treason; cursing, swearing, gluttony, drunkenness, lewdness, trespassing, mains are necessarily involved in them. Besides they render the populace, the rabble, the scum of the earth, insolent and disorderly, impudent and abusive. They give rise to lying, hypocrisy, chicanery and even perjuring among the people . . ." [33] Death was the portion of more than one returning Loyalist.[34]

[30] Alexander C. Flick, *op. cit.,* pp. 162, 163; *Canadian Archives,* B. 103, pp. 183, 203; Jones, *History of New York,* vol. II, p. 494.

[31] Fisher, *The Critical Period of American History,* New York, 1899, pp. 120, 130. Pennsylvania also indemnified a few Loyalists; see Morison, *History of the United States,* Oxford, 1927, vol. I, p. 55. The states, of course, were under no legal obligation to do so.

[32] After his return to America, Franklin, himself one of the negotiators of the treaty, advised his fellow-citizens not to permit the Loyalists to return. Bigelow, *The Life of Benjamin Franklin,* Philadelphia, 1879, vol. III, pp. 314–315. Hamilton, on the contrary, supported the treaty. Oliver, *Alexander Hamilton,* London, 1906. John Adams favored compensation. John Adams, *Works,* Boston, 1856, vol. II, p. 516.

[33] *Letters of John Quincy Adams,* vol. X, p. 63.

[34] Oswald correspondence in *Sparks Manuscripts,* no. 40, p. 179; Ryerson, *op. cit.,* vol. I, p. 92. Goldwyn Smith has described this period as follows: "The first civil war in America was followed not by amnesty but by an outpouring of the vengeance of the victors upon the fallen. Some Royalists were put to death. Many others were despoiled of all they had and driven from their country. Massachusetts banished by name 308 of her people, making death the penalty for a second return. New Hampshire proscribed 76. Pennsylvania attainted nearly 500. . . . Of the 59 persons attainted in New York, 3 were married women guilty probably of nothing but adhering to their husbands, members of the Council or Law officers, who were bound in personal honour to be faithful to the Crown. Upon the

Many of the hardships suffered by the Loyalists during the war may be condoned as unavoidable under the difficult circumstances of that time; but few extenuating facts can be adduced to excuse the post-war activities of the Revolutionary mobs. It was several years after the signing of the treaty before—"the mischief was done, thousands ruined and banished, animosities to continue for generations made certain,—the violent Whigs of Massachusetts, Virginia and New York were satisfied." (Van Tyne)

A large number of the Loyalists had left America during the Revolution. The formal end of the contest failed to bring peace to those who remained. The harsh treatment continued, and thousands more—in many instances from the best educated and most respectable classes in the community—were forced to join the swollen stream of emigration, and to seek new homes in Great Britain, the West Indies, Nova Scotia,[35] New Brunswick,[36] or Canada.[37] Thus the United States at the very outset of its independent career lost close to one hundred thousand[38] of its most reputable and conservative citizens. It may be argued that this loss has been a powerful contributing factor in producing that disrespect for law and tendency toward mob action which

evacuation of Charleston . . . the Loyalists were imprisoned, whipped, tarred and feathered, dragged through horse-ponds and carried about the town with 'Tory' on their breasts. All of them were turned out of their houses and plundered, 24 of them were hanged upon a gallows facing the quay." Goldwyn Smith, *The United States, An Outline of Political History*, New York, 1893, pp. 110–111; McMaster, *History of the United States*, London, 1885, vol. I, pp. 106–128; Haight, *Before the Coming of the Loyalists*, Toronto, 1897.

[35] *Canadian Archives Report, 1894*, pp. 404 ff; Raymond (editor), *The Winslow Papers*, St. John, 1901; *Shelburne Papers*, vol. LXXXVIII, pp. 93–125; Wallace, *op. cit.*, chapter 6.

[36] New Brunswick was created as a separate province in 1784. *Canadian Archives Report, 1895*, pp. 1–3, 5, 8, etc.; Tuttle, *History of the Dominion of Canada*, chapter 66, pp. 328 ff.; Wallace, *op. cit.*, chapter 7.

[37] Haight, *The Coming of the Royalists*, Toronto, 1899.

[38] On the number of the Loyalists, see the articles of W. H. Siebert in *Transactions of the Royal Society of Canada*, vols. VII–X; *Mississippi Historical Review*, vols. I, II, VII; *Ohio State University Bulletin*, vols. XVII, XVIII, XXI, XXIV, XXVI. See also Alexander C. Flick, *op. cit.*, p. 179; Morison, *op. cit.*, vol. I, p. 57.

have occasionally characterized American society.[39] With equal validity it may be said that, as a result of this emigration, Canada gained a solid foundation of conservatism which, although in many ways a very serious handicap, did at least bequeath that tradition of respect for law which has distinguished Canadian history.

To appreciate adequately the effects of the Loyalist emigration upon the Dominion of Canada, it is essential to understand the condition of the country at the time during which it took place. Before the coming of the Loyalists, Nova Scotia and Prince Edward Island [40] together had a population of approximately thirteen thousand. By 1790 Loyalist immigrants had raised this to thirty-five thousand. To the seven hundred settlers in New Brunswick were added ten thousand American exiles. The western settlements, later known as Upper Canada, with practically no permanent white settlers before this time, became the new home of twelve thousand Loyalists—a number that was still further increased before 1800.[41]

The movement of the Loyalists into the Canadian provinces began in the early days of the Revolution,[42] but it was during the years 1782, 1783, and 1784 that it reached the greatest proportions. The British government, which very properly held itself responsible for the welfare of those who had suffered for their loyalty, during these years found it a difficult task to provide food and shelter for these claimants upon its bounty.[43] Under the efficient supervision of Governors Haldemand and Carleton, however, the settlements in the northern wilderness progressed more

[39] The mob action condoned and encouraged by many Revolutionary leaders becomes significant in view of subsequent American history. "Lynch law" was a term first used at the time of the Loyalist persecutions. Fisher, *op. cit.,* pp. 267–268.

[40] *Canadian Archives Report, 1895,* pp. 33–39, 43, 46, etc.

[41] A. Fraser (editor), *Second Report of the Ontario Bureau of Archives,* part. I, pp. 1–25; Denison, "The United Empire Loyalists and their Influence," *Transactions of the Royal Society of Canada,* Second Series, vol. X, pp. 23–39.

[42] See "Allen's Journal" in *Proceedings of the Massachusetts Historical Society,* First Series, vol. XVI, p. 69.

[43] See Letters from Parr to Shelburne, *Canadian Archives Report, 1921,* appendix E.

rapidly than could reasonably have been expected. To tide over
the first years of low production—and it should be remembered
that many of the Loyalists knew little or nothing of the arts of
farming—the government made grants of land, food, seed, machinery, and stock.[44] The Loyalists, moreover, were not backward
in demanding indemnities for the hardships which they had suffered and the losses which they had sustained in the revolting
colonies.[45] These claims were supported by many Englishmen
in Parliament and elsewhere, with the result that a Royal Commission was appointed to inquire into the losses and to arrange
a proportionate indemnity. Thus encouraged, many of the Loyalists sullied their hitherto excellent records by the most shameless
"padding" of their claims.[46] The commission did its work
thoroughly, and generous payments were finally made to those
who could prove actual and serious loss.[47] As a balm to his
wounded dignity, the Loyalist was privileged to suffix to his name
the letters "U. E.," "alluding to his great principle, the unity
of Empire." [48]

   In spite of these material and psychic aids, however, the newly-
arrived settlers had to undergo many hardships.[49] Privations

[44] *Canadian Archives Report, 1866,* pp. 387, 393, 399, etc.; *idem, 1888,* pp.
648, 732–734, 742, etc.; *idem, 1890,* p. 80, 87, 96, etc.; Taylor, *Publications of
the Ohio Archaeological and Historical Society,* vol. XXII, pp. 222 ff.;
Canniff Haight, "Scraps of Local History," in Ryerson, *op. cit.,* vol. II,
pp. 219–226.

[45] Galloway, *Claims of the American Loyalists,* London, 1788; Kingsford,
History of Canada, vol. VII, chapter 5; *Canadian Archives,* Q. 62, A. 2,
pp. 339 ff.; Ryerson, *op. cit.,* vol. II, pp. 164–165.

[46] *Second Report of the Ontario Bureau of Archives;* Kingsford, *op. cit.,*
vol. VII, p. 217; Wilmot, *Historical View* (a report by the head of the
Royal Commission), London, 1815.

[47] Ryerson (editor), *Royal Commission on Losses and Services of the
American Loyalists, 1783–1785,* Oxford, 1915. See also *Report of the
Ontario Bureau of Archives, 1904; Canadian Archives,* B. 67, pp. 109,
168; Wilmot, *op. cit.;* Read, *Life and Times of Sir John Simcoe,* Toronto,
1890.

[48] *Canadian Archives,* Q. 44–1, p. 224.

[49] Raymond, (editor), *Winslow Papers,* St. John, 1901; Bates, *Kingston
and the Loyalists of the Spring Fleet,* St. John, 1899; Harris, *History and
Historiettes,* Toronto, 1897; MacDonald (editor), "Memoir of Colonel Joel

such as they had never known were now their daily lot,[50] and the long snowbound winter nights which they were forced to spend in rough log huts or army tents gave ample opportunity for bitter thought in reference to the authors of their misfortunes. The fierce anger with which they had resented the indignities of war gave place to a deep and acrid hatred, which pervaded every aspect of their lives and constituted one of the strongest influences in molding the outlook of their children.[51]

Another early element in the population of Upper Canada, and an element imbued with ideals and prejudices very similar to those of the Loyalists, was composed of military officers and men introduced and organized into communities by the energy of that ardent imperialist Sir John Simcoe, first Lieutenant-Governor of Upper Canada.[52]

It is worth noting that the Loyalist groups that came to Upper Canada contained fewer persons of education and social standing than those that migrated to the maritime provinces.[53]

The settlers in Canada proper were at first under the direct control of the government at Quebec but by the Constitutional Act of 1791 their political autonomy was attained, under the title of Upper Canada.[54] Nova Scotia and New Brunswick had their own political, legal, and religious institutions from the start, and the conservative tendencies of the upper class Loyalist immigrants

Stone," *Papers and Records of the Ontario Historical Society,* vol. XVIII (1920), pp. 59–90; Ryerson, *op. cit.,* vol. II, pp. 208–270.

[50] *Collections of the Nova Scotia Historical Society, 1887–1888,* vol. VI, pp. 53 ff.; Conant, *Upper Canada Sketches,* Toronto, 1898, pp. 30–51.

[51] Goldwyn Smith, *Canada and the Canadian Question,* London, 1891, pp. 98 ff.; Stark, *op. cit.,* pp. 93–98; McLeod, *A Brief Review of the Settlement of Upper Canada,* Cleveland, 1841. See also Raymond (editor), *Winslow Papers,* St. John, 1901.

[52] *Canadian Archives,* Q. 282–1, p. 6; *Canadian Archives,* Q. 280–1, p. 20.

[53] Wallace, *op. cit.,* p. 111.

[54] McArthur, "Upper Canada, 1791–1812," in Shortt and Doughty, *op. cit.,* vol. III, p. 172; 131 *George* III, chap. 31 (Imperial); Scadding, *Toronto of Old,* Toronto, 1873. It should be added that many Loyalists did not desire an Assembly. See Soward, in *Canadian Historical Review,* December, 1924; Egerton and Grant, *op. cit.,* pp. 99–148.

were soon reflected in a bureaucratic government, and an established church.[55]

4. THE LOYALISTS IN CANADA, 1784–1812

The influence of the Loyalists upon Canadian-American relations was most obviously exerted during the years between 1784 and 1815, and it reached its climax during the first critical weeks of the War of 1812. From the time of their migration to the outbreak of the war, the Canadian Loyalists were occupied in the clearing and cultivation of their new lands, in the opening of routes of travel and communication, and in the formation, development, and finally the crystallization of a social and political organism.[56] The innate conservatism of the settlers to a large extent triumphed over the frontier conditions and the society that developed in Nova Scotia, in New Brunswick, and in Upper Canada was more orderly, more stratified, and far less progressive than similar communities in the United States.[57] The social system developed in Upper Canada, with its inequalities and injustice, was to some extent, at least, the natural result of the Loyalist tradition; and it was not until after the rebellions of 1837–1838 that this system was radically modified.[58]

[55] A. W. H. Eaton, *History of Kings County in Nova Scotia,* Salem, 1910; Ryerson, *op. cit.,* vol. II, chaps. 42, 43.

[56] For conditions in Canada during this period see: W. L. Smith, *The Pioneers of Old Ontario,* Toronto, 1923; Edgar (editor), *The Rideout Letters,* Toronto, 1890, section entitled "Ten Years of Upper Canada," especially chapter 2; Weld, *Travels Through North America,* London, 1807, vol. I, p. 293, and Letter no. 30 and following letters in vol. II; Campbell, *Travels to . . . North America,* Edinburgh, 1793; Scadding, *op. cit.*

[57] There is room for a most interesting study in these contrasts.

[58] The "Family Compact" tradition, on the other hand, has certainly been exaggerated. Leadership in Upper Canada was not by any means confined solely to the Loyalists and their descendants; nor were all Loyalists supporters of the Family Compact. Neither was the government as corrupt as has sometimes been suggested. See, for example, Col. Stephen Jarvis, "Reminiscences of a Loyalist" (by the cousin of Secretary Jarvis of Upper Canada), *Canadian Magazine,* vol. XXVI, pp. 456–457.

The Loyalists maintained, as a cardinal factor in their creed, their hostility toward the United States. To this hostility gradually became linked a firm belief in the moral and political depravity of those who had left the empire. The popular acclaim with which the majority of Americans greeted the French Revolution; [59] the religious agnosticism which characterized many republican leaders; the turbulent assertiveness of the lower orders in the United States; and the radical spirit in its social, political, and religious manifestations, were the criteria upon which the Canadian based his immutable belief in the decadence of American society. Thus contempt was added to hatred.

Many Americans, in their turn, were supercilious and scornful in their attitude toward the royalist, reactionary, and religiously orthodox Canadians.

During the early years of the nineteenth century a new element was gradually appearing in the fertile acres of Upper Canada. The generous land policy of the government,[60] combined with the excellence of the soil, and the rapidly improving means of communication, proved irresistible attractions to many of the more enterprising American farmers.[61] Many of them crossed the boundary and took up farms in the newly-organized districts and townships. For the majority of these farmers this migration was made simpler by the firm belief, which was ingrained in their minds, that before many years Canada would become an integral part of the United States. As was to be expected, the new settlers tended to favor the American form of government, and were little influenced by any sentiment of loyalty toward Great Britain. For some time, however, the exigencies of frontier

[59] The majority of Canadians later condemned also the revolt of the Latin-American colonies against Spain.

[60] Paterson, "Land Settlement in Upper Canada," *Ontario Archaeological Reports,* vol. XVI (1920). For a somewhat inaccurate but interesting attack upon the land system see Gustavus Myers, *History of Canadian Wealth,* Chicago, 1914, pp. 63–97.

[61] See "Journal of William K. Beall," *American Historical Review,* vol. XVII, pp. 797 ff.; Lucas, *The Canadian War,* Oxford, 1906, pp. 15 ff. Mention should also be made of the "Late Loyalists," those who had been willing to try life in the new republic but, finding it unsatisfactory, had later removed to Canada.

life precluded any opportunity of their taking part in political matters, but as soon as the necessity of continuous physical labor was overcome, they entered more and more into the discussion of public affairs. As their numbers increased, they became more assertive, and by 1812 leaders such as Mallory (who, it might be noticed, had been a Loyalist), Marcle, and Willcocks [62] claimed to represent at least one-third of the population of Upper Canada.[63] In the crisis of 1812 many of these settlers sided with the Americans and were nearly successful in handing over the Province of Upper Canada to General Hull.[64]

When war threatened during the years from 1805 to 1812, the presence of these settlers in Upper Canada and the tenor of their reports to the American government led Congress to the assurance of an easy conquest, should the invasion of Canada be resolved upon.[65]

The influence of the Loyalists at the critical moment in 1812, and throughout the remainder of the war, was a prominent factor in the successful Canadian defense. The Executive Council which so ably assisted General Brock, the commander in Upper Canada, was composed almost entirely of Loyalists; what effective measures had been passed by the Assembly were largely the work of members of similar antecedents, and, above all, the enthusiastic support of the Loyalist settlers alone made possible the consummation of the plans of the executive. Had they been half-hearted or fearful, when the first shock came, Upper Canada could hardly have been saved. The defeat of General Hull and his invading force was the crucial test of the whole war for Can-

[62] Colquhoun, "The Career of Joseph Willcocks," *Canadian Historical Review,* December, 1926.

[63] This claim was far from being an exaggeration. See Cruikshank, "Documents Relating to the Invasion of Canada in 1812," *Canadian Archaeological Publications,* no. 7; Cruikshank, "Immigration from the United States into Upper Canada, 1784-1812," *Proceedings Ontario Educational Association,* Toronto, 1900, pp. 263-283.

[64] See *Proceedings of the Royal Society of Canada,* Third Series, vol. 6, sec. 402; McMaster, *op. cit.,* vol. III, p. 558.

[65] Cruikshank, "A Study of Disaffection in Upper Canada, 1812-1815," *Transactions of the Royal Society of Canada, 1912,* Third Series, vol. VI, sec. 2, pp. 11 ff.

ada.[66] This early victory reassured the Canadians, and steeled them to withstand every attack of the powerful but disunited enemy. The vigor and success of their defense did much to insure the continued existence of the Dominion of Canada.

It is probably just to declare that, had there been no Loyalist migration to Canada at the close of the American Revolution, the republican armies would in all likelihood have been successful in the War of 1812—in spite of French-Canadian loyalty. Great Britain, involved in a death struggle with Napoleon, could afford during 1812 and 1813 neither men nor material to defend a colony of doubtful value. Upon the Canadians themselves fell the burden of defense, and the vitality of their resistance was supplied, in large part, by the United Empire Loyalists. As the War of 1812 marked the final independence of the United States, so it marked the permanent foundation of a British state in North America. For the problems arising from this second fact Americans "have to thank their ancestors who refused amnesty to the vanquished in a Civil War." [67] The harvest sown in 1783 was reaped in the defeats of 1812.

5. THE LOYALIST TRADITION

With the close of the Napoleonic wars a great tide of British immigrants swept into Canada and the maritime provinces.[68] The virile element thus added to the population was as emphatic in its attachment to the empire as were the Loyalists, and from this time forward the spirit of the Tories was not the predominant influence tending toward imperial solidarity in the colonies. Moreover, as the original Loyalists passed from the scene there went with them their direct and dynamic personal hostility against the United States, and there arose in its stead a traditional and sentimental antipathy which exercised an undoubted influence, but

[66] See next chapter for details.

[67] Goldwyn Smith, *op. cit.*, p. 99.

[68] Lower, "Immigration and Settlement in Canada, 1812–1820," *Canadian Historical Review*, March, 1922, p. 37 ff.; Bolton and Marshall, *Colonization of North America, 1492–1920*, New York, 1920; Cowan, *British Emigration to British North America, 1783–1837*, Toronto, 1928.

which was, nevertheless, less malignant than the hatred of the veteran of 1776. From this time on, the exact extent of the Loyalist influence is a matter for speculation rather than for concrete demonstration. More and more it became merged in the common loyalty felt alike by the British immigrant and the naturalized American. The Loyalist tradition, however, did not die. At every period of Canadian crisis—in the rebellions of 1837 and 1838; in the Maine-New Brunswick dispute of 1842; [69] during the annexation discussions in 1849; at the time of the Fenian raids; in disrupting the Canada First movement of 1871; and in the political battle of 1911; [70] in trade movements, in diplomacy, and in politics—it has been a potent factor. School books, orators, and patriotic societies have done much to perpetuate the Loyalist tradition.[71]

No candid student of international relations can review the history of American-Canadian contacts without realizing that there has ever been in Canada a considerable body of public opinion hostile to the American Republic. Economic causes have been predominantly responsible for this fact, but more than casual importance must be attributed to the influence of the Loyalists

[69] See Chisholm (editor), *Speeches and Public Letters of Joseph Howe,* Halifax, 1919, vol. II, p. 399.

[70] The campaign literature of the Conservative Party continually appealed to the Loyalist tradition.

[71] As is usual in such cases, the virtues of the founders of the tradition have been acclaimed and their weaknesses or failures overlooked. The Loyalists were very far from being perfect, and it serves no good end to overlook their faults. They were in most instances undemocratic, anti-social in business affairs, hide-bound and intolerant in their religious convictions, unprogressive industrially, given to the excessive use of hard spirits, and in almost every way opposed to what is known as the "modern spirit." They were the inevitable product of their heritage and their environment, and were neither more vicious nor more virtuous than their neighbors. It is interesting in this connection to compare the publications of the United Empire Loyalist Association with those of the Daughters of the American Revolution. On this subject see Davidson, "The Loyalist Tradition in Canada," *Macmillan's Magazine,* September, 1904, pp. 390–400; *Transactions of the U. E. L. Association of Ontario, 1899,* Toronto, 1899, pp. 75 ff; Raymond (editor), *Winslow Papers,* vol. VI, p. 89.

and the Loyalist tradition. The United States is even yet reaping the harvest sown by the Whig mobs of 1783. In the national controversies of the present day can still be discerned the echo of

> "Old unhappy far-off things
> And battles long ago."

CHAPTER III

The War of 1812

I. THE CAUSES OF THE WAR

THE second and the most important military conflict between Americans and Canadians occurred in the years 1812 to 1815. The War of 1812 at first divided, but subsequently united, public opinion in the United States. It completed the work begun in the Revolution by stimulating American nationalism, and it finally destroyed any possibility of reunion with the British Empire.[1] Moreover, by its encouragement of native industry it went far toward breaking the economic ties between England and America—a fact that is evidenced by the development of the protective tariff in 1816.

The War of 1812 aroused little interest and was not taken very seriously in Great Britain, but in Canada it aroused the provinces of British North America to a consciousness of nationhood.

A by-product of the Napoleonic struggle for the domination of Europe and the world, the War of 1812 increased the existing irritation between the United States and Great Britain, and settled none of the real grievances existing in North America. To Great Britain, fighting, as she believed, for the liberties of Europe, the American declaration of war savored of treachery. The United States, injured commercially by the Franco-British blockade of Europe, its "national honor" involved in the question of impressment, and urged on, above all else, by the desire of the West for conquest and trade, disregarded the wider implications of the European conflict; disregarded also the grave injuries suf-

[1] See Gallatin's estimate in H. Adams (editor), *Writings of Gallatin,* Philadelphia, 1879, vol. I, p. 700.

fered at the hands of France; and declared war to maintain in battle the American interpretation of the freedom of the seas.[2] Selecting Great Britain as their foe—both because her offenses were more serious and because England was their "traditional" enemy, France their earliest friend—the leaders of the American people advocated the conquest of Canada as a compensation for national losses, a vindication of national worth. Careless of the danger that their action might involve for the liberties of Europe, they seized the moment of Britain's extremity to assert American dignity, and to drive, if possible, the last remnants of British monarchical rule from the continent partially won in 1783. It is true that many leading Americans vigorously opposed the declaration of war and endorsed Pickering's well-known toast, "The world's last hope—Britain's fast-anchored isle." [3] But these men were not in power and their counsel was overruled. The desires of the Canadian people were not considered—the provinces were looked upon merely as possessions of Great Britain, and not as peaceful neighboring states. To Canadians themselves, however, the causes of the war were as foreign as the war itself was undesired. But loyalty to the empire and the Crown, satisfaction with the rule of British justice, and the Loyalist repugnance to any form of union with the United States, led the Canadians to engage in a counter-struggle which resulted in the birth of Canada as a nation, and the continued hold of the British Empire on the continent of North America.

The causes of the War of 1812 were four: British interference with the European trade of the United States; the impressment of American sailors by the forces of the Royal Navy; the determination of the American frontiersmen to defend their borders against the Indian allies of Great Britain; and an imperialistic lust for the conquest of Canada. But these causes were not

[2] President Madison's argument is to be found in *American State Papers: Foreign Relations,* vol. I, p. 82; see also the vigorous modern statement of the American case in Payne, *The Fight for a Free Sea* (in *The Chronicles of America* Series).

[3] Quoted in Charles A. and Mary R. Beard, *The Rise of American Civilization,* New York, 1927, vol. I, p. 413.

as simple as they appear, and as their usual treatment would suggest.

Between 1798 and 1812 Napoleon Bonaparte was making a remarkably successful attempt to conquer the whole of Europe. One by one his adversaries were brought into subjection or alliance, until among the major powers of Europe the vacillating Alexander of Russia, chaotic Spain, and the island kingdom of Great Britain alone remained in active opposition. As the intensity of the struggle increased, every possible means of pressure was employed by the antagonists. Maritime blockade, as one of the more obvious weapons of economic warfare, was resorted to early in the conflict.[4] The Berlin and Milan decrees of Napoleon ordered the confiscation of any vessel trading with Great Britain,[5] while the British Orders-in-Council forbade commercial intercourse, except by special permit, with any continental port under the control of the French Emperor.[6] These regulations applied not only to belligerent but also to neutral vessels. Between the upper and the nether millstones thus provided, neutral commerce was threatened with disaster. Because Great Britain, by reason of her naval superiority, was able to enforce her decrees to their logical extreme, upon her was showered the more violent abuse.[7] These restrictions bore most heavily upon the trade of the United States, and under the leadership of Jefferson and Madison the American government protested with frequency and vigor.[8] This proving ineffectual, an embargo was placed upon

[4] A Schalck, *Napoleon et l'Amérique*, Paris, 1917, chap. 7; Day, *History of Commerce*, New York, 1907, chap. XLVII.

[5] November 21, 1806, *American State Papers: Foreign Relations*, vol. II, p. 806; January 7, 1807, *idem*, vol. III, p. 267; December 21, 1808, *idem*, vol. III, pp. 274, etc.

[6] *Idem*, vol. II, p. 769; *idem*, vol. III, pp. 5, 29–31, 240, 433; Updike, *The Diplomacy of the War of 1812*, Baltimore, 1915, chap. 2.

[7] It is an interesting fact, as pointed out by Professor Channing, that between 1807 and 1812 France seized 558 American vessels, while Great Britain took only 389. Channing, *op. cit.*, vol. IV, p. 453, note. The tendency among neutrals was to obey the British orders but to take chances with the French decrees. This is easily explained by a comparison of the naval strength of the two countries after Trafalgar (1805).

[8] Madison's defense of the American case is to be found in Hunt (editor), *Writings of James Madison*, New York, 1908, vol. VII, pp. 204–236. It was

all trade with the two major belligerents. When Napoleon later formally withdrew his decrees, the embargo was continued against Great Britain alone.[9] The British government, faced by conditions comparable only with those of 1914–1918, persisted in its course, ever widening the scope and tightening the enforcement of its restrictive measures. Finally, however, as a result of the repeated and emphatic protests of the United States, and wishing to avoid war with that country, the British Orders-in-Council were repealed on June 23, 1812. President Madison, however, had declared war before news of this action reached America.[10] When the news did finally cross the Atlantic, Admiral Warren in command of the British fleet in American waters at once offered to make peace; but as he could give no guarantee that impressment would be abandoned, the President decided that the war should continue.[11]

Judged by the interpretations of maritime law which were enforced by the allied and associated powers in the World War of 1914–1918, the restrictions applied by Great Britain in 1812 were lenient to the point of negligence. But judged by the chaotic juridical dicta of the early nineteenth century, a period during which an American Secretary of State could frankly argue that "free ships make free goods," it was difficult to defend the British actions.

But these trade restrictions were not as important in arousing the national temper of the United States as was the British policy of impressment.[12] The Royal Navy, grown pompous and overconfident since the victory at Trafalgar, declined thereafter to a low ebb of discipline and training. The ships had suffered from neglect, the officers suffered from pride, and the crews suffered

also published as a pamphlet in Boston in 1806. On embargoes, *see idem*, pp. 468–469; vol. VIII, pp. 17–19, 50, 63–66.

[9] This was a brilliant diplomatic manoeuvre, for by it Napoleon lost little and placed Great Britain in an exceedingly bad light. See Bemis, *op. cit.*, vol. III, p. 181.

[10] *American State Papers: Foreign Relations*, vol. III, p. 433.

[11] *Idem*, pp. 595–597.

[12] *American State Papers: Foreign Relations*, vol. I, pp. 481–482; *idem*, vol. II, pp. 147–150, 486–490, 749–750.

from lack of sanitation, decent food, and discipline. These conditions produced an inevitable deterioration in the quality of the personnel. The press-gang took the place of the recruiting officer, and so miserable was life aboard a British man-of-war that hundreds of sailors deserted when opportunity offered. This usually occurred, for obvious reasons, in American ports, and there the deserters found naturalization papers easily obtainable.[13] In many cases the deserters shipped again immediately, this time as members of an American crew. The British authorities were naturally aroused by these desertions, and refusing to recognize the validity of any form of naturalization,[14] made strenuous efforts to stop the abuse.[15] Naval vessels stopped American ships on the high seas, and on the slightest evidence the royal officers seized men whom they believed to be deserters and carried them off to the British man-of-war. Not only was this procedure illegal under the maritime code of the time, but many and grave acts of injustice inevitably occurred. The United States protested frequently and forcibly, but without satisfactory results.[16] In reply, Great Britain demanded that the United States adopt some effectual method of returning British deserters and abandon her support of the principles of naturalization and certification.[17] A deadlock ensued.[18]

[13] These papers were often forged. At one time they could be purchased *on the docks* at Baltimore for $1.00 each.

[14] Indefeasible allegiance was the theory of all European governments at this time. The United States alone, because of its need of settlers, argued in favor of the principle of naturalization. Johnson, *op. cit.,* vol. I, p. 260, discusses the problem facing the British. A few Americans defended the European contentions. See *Annals of Congress,* 13th Cong., vol. II, pp. 1555–1558.

[15] *American State Papers: Foreign Relations,* vol. II, pp. 148–150; *idem,* vol. III, pp. 576–579.

[16] *American State Papers: Foreign Relations,* vols. I, II, and III, are filled with reports of American protests. See also Payne, *op. cit.;* Updike, *op. cit.,* chapter 1, gives a clear and just statement.

[17] *American State Papers: Foreign Relations,* vol. III, pp. 579–580, etc.

[18] There is a good deal of uncertainty as to the number of men actually impressed. At an official inquiry in Boston in 1812, fifty-one of the leading shipping masters of New England would swear to only 35 impressments in 12 years. Of these, only 12 were Americans. See *Report of the Committee*

These two factors—interference with American trade and impressment—have usually been given as the real causes of the War of 1812, and this opinion still persists in many quarters. The authoritative *Cambridge History of British Foreign Policy* declares that the war was "almost entirely" due to those two causes.[19] Recent investigations, however, have radically altered this interpretation. Two other causes must also be recognized.

The Indian problem was a legacy of the War of Independence. By means of presents, the payment of comparatively high prices for furs, and, on the whole, reasonably fair treatment, the British authorities had managed to win and to hold the friendship of the Indians.[20] In every dispute with American settlers in the territory beyond the Alleghanies, moreover, the British had supported the native claims.[21] The Americans declared that British agents had not only supplied the Indians with weapons, but had urged them to attack and pillage the frontier settlements of the United States.[22] The first accusation was certainly true,

---

of the House of Representatives of Massachusetts on the subject of Impressed Seamen, Boston, 1812. In 1801 the Secretary of State reported that between 1797 and 1801, 2059 men had been seized, of whom 1042 had been released at once. *American State Papers: Foreign Relations,* vol. II, pp. 776–798; *idem,* vol. III, pp. 81–89; *Niles' Register,* vol. V, p. 343. An official report in 1812 gave the total number impressed as 6527. *Niles' Register,* vol. II, p. 119; *American State Papers: Foreign Relations,* vol. III, p. 454.

[19] *The Cambridge History of British Foreign Policy,* London, 1922, vol. I, pp. 523, 526; *idem,* vol. II, p. 221.

[20] The British or Canadian treatment of the Indians is good only in comparison with the totally indefensible record of the Americans. Judged by any absolute standard, the treatment of the Indians by the Hudson's Bay Company, the North West Company, and other British traders was far from satisfactory. See Myers, *op. cit.,* chapter 4, for a summary of the British records on this subject; also *Canadian Archives Report, 1818,* note E, pp. 59–60.

[21] Not, of course, from love of the Indians, but in order to check the American advance. Johnson, *American Foreign Relations,* New York, 1916, vol. I, pp. 276–277; *American State Papers: Indian Affairs,* vol. I, p. 776. Jefferson urged Americans to pay higher prices for furs to the Indians in order to wean the various tribes from their British allegiance. Channing, *op. cit.,* vol. IV, p. 458, note.

[22] *American State Papers: Foreign Relations,* vol. III, pp. 715–723.

and it is probable that some of the more irresponsible British traders did encourage the Indians to raid American outposts.[23] Certainly the western Americans had good cause to complain of the British relations with the Indians and, indeed, of the whole of British policy in the west.[24] The American commissioners at Ghent, however, failed to produce any evidence in support of the accusation, and there is no proof of any official encouragement of the Indians by the British authorities.[25] The desire to settle the Indian problem, to seize the Indians' lands, and to force the British to relinquish their forts in the upper Mississippi valley in accordance with the terms of the Treaty of 1783,[26] were undoubtedly strong factors in convincing the western states of the necessity of war in 1812.[27] It is significant that the American delegates at Ghent at the close of the war refused to agree to the delineation of any boundary line separating the territory of the United States from the lands claimed by the Indian nations.[28]

The three causes mentioned above were of real importance in justifying the American declaration of war; but it is now generally recognized that the determination of the western frontiersmen to expand the borders of their states and to free themselves forever from the stifling competition of the British fur traders was the fundamental explanation of the War of 1812. As Professor Pratt has definitely demonstrated, it was not the representatives of the harassed commercial interests of the East, it

[23] Morison, *op. cit.,* vol. I, p. 64; Bemis, *Jay's Treaty,* New York, 1923, pp. 16–17.

[24] Note particularly the effect of the battle of Tippecanoe, Nov. 7, 1811, which took place just as Congress was meeting to consider the problem of war. In this battle almost two hundred Americans were killed. See Bemis, *op. cit.,* vol. III, pp. 234–235.

[25] *American State Papers: Foreign Relations,* vol. III, pp. 721–723; Tupper, *Life of Sir Isaac Brock,* London, 1847, p. 95.

[26] Britain had held these posts in direct violation of the terms of this treaty, seeking thus to retain control of the western Indians and the fur trade. See McLaughlin, "Western Posts and British Debts" in *Report of the American Historical Association, 1894;* see also Morison, *op. cit.,* p. 62.

[27] See Pratt, *The Expansionists of 1812,* New York, 1925.

[28] This was the denial of a proposal made as early as 1791. *American State Papers: Foreign Relations,* vol. III, pp. 710, 715–718.

was the frontiersmen from the South and West that forced through Congress the declaration of war. "Nothing could better demonstrate the frontier character of the war spirit than to observe its progressive decline as we pass from the rim of the crescent (*i. e.,* the frontier states) to its center at the national capital." [29]

The desire to obtain Canada and to drive Great Britain forever from the continent was the natural result of the philosophy of, and the passions engendered by, the American Revolution. But it was more than that. It was a symbol of the imperialistic desire for expansion inherent in a young, confident, and successful nation. Even apart from the economic factors involved, it was natural, therefore, that the most ardent advocates of war should be found among the westerners, frontiersmen, men whose own lives were a proof of the dynamic expansive power of American society.[30] They were the real democrats; the typical product of the new frontier.[31] In the eyes of such Americans, aggressive action against Great Britain was peculiarly justified and thoroughly acceptable. The British Crown was the hereditary enemy, the malign representative of aristocracy and reaction, and blows struck against Great Britain were blows for liberty and democracy. Monarchy and republicanism could not thrive as neighbors, and until the last vestige of British control in America was removed, the union would be insecure. Furthermore, the acquisition of the Canadian provinces would compensate the United States for injuries suffered at the hands of Great Britain,[32] and it would

[29] Pratt, *The Expansionists of 1812,* p. 127; James Truslow Adams, *Revolutionary New England,* New York, 1923.

[30] See Pratt, *op. cit.;* Hacker, "Western Land Hunger and the War of 1812: A Conjecture," *Mississippi Valley Historical Review,* March, 1924. An excellently tempered and reasonable statement of this condition is to be found in Bemis, *op. cit.,* vol. III, pp. 233–235, 246.

[31] Turner, *The Frontier in American History,* New York, 1921, pp. 168, 213 (this book is an epoch-making contribution to American historiography). Paxson, *History of the American Frontier, 1763–1893,* New York, 1924, chapter 19. See also the review of Pratt's *Expansionists of 1812* in *The American Historical Review,* September, 1926.

[32] See speech of Senator Porter in Adams, *History of the United States,* vol. VI, pp. 136–137. John Randolph declared that the House of Representatives resounded to "one eternal monotonous tone—Canada, Canada,

open a new and convenient waterway for western commerce—
the St. Lawrence River.

A final incentive toward the conquest was the reputed desire
of the Canadians to be freed from British oppression, and to be
allowed to enter the American Union.[33] That Canada was united
in desiring this consummation was vouched for by Henry Clay
and his followers—those impetuous advocates of expansion known
as the War Hawks.[34]

Prominent among the overt acts which helped to make the
war inevitable were the attack of H. M. S. *Leopard* upon the
American *Chesapeake*,[35] and the publication of the Henry letters.[36]

These, then, were the causes of the War of 1812—causes in
the creation of which the Canadian people had little part. In the
result of the war, however, as elements of the British Empire,
and as the objectives of American attack, the Canadian provinces
were vitally interested and deeply involved.

Canada." Quoted in Skelton, *op. cit.*, p. 45. A modern American scholar
of distinction has declared that "the lust of land possessed us; the dream
of conquering and annexing Canada deluded us." Johnson, *op. cit.*, vol. I,
p. 281. However, James Monroe, Secretary of State, displayed no enthusiasm over the projected attack on Canada. Bemis, *op. cit.*, vol. III, pp.
247, 255–256, 269.

[33] This belief was firmly held by a large percentage of the American
people, and was based to a considerable extent upon the reports of travelers
who were nearly unanimous in declaring it to be the desire of the people of
Canada. See the many reports in Cruikshank, "A Study of Disaffection in
Upper Canada in 1812–1815," *Transactions of the Royal Society of Canada*,
vol. VI, sec. 2, 1912, pp. 11 ff. See also the report of John Howe to Prevost,
American Historical Review, vol. XVII, pp. 70 ff.

[34] See Colton (editor), *The Works of Henry Clay*, New York, 1897,
chapter 9. For a contemporary account of the methods used by the War
Hawks to influence Congress, see Gaillard Hunt (editor), "Joseph Gale's
Comments on the War Manifesto of 1812," *American Historical Review*,
vol. XIII, pp. 308–310.

[35] *Canadian Archives*, C. 673, p. 105.

[36] Henry was a British secret agent who, dissatisfied with the payment
for his letters describing American conditions, sold in copies of his correspondence to the United States government. *Canadian Archives Report*,
1896, pp. 38–64; Richardson, *Messages and Papers of the Presidents*, Washington, 1896–1899, vol. II, p. 498; *Niles' Register*, vol. II, pp. 19–27.

2. THE CANADIAN ATTITUDE TOWARD THE WAR OF 1812

To understand the attitude of the Canadian people in 1812 it is important to recall the ethnic composition of the colonial population.

As has been shown above, the inhabitants of the maritime provinces were, at this time, almost exclusively of Loyalist descent. Some few thousand emigrants from the British Isles,[37] together with a much smaller number of French-Canadians—returned Acadians, or descendants of those who had escaped the expulsion—were the only other elements in the population. New Brunswick in particular was still almost exclusively the home of Loyalists. The French-Canadian habitants, both in Nova Scotia and in Lower Canada, remained loyal to the British cause. The Roman Catholic priesthood, whose privileges and power rested very largely upon the continuance of British rule, and who were utterly antipathetic toward the skeptical, free-thinking attitude of the early United States, were primarily responsible for the fostering of this anti-American sentiment. The memory of American excesses during the invasion of 1776 was also a contributing factor.

The maritime provinces played little part in the War of 1812. The Governors of Maine and New Brunswick by concurrent proclamation, issued during the summer of 1812, prevented any military activities on that section of the international border. This truce within a war lasted until 1814 when, after the defeat of Napoleon, it was abrogated by the British, and offensive measures were undertaken with the assistance of veteran troops newly arrived from Europe.[38] Nova Scotia not only escaped suffering in the war, but actually prospered exceedingly. Halifax, the British naval station on the North Atlantic coast, was busily employed

---

[37] Cowan, *op. cit.*

[38] Bourinot, *Canada, 1760-1900*, Cambridge University Press, 1900, pp. 117-118; James. *A Full and Correct Account of the Military Occurrences of the Late War Between Great Britain and the United States of America,* London, 1818, vol. II, p. 475 ff.

in repairing and equipping His Majesty's ships, while privateer-
ing under letters of marque gave profitable employment to many
a "Bluenose" crew.[39] Supplies for the Canadian army, purchased
in New England and New York, found entrance into Canada
through the ports and border towns of the maritime provinces.
Inasmuch as a very considerable proportion [40] of the rations and
equipment for the Canadian forces was obtained from the United
States, this trade was highly lucrative for those engaged in it.[41]
Indeed, many of the traders of Nova Scotia and New England
alike prospered during the war to an unexampled extent, while
peace was temporarily disastrous.[42]

These commercial relations between the maritime provinces
and New England did not, however, lessen in any appreciable degree the hostility evidenced by the far-eastern Canadians toward
American institutions and ideals. The people of Nova Scotia,
Prince Edward Island, and New Brunswick were not less forward
than their compatriots in Upper Canada in the denunciation of
the political and territorial ambitions of Henry Clay and John C.
Calhoun. The Assemblies of Nova Scotia and New Brunswick
voted large sums of money and prepared their militia for active
service in defense of their country. The Assembly of the latter
province declared that it was "ready and determined to repel
every aggression which the infatuated policy of the American
government may induce it to commence on the soil of New Bruns-

[39] Murdock, *History of the United States,* vol. III, p. 351.

[40] Estimates ran as high as seventy-five per cent. "Lower Canada, No.
190," *British Archives,* vol. 128; *Canadian Archives Report, 1896,* p. 35.

[41] *Canadian Archives Report, 1896,* p. 37; *Annals of Congress, 1813–1814,*
p. 2021; Plattsburg *Republican,* January 15, 1813. New England's war trade
was not confined to Canada. Even during the periods of embargo and
blockade, Yankee skippers could purchase licenses in New York and
Boston (issued by Lord Sidmouth) which entitled them to pass the British
fleet. Similar licenses were forged and sold in great numbers. Stewart,
Cases in the Admiralty Court at Halifax, p. 499; *Niles' Register,* vol. III,
p. 256; "The Dearborn Letters," *Mississippi Valley Historical Review,* vol.
II, p. 422.

[42] Adams, *op. cit.,* vol. VII, pp. 147, 367–368, 264, 283; *idem,* vol. VIII,
p. 14; *idem,* vol. IX pp. 95–103, 126; *Annals of Congress, 1815–1816,* p.
1651; *American State Papers: Commerce and Navigation,* vol. I, p. 929.

wick." [43] During the critical period of the war, the 104th Regiment, recruited in large part from the Loyalist districts of the maritime provinces, made a heroic winter march through the wilderness from Halifax to Montreal, in order to aid their hard-pressed comrades in Canada.[44]

No accurate statistics relating to the population of Upper and Lower Canada in 1812 are obtainable. The census is a comparatively modern innovation on this continent. As a compromise among the many estimates, the following figures may be accepted as substantially correct:

Lower Canada (Quebec) 325,000 of whom the vast majority were of French descent.

Upper Canada (Ontario) 80,000 made up approximately as follows:

Loyalists and their descendants	35,000
American settlers	25,000
Other immigrants	20,000

The United Empire Loyalists were the most numerous as well as the most influential element in the population of Upper Canada, and Upper Canada was destined to be the main theater of the war.

The Canadian attitude toward the War of 1812 may be said to have been determined by five outstanding factors. First, the ingrained and violent dislike for the United States originating with, and fostered by, the Loyalists. Second, the natural loyalty of a weak and dependent colony to the motherland to which it is bound by ties of affection, tradition, and self-interest. Third, the favor with which the British rule was accepted by the Roman Catholic hierarchy, which in turn controlled the opinions of the vast majority of the inhabitants of Lower Canada. Fourth, Canadian resentment of the partiality which they felt was displayed in the savage attacks of the press and politicians of the United States against Great Britain, while France, though apparently

[43] *Proceedings of the Legislative Assembly,* New Brunswick, 1813.

[44] This march deserves to rank with Arnold's famous trip from Cambridge to Quebec. They were achievements unsurpassed in the military annals of this continent. Christie, *History of the Late Province of Lower Canada,* 1849, vol. II, pp. 124–125.

guilty of similar offenses against the republic, was mildly reprimanded, or even publicly applauded. Fifth, the inevitable war-
evoked conviction that the Canadian volunteers were fighting to
uphold the honor of their country, the safety of their homes, the
preservation of their ideals, and the sanctity of their religion
against an invader devoid of responsibility, subject to the mob
rule of a debased citizenry, blackened by the atheism of republican France, and destitute alike of high principles or national honor
—a nation led astray by the philosophy of Jefferson, Voltaire,
and Tom Paine.[45]

The influence of the Loyalists was the most decisive factor
in molding public opinion as the war crisis developed.[46]

The imperial loyalty of Canadians was strengthened by the imminence of a stronger and more populous neighbor. The fact that
this neighbor was not always unselfish and friendly strengthened
the imperial bonds. Love for Great Britain was linked with, and
dependent upon, a sense of security in the protection afforded
by British power, while the later development of an independent
spirit in Canada was synchronous with the growth of self-
confidence. Before the outbreak of war in 1812, perfect reliance
was placed on the ability and willingness of the motherland to
protect her domains in North America. "To expect that Great
Britain would submit to see the allegiance of her subjects stolen
from her," wrote a Canadian editor, "is to accuse her of imbecil-
ity, blindness and decrepitude." [47] The Canadian people were
convinced that "the government as well as the people of the
United States who are perfectly aware of the growing prosperity
of Canada are devising means to thwart it." [48] Against such an

---

[45] From the Canadian point of view this was purely a war of defense.
They had not willed or desired it. They felt that they were fighting for
freedom against a foreign foe. In this fact is found the basis of Canadian
success. Cf. Lucas, *The Canadian War of 1812,* Oxford, 1906, p. 24.

[46] See above, Chapter II. "The Americans were in fact to reap the harvest they themselves had sown . . . they were faced by men who above
all others in the whole world were most likely to offer a stubborn resistance." Lucas, *op. cit.,* p. 15.

[47] Montreal *Gazette,* April 27, 1807.

[48] *Idem,* April 1, 1811.

eventuality, Canada looked to the motherland for protection and assistance. A citizen of Montreal, writing to the famous Montreal *Gazette*, declared that Great Britain had given to Canada

"liberty and all the blessings arising from the protection and paternal affection of the best and happiest government the world has ever seen." If war should now be necessary, "Let government but give the word and Canadians will convince their enemies that they are loyal and brave people ready to defend their holy religion, their laws, their liberty, and their country, against any invader." [49]

Such was the spirit of Canada.

The methods by which the British administration had gained the good will of the Roman Catholic church—the guaranteeing of tithes, the freedom of worship and instruction, and complete self-government—are too well known to need recapitulation.[50]

American publicists have not always realized, do not all realize today, that critical attacks upon Great Britain arouse more resentment in Canada than they do in the country attacked. Great Britain, old and experienced in the many trials of international intercourse, accepts these attacks as matters of routine, while Canada, young, impetuous, and sensitive, feels the sting in all its bitterness. In 1812 the attitude of the American government and press was rendered even more obnoxious in Canadian eyes by the obvious discrimination made between England and France.[51] The editor of the "Gazette" summed up the matter thus:

"When it is self-evident that the American Government is decidedly hostile to Great Britain, we must conclude (from its being elective) that the majority of the people approve of the measure of their rulers. . . . How can a British subject restrain his indignation when he perceives the perfidy of the American Government

[49] "Calm Observer" in the Montreal *Gazette,* July 4, 1807.
[50] See above, Chapter I.
[51] It is now generally recognized that the French offenses were nominally more serious than the British, though France was not in a position to carry them out so completely. "The British policy gave neutral traders fair warning and a chance to go elsewhere with their cargoes. The French policy was that of arbitrary confiscation." Johnson, *op. cit.,* vol. I, pp. 261–262.

in their relations with England and their treacherous subserviency
to such despotism" (France).[52]

"From the mortal enemy of Great Britain," wrote the same editor
on another occasion, "America has tamely put up with every insult even when offered in the presence of her household Gods.
When the French and Spaniards capture and condemn her vessels,
where is her indignation, her national energies, her honorable impartiality? From these friends she has been offered the very dregs
of humiliation and she has not refused the cup." [53]

The solution of this perplexing attitude as explained by the editor
of the Montreal *Gazette* was found in the employment of "French
gold"—a medium of exchange in 1807 with characteristics very
similar to those attributed to the "tainted gold" of Russia by
the American State Department after 1917. The people of the
United States were particularly susceptible to such influences, declared the *Gazette,* for they were remarkable "for prudence and
sagacity in all matters in which their pockets were concerned." [54]
Canadians were firmly convinced that the United States took a
peculiar and exclusive delight in slandering the British Empire,
and Governor Craig clearly expressed this view, when he declared
to the Assembly of Lower Canada: "I fear that there can be no
difference of sentiment as to its being a branch of that system
of partial and irritating policy which has so long marked their
public proceedings toward us." [55] Slander replied to slander and
opinion became more and more inflamed on either side of
the boundary.

"The United States may continue to boast," wrote a Canadian
paper, "but without any of the bluster and gasconade which is
characteristic of democracies, the people of Canada will be ready
for any event which the temerity or folly of the American government may produce." [56]

[52] Montreal *Gazette,* April 1, 1811.
[53] *Idem,* April 27, 1807.
[54] *Ibid.*
[55] *Idem,* April 1, 1811.
[56] *Canadian Courant,* August 10, 1807.

Five years later the same paper, answering an American assault against the moral and ethical standards of Great Britain, declared:

"This opprobrious system of national slander; this new system of warfare against which neither virtue nor valour can always furnish an adequate defense, has been transplanted with other noxious productions from the polluted soil of France to the political hotheads of the United States, where for some time they have been shooting and spreading it with . . . natural exuberance. They have ascribed to Great Britain acts of atrocious wickedness, for the utter abhorrence of which she has ever been preëminently conspicuous." [57]

The last and a very important influence in forming the Canadian attitude toward the War of 1812, was that arising from the fundamental differences between society in the two nations. This difference led the Canadians to look upon themselves as the defenders of Christianity in its battle against French scepticism; as upholding law and order against the attacks of mob rule; as representing all that was sane, conservative and traditional, in contrast with the revolutionary, democratic and chaotic social and political conditions of the United States.

In every society there is a constant conflict between the radical and the conservative. The latter demands a proper appreciation of the thought and custom of the past, while the radical is eager to improve the present by the introduction of the new and idealistic. Held in proper equilibrium, these two forces would produce a society which, while retaining the elements of value from the past, would ever move forward to a more worthy future. Unbalanced by a radical predominance, the result would be a lack of respect for law, tradition and authority, costly experiments, and eventual chaos.[58] When the scales are depressed by the weight of conservatism the result is stagnation, reaction, and suppression followed inevitably by the revolt of those oppressed. Every social revolution in history—from Iknoton III to Nicholas II—has been caused by the conservatives.

[57] *Idem*, July 27, 1812.
[58] A radical society is a most unusual phenomenon and seldom persists after the subsidence of the strain or enthusiasm which gave it birth.

In the Loyalist immigration Canada received a foundation of conservatism which stood her in good stead during the early years of her formative period.[59] It made possible the establishment of an orderly society, the foundation of those institutions by which civilization is commonly judged—although the Loyalists' interest in education, for example, was not as extensive as is frequently supposed—and it made certain the adherence of the new nation to the established, traditional authority, that of the British Crown. Thus a great bulwark of imperial authority was erected on the continent of North America. Respect for law, obedience to the government, attachment to the church, and loyalty to the empire were the outstanding characteristics of early Canada.

Conditions in the United States were quite different. Here the forces of law and order had indeed won a victory in the establishment of the Constitution, but the hostility toward authority which had been engendered and expressed by the Revolution was still everywhere apparent. The forty years following the War of Independence were characterized by an excessive hostility to legal and—to a certain extent—moral restrictions.[60] The Federalist leaders—Washington, Hamilton, Adams, and Jay—had favored a strong centralized government, and had vigorously opposed anything approximating mob rule, but after 1800 they were not in the majority and consequently could not control the particularist activities of the citizens as a whole. The spirit of the time was individualistic, aggressive, and confident, and, as has been almost invariably the case, the period of war was followed by a general relaxation of the ethical code of the nation—a psychological reaction after a period of moral and physical stress. That this relaxation did not affect the Loyalists to an equal degree was due

---

[59] And which in excess very quickly stultified Canadian progress, and led to the rebellions of 1837–1838.

[60] Some exception should be made for federalist New England. It is interesting to note that, in spite of the prominent part played by New England in the Revolution, Canadians generally considered these states to be superior in morality and in government to the remainder of the Union. As one editor put it, the New England states were inhabited by the descendants of Englishmen and furnish the best specimens of American morals, talents, and unmixed character." *Canadian Courant,* Aug. 19, 1817.

to the conditions of their new environment. Hard and continuous labor is not conducive, among groups with the social and religious traditions of the Loyalists, to lax morality.

Thus the Canadian provinces and the United States, in the period before the War of 1812, were inhabited by radically different classes of society. The conservatism and formalism of the Canadians led them to look upon the political, social, and religious liberalism of the United States as symptoms of degeneracy and decay. In no way can the contrast of the two peoples be better exemplified than in their attitudes toward the French Revolution. The admiration for the French republic expressed by Jefferson and his followers is notorious, and the Jeffersonian Democrats constituted the majority party in the United States from 1800 to 1812.[61] On the other hand, the typical attitude of Canadians toward this great movement was distinctly hostile. "The violent revolutionists of France," declared the Montreal *Gazette*, "have made a merit of proscription; of equality a preparation for tyranny; of maxims of morality a language of hypocrisy; of religion an insult to the Supreme Being; and of the purest blood the most inexorable orgies." [62] Similar in kind, though modified in degree, was the Canadian opinion of the United States. The Rev. John Strachan, the able but violent bishop of the Anglican church in Upper Canada, declared that the seceded colonies, "instead of possessing the happiest government in the world, possess one of the worst, for who is so ignorant as not to know that the unhappy country is subject to a Virginia oligarchy? We may despise this degenerate government, equally destitute of national honor and virtue, and leave them in silent contempt to brood over their selfish and iniquitous proceedings." [63] Nourished on such sentiments from a pulpit consecrated to the service of the Prince of Peace, and from the pen of one whose duty it was to

[61] Americans generally agreed in applauding the Revolution as a continuance of the struggle for liberty commenced in 1776, although it must not be forgotten that many of the Federalists were just as hostile to many aspects of French republicanism as were any Canadians.

[62] Montreal *Gazette*, April 21, 1803.

[63] Strachan, *A Discourse on the Character of King George III*, Toronto, n.d.

proclaim the brotherhood of man as well as the fatherhood of God, it need cause little surprise to find that the Canadians were convinced that in 1812 they were fighting against a nation whose society was governed by evil and whose moral standards were debauched.

3. THE ATTITUDE OF THE UNITED STATES

Pity, not unmixed with contempt, was the general attitude of Americans toward the Canadian colonists. Having themselves battled against and overthrown the power of the British Crown within their respective states, the Americans could not understand the attachment of Canadians to the "effete" monarchy of Great Britain, and laid the cause to a lack of energy, initiative, and valor. Thus it was that in planning the conquest of Canada the American leaders sincerely believed that they were conferring a favor upon the less vigorous inhabitants of North America. It was to be a crusade to spread the culture of the democratic republic. That the Canadians might not wish such liberty and culture, or that the American armies would be faced with any great difficulty in accomplishing their task, was beyond the comprehension of the democrats of Kentucky or New Jersey.[64] There were, of course, other attractions in this plan of conquest: the Indian trouble would be settled as the Americans desired,[65] the addition of a rich and extensive territory would add to American prestige, and above all, Americans once again would be fighting against the hereditary foe; and all the auguries and portents promised victory.

The people and government of the United States were alike

[64] For a clear picture of the American attitude toward the war see Hunt (editor), *The Writings of James Madison,* New York, 1908, vols, VII, VIII. For interesting sidelights on the war from the diplomatic point of view see Paul Leicester Ford (editor), *The Writings of John Quincy Adams,* New York, 1915, vols. IV, V. Canada was invariably treated as a commodity belonging to Great Britain to be taken, captured, or sold without regard to the wishes of the inhabitants.

[65] Paul Leicester Ford, *Adams,* vol. V, pp. 8–9.

completely misled in regard to the sentiment of the Canadians. Americans could not comprehend how any people could prefer the monarchical system of Great Britain, with its restrictive colonial regulation, to the free, independent, and democratic political economy of the United States. The American settlers in Upper Canada added to the delusion. Segregated to a great extent in townships of their own, these emigrants soon came to believe that their own desire for union with the republic was shared by all Canadians. They so reported to the United States government, leading Jefferson to speak of Canada "which wants to enter the Union." [66] Eustis, American Secretary of War, after an examination of all the information obtainable, declared: "We can take Canada without soldiers! we have only to send officers into the Provinces, and the people, already disaffected toward their own government, will rally to our standard." [67] John Henry, sent into the United States by Governor-General Prevost on a mission of observation, reported that Americans unanimously considered "the disposition of Canadians as friendly to them," while John Mellish, an American who visited Canada in 1811, declared that "were five thousand men to be sent into the Province with the Proclamation of Independence the great mass of the people would join the American government." [68] Colonel Cruikshank, a Canadian historian who has done invaluable work on this period, has written that "travellers from the United States, who visited Upper Canada during the first decade of the nineteenth century, generally agreed in reporting that they had observed among the inhabitants a determined partiality to the United States, and an avowed hostility to the British government." [69] Many Americans, moreover, believed that even Great Britain itself would not be averse to an American-Canadian union. "That the Canadas should be attached to the United States was the unanimous opinion of all intelligent statesmen in Great Britain in the years 1809–1811,"

[66] Henry Adams, *op. cit.,* vol. VI, p. 149.

[67] Quoted in Denison, *The Influence of the United Empire Loyalists,* Toronto, 1905. See Cruikshank, *op. cit.*

[68] *Proceedings of the Royal Society of Canada,* Third Series, vol. VI, sec. 402, p. 11.

[69] Cruikshank, *op. cit.*

declared the *National Intelligencer*.[70] These opinions, both American and Canadian, are further proof of the old adage, "A man believes that which he wishes to believe."

Not only did Americans believe that Canada would welcome intervention by the United States, but they were confident, should any defense of Canada be attempted, that the American forces could easily overcome the opposition. A comparison of the relative strength of the combatants goes far to prove the justice of drawing such a conclusion.[71]

In 1812 the British colonies on this continent possessed a practically undefended boundary line one thousand miles in length; and a population of less than 500,000, of whom only some 80,000 were domiciled in Upper Canada—the inevitable point of attack. To defend this territory there were in Canada 4450 regular soldiers, and a possible militia strength of about 65,000 men. Of these Upper Canada could provide, at most, 11,000. Canada did, in truth, appear to be in no condition for self-defense.

In the United States, on the other hand, was a white population of over six million.[72] In April, 1808, the American standing army had been increased to about 6000 men,[73] and on June 6, 1812, there were under arms a total of 6744 men.[74] But the potential strength of the country was shown by the war measures and the militia returns. An order of January 11, 1812, provided for the enlistment of 25,000 additional men,[75] and other acts authorized the President to raise this total to 50,000,[76] and to demand of the states 100,000 militia.[77] The total militia enrollment (on paper) at this time reached the enormous number of 694,735.[78]

[70] *National Intelligencer*, January 6, 1814.

[71] See comparison in W. Wood, *The War with the United States*, Toronto, 1915, chapter 2.

[72] *Canadian Archives*, C. 1168, p. 2; Garneau, *op. cit.*, vol. II, p. 491.

[73] *American Statutes at Large*, Washington, 1845, vol. II, p. 481.

[74] *American State Papers: Military Affairs*, vol. I, p. 319.

[75] *American Statutes at Large*, vol. II, pp. 671, 676, 705.

[76] *American State Papers: Military Affairs*, vol. I, p. 320.

[77] *American Statutes at Large*, vol. II, p. 676.

[78] *American State Papers: Military Affairs*, vol. I, pp. 298–300 ff. American enlistments during the war exceeded the total population of Canada. For a comparison of military strength see: Madison's address in *Annual*

Fortunate it was for Canada that, through the opposition of New England, and the almost complete lack of competent leaders, this huge strength could not be exerted on the northern frontier.

Thomas Jefferson characterized the proposed conquest as "a mere matter of marching," [79] while Calhoun declared that "in four weeks from the time that a declaration of war is heard on our frontiers the whole of Upper Canada and a part of Lower Canada will be in our possession." [80] But it was left to Andrew Jackson to picture the conquest in its most alluring colors:

> "We are going," he declared, "to vindicate our right to the fur trade, and to open a market for the productions of our soil . . . to seek some indemnity for past injuries by the conquest of all the British dominions upon the continent of North America. Should the conquest of Canada be resolved, how pleasing the prospect that would open to the young volunteer, while performing a military promenade into a distant country. A succession of new and interesting objects would perpetually fill and delight his imagination, the effect of which would be heightened by the warlike appearances, the martial music, and the grand evolutions of an army of fifty thousand men. But why should these inducements be held out to the young men of America? They need them not, animated as they are to rival the exploits of Rome, they will never prefer an inglorious sloth, a supine inactivity to the honorable toil of carrying the Republican standard to the Heights of Abraham." [81]

It is obvious that the American interpretation of the Canadian viewpoint was entirely incorrect, and it was so proven by the outcome of the invasion.

All of the United States, however, did not view the projected war with such enthusiasm. It is an extraordinary fact that the very persons upon whose behalf the war was nominally being fought (the harassed shopkeepers of New England and New York) were

---

Register, 1813, p. 395; Wood, "Canada in the War of 1812" in Shortt and Doughty, *op. cit.,* vol. III, p. 204.

[79] Adams, *op. cit.,* vol. VI, p. 337.

[80] Paul Leicester Ford (editor), *The Writings of Jefferson,* vol. VIII, p. 450.

[81] Andrew Jackson in the Essex *Register,* May 6, 1812.

the leaders in opposition to the war policy. Evidently the influence
of the western "expansionists" was greater than has sometimes
been suggested. The merchants of New England and New York,
whose commerce had been so seriously disrupted by the embargo
laws enacted by the Madison administration, were almost unanimous in their opposition.[82] The British Orders-in-Council and
policy of impressment were annoying, but they feared that war,
with Great Britain in command of the seas and the British market
closed, was likely to prove disastrous.[83] "Nothing but their fears,"
wrote General Dearborn in regard to the citizens of Massachusetts,
"prevent them from going to all lengths," in opposition to the
government.[84] Two weeks after the declaration of war the General reported again: "There has been nothing yet done in New
England that indicates an actual state of war, but every means
that can be devised by the Tories is in operation to depress the
spirits of the country."[85] The Governors of Massachusetts and
Connecticut refused to supply the militia necessary to guard the
coast,[86] and the former issued a proclamation (June 26) for a

[82] 34 Members of Congress issued a proclamation stating that if the
United States entered such a war, it would do so "as a divided people
. . . from the moral and political objections of great weight and very
general influence." *Niles' Register,* vol. II, pp. 309–315. The elections of
1812 were fought primarily on the war issue and De Witt Clinton, the
Federalist candidate, won New England, New York, New Jersey and
Delaware. Madison carried all the other states and the election. Adams,
op. cit., pp. 409–414; Walker, *The Making of the Nation,* New York, 1895,
pp. 240–247.

[83] See above, pp. 57, 66. Great Britain wished to persuade New England
to leave the Union. She also wanted to have her ships supplied from New
England ports. As a result trade from these ports flourished during the
Napoleonic struggle. Henry, a British agent sent to New Engalnd to report
on conditions, declared, "there is good ground to hope that . . . Mass.,
R. I., Conn., New Hampshire, and Vermont will resist every attempt of
the French party to involve the U. S. in a war with Great Britain." *Report
on Canadian Archives, 1896,* note B; McMaster, *op. cit.,* vol. III, pp. 550–
553.

[84] Dearborn to Eustis, June 26, 1812. War Department manuscript.

[85] *Idem,* July 1, 1812.

[86] *Massachusetts State Papers: Military Affairs,* vol. I, p. 324; Richardson (editor), *Messages and Papers of the Presidents, 1789–1907,* vol. I,
p. 516; *idem,* vol. X, p. 43.

public fast in consequence of the Federal declaration of war—
a wrong committed "against the nation from which we are descended and which for many generations has been the bulwark
of the religion we profess." [87] The Governor of Vermont threatened to use force if the Federal government attempted to compel
that state to aid in the prosecution of the war.[88] Under the vigorous leadership of Josiah Quincy [89] the Federalists openly and
violently accused Madison and Monroe of having sold the honor
of the United States to France.[90] New England Congressmen who
had voted for the war were publicly insulted; [91] the Massachusetts House of Representatives issued an address proclaiming the
war a wanton sacrifice and advising the people to organize locally
to "express your sentiments without fear, and let the sound of
your disapprobation . . . be loud and deep . . . let there be no
volunteers except for defensive war." [92] An attempt made to call
a state convention to arrange for the withdrawal of Massachusetts
from the Union was narrowly defeated.[93] The action of President
Madison in denouncing the armistice arranged by Governor Prevost and General Dearborn (in consequence of the repeal of the
British Orders-in-Council) provided the Federalists with further
ammunition.[94] New England Puritanism, still extant in some
degree, was as vigorously opposed to a war which strengthened
the hands of "atheistic France" as was Canada itself.[95]

New England was, perhaps, even more opposed to the Republican (Jeffersonian Democratic) Party than it was to the war,
but this does not alter the fact that the opposition was a vital
factor in restricting the energies of the United States, and the
movement continued to grow after 1812, to culminate in the Hart-

[87] *Niles' Weekly Register,* Baltimore, 1811–1845, vol. II, p. 355.

[88] *Idem,* vol. V, pp. 212–230.

[89] *Annals of Congress,* 11th Cong., 3rd sess., pp. 524, 540, etc. E. Quincy,
Life of Josiah Quincy, Boston, 1867, chaps. 9–14.

[90] Adams, *op. cit.,* vol. VI, p. 400.

[91] Boston *Patriot,* August 19, 1812.

[92] *Address to the People of the State,* Boston, June 26, 1812.

[93] *The Palladium,* August 7, 1812; *The Patriot,* August 8, 1812.

[94] *State Papers,* vol. III, p. 587.

[95] Adams, *op. cit.,* vol. VI, p. 399.

ford Convention of 1814.[96] But the Federalists, defeated and discredited in the country at large, could produce no effect on the national policy, could not prevent the southern and western states from waging an offensive war.[97]

4. WAGING THE WAR

War was declared by the United States on June 18, 1812.[98] When the news reached America that the British government had revoked its Orders-in-Council, President Madison refused to agree to an armistice, but he did authorize Jonathan Russell, American *chargé* in London, to offer definite terms of peace. Lord Castlereagh, however, expecting Admiral Warren and President Madison to settle the whole problem in America itself, refused to negotiate with Russell.[99] This deadlock wasted so much time that the continuation of the war became inevitable. An Atlantic cable might easily have ended hostilities, although the problem of impressment would have had to be faced.

The exposed situation of Upper Canada led inevitably to its selection as the theater of war.[100] With its long and undefended

[96] Strange as it may seem, despite this opposition, New England and New York contributed their proportionate share of man power and money before the end of the war. See Adams, *op. cit.*, vol. VIII, pp. 233–236; Morison, *Harrison Grey Otis*, vol. II, pp. 52–124 (a vivid description of these years).

[97] Morison, *op. cit.*, vol. II, p. 84. G. Morris advocated calling a convention to decide whether or not it was wise for the "Northern and Eastern States to continue in Union with the owners of slaves." Separation was freely advocated and justified. Cf. Anderson, "A Forgotten Phase of the New England Opposition to the War of 1812," *Proceedings of the Mississippi Valley Historical Society*, vol. VI; *The Public Documents of the Massachusetts Senate, Containing Proceedings of the Hartford Convention of Delegates*, Boston, 1815.

[98] The divided opinion of the country is clearly reflected in the congressional vote on the declaration of war. Both houses voted in favor of war, the Senate by 19 to 13, the House of Representatives by 79 to 49. Walker, *op. cit.*, p. 225; Richardson (editor), *Messages and Papers of the Presidents, 1789–1907*, vol. I, pp. 499–504.

[99] *American State Papers: Foreign Relations*, vol. III, pp. 587, 590, 595.

[100] An interesting, although not entirely accurate description of the influence of geography on the War of 1812 may be found in Ellen Semple,

border, its weak military strength,[101] the large percentage of Americans in its population, and its difficult communications,[102] Upper Canada appeared to be incapable of any resolute defense. Almost every prospect appeared to favor a speedy and practically uncontested victory for the American forces. Internal dissensions in the United States, and the enthusiasm with which the Loyalists of Upper Canada supported General Isaac Brock, who was probably the most capable leader to participate in the war, alone indicated the possibility of a successful defense of Canada.[103]

The declaration of war precipitated a real crisis in Upper Canada. General Brock, apart from his 1450 regulars, was forced to rely upon a scanty militia force, which in many districts refused to obey his orders, and a legislature so evenly divided between Loyalists and American sympathizers as to be practically useless. His troops, moreover, were lacking in the essential materials of war; their artillery was weak, supplies were meager, uniforms and shoes were not available for all. Thus Canada was defended in its most vulnerable spot by less than two thousand soldiers and a populace at least one-third of which was in sympathy with the invaders.[104] The only favorable omens, as noted above, were the hostility of New England to the war, the character and ability of General Brock, and the enthusiastic coöperation of the Loyalists and their sons.[105] The American leaders in their optimistic references to the conquest of Canada had forgotten

American History and Its Geographic Conditions, New York, 1903, chapter 8.

[101] Counting Canadian irregulars, there were 6360 soldiers in Canada, of whom 1473 were in Upper Canada. "Abstracts of General Returns of Troops in Upper and Lower Canada, July 30, 1812," *Freer Papers*, 1812–1813, *Canadian Archives Manuscripts;* James, *op. cit.*, vol. II, p. 55; MacDonell, *op. cit.*, pp. 162 ff.

[102] *Canadian Archives Report, 1896*, p. 36.

[103] McMaster, *op. cit.*, vol. III, p. 558.

[104] *Canadian Archives*, Q. 107, p. 236.

[105] Not all those who supported General Brock in 1812 were Loyalists or the descendants of Loyalists; many were recently-arrived British immigrants. But the Loyalists supplied the hatred and inspired the enthusiasm which turned the scales.

the exiles of 1783. The Loyalists had suffered too acutely to forget with such dispatch.

War had been declared on June 18, 1812.[106] On July 12th General Hull, a venerable relic of the Revolutionary struggle, advanced with some two thousand men from Detroit into Upper Canada. The settlers on the western end of the Ontario peninsula offered little resistance, and within two days his cavalry had penetrated one hundred miles into British territory. One of the first acts of General Hull after the invasion started, was to issue a grandiloquent proclamation to the Canadian people, offering them freedom, justice and the other prerogatives of a republican people, if they would refrain from interfering with his operations against the minions of British tyranny.[107] General Brock replied with a counter-proclamation, and ordered out the militia.[108] This order was obeyed only in the Loyalist districts,[109] and the apparent success of General Hull tended to make the people as a whole disheartened and fearful.[110] The pro-American element rejoiced, and on July 26th General Brock reported that "numbers had already joined the invading army." [111]

In this predicament the British Commander saw the necessity of rallying public opinion behind his efforts, and on July 27th he summoned an extraordinary session of the Assembly.

The legislative body which assembled at York in answer to the summons of General Brock was divided almost equally between Loyalists and representatives who either did not wish or feared to oppose the American advance. Five months previously [112] Brock had appeared before this same body and had urged immediate action to place the country in a position of defense. Specifically he had demanded the recruiting of a larger militia

[106] Updike, *op. cit.,* pp. 125 ff.

[107] *Canadian Archives,* Q. 676, p. 168; W. Wood, *Select British Documents of the Canadian War of 1812,* Toronto, 1920, vol. I, pp. 26–28.

[108] W. Wood, *op. cit.,* vol. I, p. 371; *Canadian Archives,* Q. 315, p. 152.

[109] Kingsford, *op. cit.,* vol. VIII, p. 191.

[110] Cruikshank, *op. cit.; Canadian Archives Publication* no. 4, pp. 99, 107.

[111] Brook to Prevost, July 26, 1812, *Canadian Archives,* C. 676, p. 408.

[112] On February 4, 1812. See Edgar, *General Brock,* Toronto, 1909, chapter 15; Wood, *op. cit.,* vol. I, p. 22.

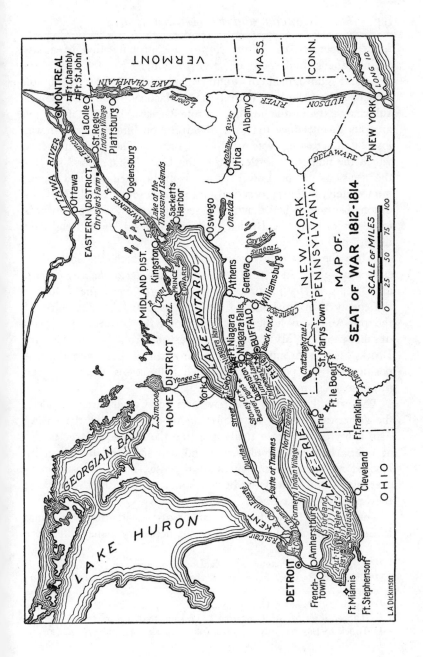

MAP OF.

SEAT OF WAR 1812-1814

SCALE of MILES

0   25   50   75   100

L.A Dickinson

force, suspension of *habeas corpus,* the promulgation of a law against aliens, and more effective machinery for the apprehension and punishment of military offenders.[113] The legislation which resulted had been entirely unsatisfactory. "The many doubtful characters in the militia," wrote General Brock, "made me anxious to introduce the oath of adjuration into the Bill. It was lost by the casting vote of the Chairman. The great influence which the numerous settlers from the United States possess over the decisions of the Lower House is truly alarming, and ought, immediately, by every practical means, to be diminished." [114] Conditions became so bad that the Assembly actually offered rewards to deserters from the British forces.[115] The session had ended in discord and chaos.

When the Assembly reconvened, on July 27th, the same difficulties arose. Again it refused to repeal the act of *habeas corpus,* and "appeared by its proceedings rather to court the favor of the enemy than fearlessly to perform its duty." [116] The spirit of the pro-American leaders was beginning to permeate the mass of the people. "My position is most critical," wrote General Brock, "not from anything the enemy can do but from the disposition of the people. A full belief possesses them that the province must inevitably succumb." [117]

The critical moment had now arrived. Canada was invaded; the American settlers were offering no resistance to the enemy —in many cases were actually assisting the invaders; large bodies of militia had refused to serve; and opposition in the Assembly blocked all energetic measures of defense. The Loyalists, however, were still united in their hostility toward the Americans; they needed only a leader.

The leader demanded by the danger of the situation was found in General Brock. Almost by force the necessary money bills were

---

[113] Edgar, *op. cit.,* chapter 15; MacDonell, *op. cit.,* pp. 165 ff.

[114] Brock to Prevost, February 6, 1812, quoted in MacDonell, *op. cit.,* p. 166.

[115] *Canadian Archives,* Q. 315, pp. 4-28.

[116] Tupper, *Life of Sir Isaac Brock,* London, 1847, p. 203.

[117] Brock to Baynes, July 29, 1812, *Canadian Archives,* C. 676, p. 239.

rushed through the Assembly, which was then summarily dismissed.[118] Calling together the Executive Council, Brock outlined the situation and, with its hearty concurrence, declared martial law. Orders-in-Council were promulgated to provide for the control of aliens and the deportation of those who refused to take the oath of adjuration and allegiance.[119] Imbued with their traditional antipathy toward Americans, and inspired by the challenge of Brock's leadership, the loyal elements of the Upper Canadian population rallied against the invaders.[120] Troops and supplies were collected, with a new enthusiasm regulars and militia united, and between the 4th and 27th of August the timid Hull was forced to retire over the border; Detroit was invested and captured; Upper Canada was consolidated and made secure.[121]

The expulsion of General Hull and the capture of Detroit constitute one of the most extraordinary feats in the military history of Canada. Brock's force was barely half the size of the American army, but it was disciplined, enthusiastic, and brilliantly led. General Hull was subsequently court-martialed and sentenced to death. On account of services in the Revolution, however, he was pardoned by President Madison.[122]

The success of General Brock in this action against Detroit was greatly facilitated by the capture of Fort Michillimakinac by a small detail of soldiers under Captain Roberts—a bold operation which confirmed the western Indians in their allegiance to

[118] Prevost to Bathurst, August 17, 1812. *British Archives Manuscripts,* quoted in Adams, *op. cit.,* vol. VI, p. 318.

[119] MacDonell, *op. cit.,* pp. 168 ff; Adams, *op. cit.,* vol. VI, pp. 316–320; Robinson, *Life of Sir John B. Robinson,* chapter 2.

[120] See *Address of the House of Assembly,* quoted in Ryerson, *op. cit.,* vol. II, pp. 342–345; Coffin, *1812,* Montreal, 1864, p. 40.

[121] Adams, *op. cit.,* vol. VI, pp. 320 ff.; *Niles' Register,* vol. III, p. 53.

[122] *Canadian Archives,* C. 677, p. 46; *idem,* Q. 118, pp. 227, 237; Cruikshank, "General Hull's Invasion of Canada in 1812," *Publications and Transactions of the Royal Society of Canada,* 1907; *Niles' Register,* vol. VI, pp. 154 ff.; Forbes, *Report on the Trial of Brigadier General Hull,* New York, 1914, chapter 2; Hull, *Defense of Brigadier General Hull,* Boston, 1914; Hull, *Memoirs of the Campaign of the Northwest Army of the United States, 1812,* Boston, 1824.

Great Britain.[123] The dilatory antics of another incompetent republican—General Dearborn—who had been expected to aid Hull by vigorous action on the Niagara frontier, also contributed to the American defeat.[124] The only American success in the early weeks of the war was a minor victory at Fort Erie.[125]

The second attack upon Canada was launched at Queenston by Generals Smyth and Van Renssalaer. Having collected 5000 men on the American side of the Niagara River, they crossed over and succeeded in occupying the heights above the Canadian village. Owing, however, to a difference of opinion between the commanders, the refusal of the New York troops to leave the territory of their own state, and the energetic and able opposition of Generals Brock and Sheaffe, the Americans were expelled from the heights which they had captured, were driven into the river, or forced to surrender.[126] The Canadians captured 900 prisoners, but the death of General Brock was heavy payment for their victory.[127]

In the early months of the war Russia proposed to mediate between the combatants, but, as in the case of the armistice desired by Admiral Warren, no assurance was forthcoming from the British government that the policy of impressment would be abandoned, and President Madison in consequence refused to discuss peace.[128] It is only just to add that the war enthusiasm which had by this time affected the majority of the American

[123] This was the first action of the war and took place on July 17, 1812. *Canadian Archives,* C. 676, pp. 232–236. The dispatches of Captain Roberts and his American opponent, Hanks, are also to be found in James, *op. cit.,* vol. I, Appendix I, no. 3.

[124] Adams *op. cit.,* vol. VI, pp. 310, 322, 339.

[125] Mahan, *Sea Power in its Relation to the War of 1812,* Boston, 1905, vol. I, pp. 354–356.

[126] Cruikshank *The Battle of Queenston Heights,* Lundy's Lane Historical Society, Welland, 1904; *Canadian Archives,* Q. 119, pp. 14–17; *idem,* Q. 118, pp. 278–288.

[127] One of the chivalrous actions of the war was the salute fired by order of General Van Renssalaer on the day of Brock's funeral. W. Wood, *Select British Documents,* vol. III, pp. 623–627; Updike, *op. cit.,* p. 143.

[128] *American State Papers: Foreign Relations,* vol. III, pp. 623–627; Updike, *op. cit.,* p. 143.

people—including the leaders of the government—made them impatient of any peace proposals. Less than three years later they accepted terms that they had refused to consider in 1812.

After the defeat at Queenston Heights, Van Renssalaer retired and General Smyth took complete command of the American troops on the Niagara frontier. He immediately assured himself of a prominent place in the records of military incompetence. Although he had 4000 troops in his command, he was badly defeated in a second attempt to cross the river into British territory —by a force of 400 Canadians.[129] This travesty on the art of warfare occurred at Black Rock, and General Smyth was shortly afterwards relieved of his duties.[130] It was now too late in the year for profitable campaigning, and except for a few small and unimportant engagements, both armies retired to winter quarters.[131]

In contrast with these defeats by inferior forces on land, the record of the small and largely disregarded American navy was replete with brilliant victories. The inventive genius of the republic had produced a type of frigate that was heavier in construction, better adapted for speed, designed to carry more men and to mount more guns, than vessels of the same nominal class in the French and British fleets.[132] The American ships, moreover, were manned by volunteers, the majority of whom had been trained in the mercantile service of the eastern states.[133] Too

[129] *Niles' Register,* vol. III, p. 284.

[130] *Canadian Archives,* C. 677, p. 219. General Smyth was probably the most stupid of the many incompetent generals employed by the United States in the war.

[131] Cruikshank, *Documents Relating to the Invasion of Canada in 1812,* Lundy's Lane Historical Society, is an excellent collection of source material on the campaign of 1812. See also *American State Papers: Military Affairs,* vol. I, pp. 490 ff; *Canadian Archives,* Q. 119, pp. 52–65, 112–114, etc.; *Niles' Register,* vol. III, pp. 264–265, 284 ff.

[132] Mahan, *op. cit.,* vol. I, pp. 334, 414–416. The superior power of the American frigates, while it excuses to some extent the defeat of individual British ships, does not in any sense exonerate the British navy as a whole. The navy was caught unprepared; the incompetence of its higher command cost the lives of many valiant seamen and severely damaged the national reputation. Trafalgar had killed Nelson and put the Lords of the Admiralty to sleep.

[133] James, *An Enquiry into the Merits of the Principal Naval Actions*

many of the British crews, on the other hand, were the off-scourings of city slums—the type most likely to constitute the "catch" of the press-gangs.[134] Three great American frigates—the *Constitution, President,* and *United States*—during the first few months of the war won decisive victories over the hitherto undefeated vessels of the British navy. Their success in these single combats aroused intense enthusiasm in the United States, while defeat came as a stupefying shock to the British.[135] These spectacular victories, however, had very little effect on the course of the war as a whole, and after January, 1813, the British navy not only controlled the seas by reason of its superior numbers, but also retrieved some of its lost prestige by victories in single combats.[136] In 1813 and 1814 the American coast was securely blockaded by a vast fleet of vessels under the White Ensign.

The naval policy of the United States in 1813 was aimed primarily at gaining control of Lake Erie and Lake Ontario. In this way it was hoped to facilitate the military occupation of Upper Canada. Captain Chauncey was sent to Lake Ontario and under circumstances of great difficulty he constructed, armed, and manned a small fleet. Across the lake at Kingston, Commodore Yeo was engaged upon a similar task. The result was a stalemate; neither officer wished to risk the chance of a decisive defeat, and no serious engagement took place.[137] A different result was obtained on Lake Erie. Here Commander Perry succeeded in building a fleet that was definitely superior to that of his British opponent, Captain Barclay. In the Battle of Lake

Between Great Britain and the United States, Halifax, 1816. This is an attempt to prove that in each American victory the larger ship won.

[134] Channing, *op. cit.,* vol. IV, pp. 476–478 (this is a very fair discussion). *American State Papers: Naval Affairs,* vol. I.

[135] The Duke of Wellington wrote: "I have been very uneasy about the American naval successes. I think we should have peace with America before the season for opening the campaign in Canada if we could take one or two of these damned frigates." Gurwood (editor), *Wellington's Dispatches,* London, 1838, vol. X, p. 92; quoted also in Lucas, *op. cit.,* p. 68.

[136] Mahan, *op. cit.,* vol. I, pp. 405–406; vol. II, pp. 140 ff.; *Biography of James Lawrence, Esq.,* New Brunswick, New Jersey, 1813.

[137] *Canadian Archives,* C. 729, p. 132; Mahan, *op. cit.,* vol. I, pp. 354–366.

Erie the Americans were completely victorious.[138] As a result of this battle the United States gained full control of the lake, and consequently were able to force the British troops to retire eastward, abandoning Detroit and Amherstburg.[139]

On land the United States was somewhat more successful in 1813 than it had been in 1812, although the final balance was not materially altered. General Harrison, now in command of the American forces in the northwest, advanced his troops toward Upper Canada in three divisions. General Winchester, in command of 1000 men, took the most westerly route. Near the village of Frenchtown, at the extremity of Lake Erie, he was met and defeated by General Proctor, who had a force of 500 regulars and a similar number of Indians. Some 560 of Winchester's men were captured, and the British were accused of allowing their Indian allies to kill many of the American wounded.[140] After his victory at Frenchtown, General Proctor twice crossed Lake Erie to attack the pompous but timid Harrison (at Forts Meigs and Sandusky), but actually succeeded in capturing only a few American militiamen.[141] After Perry's victory on Lake Erie, Proctor was forced to retire. General Harrison followed and defeated him at Moravian Town, where the famous Tecumseh,[142] a national hero in the history of Canada, was killed.[143]

[138] Bancroft, *History of the Battle of Lake Erie*, New York, 1891; *Canadian Archives*, Q. 122, p. 199; *idem*, C. 680, pp. 71 ff; *idem*. C. 731, pp. 116 ff; *American State Papers: Naval Affairs*, vol. I, pp. 294–295; Wood, *Selected British Documents*, vol. II, pp. 243–319.

[139] *Niles' Register*, vol. V, p. 60; *idem*, vol. VIII, p. 236.

[140] *Canadian Archives*, Q. 121, pp. 68–77; *idem*, C. 678, pp. 23–31; Atherton, *Narrative of the Suffering and Defeat of the Northwestern Army under General Winchester*, Lexington, 1818. The employment of Indians was a constant cause of bitterness and recrimination. Lucas, *op. cit.*, pp. 73–74, 80–82.

[141] *Canadian Archives*, C. 679, p. 371.

[142] Raymond, *Tecumseh*, Toronto, 1915, chapter 10. The death of Tecumseh, one of the few Indian statesmen, ended the anti-American confederacy of Indian tribes which he had organized. General Jackson simultaneously defeated the southern Indians and this removed another menace to American success. *American State Papers: Indian Affairs*, vol. I, p. 827; *Niles' Register*, vol. V, pp. 218, 240.

[143] *Canadian Archives*, Q. 123, p. 5; *Niles' Register*, vol. V, p. 130.

This battle destroyed the reputation of General Proctor but failed to provide one for Harrison. The latter had, however, in conjunction with Perry regained control of the Michigan territory for the United States. He now transferred his troops to the Niagara frontier.

In this region the first important action of the year was the capture and partial destruction of York (now Toronto), the capital of Upper Canada, by the combined forces of General Dearborn and Commodore Chauncey.[144] The Library and Parliament buildings were burned, the public records were destroyed, plate was carried off from the churches, and many private dwellings were pillaged by the American soldiery. It is probable, in the light of recent researches, that the American commanders did not order or even encourage this destruction, but they cannot be held blameless for the actions of their soldiery.[145] On the other hand, the American General McClure declared after the war that York had been officially destroyed in reprisal for the burning of Washington by the British. The amusing feature of this testimony is found in the fact that York was destroyed in 1813—Washington in 1814.[146]

After the reduction of York, General Dearborn proceeded to Fort George, which he captured with little difficulty. But while these events were taking place, Governor-General Prevost sought to create a diversion by crossing the lake in Yeo's squadron to raid the American naval base at Sackett's Harbor. No startling success was achieved, although one ship which was building was destroyed on the stocks.[147]

When General Dearborn captured Fort George, he drove out the British commander General Vincent, who was in charge of

[144] *Canadian Archives*, Q. 121, pp. 209–219; *Canadian Archives*, C. 678, pp. 172a, 178.

[145] See the brief but excellent article by W. B. Kerr, "The Occupation of York," *Canadian Historical Review*, vol. V. (1924), pp. 9–21.

[146] *Canadian Courant*, April 5, 1823.

[147] *Some Account of the Public Life of the Late Lieutenant-Governor, Sir George Prevost*, London, 1823, p. 88; *Canadian Archives*, C. 678, pp. 347 ff.; *idem*, M. 389, 6, p. 22; *Niles' Register*, vol. IV, pp. 260 ff. (this is a complete account).

a force of 1600 regulars and volunteers.[148] Generals Winder and Chandler with 3000 men were sent in pursuit. Vincent retired as far as Stony Creek, where he took up a defensive position. Acting on the advice of Lieutenant-Colonel Harvey, a conceited but energetic subordinate, General Vincent sanctioned a night attack on the American forces. Under the command of Harvey himself, this attack was carried out on the night of June 5th–6th with complete success.[149] Once again American leadership had failed, while the Canadian volunteers, as always when fighting defensive actions in Canada, were valorous and effective.[150] The Canadian forces now divided, thus paving the way for one of the most spectacular events of the war. The main body encamped at Beaver Dam, while Lieutenant FitzGibbon with fifty men took up an advanced position some miles away.

Having been warned [151] that he was about to be attacked by a force of over 600 men, FitzGibbon placed his fifty followers in ambush and, with the aid of a small band of Indians, succeeded in deluding the American leader as to the number of his opponents. As a result the whole column surrendered.[152]

In August, 1813, General Wilkinson, a pompous, incompetent and unprincipled militarist, arrived at Sackett's Harbor to take command of the American armies in the west.[153] All of the available troops were collected here in preparation for a descent upon Montreal by way of the St. Lawrence River. This advance was to be made in conjunction with the forces of General Hampton—the latter entering Canada from his headquarters at Platts-

[148] *Canadian Archives,* C. 678, p. 332; Cruikshank, *The Battle of Fort George,* Niagara Historical Society, 1904.

[149] *Canadian Archives,* C. 679, pp. 38 ff.; *idem,* Q. 122, pp. 22 ff.

[150] Cruikshank, *Documentary History,* pt. 11, pp. 7 ff.

[151] *Canadian Archives,* C. 679, pp. 135 ff.; M. A. FitzGibbon, *The Life of James FitzGibbon,* contains an interesting account of Laura Secord, who is supposed. to have given the warning. The American force was under the leadership of Colonel Boerstler.

[152] Cruikshank, *op. cit.,* pt. II, pp. 115 ff.; *Canadian Archives.* Q. 122, pp. 52–62; *idem,* C. 679, pp. 130–140; *American State Papers: Military Affairs,* vol. I, pp. 445–449.

[153] Mahan, *op. cit.,* vol. II, p. 104.

burg on Lake Champlain. At last success seemed ready to crown the American efforts. An imposing force had been collected, and an intelligent plan of action had been developed. But once again the stupidity of American generals, combined with the enthusiastic and persistent defense of Canadian volunteers, saved Canada from the threatened disaster and blasted the hope of American success.

On October 26th a force of about 1000 Canadians, under the command of a French-Canadian officer—Colonel De Salaberry—ambushed and defeated Hampton's army at Chateauguay.[154] A few weeks later General Wilkinson, having allowed his army to become divided, was badly defeated on the banks of the St. Lawrence, at Chrystler's Farm.[155] Had Wilkinson been blessed with the virtue of courage, he might still have pushed on. His forces were scattered but not destroyed. Hearing, however, that General Hampton had retreated, he followed suit.[156] The close of the year's operations was marked by the withdrawal of the American forces from Canadian territory along the Niagara River, after a harsh display of useless severity at Newark, and the burning of Sandwich by General McClure.[157] Fort Niagara, on the American side of the river, was captured by the Canadians, and a number of small villages were destroyed as retaliation for Sandwich, York, and Newark. [158] Fort Niagara was retained until the end of the war under Canadian control.

[154] This victory is particularly important because of its proof of French-Canadian loyalty and valor. Sulte, *La Bataille de Chateauguay,* Quebec, 1899; *Canadian Archives,* Q. 122, pp. 199–261; Coffin, 1812, *The War and Its Moral,* pp. 244–251. On De Salaberry's claims to the credit of victory see W. Wood, *Selected British Documents,* vol. II, pp. 359–429. On the French-Canadian efforts in the War of 1812 see Sulte, *Histoire de la milice canadienne française, 1760–1897,* Montreal, 1897.

[155] *American State Papers: Military Affairs,* vol. I, pp. 462 ff.; *Canadian Archives,* Q. 123, pp. 11 ff.; *idem,* C. 681, pp. 62 ff.

[156] *American State Papers: Military Affairs,* vol. I, pp. 458–463.

[157] The inhabitants, including women and children, were driven into the snow-covered forest while their homes were burned. *Canadian Archives,* C. 681, p. 217; Lucas, *op. cit.,* p. 144.

[158] Nowhere can the degrading effect of war be better illustrated than in these mutual attacks on defenseless and essentially peaceful villages. *Canadian Archives,* C. 681, p. 253 ff.; *Niles' Register,* vol. V, p. 394.

In the campaigns of the next year (1814) the American troops, for the first time in this war, were led by reasonably competent commanders. In the summer of that year, fortunately for Canada, British reinforcements, released from European duty by the banishment of Napoleon to Elba, began to arrive in North America.[159] But Yeo and Chauncey still disputed, without deciding,[160] the supremacy of Lake Ontario. American invasions of Canada were again repulsed, while Great Britain maintained, and made even more secure, her control of the sea.

The first important movement of the year was initiated by one of the newly-appointed American leaders—General Brown. With 4500 soldiers under his command,[161] he crossed the Niagara and on July 5th defeated General Riall who, with 1500 men, was awaiting him at Chippewa.[162] Due to the failure of Commodore Chauncey to bring his naval forces into proper coöperation, General Brown was unable to profit by this victory and retired westward to the Niagara. At Lundy's Lane, within sound of the cataract itself, was fought the most bitter engagement of the whole war. The battle began late in the afternoon, and neither army had any great preponderance of either guns or men. At first the Americans were victorious; they drove the British from their positions and captured guns and ammunition. Under the leadership of General Drummond, reinforced and reinspired, the Canadians returned to the attack at 9 P. M. and continued the hostilities until midnight. Both sides were thoroughly worn out, but it was the Americans who retired; the Canadians were left in possession of the field. The next morning the American camp was found deserted. General Brown had retired to Fort Erie.[163] This post was soon abandoned, and at the end of the year Amherstburg

159 It is worth noting that the Canadian volunteers were less vigorous and less determined in the offensive operations undertaken after the arrival of these reinforcements than they had been when fighting alone in a defensive war. When the character of the war changed, they tended to leave it all to the professionals. Their homes were no longer in danger.

160 Until October.

161 They were not all present at the battle of Chippewa.

162 Cruikshank, *Documentary History . . . 1814*, vol. I, pp. 31, 38–47, 54.

163 The details of this battle have long been in dispute. There has been little agreement as to the numbers involved, the losses, and the identity of

and Malden alone of Canadian towns remained under American control.

In August, 1814, Sir George Prevost found himself at the head of more than 11,000 seasoned troops—veterans of the Peninsular campaign. Having decided upon an aggressive movement against the United States by way of Lake Champlain, he moved slowly across the border, and invested and captured Plattsburg with little opposition. There he hesitated, waiting for Captain Downie, who was in command of the British naval forces on the lake, to defeat the American squadron and thus assure the safety of the British lines of communication.[164] Unfortunately for his plans, Downie was killed and the British ships were defeated by an American flotilla under the command of Thomas Macdonough.[165] Thereupon Prevost departed at once for Canada. Although this retreat has been partially condoned by Wellington himself, it seems obvious that had an able, determined, and resourceful commander occupied Prevost's position, the 1500 Americans who opposed him and the temporary loss of control on Lake Champlain would not have stopped the finest army ever collected (up to that time) on American soil.

The final naval action of the war on Lake Ontario occurred in October, 1814. In that month Yeo, having constructed a great vessel of 102 guns (the *St. Lawrence*) blockaded Chauncey in Sackett's Harbor. This blockade was maintained during the few remaining months of the war.

Throughout 1814 the British navy controlled almost completely

the victors. American historians, in the past, have claimed Lundy's Lane as a victory, explaining that the troops of Gen. Brown retired—after the battle was won. This argument is now being abandoned. While the losses were about equal, there can be no doubt that in its larger effect Lundy's Lane was a real Canadian victory, as it ended a very serious threat against the safety of Upper Canada. Cruikshank, *op. cit.*, pp. 87 ff.; Babcock, *The War of 1812 on the Niagara Frontier*, Buffalo, 1927; Channing, *op. cit.*, vol. IV, p. 501; Cruikshank, *The Battle of Lundy's Lane*, Lundy's Lane Historical Society, Welland, 1895; *Canadian Archives*, Q. 128-1, pp. 119 ff.

[164] *Canadian Archives*, M. 389, pp. 176-183.

[165] *Idem*, Q. 128-1, p. 220; Mahan, *op. cit.*, vol. II, pp. 360-382; *American State Papers: Naval Affairs*, vol. III, pp. 309 ff.; R. Macdonough, *Life of Commodore Thomas Macdonough*, Boston, 1909.

the eastern coast of the United States. Raids were made at many places along the seaboard,[166] and these culminated in the battle of Bladensburg and the capture of Washington. For some unknown reason no provision had been made for the defense of the capital. The hastily-gathered militia fled at the first volley, and as a result Sir George Cockburn and Admiral Cochrane had little difficulty in taking the city.[167] The Capitol, the Library, and the President's mansion were burned, although no private property was destroyed, nor were personal injuries suffered by any of the citizens.[168] Admiral Cochrane wrote to Secretary of State Monroe that this action was taken as a measure of retaliation for the atrocities committed by American troops in the destruction of Canadian towns and the mistreatment of inhabitants.[169] This explanation has been generally accepted by British historians;[170] but, while the destruction of government property is permissible under the laws of war, there are few reasonable men who applaud this or similar actions of the War of 1812. It is particularly difficult to find any real excuse for the destruction of the Congressional Library. This, in common with the American actions at Sandwich and the other excesses of the war, must simply be charged to the anti-social insanity, the destruction psychosis, which is an invariable accompaniment of war. An abortive attack on Baltimore ended the warfare on the eastern coast.[171]

[166] In the New England district the raiders were frequently welcomed and supplied by Yankee merchants. Cf. *Annals of Congress,* 12th Cong., 2nd sess., p. 1116; *idem,* 13th Cong., 2nd sess., p. 2781.

[167] *American State Papers: Military Affairs,* vol. I, pp. 524–599; King, "The Battle of Bladensburg," *The Magazine of American History,* vol. XIV, pp. 438 ff.

[168] *American State Papers,* 13th Cong., 3rd sess., no. 24; *idem,* Appendix, pp. 51–370. This volume contains the official documents of the committee of inquiry.

[169] *American State Papers: Foreign Relations,* vol. III, p. 694.

[170] Bourinot, *op. cit.,* p. 117; Lucas, *op. cit.,* pp. 229–233. The latter book offers the best treatment from the British point of view.

[171] *The Citizen Soldiers at North Point and Fort McHenry, September 12 and 13, 1814,* Baltimore, 1862; Carpenter, "The Star-Spangled Banner," *Century Magazine,* vol. XLVIII, pp. 358 ff. An incident in this battle inspired the author of the famous national anthem.

On December 17, 1813, the American Congress had passed a new Embargo Act designed to prevent the trade which had grown up between New England and the enemy ports and fleet.[172] As a result this illegal trade began to decline in volume, and Sir John Sherbrooke, Governor of New Brunswick, was ordered to invade Maine. It was hoped that in this way a new trade channel would be opened. The Americans offered little opposition, as the conquest gave promise of peace and increased commerce.[173] The territory thus captured—the whole eastern section of Maine—was retained until the end of the war.

The battle of New Orleans was the final land action of the war. It took place after the signing of the treaty of peace, but before the news of this event reached America, and it resulted in the decisive defeat of General Pakenham and his European veterans. It also resulted, ultimately, in the provision of a new candidate for the American Presidency—General Andrew Jackson.[174]

By the middle of 1814 both nations were heartily sick of the war, and in August peace negotiations were opened at Ghent.[175] A treaty was agreed upon and ratifications were exchanged on February 18, 1815.[176] In the negotiation of the Treaty of Ghent, British diplomacy is seen at its lowest ebb. Castlereagh, Liverpool, and the others influential in deciding British foreign policy, were concentrating their attention on the Congress of Vienna, and had little time to spare for the minor drama at Ghent. By all rules of logic and the precedent of diplomacy, Great Britain

[172] *Annals of Congress,* 13th Cong., vol. II, p. 2781.

[173] Essex *Register,* August 3, 1814.

[174] Latour, *Historical Memoir of the War in West Florida and Louisiana, 1814–1815,* Philadelphia, 1816; Davis, *An Official and Full Detail of the Great Battle of New Orleans,* New York, 1836; Cooke, *Narrative of Events . . . in 1814 and 1815,* London, 1835, pp. 224–237; Bassett, *The Life of Andrew Jackson,* New York, 1911, vol. I, pp. 126–207.

[175] *American State Papers: Foreign Relations,* vol. III, pp. 621–622; Ford, *The Treaty of Ghent and After,* Wisconsin Historical Society, Madison, 1914.

[176] Updike, *op. cit.,* chaps. 5–9 describes the negotiations.

should have been able to enforce her claim at least in regard to the cession of northern Maine. The British navy was in command of the sea and was enforcing a fairly complete blockade along the whole eastern coast of the United States; the British army held a large part of Maine, several posts on the American side of the Niagara frontier, and controlled the Oregon territory.[177] Amherstburg and Malden alone of Canadian towns were in American hands. The cession to Canada of the northern half of Maine would have linked up the maritime provinces with Canada in a direct way, and had the cession been insisted upon it might well have been achieved. The demand was made, but quickly withdrawn. Gambier, Goulburn, and Adams were men of little ability, less experience, and no determination. The United States, on the contrary, was represented by an exceptionally able group of men—Gallatin, Clay, Russell, Bayard, and John Quincy Adams composed what was probably the strongest diplomatic delegation in American history. Gallatin and Adams alone were more than a match for the British delegates. They did not succeed in persuading Great Britain to abandon Canada to the United States,[178] nor did they gain a specific undertaking that Britain would end the system of impressment,[179] but they did succeed in gaining peace without paying by concessions.[180] Canada was not directly represented at Ghent.

The treaty was signed on December 14, 1814. It decreed a

[177] See below, Chapter IV.

[178] On this point, the British delegates were emphatic. See Bayard Manuscripts in the *Reports of the American Historical Association, 1913,* vol. II, pp. 263–265. The instructions to the American delegates as to the cession of Canada were elided from *American State Papers: Foreign Relations,* but may be found in *Unclassified Instructions,* vol. VII, Bureau of Indexes and Archives, "Monroe to Plenipotentiaries, January 28, 1814." Jefferson in 1812 had declared this to be a *sine qua non* of peace. Paul Leicester Ford (editor), *Works of Jefferson,* vol. VI, p. 70.

[179] *American State Papers: Foreign Relations,* vol. III, pp. 695–703, 735; see Mills, "The Duke of Wellington and the Peace Negotiations at Ghent in 1814," *Canadian Historical Review,* March, 1921.

[180] The treaty was denounced as a surrender in London and in Canada. London *Globe,* December 27, 1814; London *Times,* December 30, 1814.

complete return to the *status quo ante bellum;* impressment was not mentioned, nor was the subject of blockade, while the problem of the boundaries was postponed.[181]

5. THE RESULTS OF THE WAR

The War of 1812 had little or no effect on the history or constitution of Great Britain—it was a minor problem quickly forgotten in the rush of stirring events on the continent of Europe. But upon the United States, and Canada, and upon the relations of the two, it had a vital and enduring influence.

During the early months of the war there appeared to be some real danger of its destroying the American Union. New England openly talked of secession.[182] As the struggle continued, however, more and more of the Federalists united with the Democrats in support of the national policy. Those who continued in opposition were finally defeated in the hour of victory—as most Americans considered it—when the Hartford Convention, designed· as the first step toward secession, ended as a complete fiasco on the arrival of the news of peace. On the signing of the Treaty of Ghent, differences of opinion were submerged in common rejoicing over the "victory." The Democratic candidate (Monroe) was returned in the election of 1816 by an electoral vote of 183 to 34, and this triumph inaugurated the national "Era of Good Feeling." From this time on the American people "felt and acted more as a nation . . . they were more Americans." [183] The new nationalism produced by the war was characterized by the triumph of

[181] Malloy, *op cit.,* vol. I, pp. 612 ff. On the negotiations see also: Mahan, "The Negotiations at Ghent in 1814," *American Historical Review,* vol. II, pp. 68–87; "The British Instructions," taken from the *British Archives,* in Ford (editor) *Proceedings of the Massachusetts Historical Society,* December, 1914–January, 1915, pp. 138–164; *Proceedings of the American Antiquarian Society,* 1913, pp. 110–169; Dunning, *The British Empire and the United States,* New York, 1914.

[182] von Holst, *Constitutional and Political History of the United States,* Chicago, 1877, vol. I, pp. 209–223.

[183] Adams (editor), *The Writings of Gallatin,* vol. I, p. 700.

centralized government,[184] by the introduction of permanent military and naval establishments, and by the inauguration of that great American institution, the high protective tariff.[185] Thus the military, economic, and sentimental life of the nation joined with the political interests in centralization at Washington. It is, then, true in more than one way that "the country entered the war distracted, indifferent and particularistic; it emerged from it united, enthusiastic and national." [186]

Important as was the effect of the war upon the United States, it was even more vital in its influence on the history of the British colonies in North America. The defense of Canada was so unexpectedly successful, and was carried out in the face of such enormous odds, that the War of 1812 has become a national tradition, the power of which tends to increase as the years pass. "This war, together with the United Empire Loyalist traditions in which British Canada was founded, accounts for many things that the modern visitor to Canada cannot understand. . . . They are the 'atmosphere.' " [187] Before the war Canada had consisted of five geographically separate and politically independent colonies —all weak, all undeveloped, all apparently destined to ultimate absorption in the United States. At the close of the successful war of defense the colonies were still disunited, but they possessed a common tradition of more than ordinary virility, and a remembrance of victory against overwhelming odds, that gave confidence to the present and assurance to the coming generation. With the record of 1812 before him, no future Canadian had cause for despair. The struggle had been, in Canadian eyes, a

[184] The struggle over state rights, of course, continued, to culminate in the Civil War; but the ultimate triumph of the federal government was clearly foreshadowed by the events of 1803–1816.

[185] First started in 1816 to protect industries developed during the war. This is another reason for looking upon the War of 1812 as the "Second War of Independence."

[186] Nicholas Murray Butler, *The Effect of the War of 1812 on the Consolidation of the Union* (Johns Hopkins University Studies, series 5), pp. 251–276. As has been said, "The first war with England made the United States independent; the second made them a nation."

[187] Bradley, *Canada,* London, 1911, p. 96,

desperate defense of home and political integrity; a fight for liberty against submersion in the American Union; a defensive war against a foreign invader. In the struggle, French and British Canadians were drawn together as would not have happened in fifty years of peace—"it did more than any other event, or series of events, could have done to reconcile the two rival races within Canada to each other." [188] Although the Canadian nation was not formally inaugurated until half a century later, the political divisions then united found their common basis on the fields of Chateauguay and Lundy's Lane. To the War of 1812 the British Empire owes a debt of gratitude too often unrecognized. It is almost a national epic in the Dominion.

In one respect, however, the effect of the war on Canada was seriously detrimental: it retarded the growth of responsible government by at least a generation. Democracy, as an American invention, was in serious disrepute and the leaders in the movement for constitutional reform were inevitably denounced as annexationists in disguise.[189] Indeed, this tendency among a certain class of Canadians to condemn all political changes as American inventions still exists—in spite of the fact that today Great Britain is, from a political point of view, infinitely more radical than the United States.

The effects of the war, so far as the relations of Canada and the United States were concerned, were far from satisfactory. The schism between the two branches of the Anglo-Saxon race was broadened and intensified. Mutual charges of atrocity were exchanged, confirming Americans in their hatred of Great Britain; while in Canada "two generations did not suffice to efface the evil memories of 1812." [190] Thomas Jefferson declared that the British had indulged "in acts of barbarism which do not belong to a civilized age," [191] while Canadians were "convinced of the future

[188] Lucas, *op. cit.,* p. 259.

[189] See Chapter IV. See also Dafoe, "Canada and the United States," in *Great Britain and the Dominions* (Harris Foundation Lectures), Chicago, 1928.

[190] Goldwyn Smith, *Canada and the Canadian Question,* New York, 1891, p. 108.

[191] Quoted in Montreal *Herald,* April 15, 1815.

necessity of keeping their neighbors at a respectable distance, whether in peace or war." [192] The influence of the Loyalists became more pronounced, and at the same time there was increased acceptance of their creed and its essential foundation—opposition to the United States. The bitterness engendered by the Revolution was renewed and intensified by the War of 1812.

[192] Montreal *Herald,* April 15, 1815.

CHAPTER IV

Moments of Crisis

THE century of continuous peace that has been maintained between the United States and Canada has so often been eulogized by the professional orator that there is danger that its real significance will be unduly discounted. The "Peace Arch" recently dedicated on the boundary between the State of Washington and the Province of British Columbia commemorates a true achievement in the conduct of international affairs, and the record is even more remarkable in view of the possibilities of conflict presented by the historic, geographic, and economic contacts of the two nations. Had there been no incentive to war, peace could hardly be called a virtue.

On more than one occasion since 1815 the maintenance of peace has been by no means easy or automatic. Chronic dislike, fanned into glowing hostility by some unfortunate series of circumstances or some unusually knavish politician, has seemed potent with the threat of war. In 1838, in 1842, in 1846, the tranquil intercourse of the two peoples was rudely destroyed, and only by the determined efforts of the true patriots in Great Britain, Canada, and the United States were armed conflicts averted. American exponents of the theory of "Manifest Destiny" (the rationalization that justifies the casting of covetous eyes upon all territories from the North Pole to Panama) have ever seen in the annexation of Canada a logical and mutually beneficial step toward the consummation of their desires. Thus, during times of crisis in the history of British North America—in the rebellions of 1837–1838, in the extreme depression of 1849, in the critical days of British Columbia from 1868 to 1871—these advocates of expansion have tended to aid that party in the Dominion which seemed most likely to favor union with the United

States. More than once such aid took the form of money and of arms. The development and solution of problems thus aroused form no small part of the history of the relations of the two countries. It is, then, desirable to have some knowledge of the more important of these critical periods.

I. THE UNITED STATES AND THE CANADIAN REBELLIONS

Long before the War of 1812 the more radical among the settlers of Upper Canada were protesting against both the form and the spirit of their government. The great power vested in the person of the Governor and the strength of the appointed Executive Council far outweighed the limited rights accorded to the elected Assembly. Many of those who were dissatisfied had been accustomed to the more democratic conditions that had pertained in some of the American colonies, and they now objected strongly to a governmental system that was neither responsible nor even fully representative.

For some years after their great migration, the leaders of the Loyalists found no one in Upper Canada to dispute their rule, but the gradual influx of other settlers foreshadowed the coming attack upon their control. As the less wealthy among the Loyalists and the later settlers from the United States and Great Britain [1] slowly overcame the hardships of their pioneer life, they found more time to devote to political affairs and their challenge to the bureaucracy became audible.

The War of 1812 at first appeared to have welded Canadian society into a homogeneous unit, but with the relaxation of external pressure after the signing of the Treaty of Ghent, the cohesive bonds were sundered, and criticism again became vigorous and insistent. But the leading Loyalists, conscious of their

---

[1] See *supra,* Chapter II. The number of British settlers was small. Buchanan's report on immigration for 1831 estimated that only 5000 British immigrants had arrived in Upper Canada before 1815; quoted in Lower, "Immigration and Settlement in Canada, 1812–1820," *Canadian Historical Review,* March, 1922, p. 37.

patriotic service in the defense of Canada during the war, were more than ever imbued with a spirit that caused them to look upon Upper Canada as their "special heritage," and its government as their prescriptive right.[2] Related in some instances by ties of blood, but bound together far more effectively by their social, political, and economic interests, the "Family Compact" held in one central authority the attributes of social prestige, economic advantage and political control. Into this circumscribed body were admitted some of the more able, forceful or genteel of the immigrants from the British Isles, while the Royal Governor became, perforce, a part of the system.[3] The evils of the bureaucratic system that was thus developed were followed by the inevitable protests of those whose ambitions were fettered by their exclusion from the charmed circle. The criticism became more and more widespread, and many of the Loyalists themselves took part in the attacks upon the ruling clique.[4] As the criticism increased, the grasp of the bureacracy upon law, finance, state and church became more tense.[5] Revolution was inherent in the situation that developed.

As is frequently the case, the most perfect example of reactionary control was found in the church. By the Constitutional Act of 1791 large land endowments had been set aside for the benefit of the "Protestant clergy."[6] This term was interpreted by the colonial officials to refer only to the members of the Church of England—although it was later modified to include the Church

[2] Goldwyn Smith, *Canada and the Canadian Question*, New York, 1891, pp. 109–111.

[3] Professor W. Stewart Wallace has written an excellent brief account in *The Family Compact* (The *Chronicles of Canada* Series). See also "Personnel of the Family Compact," *Canadian Historical Review*, September, 1926; *Sir Francis Bond Head's Narrative of His Government in Upper Canada*, Toronto, 1838–1839; Bethune, *Memoir of the Right Reverend John Strachan*, Toronto, 1870. The latest study is Dunham, *Political Unrest in Upper Canada, 1815–1836*, London, 1927.

[4] See above, p. 50 n.

[5] D. McArthur, "The Reform Movement in Upper Canada" in Shortt and Doughty, *op. cit.*, vol. I, pp. 327–359; *Canadian Archives Report, 1892*, note D, pp. 73–74, 89, 97–99, etc.

[6] A. Dunham, *The Constitutional Act*, Toronto University Library, 1921.

of Scotland.[7] Not only were non-conformist bodies refused assistance from this endowment, but they were forced to labor under other restrictions as well. As late as 1828, Methodist ministers were not allowed to conduct the marriage ceremony, although the non-conformists far surpassed the Anglicans in number.[8] Especially under the leadership of the famous Bishop Strachan, the established church interfered in political and social matters and displayed a bigotry almost as tyrannical, if not as complete, as that of the church in early New England.[9]

For over twenty years this governmental system prevailed, in spite of protests and active opposition.[10] From every district came the voice of remonstrance, but for a quarter of a century, in spite of bureaucratic interference and absolutism, the citizens of Upper Canada endured without violence, though the black clouds of protest bore witness to a coming storm. Opposition was crushed by legal or illegal means, by persuasion, bribery, and force.[11] Here, as ever, extreme conservatism was forcing revolution.

Yet it must not be supposed that the Canadian populace was unanimous in opposition to the Family Compact, or that there was

[7] Lindsey, *History of the Clergy Reserves,* Toronto, 1851; Ryerson (edited by Hodgins), *The Story of My Life,* Toronto, 1883; Goldwyn Smith, *op. cit.,* p. 112.

[8] The Anglicans declared that many Methodist clergymen were Americans and favored annexation. This was strongly denied by Dr. Ryerson, editor of *The Christian Guardian* and father of Canadian Methodism. The first statement, however, was partially true. *Canadian Archives,* Q. 325, p. 342; *idem,* Q. 188, p. 345; *idem,* Q. 330, p. 99; *idem,* Q. 382, p. 481; Lindsey, *Life and Times of William Lyon Mackenzie,* Toronto, 1862, vol. I, pp. 44 ff.; Sanderson, *First Century of Methodism,* Toronto.

[9] Scadding, *Dr. Strachan, the First Bishop of Toronto—A Review and a Study,* Toronto, 1808; Roberton, *The Fighting Bishop,* Ottawa, 1926; W. S. Wallace, *op. cit.,* pp 29, 31, 60–62, 66–94.

[10] See *The Colonial Advocate,* June 28, 1824, for a typical protest. See also *Seventh Report of the Grievance Committee of the Legislature of Upper Canada,* Toronto, 1835, which gives a digest of political and social ills.

[11] For details of the attack upon *The Colonial Advocate,* see Lindsey, *op. cit.,* vol. I, pp. 78 ff. See also *Canadian Archives Report, 1892,* note D, pp. 32–135, which contains a great deal of information relating to conditions in Canada during the early days of the Family Compact.

always even a majority against the existing rule. By the use of one magic word, asssisted, it is true, by a high technical perfection in the arts of political manipulation, many a hostile district had been won to enthusiastic support of the existing regime. The magic word was "Loyalty." The record of the bureaucracy was consistent in this matter—it had not varied in its support of the imperial bond, and had opposed with unrelenting vigor any scheme of independence, any thought of annexation. Its hostility to the United States was ingrained and bitter, and this was the one issue upon which Canadian opinion, of whatever social or economic strata, approached unanimity.[12] With consummate skill the leaders of the Tory group cast doubt upon the loyalty of every one who offered criticism—a protest against the Clergy Reserves was invariably followed by an attack upon the protestant as a propagator of American doctrine, as an advocate of annexation. Thus the prejudice of the people was utilized by the government, and for many years with great success. The task of the administration was made more simple, when in 1835 William Lyon Mackenzie,[13] the picturesque and fiery Scotchman who had led the forces of opposition, driven to desperation by his fifth illegal expulsion from the Assembly, and enthused by the doctrines of Hume and other English liberals whom he had met during an unsuccessful pilgrimage to London, threw off all restraint and became an open advocate of independence.[14]

Throughout this period the attitude of Canada toward the United States was one of unremitting hostility, and this sentiment not only permeated the press, pulpit, and legislature, but was fundamental in the people themselves.[15] They felt, and with

[12] Goldwyn Smith, *op. cit.*, p. 108.

[13] On Mackenzie, see Dent, *The Story of the Upper Canada Rebellion*, Toronto, 1885; King, *The Other Side of the "Story,"* Toronto, 1886; Lindsey, *The Life and Times of William Lyon Mackenzie*, Toronto, 1862.

[14] Mackenzie went to London to try to persuade the imperial authorities to intervene in Canada. He was then Mayor of Toronto, the capital city. Despite his position, he was unsuccessful, and this made him even more determined in his views. Cf. Goldwyn Smith, *op. cit.*, pp. 113, 118; for dangers in Canada, see *Canadiana*, London, 1837.

[15] Cf. "Memorial of Montreal Business Men, 1818," *Canadian Archives*, Q. 149, p. 142.

some show of reason,[16] that the United States was not only willing, but eager to take advantage of any favorable opportunity to
annex the British provinces. Many Americans could not feel
comfortable until "British despotism" was finally removed from
this continent.[17] To any close relationship, either political or
economic, the Canadian people were distinctly opposed, and the
record of hostility which characterized the Canadian attitude toward the American contentions in fishery, boundary, and trade
discussions from 1815 to 1846 was, in no small measure, a result
of this ingrained national sentiment. Revolutionary America's
treatment of the Loyalists was still bearing fruit. Not only did
Canadians fear armed aggression from the United States, but
they were keenly alive to the danger of permitting the establishment of a large American community in the Upper Province,[18]
the possibility of "peaceful penetration," [19] and the introduction
of the "loose demoralizing principles" [20] of the Republic.

American opinion of Canada throughout the same period was
very far from complimentary, and American newspapers and
journals have been no more noted for reticence in the statement
of popular prejudices than has the press of Canada—perhaps even
less.[21] The sympathy of the Union, so far as Americans knew
what was transpiring in Canada, was naturally bestowed upon the
radical and anti-imperial elements in the Canadian population.[22]

[16] The United States were "influenced by a spirit of aggrandizement not
necessary to their own security but increasing with the extent of their
empire, . . . and the conquest of Canada and its permanent annexation to
the United States was the declared object of the American government."
Statement of the British delegates at The Hague, *American State Papers:
Foreign Relations*, vol. VIII, pp. 713 ff.

[17] D. R. Moore, *Canada and the United States, 1815–1830*, Chicago, 1910,
pp. 65, 73, gives a good *résumé* of some phases of Canadian-American relations.

[18] General Drummond reported to Bathurst that the Americans were "bitterly inimical" to British America. *Canadian Archives*, Q. 136, p. 222.

[19] *Canadian Archives*, Q. 167, pp. 57, 147, 244, 319.

[20] Sherbrooke to Bathurst, January 6, 1823. *Canadian Archives*, Q. 332,
p. 114.

[21] Cf. *Niles' Register*, February 11, 1832.

[22] *Canadian Archives Reports, 1922–1923*, p. 127.

Any movement which seemed to promise opposition to British or Loyalist authority received hearty encouragement from "across the line." Willcocks, a Canadian traitor of the War of 1812, had escaped to the United States, whence he devoted himself to the task of influencing Canadian opinion in favor of annexation. This he tried to accomplish by a sheet known as *The Upper Canada Guardian,* which he published in the United States and circulated in Canada. The whole venture was financed by American funds.[23] In Plattsburg, New York, was published *L'Ami du Peuple,* a paper intended for the consumption of the French-Canadian habitant, and designed to stir him to rebellion by its recital of the diabolical plots in preparation by the British government.[24] Generalization is always difficult, and seldom exact, but it can be stated without exaggeration that the majority of the American people in 1835 not only favored the annexation of Canada but felt that any indirect aid which could be given to Canadian revolutionists would be not only justifiable but highly praiseworthy.[25] Thus, during the conflicts of 1837–1838 there was very little popular objection to the violation of Canadian territory by armed American bands.[26] On the other hand, the greatest enthusiasm was aroused by the presence of Mackenzie, Nelson, Papineau, and other Canadian rebels in American cities. The American as a rule rather despised the Canadian as a man without spirit who allowed himself to be ruled by a tyrannous and "effete" monarchy. The revolutionists were Canadians in whom "the slumbering genius of freedom" [27] had at last awakened. Moreover, independence with Canada in its then-existing condition meant inevitable annexation. Sentiment and interest united to mold American opinion.

So matters stood when writs were issued for the election of members to the Upper Canada Assembly in 1835. Mackenzie had

[23] *Canadian Archives,* Q. 312, p. 237; *idem,* Q. 311, p. 53.

[24] Kingsford, *History of Canada,* vol. IX p. 355, note.

[25] *Canadian Archives Reports, 1922–1923,* pp. 133 ff.

[26] E. A. Theller, *Canada in 1837–1838,* Philadelphia, 1841. This book displays an attitude typical of contemporary American thought. See also *Canadian Archives Reports, 1922–1923,* pp. 314–315.

[27] Rochester *Democrat,* date uncertain.

been irritated into declaring for independence, and this fact had alienated the vast majority of the voters, in spite of the appeal held forth by his demand for internal reform. Even ardent liberals such as Dr. Ryerson and Alexander Perry evidenced the popular belief that in this election the people were "called upon to decide the question of separation by their votes." [28] The inevitable result was achieved—by an overwhelming majority the Family Compact was confirmed in its position. Mackenzie himself was defeated.

The convocation of the Assembly was followed by some months of futile debate, in which the cause of reform was hopelessly beaten. Gradually, however, public opinion, in its reaction from the patriotic heat of the election, regained its old attitude of hostility toward the existing order. But Mackenzie was now ready for more drastic measures, and he was energetically preparing for the employment of force to accomplish his desires. When, as a result of an armed insurrection under Papineau [29] and Dr. Wolfred Nelson in Lower Canada, the regular troops had all been moved to Montreal, he seized the opportunity presented to him.[30] Against the advice of many of his friends and advisers, on December 4, 1837, Mackenzie organized a provisional executive, raised the standard of revolt, and called upon the citizens to support a democratic government.[31]

---

[28] See Lord Durham's report in appendix to *Journal of the House of Assembly of Upper Canada,* Toronto, 1839; it appears also in *Sessional Papers, Reports from Commissioners,* vol. XVII, London, 1839, and in Kennedy *Documents of the Canadian Constitution,* London, 1918.

[29] For Papineau see F. Taylor, *British Americans,* vol. III, Montreal, 1868; De Cellis, *Papineau,* Toronto, 1909. For causes of the revolution in Lower Canada see: A. Gerin Lajoie, *Dix Ans au Canada de 1840 à 1850,* Quebec, 1891, chap. 1; Garneau, *Histoire du Canada,* Montreal, 1882, vol. III, book 6, chapter 2. A description of conditions in Lower Canada from October, 1835 to November, 1837 is to be found in *Canadian Archives Reports, 1922-1923,* pp. 214-313.

[30] Winsor, *op. cit.,* vol. VIII, pp. 160-161, contains an article by Professor George Bryce on this subject, *Canadian Archives Report, 1922-1923,* p. 314.

[31] Winsor, *op. cit.,* vol. VIII, pp. 160-161; Lindsey, *op. cit.,* vol. II, pp. 63 ff.

From the first the enterprise was doomed to dismal defeat. The government sent out a call for loyal volunteers, and these poured into Toronto in almost unmanageable numbers. A few insignificant skirmishes, one real fight at Montgomery's Tavern, and the rebels were completely routed.[32]

Mackenzie himself escaped to the United States, and at Buffalo his movement received cordial and material support. Here four public meetings were held with the object of gaining volunteers and supplies for the Canadian rebels. One of these meetings was the largest gathering held, up to that time, in the city of Buffalo.[33] The utmost enthusiasm prevailed, and the representatives of the federal government, if they did not sympathize, at least made no attempt to preserve the strict neutrality of the United States. Mackenzie made an eloquent appeal for supplies, for arms, and for volunteers. Many of the audience enlisted immediately, while ammunition and field pieces were taken from the United States arsenal without any show of opposition.[34] The number of recruits increased during the following week until a full thousand men were under arms, and "General" Renssalear Van Renssalear of Albany, took over the command.[35]

On the other side, however, notice must be given to a meeting of the American-born residents of Montreal, at which a resolution was passed declaring that neither their support nor their sympathy would be given to the rebels. But at a score of places across the American border—at Troy, Burlington, Middlebury, Rochester, Ogdensburg, Montpelier—this resolution was denounced and votes of money and supplies were passed in favor of the Canadian "patriots." [36]

[32] Lindsey, *op. cit.*, chapter 4; *Michigan Pioneer Collections,* vol. VII, p. 89.

[33] John Bassett Moore, *International Arbitrations,* Washington, 1898, vol. III, p. 2425; Lindsey, *op. cit.*, vol. II, p. 124.

[34] *House Executive Document,* no. 74, 25th Cong., 2nd sess.

[35] *House Executive Document,* no. 64, 25th Cong., 2nd sess; see also Kingsford, *op. cit.*, vol. X, pp. 430 ff. The actual number of Americans who took part in the border warfare is not known; at Navy Island there were more than 350. Many of those who volunteered apparently did nothing more. Lindsey, *op. cit.*, vol. II, pp. 138–139.

[36] McMaster, *op. cit.*, vol. VI, pp. 434–435.

Mackenzie and his supporters were now determined to carry on the struggle from an American base, "secure in the protection of American unfriendliness to Canada." [37] To give an appearance of legality, however, Navy Island, a Canadian possession in the Niagara River situated a short distance above the falls, was fortified as a base. Thence was issued a Canadian Declaration of Independence. This document offered land and money to all who would join the new government. On the American side volunteers gathered in considerable numbers; material of every sort was provided by individuals, by societies, and by town and city officials. [38] The encampment at Navy Island was, of course, of little importance—the real work was performed at Buffalo and Black Rock on the American shore. "The whole border" was in arms or actively supporting those who had enlisted. [39]

Throughout the northeastern states "Hunter's Lodges" were organized, membership being contingent upon subscription to an oath "never to rest until all tyrants of Great Britain cease to have any Dominion or footing whatever in North America." [40] There can, of course, be no question whatever as to the total illegality of the raids which ensued—raids organized by Americans, on American territory, and directed against a neighboring country with which the United States was not at war. The American government was, moreover, distinctly negligent in failing to take effective action to the end of checking these enterprises. It is true that orders prohibiting actions contrary to international law were issued, but they were not adequately enforced. [41] No vigorous action was taken until after the destruction of the *Caroline*. [42]

[37] W. L. Griffith, *The Dominion of Canada*, London, 1911, p. 35.

[38] Lindsey, *op. cit.*, vol. II, pp. 131–139; *House Executive Document*, no. 74, 25th Cong., 2nd sess.

[39] McMaster, *op. cit.*, vol. VI, p. 437.

[40] Webster wrote to Tyler that these Lodges were organized from Maine to Wisconsin and that they had ten thousand members. Van Tyne (editor), *Letters of Daniel Webster*, New York, 1902, p. 233; Bourinot, *op. cit.*, p. 154.

[41] *Canadian Archives Reports, 1922–1923*, pp. 314 ff.

[42] Mackenzie himself was imprisoned in Rochester for almost a year. Lindsey, *op. cit.*, vol. II, chapter 13; Bourinot, *Canada and the United States*, pp. 108–109. But "at Buffalo, arms and ammunition were openly

2. THE *CAROLINE* INCIDENT

The *Caroline* incident added no little to the already violent prejudice cultivated against Great Britain by the authors and politicians of the United States. At the same time it equally inflamed the Canadian hostility to the Republic.[43]

The Navy Island base was supplied with all necessary materials by small boats loaded on the American side of the river. One of these vessels—a steamer known as the *Caroline*—was used by the insurgents to transport men and ammunition from Fort Schlosser in the United States to the island headquarters.[44] Faced with the necessity of destroying this rendezvous, on December 30, 1837, a party of Canadian soldiers under Captain Drew crossed the river in small boats, cut the *Caroline* from her moorings at the wharf of Fort Schlosser, and towed her to the middle of the stream—whence, a burning wreck, she drifted toward the falls. In the skirmish on the American side at least one citizen of the United States was killed.[45]

This action produced a violent repercussion in the United States.[46] For a short time it appeared as though the border counties would themselves promote a war against Upper Canada. At last the President was forced to action; the militia of New York were placed on duty, General Winfield Scott was sent to the border, and orders were issued providing for the strict enforcement

taken from the arsenals of the government, and a regiment of militia was quietly looking on while all these preparations were being made for the invasion of Canada."

[43] *House Executive Document,* no. 302, 25th Cong., 2nd sess; *idem,* no. 64; Moore, *op. cit.,* vol. III, pp. 2426-2427; Dent, *The Last Forty Years,* vol. I, Toronto, 1871, pp. 165-170.

[44] "Fort Schlosser" was the site of an old French fortress, long since destroyed. At this time an inn, a warehouse and a wharf alone gave evidence of the proximity of civilization. McMaster, *op. cit.,* vol. VI, p. 439.

[45] See *Gould's Reporter,* vol. II, p. 121 ff. The exact details of this raid have remained obscure. It is to be found described in most texts on international law; see, for example, Hall or Hershey.

[46] Dent, *Canada Since the Union,* vol. I, p. 162.

of the laws of neutrality.[47] The American government then demanded redress from Great Britain, for the violation of American territory.[48] Great Britain replied, justifying the action on the ground that it was a necessary precaution undertaken in defense of the realm, and legal under the rules of international law.[49]

For three years the controversy which this reply aroused was carried on by the two governments, while the excitement on each side of the border gradually subsided. In 1840, however, the whole problem was again dramatically brought to the public attention by the arrest of a certain Alexander McLeod, who, apparently in a fit of drunken bravado, had boasted in a New York saloon that he had killed an American in the attack upon the *Caroline*. The British government requested that McLeod be immediately released on the ground that whatever he had done had been done under the orders of his superior officer, and that the British Crown itself assumed all entailed responsibility. The "national honor" was involved. The Department of State replied that the American government was unable to interfere in a state trial,[50] and once more war seemed to be the only solution of the impasse.[51]

[47] These restrictions were presently relaxed, and matters again assumed their natural state of unrest. President Van Buren suffered heavily in the public esteem for this single act of upright statesmanship. Public sentiment in New York unanimously favored retaliation and the provision of aid to the Canadian rebels. Foster, *A Century of American Diplomacy*, Boston, 1900, p. 280; Dodd, *Expansion and Conflict*, New York, 1915, p. 105.

[48] *House Executive Documents*, no. 302, 25th Cong., 2nd sess.

[49] *House Executive Documents*, no. 302, 25th Cong., 2nd sess.; Richardson (editor), *Messages and Papers of the Presidents, 1789–1907*, vol. III, pp. 401–404.

[50] Bryant and Gay, *A Popular History of the United States*, New York, 1880, vol. IV, p. 356. The Attorney-General was sent to watch the trial and to aid McLeod in any way possible, for war would have resulted from his death. Winsor, *op. cit.*, vol. VIII, p. 494; Johnson, *America's Foreign Relations*, New York, 1916, p. 385. As a result of this trial, Congress on August 29, 1842 passed an act giving the federal government jurisdiction in all future cases of this nature. *U. S. Revised Statutes*, secs. 752–754. Lord Sydenham wrote to Lord John Russell, "If the Yankees really hang him it will be a cause of war." Scrope, *Life of Sydenham*, p. 235, note.

[51] Webster wrote to Tyler that there was great danger that McLeod might be lynched, and that if this occurred, "war would be inevitable in ten

A United States district attorney was supplied to McLeod as counsel in an attempt to assure his acquittal, although Governor Seward and other ardent patriots vehemently protested. Fortunately it was proven at the trial that if McLeod had ever made the alleged boast, he was an unvarnished liar, for at the time of the raid he had not even been near Fort Schlosser. He was finally released.[52]

The discussion then returned to the original question of the legality of the invasion of American soil. Calhoun led the public attack upon the Canadian case, stating that it could in no sense be claimed to have resulted from necessity, and that it was, therefore, illegal.[53] The matter was finally submitted to the arbitration of Daniel Webster and Lord Ashburton in 1842. Webster insisted that to justify the action Great Britain must show "a necessity of self-defense, instant, overwhelming, and leaving no choice of means, and no moment for deliberation." Further, the British agents must not have been guilty of any "unreasonable and excessive" action. Lord Ashburton agreed with this statement of the legal principle, and declared that all these conditions were apparent in the case in hand. Viewed objectively, this statement must be considered too sweeping, for the Canadian forces might easily have delayed and accomplished their purpose at a more seasonable time. Navy Island might have been taken from the Canadian shore without troubling to scuttle the *Caroline*. The difficulty was finally settled when Ashburton "expressed regret that explanation and apology for the occurrence was not immediately made," and there the matter was left.[54]

For some time after the destruction of the *Caroline,* untoward incidents continued to occur along the Canadian border. President Van Buren's proclamation urging the observance of strict days." Van Tyne (editor), *Letters of Daniel Webster,* New York, 1902, p. 233.

[52] For this case see Curtis, *The Life of Daniel Webster,* vol. II, p. 53, 61, 62, 64, 69, 85, and any good text on international law. Dent, *op. cit.,* pp. 170–171 declares that McLeod did not make this boast, but was so accused by personal enemies.

[53] *Calhoun's Works,* vol. III, p. 618.

[54] *Webster's Works,* vol. VI, pp. 292–303.

neutrality was of little avail, though at first an honest effort had been made to carry it into effect.[55] Raids into Canadian territory were finally stopped by a realization of their futility and by the severe treatment accorded prisoners by the Canadian authorities.[56] These raiders had, in reality, the status of brigands, so severe punishment was legally just. A number of them were executed and over one hundred and fifty were deported to Van Dieman's Land.[57] Whether or not the British officials might have displayed more leniency is still a topic of Canadian debate.[58] A rather humorous recognition of the efficiency of Canadian methods is found in the following resolution passed by a public meeting in the city of Buffalo: Resolved "that Great Britain, in hanging, shooting or transporting American citizens who were assisting the Canadian revolutionists has infringed upon the rights of free men." [59]

Thus was ended one of the most critical periods in the history of American-Canadian relations. That it did not result in war is decidedly creditable to those political leaders who braved the anger of the mob in order to preserve international peace. Internal conditions in the United States, especially after the burning of the *Caroline,* might very easily have plunged the English-speaking

[55] Kingsford, *op. cit.,* vol. X, pp. 430–445; Tiffany, "Relations of the United States to the Canadian Rebellion of 1837–1838," *Publications of the Buffalo Historical Society,* vol. VIII (1905); Shepard, *Van Buren,* pp. 350–356.

[56] For a complete account see *Report of the State Trials Before a General Court-Martial at Montreal, 1838–1839, Exhibiting a Complete History of the late Rebellion,* Montreal, 1839; Fry, *Case of the Canadian Prisoners,* Montreal, 1839.

[57] See an excellent paper by F. Landon, "The Exiles of 1838 from Canada to Van Dieman's Land." *Transactions of the London and Middlesex Historical Society,* pt. 12, 1927.

[58] Bourinot, *op. cit.,* p. 155. The execution of distinguished reformers such as Blount and Matthews by the brutal and stupid Sir George Arthur is now generally condemned; less sympathy is granted to the American raiders who, in many instances at least, were simply seeking adventure or profit. R. C. Watt, "The English Prisoners in Upper Canada, 1837–1838," *English Historical Review,* October, 1926; Shortridge, "The Canadian American Frontier During the Rebellion of 1837–1838," *Canadian Historical Review,* March, 1926.

[59] Quoted in Halifax *Morning Herald,* February 23, 1842.

world in war. Here was a people proud, exultant, youthful; still glorying in the winning of their freedom from the world's greatest empire; filled with a passion for republican institutions; and still looking with disfavor upon the authors of their ancient wrongs. On the northern side of the boundary dwelt a people of equally intense pride, a people who had created a new nation in a wilderness because of ill-treatment suffered at the hands of their southern neighbors, and because of loyalty to their king. The Canadian nation was divided in race, and gripped in the travail precedent to the birth of free and responsible institutions. On neither side of the border was prudence held in high esteem; it was a time of hot words and energetic action; not of reason and of philosophic calm. It is fortunate, and even surprising, that war did not ensue.

3. THE ANNEXATION MOVEMENT OF 1849

The importance in Canadian history of the revolutionary movements of 1837 and 1838 is to be found not in the events themselves, but rather in the psychological result produced by the revolts. So effectually did these eruptions in the body politic draw the attention of the statesmen of Great Britain to the problem of Canadian government that Lord Durham, soon to become an outstanding figure in British colonial history, was delegated to proceed to the American colonies, to inquire into and report upon conditions there existing.

It was no simple problem with which Lord Durham had to deal, and although in its ultimate effect the result of his counsel was beneficial to the colony, the political and especially the economic disturbances of the decade following his appointment as Governor-General led Canada in 1849 to the serious consideration of annexation to the United States.

One of the first acts of Lord Durham upon taking office as Governor-General was to issue a general pardon to all those who had taken part in the late revolts, with the exception of some few leaders including Papineau, Nelson, and Mackenzie.[60]

---

[60] Bourinot, *op. cit.*, p. 137.

At the same time he was conducting an extensive inquiry into the causes of political and social unrest in both Upper and Lower Canada. Late in 1839, failing to receive the complete support from the home authorities which his haughty spirit demanded, Durham resigned, but his report,[61] soon to become one of the celebrated documents of Canadian constitutional history, was already in the final stages of preparation. Upon his return to Great Britain his recommendations were presented to the ministry at Westminster.

The most important item in Lord Durham's report was his proposal to unite the provinces of Upper Canada and Lower Canada in a federal union. This recommendation was made effectual in the Act of Union of 1840. The act, moreover, provided for a system of semi-responsible government, and by liberal interpretation and insistence the practices of real responsibility were gradually introduced, strengthened, and accorded the authority of precedent.[62] The appointment of Lord Elgin, a pronounced liberal, as Governor-General in 1847, indicated beyond all possibility of mistake that the British government was now prepared to permit the establishment in Canada of a thoroughly responsible system of government.[63] In the general elections of that year the Governor-General assumed a strictly impartial attitude and largely as a result of this fact, the Tory party was decisively defeated.[64] The Reformers were returned to power and a ministry was formed from among their leaders.

Now for the first time the power of the Family Compact and

[61] *Sessional Papers: Reports from Commissioners,* London, 1839, vol. XVII; Kennedy, *op. cit.*

[62] On the growth of responsible government in Canada see Kennedy, *The Constitution of Canada,* and *The Winning of Responsible Government;* Morison, *British Supremacy and Canadian Self-Government, 1839–1854,* Glasgow, 1919.

[63] Winsor, *op. cit.,* vol. VIII, p. 166; Walrond, *Letters and Journals of James, Eighth Earl of Elgin,* London, 1872, pp. 54, 86, 89; Morison, *op. cit.,* chapter 6.

[64] In previous elections the Governor had almost invariably thrown his influence on the side of the Tory ministries, and had assisted greatly in the defeat of the "disloyal" Reformers. See Mackenzie, *Life and Speeches of Hon. George Brown,* Toronto, 1882, p. 20.

of the so-called "Chateau Clique"[65] was shattered; a Reform
administration was in office and an impartial Governor-General
occupied the official residence.[66] This was a bitter experience for
those who had long enjoyed the perquisites of office and authority; who had come to view themselves as the sole Canadian re-
positories of loyalty; and who now perceived that the government
of their country had fallen into the hands of those whom they
considered the low-born and the malcontent. Some explanation of
this dramatic overturn was necessary, and the Tories found the
explanation that they desired in the almost solid delegation sent
to swell the Reform majority *from French-Canadian constituen-
cies.* Immediately the cry of "French domination" was raised
throughout the land, and the decades of Anglo-French dissension
—dissension which is still far too common in Ontario and Quebec
—can be traced in no small measure to the bitterness here engendered.

The new ministry introduced as one of its first measures a
bill to indemnify the citizens of Lower Canada for losses sustained in the outbreaks of 1837 and 1838. Similar legislation had
already been enacted in Upper Canada, but the new bill was violently opposed by the Tories on the ground that, owing to the
widespread nature of the revolts in Lower Canada, the proposed
indemnity would, in fact, be subsidizing revolution.[67]

The attack on the Rebellion Losses Bill was characterized by a
bitterness and a violence never since equalled in a political struggle in Canada. Amid the fierce protests against "French rule,"
and accusations of personal corruption, began to be heard the
prophecy of armed revolt, the muttered wish for annexation.[68]
The threats used a decade before by Papineau and Mackenzie
were now heard in the mouths of Tories—many of the ultra-
Loyalists of 1837 were flirting with revolt in 1848. If the Re-

[65] The "Family Compact" of Lower Canada.

[66] Walrond, *op. cit.,* p. 71. For amusing sidelights on the politics of this
period see Bengough, *A Caricature History of Canadian Politics,* Toronto,
1886.

[67] Mackenzie, *op. cit.,* pp. 18–19; L. O. David, *L'Union des Deux Canadas, 1841–1867,* Montreal, 1898, pp. 99–107.

[68] *Idem,* pp. 109 ff.

formers had been extravagant in their denunciation of the government in 1837, the Tories were no more rational now—and they had infinitely less excuse for violence. "Civil war is an evil," wrote one Tory editor, "but it is not the worst of evils, and we say without hesitation that it would be better for the British people of Canada to have a twelvemonth of fighting . . . and lose five thousand lives, than submit for ten years longer to misgovernment induced by French domination." [69] Another paper was reported by Lord Elgin to have said: "When we can stand tyranny no longer, we shall see whether good bayonets in Saxon hands will not be more than a match for a race and a majority." [70] As Lord Durham had half foreseen, the Tories' hostility to the French was so great that many of them in order "to remain English" were willing "to cease being British." [71] For reasons which will shortly become more apparent, Montreal was the center of disloyal movement. In March, 1849, the Toronto *Patriot* declared that there was an "undercurrent leaning of the Anglo-Saxons there (in Montreal) towards an annexation with their brethren of the United States." [72] But the agitation was not entirely confined to Lower Canada. In Kingston a petition in favor of annexation was circulated,[73] while the Toronto *Mirror* and the Hamilton *Spectator* advocated "an alliance with a kindred race." [74] But Montreal was the center of the disturbance and both the *Colonist* and the *Spectator* declared that a continuance of the existing situation would inevitably lead to separation from Great Britain and union with the United States.[75]

The dispossessed Tories focused their attacks most pertina-

[69] Montreal *Courier*, April 2, 1849.

[70] Elgin to Gray, April 30, 1849, quoted in Allin and Jones, *Annexation, Preferential Trade and Reciprocity*, Toronto, 1911, p. 6. This book, which is by far the most exhaustive study of the annexation movement of 1849, is the source of many of the newspaper and other quotations used in this section. The author is deeply indebted to Professor Jones for permission to use this material.

[71] Skelton, *Life and Times of Sir A. T. Galt*, Toronto, 1920, p. 148.

[72] Quoted in Allin and Jones, *op. cit.*, p. 45.

[73] Kingston *Argus*, March 3, 1849.

[74] Allin and Jones, *op. cit.*, p. 7; Walrond, *op. cit.*, p. 116.

[75] *Colonist*, July 3, 1849; Hamilton *Spectator*, April 7, 1849.

ciously and most violently against the government's Rebellion Losses Bill; their leader, Sir Allan McNab, declared on one occasion that he would rather join the United States than agree to its passage.[76] A part of this opposition was undoubtedly caused by a genuine fear of French control, but it is not unfair to consider this a comparatively minor factor in the situation. The real explanation of the attitude of the Tories is probably to be found in their chagrin at the loss of office after so many years of uninterrupted power,[77] in an intense desire to discredit the government, and in the hope of intimidating Lord Elgin into vetoing the bill.[78]

In spite of all opposition, the government persisted, the bill was passed, and Lord Elgin gave his consent. Thereupon ensued the most disgraceful scenes in all Canadian political history. Lord Elgin's carriage was stoned, the Governor-General himself was insulted and reviled, and as a final act of revenge the Tory mob stormed and fired the Parliament buildings.[79] Since that day no provincial or federal legislature has been convened in Montreal.

As might be expected, such actions as these merely served further to inflame the popular passions. The editor of the Quebec *Gazette* declared that the Tories had "destroyed their own reputation for consistent loyalty, ruined the character and credit of the country abroad, and retarded its prosperity. . . ."[80] George Brown, the father of Canadian liberalism and editor of the Toronto *Globe,* had some justification for writing that "the Tories have not been a year out of office, yet they are at the rebellion point. . . . Withdraw the supplies and the Tory soon lets you

[76] Brunet, *op. cit.,* p. 167; Sir Francis Hincks, *Reminiscences,* Montreal, 1834, pp. 189–200; Dent, *The Last Forty Years,* Toronto, 1881; vol. II, pp. 143 ff.

[77] Waldron, *op. cit.,* p. 75.

[78] *Ibid. The Question Answered,* a pamphlet published in Montreal in 1849 provides an interesting contemporary analysis of the situation.

[79] Lord Elgin's own description of these scenes is to be found in Egerton and Grant, *Selected Speeches and Despatches Relating to Canadian Constitutional History,* Toronto, 1907, pp. 313 ff.; Dent, *op. cit.,* vol. II, chap. 27; David, *op. cit.,* p. 108.

[80] Allin and Jones, *op. cit.,* p. 8.

know it is not the man or his principles which he loved, but the solid pudding which he could administer." [81]

It would, of course, be manifestly unjust to hold the whole Tory Party responsible for the statements of its leaders or the actions of its mobs. The vital fact in the Canadian political situation in 1849 was the existence of a violently inflamed hostility between the two major parties—a condition so acute that many members of the party which had always been foremost in voicing its loyalty were now ready to discuss annexation to the United States, to toy with the idea of revolt.

The Canadian disorders of 1849, however, were not solely the result of political and constitutional difficulties. These difficulties were inevitable, but economic causes made them important.[82] By the year 1846 the political and economic philosophy of the "Manchester School" had triumphed in Great Britain.[83] In that year the Corn Laws were repealed, and during 1847 and 1848 tariff duties were removed from practically all commodities of commerce and industry. The reaction of this British policy upon Canadian economic life was almost immediately disastrous. Prior to 1846 Canadian farm and forest products had enjoyed preferential treatment in British markets,[84] a fact that gave assurance to the farmer or lumberman, and facilitated the procuring of credit.[85] Now this preference was wiped away and the products of Canada were forced into competition with the output of the United States and other countries. Lord Elgin, in writing to the Colonial Secretary, described the conditions in Canada as follows:

"I do not think that you are blind to the hardships which Canada is now enduring; but, I must own, I doubt much whether you fully appreciate their magnitude, or are aware of how directly they are chargeable on Imperial legislation. Stanley's Bill of 1843

[81] Toronto *Globe*, March 3, 1849.

[82] For a detailed description of conditions in Canada in 1849 see Brown, *Views on Canada and the Canadians* (second edition), Edinburgh, 1851.

[83] For British opinion regarding the colonies see Morison, *op. cit.*, chapter 7.

[84] Under the Canada Corn Bill, 1843; see Shortt and Doughty, *op. cit.*, vol. X, pp. 372–373.

[85] Shortt, *Imperial Preferential Trade*, p. 30.

attracted all the produce of the West to the St. Lawrence, and fixed all the disposable capital of the province in grinding mills, warehouses and forwarding establishments. Peel's Bill of 1846 drives the whole produce down the New York channels of communication, destroying the revenue which Canada expected to derive from canal dues, and ruining at once mill-owners, forwarders and merchants. The consequence is that private property is unsaleable in Canada, and not a shilling can be raised on the credit of the province.

. . . .

"What makes it more serious is that all the prosperity of which Canada is thus robbed is transplanted to the other side of the line, as if to make Canadians feel more bitterly how much kinder England is to the children who desert her, than to those who remain faithful. . . . I believe that the conviction that they would be better off if they were 'annexed' is almost universal among the commercial classes at present, and the peaceful condition of the province under all the circumstances of the time is, I must confess, often a matter of great astonishment to myself." [86]

The difficulty was enhanced, moreover, by the fact that Colonial shipping was still hampered by the Navigation Acts—Acts already famous as major causes of the American Revolution.[87] Canadian protests against the new British policy were unavailing,[88] and to many observers separation from the mother country and union with the United States, whose tariff wall was one of the chief obstacles to Canadian prosperity, seemed inevitable.[89] Banks refused to extend credit to the farmer, for he was no longer certain of a market for his grain and fruit. The lumbering and dairying industries were faced with a similar problem, while exporting firms and allied corporations were forced into liquidation. To quote Lord Elgin again:

[86] Walrond, *op. cit.*, p. 60.
[87] Egerton and Grant, *op. cit.*, p. 335.
[88] Shortt and Doughty, *op. cit.*, vol. V, pp. 234–235; *idem*, vol. XV, p. 106. The full text of one such protest is to be found in *Hansard*, vol. LXXXVI, pp. 556–557. The Canadian Assembly in 1846 warned Great Britain that if Canada lost her preference she might seek separation. Skelton, *Galt*, p. 153.
[89] Shortt and Doughty, *op. cit.*, vol. V, p. 53.

"Property in most of the Canadian towns and more especially in the capital, has fallen fifty per cent in value within the last three years. Three quarters of the commercial men are bankrupt, owing to Free-Trade; a large proportion of the exportable produce of Canada is obliged to seek a market in the States. It pays a duty of twenty per cent on the frontier. How long can such a state of things be expected to endure?" [90]

The British government, realizing the difficulties which were besetting its premier colony, was seeking means which would alleviate this distress and at the same time enable the government to remain true to its own political philosophy. The repeal of the Navigation Laws seemed to fulfil both requirements, and in consequence this was done.[91] The St. Lawrence River was now thrown open to the traders of the world and *ultimately* this action conferred important benefits upon Canada. It was some months, however, before foreign powers took advantage of their new opportunity, and the immediate effect was almost negligible.[92]

The most direct and obvious means of ameliorating Canadian conditions was that suggested by the British ambassador at Washington who, at the instigation of Canadian advisers, proposed the negotiation of a reciprocal trade agreement with the United States. The effect of such an enactment would be to open the American market to Canadian raw material, and the United States would supplant Britain as Canada's chief customer. To this proposal the American administration agreed and a bill to implement the agreement was introduced and passed by the House of Representa-

[90] Walrond, *op. cit.*, p. 70. Conditions were summarized in a memorial to the Queen from the Montreal Board of Trade, published in the Quebec *Gazette*, January 8, 1849.

[91] Galt, *Canada, 1849–1859*, Quebec, 1860.

[92] Canada was now given full control over her tariff laws, and she began to levy duties against British as well as foreign goods. It was the beginning of a new era in Canadian self-government. See Davidson, *Commercial Federation and Colonial Trade Policy*, p. 15. See also Lucas's introduction to Lewis, *Government of Dependencies*, p. 33. Duties against the United States were somewhat lowered at this time. *United States Executive Document*, no. 64, 31st Cong., 1st sess.; Haynes, *The Reciprocity Treaty with Canada of 1864*, p. 12.

tives in 1848. Owing to a general lack of interest and the pressure of other business, however, the session closed before the Senate had taken any action with regard to it.[93] An equally abortive effort marked the following session.[94]

While the Senators procrastinated at Washington, conditions on the St. Lawrence grew steadily worse, and sentiment in favor of annexation became more and more common as the economic situation became more stringent.

Nor was the condition of the loyal Canadian made easier by the news now emanating from Great Britain, for the London *Times,* the Edinburgh *Review* and other equally prominent journals were giving voice to the colonial philosophy of Cobden and Bright. Loyalty to the empire was no longer considered—even in the heart of the empire—to be, of necessity, a virtue. Political leaders and public opinion seemed at one in resigning colonial destiny to the colonies themselves.[95] Lord John Russell, Prime Minister of Great Britain, declared with the applause of a full House that "he looked forward to the day when the ties which he was endeavoring to render so easy and mutually advantageous would be severed"; he and the people of England generally assumed that "the colonial relation was incompatible with maturity and full development."[96] Other English politicians favored separation on the ground of expense.[97] Indeed, the reaction against Tory imperialism seemed complete, and it was not surprising to find a Canadian annexationist editor summarizing it thus: "The whole current of opinion among England's most influential statesmen is evidently tending toward that point when they will bid adieu to the colonies, with wishes for their prosperity and hopes for continued friendship.[98] As became evident later, British opinion was not united in willingness to bid the colonies adieu, but there was

[93] *United States Executive Document,* no. 64, 31st Cong., 1st sess.; Porritt, *op. cit.,* p. 89.

[94] *Idem,* pp. 90–94; Walrond, *op. cit.,* p. 107.

[95] Allin and Jones, *op. cit.,* chapter 10; Morison, *op. cit.,* pp. 233 ff.

[96] Walrond, *op. cit.,* p. 115.

[97] See *Annual Register, 1849.*

[98] Montreal *Herald,* April 13, 1849.

enough of this spirit extant and expressed to give real cause for worry to the Canadian opponents of separation.[99]

In spite of these conditions, however, Canada was by no means ready for immediate annexation to the United States. Lord Elgin in describing conditions declared:

"There has been a vast deal of talk about annexation as is unfortunately the case when there is anything to agitate the public mind. If half the talk on this subject were sincere I should consider an attempt to keep up the connection with Great Britain as Utopian in the extreme. . . . A great deal of this talk is, however, bravado, and a great deal more the mere product of thoughtlessness. Undoubtedly it is in some quarters the utterance of every serious conviction; and if England will not make the sacrifices which are absolutely necessary to put the Colonists here in as good a position commercially as the citizens of the United States . . . the end may be nearer than we wot of." [100]

It was at this juncture in Canadian affairs, early in the year 1849, that the British American League was organized at Brockville, whence its headquarters were shortly moved to Montreal.[101] The League was organized by the Honorable George Moffatt, and its objectives were stated to be, the promotion of the commercial and industrial life of the colony; the organization of the moderate elements of the British population into one party; and a united opposition to French-Canadian domination. The advertisement issued by the League further proclaimed that "to maintain the British connection inviolate, has been, and still is, the ardent wish of every member of the League." [102] The latter statement, however, was soon proven to be far from accurate.

The League was, in fact a conglomerate body, composed of all

[99] Elgin over and over again protested against the assumption that all Englishmen were willing to see Canada leave the empire. He persistently urged the home government to deny the assertions of those who "admitted that separation *must* sooner or later take place." Walrond, *op. cit.,* p. 112.

[100] Quoted in Allin and Jones, *op. cit.,* p. 48.

[101] On League see Dent, *op. cit.,* vol. II, pp. 172–173; Montreal *Gazette,* April 19, 1849.

[102] Quoted in Allin and Jones, *op. cit.,* p. 54.

the elements in Canadian society hostile to the existing regime, and it included Annexationists, Tories, Independents (those desiring Canadian independence, but not annexation), Federal Unionists (proponents of a union including the maritime provinces and Newfoundland), and Provincial Partitionists (those in favor of annulling the Act of Union of 1840). One of the vice-presidents was an American citizen who openly favored annexation.[103]

An organization composed of such discordant elements could not long resist the centrifugal forces embodied in itself. A convention was called, and when it became evident that the majority of delegates supported the British connection,[104] many members left to join another body, known as the Annexation Association.[105] At this convention,[106] the tenets of the League were expressed in the formula, "Protection, Retrenchment, and Union." This, for the time being, ended the attacks upon the loyalty of the League.

The agitation for annexation was centered in Montreal, and it was here on October 10th that an "Annexation Manifesto" was prepared and published.[107] This document contrasted conditions in the United States and in Canada; placed the responsibility for the prevailing depression in the latter country upon the British government; considered and discarded all proposals for relief which included membership in the empire; and concluded that a true solution could be found only in "a friendly and peaceful separation from the British connection, and a union upon equitable terms with the great North American Confederacy of sovereign States." The benefits to be derived from such a union were then enlarged upon, and the manifesto ended with an appeal to all true citizens to unite under the banner of the Annexation Association in working out the "common destiny" of the North American continent. In ten days, over one thousand names were

[103] The Montreal *Pilot,* May 17, 1849.
[104] *Idem,* July 19, 1849.
[105] Toronto *Globe,* June 25, 1849.
[106] Held at Kingston.
[107] Egerton and Grant, *op. cit.,* pp. 335 ff. Finally signed by about 1000 persons.

appended to this document, and many of them were those of leaders in the social and commercial life of Lower Canada.[108] Combined with these were the signatures of Americans, extremists of the Rouge party, and others who had suffered politically, economically, or both, by the recent events.[109]

The publication of the Annexation Manifesto served to bring the problem directly to public attention, and it did much to crystallize opinion either for or against the movement.[110] The combination of forces favoring annexation was indeed a strange one. The business interests of Montreal—predominantly British by birth and extreme conservatives in politics—were, on this one question, linked with the ultra-radical elements of the French-Canadian populace, although on every other conceivable issue the two groups were diametrically opposed.[111] Many members of the Tory party, fearful of French domination, enraged by their own expulsion from office, and bitterly incensed over the enactment of the Rebellion Losses Bill, were united in the advocacy of annexation with those who had been their most fervent opponents on all other issues.

The Montreal press at once became involved. The *Witness,* religious in tone and Tory in spirit, endeavored to give the sanction of theology to the proposed union: "It is precisely because we think the indications of Divine Providence are pointing directly, constantly and urgently in the direction of annexation that we have felt constrained to discuss it." So wrote the editor on October 5, 1849. The *Herald, Courier,* and *Gazette* favored annexation, while the *Transcript* and *Pilot* remained loyal to the

[108] The signatories included a future Prime Minister of Canada (J. J. C. Abbott), three future Cabinet ministers, two Queen's Counsellors, several Justices of the Peace, together with Redpath, Molson, Galt, Torrance and other famous leaders in the Canadian business world. See Egerton and Grant, *op. cit.,* p. 335, note; Allin and Jones, *op. cit.,* p. 170.

[109] Skelton, *op. cit.,* p. 145; Grey, *Colonial Policy of Lord John Russell's Administration,* London, 1853, vol. I, pp. 219–220.

[110] Some interesting sidelights on this movement are to be found in the recently-discovered Penny letters, printed in *The Canadian Historical Review,* vol. V (1924), pp. 236–261.

[111] Turcotte, *Le Canada sous l'Union,* Quebec, 1871, pt. 2, p. 121.

British connection.[112] The French-Canadian papers were similarly divided.[113]

Although many of the more radical French-Canadian democrats were in favor of annexation, the majority of the French populace was hostile to the movement. Following the leadership of their church officials, these citizens of Lower Canada were definitely opposed to a policy that would have led to their submersion in the huge population of the United States. They felt, and probably with justice, that no American Congress would ever grant to any section of its populace the peculiar rights which Britain had granted to the inhabitants of Quebec.[114] As one of their own historians has expressed it:

"Les Canadiens-Français n'avaient aucune sympathie pour les Américains avec lesquels leurs ancêtres avaient été souvent aux prises sur le champ de bataille. Monarchiste et conservateur par leurs institutions, leurs moeurs et leur education, ils detestaient les principes républicains. Ils savaient que, sous le drapeau britannique, ils trouveraient une sécurité parfaite pour leurs institutions et leurs privilèges, tandis qu'avec l'annexion, leur existence national courrait de grands dangers." [115]

Apart from Montreal, the movement in Lower Canada was centered in the eastern townships.[116] The movement, on the whole, as subsequent developments clearly demonstrated, was not the expression of a united public sentiment, but rather the action of an ardent minority coerced from their old beliefs and convictions by the pangs of a bitter experience, and temporarily beguiled by the specious arguments of those few individuals to whom annexa-

[112] Montreal *Courier,* October 5, 1849. The *Pilot* and *Transcript* were both Reform journals; the others were Tory. Skelton, *op. cit.,* pp. 153–154; Allin and Jones, *op. cit.,* p. 74 ff.

[113] Turcotte, *op. cit.,* pp. 126–127; *L'Echo des Campagnes,* November 2, 1849.'

[114] *L'Ami de la Religion,* October 16, 1849; Gerin-Lajoie, *op. cit.,* p. 598.

[115] Turcotte, *op. cit.,* pt. 2, p. 124.

[116] Predominantly British in population. See the speech of Mr. Galt, then Member of Parliament for Sherbrooke in *Minerve,* November 15, 1849,

tion really appeared to be the logical, inevitable, and attractive destiny of British North America.[117]

The publication of the manifesto did more than arouse public opinion; it introduced the very practical problem of ways and means. And this in turn demanded a discussion of the *terms* upon which union should be based. The Montreal *Gazette* had at first favored union, but it soon came to the point of declaring: "We must have an opportunity to understand what we are called upon to participate in before we can with prudence or honour throw ourselves unreservedly into the annexation fad." [118] This discussion of terms did something toward cooling the excitement of the more volatile annexationists, and it served to arouse many of the old anti-American prejudices of those whose Loyalist traditions had been momentarily forgotten in a temporary hostility toward Great Britain. Nevertheless, the movement did not collapse. The manifesto was followed by the formation of a political party; papers were published, pamphlets printed and distributed, and a platform campaign was carried on throughout the country.[119]

As the campaign went on, the two sides drew farther and farther apart. The members of the government issued a vigorous denunciation of the Annexationists and all officials of the state who had been in any way connected with the movement were summarily dismissed—an action which was vigorously supported and defended by Elgin in Canada and Grey in England.[120] This step was, however, severely criticized by the parliamentary opposition and even some of the Reform Party felt that it was somewhat too drastic.[121] For the most part, however, the press and people ap-

[117] *Memoirs of the Rt. Hon. John A. Macdonald*, Ottawa, vol. I, p. 70.

[118] Montreal *Gazette*, October 20, 1849.

[119] See *L'Avenir*, November 30, 1849. All issues of this paper in 1849 and 1850 were filled with propaganda material. *The Independent* was published by the annexationists in Upper Canada, but soon suspended for lack of support. See *Papers and Records of the Ontario Historical Society*, vol. XIII, p. 74.

[120] Walrond, *op. cit.*, p. 101; Grey, *op. cit.*, p. 232; Montreal *Gazette*, October 31, 1849.

[121] Toronto *Colonist*, November 12, 1849; Quebec *Mercury*, November 14, 1849; *L'Avenir*, October 18, 1849.

plauded the action of the administration; the annexationists were apparently losing ground.[122] Early in October prominent members of the British American League joined with the Loyalists of Montreal in issuing a Counter-Manifesto which received one thousand signatures without the formality of a canvass.[123]

The Canadian Orangemen, though the vast majority of them were intensely opposed to the existing government, declared themselves in favor of unswerving allegiance to the British Crown.[124] Many of those who had signed the original manifesto refused to continue their support.[125] An enormous harvest and a slight stimulation to trade began to create an interest in business and to lessen the interest in political affairs.[126] Conditions were such that the Montreal correspondent of the London *Times* felt justified in writing to his paper that he was becoming

> "more confident every day that the late movement is a bubble which will have burst before next summer. . . . Nine-tenths at least of the Annexationists are so reluctantly. They believe that this incorporation with the United States will act in a magical manner on the value of property and labour in Canada, and on commerce; that it will, in short, restore their own dilapidated fortunes. Show them a revival of prosperity without it, and annexation will be laid on the shelf until the next rainy day." [127]

Doubtful as was the reception of the Annexation Manifesto in Montreal, it was received with even less enthusiasm in Upper Canada. The Toronto papers were almost unanimous in opposition to the proposal,[128] *The Church* even going so far as to reassert the Revolutionary Loyalists' doctrine of indefeasible allegiance.[129] Lord Elgin, nevertheless, was of the opinion that the

[122] Toronto *Globe,* October 16, 1849; Montreal *Pilot,* October 25, 1849.
[123] Gerin-Lajoie, *op. cit.,* p. 598.
[124] London *Times,* November 23, 1849.
[125] Allin and Jones, *op. cit.,* pp. 164, 274.
[126] *The Transcript,* December 1–22, 1849.
[127] *The Times,* December 20, 1849.
[128] *The Mirror,* an Irish-Catholic organ stood almost alone in favoring annexation. *The Independent,* publication of which was commenced by the Annexationists, soon failed.
[129] *The Church,* October, 1849.

large majority of those persons in Upper Canada who were protesting against the manifesto "firmly believe that their annexation to the United States would add one-fourth to the value of
the produce of their farms."[130] The attacks on the annexation
movement were not, in general, based on economic grounds. The
Globe and the *Patriot* reiterated time after time in good Loyalist
style the old charges against the morals, religion and civilization
of the United States, paying particular attention to the question
of slavery.[131]

At this juncture a most interesting event occurred. William
Lyon Mackenzie, the exiled revolutionary leader of 1837, in a
letter from New York to the Toronto *Examiner* stated that his

"sojourn in the United States had wrought a disillusionment. American democracy as it presented itself in the form of political corruption, crass materialism and human slavery, filled his soul with
righteous indignation. He was convinced that the vaunted liberty
of the United States was merely a sham; that neither the grandiloquent principles of the Declaration of Independence, nor the unctu-
ous guarantees of the American constitution assured to the private
citizen the same measure of civil and political freedom' as was enjoyed
by the humblest Canadian subject under the British Constitution."[132]

This from the man who a decade before had favored annexation
and had led a rebellion against the representatives of the Crown.
Throughout the Upper Canadian peninsula this sentiment prevailed, the proponents of annexation being few and scattered.[133]
The British American League, both in convention and by vote of
the local chapters, expressed itself as definitely opposed to union
with the United States.[134]

One of the strongest arguments of the annexation party, and
one that was used with considerable effect, was that many British
leaders had expressed themselves as favorable to Canadian separa-

[130] Walrond, *op. cit.,* p. 104.

[131] *The Patriot,* January 19, 1850; *The Globe,* October 20, 23, 24, November 17, 1849.

[132] Toronto *Examiner,* January 31, 1850.

[133] Allin and Jones, *op. cit.,* pp. 223–242.

[134] Allin and Jones, *op. cit.,* pp. 59, 61–3, 241, 243, 255.

tion, and that England, in effect, would be glad to see Canada go. This argument was finally overthrown in January, 1850, when Earl Grey, the British Colonial Secretary, stated that the Queen was prepared "to assert all the authority which belongs to her for the purpose of maintaining the connection of Canada" with the mother country.[135] This declaration went far toward ending the discussion: the practical difficulties were now too great to be overcome.

The session of the Assembly which opened on January 18, 1850, was to see the final defeat of the annexation movement. Only seven Annexationists had been elected to the House in a total membership of eighty-three. Motions in favor of both independence and annexation were presented and overwhelmingly defeated. But the fundamental reason for the ending of interest in annexation, which took place during the spring and summer of 1850, was the revival of trade consequent upon the discovery of the Canadian market by foreign purchasing agents, and the activity of American buyers in taking up the immense Canadian crop of 1849. As soon as navigation opened, the St. Lawrence became crowded with shipping, and the grain deliveries presaged a great revival in every branch of commerce. Credit was again obtainable, property value increased, and a wave of confidence swept over the whole country.

The annexation movement of 1849 was merely one of the growing pains of Canadian evolution. It was based on no fundamental hostility to the British connection, or on any compelling and persistent desire for union with the United States. The progress from colonial to Dominion status in Canada, and from protection to free trade in Great Britain, produced a natural, but temporary, dislocation of the economic and political vested interests in the colony.[136] The movement failed because it was—in a fundamental sense—insincere. As Sir John A. Macdonald said at a later time, the leaders of the movement, chagrined at their loss of political power and suffering from serious economic difficulties, tempora-

[135] Quoted in Allin and Jones, *op. cit.*, p. 268. Grey to Elgin, January 9, 1850.
[136] Skelton, *op. cit.*, p. 145.

rily "lost their heads." [187] The fact is that the vast majority of Canadians were too much satisfied with their recently gained autonomy to be willing to sacrifice it by annexation to the United States.[188] As Elgin wrote, "the existence to an unwonted degree of political contentment among the masses has prevented the cry for annexation from spreading . . . through the Province." [139]

Supplementary explanations of the defeat of annexation may be found in the following facts: *First.* The party favoring union with the United States was composed of totally irreconcilable elements with no common ground except hostility to the government of the day. *Second.* The firm attitude adopted by the Baldwin-Lafontaine government, the tireless efforts of Lord Elgin and the tardy but powerful support of the British Colonial Office. *Third.* The inherited and deeply-rooted dislike for the American institutions and people so firmly implanted in the minds of Canadians—a dislike made more potent by the influence of the Roman Catholic church, and crystallized by recent developments in connection with slavery in the United States. *Finally, and most decisive,* was the revival of trade in the spring and summer of 1850. The winning of reciprocity in 1854 gave to Canada most of the advantages of annexation without its defects.

The Movement in the Maritimes.—In the maritime provinces an agitation somewhat similar to that in Canada was carried on during 1849 and 1850. The principal grievance here was the removal of the tariff preference hitherto extended to New Brunswick lumber by Great Britain. The whole economic fabric of the colony may be said to have been based on this trade.[140] Here, also, the old conservative bureaucracy had been defeated upon the introduction of responsible government, and its discontent synchronized with that of the commercial classes. The revival of trade and the successful working of responsible government, however, ended "the silly fever of annexation which had

---

[187] Pope, *op. cit.*, p. 71. Sir John Abbott, who had himself signed the Manifesto, gave a similar explanation. *Idem*, pp. 70–71.

[188] Walrond, *op. cit.*, p. 109.

[139] *Idem*, p. 103.

[140] *The Newbrunswicker*, February 8, 1850.

prevailed for a time" amongst a disappointed clique, "for the Colonists had no liking for American slavery." [141]

American Sentiment Regarding Annexation.—What, during this time of stress in Canada, was the attitude of the United States?

The Republic was, at this time, going through a period of militaristic expansion comparable in American history only with the course of events since 1898. Texas and California had lately been annexed to the Union, as had also a considerable portion of the long-debated Oregon Territory. It was not alone the oratorical patriots of the period who could visualize a continent over which the stars and stripes should wave alone, supreme. With the coming struggle over slavery and states' rights casting its ominous shadow before, political leaders were not averse to directing the public gaze toward foreign affairs. New York and New England merchants were glancing with covetous eyes upon the Canadian trade, and they were ever ready to welcome the northern provinces within the American customs wall. General Winfield Scott, whose previous connections with Canadian affairs had been marked by a high degree of intelligence and understanding, now published an open letter advocating the annexation of the provinces —by agreement with Great Britain, if possible.[142] For a time this proposal threatened to become a plank in the Whig platform, for as a politician of the time declared, "it would be a great honour and glory at this time to deliver Canada from the British yoke, for a great part of the Canadian people, and all of Lower Canada, have been despoiled of their political liberties." Certainly it may be said that a firm and unequivocal belief in the "manifest destiny" of the United States possessed the majority of the American people.[143] "Both Cuba and the British Colonies," wrote a Washington paper, "at the proper time and in the proper manner will ultimately be annexed to the American Union." [144] Secretary Seward, recognizing the tendency of the times, wrote that "the

[141] *The New Brunswick Reporter,* quoted in Toronto *Globe,* September 27, 1849.

[142] Quoted in Gerin-Lajoie, *op. cit.,* p. 599.

[143] Cf. Adams, *The Power of Ideals in American History,* New Haven, 1913, chapter 3.

[144] Quoted in Allin and Jones, *op. cit.,* p. 376.

popular passion for territorial aggrandizement is irresistible." [145]
The old antipathy toward England, aroused by the many recent
controversies, had not been allowed to die down, and an American
correspondent of the London *Times* is found writing that "to fight
the Britishers, all the States are one." [146]

Native-born Americans, however, were not alone in their interest in Canada. French-Canadian immigration to the United
States had already become an important movement, and at a
meeting held in New York, a society was formed by members
of this group, with the object of bringing about a political union
of the two countries. An address was prepared urging all French-
men in Canada and in the United States to band together to
achieve this object. The address was circulated throughout the
continent, and branch societies were formed in many of the northern states.[147]

It was, very naturally, in the northern states of the Union that
the Canadian question became most prominent. American papers
quoted the Annexation Manifesto, and all the information they
could acquire tending to prove the dissatisfaction of Canadians
with British rule, and their desire for union with the United
States.[148] The Democratic State Convention, held in Montpelier,
Vermont, adopted the following resolution:

"That, in the true spirit of Democracy, deeply sympathizing
with the downtrodden, oppressed, and over-restricted of every clime
and country, we hail with joy the rising spirit of liberty in the
provinces of Canada as expressed recently in the published opinions
of its citizens on the subject of annexation; that we appreciate the
efforts and emulate the movements of the friends of Republicanism
in Canada, and that we cordially extend to them the hand of friendship, fellowship, and brotherly love; that we will use all peaceable
means in our power to further their object in becoming members of
this our glorious union of free, independent and sovereign states." [149]

[145] Seward, *Works,* New York, 1884, vol. III, p. 409.
[146] London *Times,* November 21, 1845.
[147] *L'Avenir,* January 11, 1850.
[148] For example, *New Hampshire Statesman,* October 28, November 2,
1849.
[149] Burlington *Daily Sentinel,* October 22, 1849.

Not to be outdone, the Whigs of Vermont adopted a similar resolve.[150] The Burlington *Sentinel* was even prepared to use force
in the accomplishment of this glorious act of liberty, "after a
fair trial" of "other means." [151] The Legislative Assembly of
New York resolved "that the annexation of Canada, and other
provinces of Great Britain in North America . . . is an object
of incalculable importance to the people of the United States." [152]

President Taylor was scrupulously correct in his attitude toward the whole problem. He even made strenuous efforts to pass
the Reciprocity Bill which was designed to aid Canada by fostering the return of prosperity. This bill was defeated, however, because of poor management in Congress and because the southern
representatives feared that it would lead to annexation which they
did not desire (Canada being "free" soil), and because a few of
the northern Congressmen believed that annexation, which they
did desire, could best be obtained by making Canada realize the
hardships of separate existence. The slave states approved the
annexation of Cuba, which was slave territory, but opposed the
taking of Canada; in the North the converse was largely true.

Such was the annexation movement of 1849. True, it was not
an event of primary importance, for from the first its prospects
of success were far from convincing. Nevertheless, it deserves
much more attention than is generally paid to it in conventional
histories, for it signalized the entrance of Canada on free and
equal terms into the ranks of commercial nations. No longer were
the provinces a commercial adjunct of the mother country. Moreover, the movement gave a glimpse into the thoughts which were
in the background of Canadian minds for many years; and at
the same time gave American imperialists the opportunity to express themselves yet again on the "manifest destiny" of the United
States. It was not until almost the beginning of the twentieth
century that loyal Canadians ceased to fear the possibility of
absorption by the United States; and even yet many Americans

[150] Burlington *Daily Sentinel*, October 31, 1849.
[151] *Idem*, November 6, 1849.
[152] *Journal of the House of Assembly*, New York, 1850, pp. 206–207.

believe that the Constitution will ultimately apply to the whole of North America.

4. THE AMERICAN CIVIL WAR AND THE FENIAN RAIDS

A. The Civil War and the British Empire.—In 1860 British-American relations appeared to be more firmly established on a basis of mutual toleration than had been the case at any time since the American Revolution. True, there was no great cordiality either expressed or instinct between the two peoples. Many Britons still looked upon the American as an uncouth and boisterous ruffian, engaged in a political experiment which was doomed to failure and dissolution; while, on the other hand, the American was prone to look upon the British aristocracy as the product of many centuries of disastrous in-breeding—"effete," "decadent," and "rapacious." [153] In spite of these mutually uncomplimentary estimates, however, the American Department of State and the British Foreign Office had at last succeeded in settling the outstanding difficulties which had embarrassed the two nations since 1776, and for a time there appeared to be no necessity of propagating an anti-American or anti-British sentiment in either country. The various boundary problems had been settled [154]; Britain had virtually abandoned the right of search; the fisheries dispute was temporarily dormant, and in general the future gave promise of a more peaceful intercourse than had marked the past. Relations with Canada were particularly satisfactory as a result of the mutual benefits being derived from the reciprocity agreement of 1854.[155] Yet in the five years from 1861 to 1866 these conditions were utterly changed. By the latter year the reciprocity treaty was abrogated; the American people were seriously considering the advisability of war against Great Britain; notice of repeal of the Rush-

[153] Cf. Dickens, *Martin Chuzzlewit, American Notes,* etc.

[154] Except the San Juan affair, which was not considered important.

[155] Many Americans were desirous of enlarging this to include Vancouver Island and British Columbia, and to apply to a greater list of commodities. Watkins, *Recollections of Canada and the United States,* chapter 18.

Bagot agreement had been sent to London,[156] and the tension on the Canadian border exceeded that of 1837–38.

The causes for this abrupt and all-inclusive change are almost too well known to need recapitulation. During the American Civil War, Great Britain came to be so generally hated by both the North and South that there was a very real possibility that the two sections of the Union might join in an offensive war against the common and "hereditary" foe.[157] The Northern enmity was based upon Great Britain's recognition of Confederate belligerency;[158] upon official laxity in allowing the escape of the *Alabama* and other cruisers;[159] upon the Confederate raids from Canada;[160] upon the consistent policy of blockade-running fostered by the British navy;[161] upon the generally expressed sympathy for the South common in British "society";[162] and, above all, upon the action taken by Great Britain in the case of the S. S. *Trent*.[163] The basis of Southern hostility was found in the refusal of Great Britain to join France in recognizing the Confederacy, and her refusal to intervene on behalf of the South even for the sake of cotton, the lack of which had paralyzed industry in northern Britain. It was largely on the hope of British and French aid that the South had built her confidence of success, and when the formal neutrality of the British government made

[156] Limiting naval armament on the Great Lakes.

[157] Dunning, *The British Empire and the United States*, New York, 1914, chapter 5.

[158] Hart, *American Journal of American Law,* 1907, vol. I, pt. 1, p. 631; Earl Russell, *Recollections and Suggestions*, p. 235.

[159] John Bassett Moore, *op. cit.*

[160] It is an extraordinary fact that Great Britain, for comparatively trivial offenses against the Union in this war, is universally condemned in the United States; while France, whose offenses were infinitely more serious, and who would probably have intervened by force if Great Britain had not prevented it, is never mentioned in connection with the American Civil War.

[161] *American Journal of International Law*, vol. I, pt. 1, p. 61 (1907).

[162] Dunning, *op. cit.*, chapter 5.

[163] C. F. Adams, "The Trent Affair," *Proceedings of the Massachusetts Historical Society,* vol. XLV; T. L. Harris, *The Trent Affair*, Indianapolis, 1896; Blaine, *Twenty Years of Congress*, vol. I, p. 585.

a Confederate victory impossible, the Southern hostility became correspondingly bitter.

The result of this feeling in the United States was, at the close of the Civil War, viewed with some concern in Canada. If a rapprochement had been consummated between the recent foes for the purpose of attacking Great Britain, Canada and the maritime provinces would have been the first points of attack. And many reports from south of the border served to convince Canadians that the people of the United States, as well as many of the more violent public officials, would not be averse to such a conflict. As a northern marching song expressed it—

> "Secession first he would put down
> Wholly and forever,
> And afterwards from Britain's crown
> He Canada would sever."

> (*From a popular version
> of "Yankee Doodle."*)

As a result of this attitude on the part of the American people, the reciprocity treaty was abrogated in 1866, and a bill was actually introduced in Congress to allow the entrance of Canada and the other provinces into the Union—a proceeding which was expected to result from the cancellation of the trade agreement.[164] The real effect of this move was far different, for it was one of the prime factors in causing the formation of the Dominion of Canada [165]—an event which ended, apparently forever, the possibility of the political union of these two North American nations.

Modern historical investigation has served to correct many of

[164] Bourinot, *Canada and the United States,* pp. 125–126.

[165] Gray, *Confederation,* pp. 290–304; Landon, "The American Civil War and Canadian Confederation," *Transactions of the Royal Society of Canada,* 1927, sec. 2, pp. 55–62. The name "Dominion" was adopted rather than "Kingdom" in order to avoid offending American opinion. Such Americans as Sumner, Chandler, and Seward were strongly opposed to Canadian federation, and this opposition so frightened Lord Derby that he refused to allow the use of the stronger term—an event that has definitely retarded the growth of Canadian self-government. See Dafoe, "Canada and the United States," in *Great Britain and the Dominions,* Chicago, 1928.

the earlier misapprehensions in regard to the attitude of Great
Britain toward the American Civil War. It has been shown that
English society at that period cannot be treated as a homogeneous
whole—that there were at least two widely divergent views of
the American struggle. While the aristocratic Tories were expressing their disdain for the North and sneering at the complete
renunciation of the principles of 1776 which the policy of Lincoln seemed to entail, the textile operators of Lancashire and the
northern counties were cheerfully enduring unemployment and
its concomitant ills, inspired by the messages of Henry Ward
Beecher and other apostles of abolition, who portrayed the struggle, not as a contest between free trade and protection, not as a
forceful denunciation of the liberties of sovereign states, but as a
crusade against that most vicious of institutions, human slavery.[166] And this was accepted by many Englishmen, in spite of
Lincoln's repeated assertions that slavery was not the issue; that
union was the principle at stake.[167]

A very similar social alignment had taken place in Canada.[168]
The Tory classes were as hostile to America as ever, and openly
rejoiced at the apparent disruption of the Union. On the other
hand, the majority of Canadians, looking beyond the expressed
cause of the war, could see the inevitable effect which a Northern
victory would have upon the hated institution of slavery. It was
this class that, while not animated by any strong friendship for
the North, was generally favorable to the cause of emancipation.
It was from this class also that the thousands of Canadians who

166 Goldwyn Smith in *Atlantic Monthly,* December, 1864, vol. XIV, p.
763; *Littell's Living Age* (3rd series), vol. XIX, p. 381; W. J. Barr,
Anglo-American Relations, Clark University Library (unpublished), 1920,
pp. 29–30.

167 Villers and Chesson, *Anglo-American Relations, 1861–1865,* p. 189;
Nicolay and Hay (editors), *Complete Works of Abraham Lincoln,* New
York, 1902, vol. II, p. 227; Logan, *The Great Conspiracy,* New York,
1886, pp. 180–181, 367–368; Goldwyn Smith in *Atlantic Monthly,* March,
1902, vol. LXXXIX, p. 305.

168 "When the Civil War broke out, the sympathies of Canadians were
overwhelmingly on the side of the North." Skelton, *The Canadian Dominion,* Yale, 1919, p. 125.

enlisted in the Union armies were drawn.[169] But the attitude generally assumed by the average citizen of Canada was probably well summarized by the Montreal editor who wrote:

"The Canadian people, heartily as they are opposed to slavery, have not seen, cannot yet see, why they should be friends with a people who have taken such pains to proclaim themselves our enemies; and to pander to every anti-British prejudice,[170] every action of their own people most imbued with such prejudice or hatred." [171]

That the Canadian people were thus affected toward the United States cannot be a cause of wonder to one who has followed the course of American political activities after the immense influx of German and, particularly, Irish immigrants after 1848. The manipulation of this great foreign vote could most easily be accomplished by an appeal to their native prejudices, and as a result many American political leaders allowed themselves to be drawn into a contest of villification, with Great Britain as the object of assault. The Canadian reaction to these attacks, naturally, was not favorable.

[169] Bourinot estimated that twenty Canadians enlisted in the Northern army to one who enlisted in the Southern. *Op. cit.,* p. 126. It is generally believed that forty thousand Canadians enlisted in the Northern army. Cf. Skelton, *op. cit.,* p. 128; see also Landon, "Canadian Opinion of Abraham Lincoln, *Dalhousie Review,* October, 1922.

[170] This identity which Canadians feel with Great Britain is not even yet understood in the United States. Americans do not realize that a denunciation of "England" is felt as an insult in Canada, and they cannot, therefore, understand the typical Canadian feeling of hostility to the United States.

[171] Montreal *Gazette,* Dec. 5, 1864. This reaction was due to attacks by The New York *Herald* and other papers which tried to force Great Britain and the United States into War. In August, 1861, Canada's leading newspaper, the Toronto *Globe,* said: "The insolent bravado of the Northern press towards Great Britain and the insulting tone assumed towards these Provinces have unquestionably produced a marked change in the feelings of our people. . . . People have lost sight of the character of the struggle in the exasperation excited by the injustice and abuse showered upon us by the party with which we sympathized." Toronto *Globe,* August 7, 1861.

B. Canada and the War.—Canadian hostility, however, was soon mingled with something of distrust and fear. At the conclusion of the war the presence of some million soldiers imbued with a resentful and retaliatory spirit, just south of the international border, caused no little anxiety in Canada. The memory of the Texas War was frequently recalled.[172] "Even were the American government noted for its conciliatory foreign policy, and free from mob dictation," wrote an aristocratic Canadian editor, "and were we stronger in numbers and position—the absence of all defensive preparations might well be thought perilous."[173] And these fears seemed fully justified, for the American people, flushed with victory, and deeply conscious of the real and also the imaginary wrongs inflicted upon them by the other branches of the English-speaking peoples, were in a mood that seemed to foreshadow vigorous action.[174]

The Northern states, in particular, had special grievances against Canada—grievances based on raids into Northern territory undertaken by Confederate soldiers acting from a Canadian base. The first plot of this sort was directed against Johnson's Island in Sandusky Bay, and was forestalled by a warning sent out from the British Embassy at Washington.[175] This was followed, however, by a much more important event—the Confederate raid on St. Albans, Vermont.

"President" Jefferson Davis had commissioned a certain Jacob Thompson to proceed to Canada and there to carry on such operations as "shall seem most likely to conduce to the furtherance of the interests of the Confederate States of America."[176] The first plan of Mr. Thompson and his confederates was to capture the steamer *Michigan,* the only armed American vessel on the Great Lakes. This project failed, though two smaller boats were cap-

[172] In this war, which broke out in 1848, the United States had seized and incorporated in the Union large stretches of Mexican territory. See Smith, *The War with Mexico,* New York, 1921.
[173] Clinton *New Era,* February 21, 1867.
[174] Dunning, *op. cit.,* pp. 208 ff.
[175] *American Cyclopaedia, 1863,* p. 765.
[176] *Official Records of the Rebellion,* vol. III, series 4, p. 322.

tured, and later lost.[177] Turning then to land operations, the attack on St. Albans was planned. On October 19, 1864, Bennett H. Young, a lieutenant in the Confederate army, with a party of about twenty-five Southern soldiers—armed but not in uniform —descended on the little town of St. Albans, situated about fifteen miles from the Canadian border. After wounding two citizens and setting fire to a portion of the town, the detachment seized all of the money in the local banks, amounting to about $200,000, and left for their secret base in Canada. Pursued across the Canadian line, they were captured with the aid of the Canadian authorities, and about $75,000 was immediately recovered. The raiders were placed in a Canadian jail.[178]

There is no evidence that the Canadian authorities had any foreknowledge of this raid. After the capture of the raiders a body of militia was placed along the border, and every precaution taken to prevent a repetition of such an event.[179] Nevertheless, the whole northern part of the United States was thrown into something of a panic; Canada was harshly criticized,[180] and Seward gave six months' notice of the abrogation of the Rush-Bagot convention.[181] Fortunately this last threat was never carried into execution, the notice being withdrawn in March, 1865.[182] One other raid was planned by Confederates working in Canada, but the activity of American officials in Chicago brought about the arrest of the raiders who had left Canada separately and in dis-

[177] *Idem.* vol. XLIII, pt. 2, pp. 225 ff.; *idem,* vol. III, series 4, p. 444; Headley, *Confederate Operations in New York and Canada,* New York, 1906.

[178] Sowles, *History of the St. Albans Raid;* New York *Times,* February 19, 1865; *Official Records of the Rebellion,* vol. XLIII, pt. 2, pp. 420, 423, 435–436, 455; *Appleton's Annual Cyclopaedia, 1864,* p. 807.

[179] Dent, *Canada,* vol. II, pp. 446–447.

[180] Callahan, *American Historical Association, 1891,* vol. I, p. 352; *Official Records of the Rebellion,* vol. XLIII, pt. 2, p. 934; Sowles, *op. cit.,* p. 19; Chicago *Tribune,* October 21, 1864; New York *Herald,* October 20, 1864.

[181] Nicolay and Hay, *op. cit.,* vol. II, p. 607; *Messages and Documents: State Department, 1865–1866,* pt. 1, pp. 77, 177.

[182] *Idem,* vol. I, p. 69.

guise. The object of this attack was Camp Douglas, in northern Illinois.[183]

The St. Albans raid was undoubtedly an outrageous act, justified neither by the laws of war nor by commonsense. It was roundly condemned by Lord John Russell, by the London *Times,* and by the Canadian press.[184] Although it is the consensus of instructed opinion that the Canadian government was not at fault in the matter, due to the secrecy of the preparations, and the immense length of the line to be guarded, nevertheless the raid did produce a sharp and bellicose reaction in the United States— an irritation that did not soon subside.

These events constituted the direct and overt acts upon which much of the American hostility to Canada was based. The bitter animosity against the United States which again flared up in Canada after the Civil War was due more particularly to events which occurred *at the conclusion* of that epoch-making struggle. These events were the Fenian Raids.

C. The Fenian Movement.—The Fenian movement was a byproduct of the agitation which for many centuries has marred the beauty of one of the world's most lovely gardens. The peculiar character of the conflict with England, combined with the national characteristics of the Irish people, have made Ireland a conservatory in which secret orders have flourished in profusion. Many of the objectives for which they fought and schemed were laudable and just, but revolution, murder, assassination, and graft have been the outward manifestations of the presence of some of these societies.

Emigration from Ireland to the United States had been in progress since before the American Revolution.[185] It was not,

[183] *Official Records of the Rebellion,* vol. XXXIX, pt. 3, pp. 678, 696, 739; *idem,* vol. XLV, pt. 1, pp. 1079, 1082.

[184] Nicolay and Hay, *op. cit.,* vol. II, p. 607; *Messages and Documents: State Department, 1865–1866,* pt. 1, pp. 77, 177.

[185] The majority of these early emigrants were the industrious Scotch-Irish from Ulster. Schlesinger, *New Viewpoints in American History,* New York, 1922, chapter 1; Innes, *England and the British Empire,* London, 1915, vol. IV, pp. 316 ff.

however, until the period of the potato famines in 1845–1848, and the disastrous revolutionary movement of the latter year, that this migration assumed truly important dimensions.[186] During these and later years the eastern states were inundated by a steady stream of immigrants, until at the present time the Irish-American population far exceeds in numbers and in wealth the population of the homeland. To the revolutionary leaders who, in spite of their defeat in 1848, had remained in Ireland, the possibility of using the wealth and personal services of this American community was an opportunity not to be passed by. Already imbued with a fanatical hostility toward England, the Irish-American immigrants needed only direction and inspiration to become a vital factor in British-American relations. To this end James Stephens, leader of the Irish Republican Brotherhood, or Phœnix Society, dispatched John O'Mahony to the United States for the purposes of organizing the Irish migrants. O'Mahony arrived in New York in 1853, and after conversations with leaders of the Irish already there, the Fenian Brotherhood was organized. By 1857 the organization was complete and O'Mahony was elected as its first national president.[187] The members of the Order bound themselves by an oath of "allegiance to the Irish Republic now virtually established" and further swore to "obey implicitly the commands of their superior officers" and to take up arms against Great Britain when so ordered.[188] Although condemned by the Pope and his American subordinates, the society flourished and increased in numbers and influence. The Fenians enlisted in large numbers during the Civil War, and when James Stephens himself visited the United States in 1864 he was received with marked cordiality by American civil and military officials.[189] It has been stated, and by a discriminating authority, that certain American political leaders at this time assured the Fenian Brotherhood of

[186] Rutherford, *The Secret History of the Fenian Conspiracy*, London, 1877, vol. I, chaps. 2, 3.
[187] See McNeill, "Fenians," *Encyclopaedia Britannica* (11th edition), vol. V, p. 254.
[188] Rutherford, *op. cit.*, vol. I, pp. 216–224.
[189] *Idem*, vol. I, p. 234.

"material aid in the struggle they proposed to open with England."[190] Canada was the obviously indicated point of attack,[191] and from 1864 on the Canadians resident along the border were periodically alarmed by rumors of Fenian raids.[192]

A great convention was held in Chicago in 1863 and here the Irish Republic was formally proclaimed. A President was elected, Senate and House of Delegates organized, bonds and notes issued in the name of the Republic; an army was constituted, uniforms and flags were provided, and drilling soon commenced in various parts of the Union, without concealment and virtually without interference.[193]

With the ending of the Civil War in 1865, still greater impetus was given to the movement. On the disbanding of the armies thousands of Irish-Americans—for the most part of the independent and adventurous immigrant type—were turned back into civilian life. The majority of them were unlearned in any trade or profession, and did not fit readily into the new life. Having received a good military training and having had many of their old contacts and old habits broken and interrupted by four years of warfare, they proved excellent tinder, ready for the spark of the demagog. Now when the call of their national tradition was accentuated by the love of adventure so lately stimulated, few there were who could withstand it. An attack upon Canada, which many believed would prove completely and easily successful, would gratify at once their longing for excitement, their hatred of Great Britain, and their ideals of freedom. As a marching song expressed it:

"We are the Fenian Brotherhood, skilled in the art of war,
And we're going to fight for Ireland, the land that we adore.

[190] *Idem*, p. 235.

[191] O'Mahony desired to send an army to Ireland to strike a blow at the heart of the empire, but he was overruled. Skelton, *Life of Thomas D'Arcy McGee*, Gardenvale, 1925, p. 441.

[192] Canadian volunteers were called for frontier service on December 20, 1864. Headquarters were established at Windsor, Niagara, and La Prairie. Hunter, *Reminiscences of the Fenian Raid*, Niagara Historical Society Publications, no. 20, pp. 1–20.

[193] "Privy Council Report on Fenian Activities." *Sessional Papers, 1872.*

Many battles we have won along with the boys in blue,
And we'll go and capture Canada, for we've nothing else to do." [194]

In the spring of 1866 Major T. W. Sweeney, late of the Union
Army, became Secretary of War in the Fenian cabinet, and definite
plans for the invasion of Canada were announced from Fenian
headquarters.[195] Arms and ammunition were collected at many
places along the border [196] in Buffalo and other northern cities
troops were drilled daily, in Fenian uniforms and carrying the
Fenian flag.[197] In Cincinnati committees had been appointed to
visit all citizens "for the purpose of raising funds for the purchase
of rifles to be used by the Irish army." [198]

On March 14th the British Ambassador at Washington brought
these events to the attention of the American Secretary of State,
and pointed out that American army officers were participating
in them.[199] There can be no reasonable doubt that the American
officials already knew of the Fenian activities, and in failing to
take more strenuous action to prevent the raids they were guilty
of an offense against a peaceful neighbor, as well as a violation
of the law of nations.[200] Many prominent Americans, indeed,
had openly encouraged the Irish leaders. In 1864 an "Irish National Fair" had been held in Chicago for the purpose of raising
funds to finance the attack on Canada and the rebellion in Ireland which was to follow. To the directors of this Fair Postmaster-
General Blair—a member of Lincoln's cabinet—wrote: "I rejoice
in the conviction that the days of Ireland's oppressor . . . are

[194] Quoted in Macdonald, *Troublous Times in Canada,* Toronto, 1910,
p. 15.
[195] Details are to be found in Somerville, *Narrative of the Fenian Invasion of Canada,* Hamilton, 1866, pp. 9–14.
[196] Macdonald, *op. cit.,* p. 15. Quebec alone was expected to offer serious
resistance. The Fenians believed, moreover, that Secretary of State Seward
and other American officials would not in any way interfere with their attack upon "England."
[197] "Report on Fenian Activities," *Sessional Papers, 1872;* Macdonald,
op. cit., p. 12.
[198] Cincinnati *Daily Engineer,* September 28, 1865.
[199] "Report on Fenian Activities," *loc. cit.*
[200] Hall, *International Law,* London, p. 215, note; Dunning, *op. cit.,* p.
224.

numbered. Let us conquer in this struggle and there will soon be an end put to the sway of the oppressors of Ireland." [201] To hasten this victory he enclosed twenty-five dollars.[202] Three American generals, two State governors, the Speaker of the House,[203] and numerous Senators and Representatives sent letters of commendation, many of them following Blair's example and enclosing cheques.[204] The 19th Illinois regiment prayed "to be in at the finish" with England, and enclosed $507.00. Another regiment desired "to flesh their bayonets in the corpulent Mr. Bull." [205]

All Americans, however, were not engaged in egging on the Fenian battalions. The majority of them in all probability looked upon the whole thing as being a bit unreal and fantastic. Many of the better class of American citizens were definitely opposed to the whole movement.[206] There was, however, a widespread antipathy to Great Britain and the empire, and many Americans would probably have agreed with the Buffalo editor who wrote:

"Looking back two or three years to the time when Buffalonians were in hourly expectation of Confederate soldiers from Canada we can 'phancy the phelinks' of Victoria's loyal subjects. We don't wish them any ill but a little healthy scaring won't do them any harm." [207]

This feeling was even more clearly expressed by the editor of the New York *Citizen:*

"All American citizens who are not enamored with the course of England and Canada towards the United States during the late rebellion . . . (find in the Fenian activities) . . . an opportunity to have avenged the wrongs of British pirate vessels without costing the American government one dollar. Here the Canadians might have been allowed to realize the scoundrelism of their conduct in

[201] *All the Year Round,* June 4, 1864.

[202] Cooper, "The Fenian Raid of 1866," *Canadian Magazine,* vol. X, no. 1, November 1897.

[203] *Ibid.*

[204] Skelton, *The Canadian Dominion,* p. 129, speaks of "the connivance of American authorities in the Fenian raids of 1866 and 1870."

[205] *All the Year Round,* June 4, 1864.

[206] Skelton, *Life of McGee,* pp. 441, 443, 454, etc.

[207] Quoted in Somerville, *op. cit.,* p. 53.

sheltering the raiders of St. Albans and the yellow fever and assassination conspirators. What Mr. Seward may think about it we do not know, but are well satisfied a majority of the American people regret that the Fenian flag is not today floating over the steeples of a captured Montreal." [208]

The explanation of the failure of American officials to put a stop to the whole movement is usually ascribed to the size and unity of the Irish vote.[209] Hostility to Britain, moreover, was just as prevalent among the officials as among the common people.

Originally there had been a good deal of sympathy for the Irish cause among the radical groups in Canada. When first organized, the Fenian Brotherhood had actually enrolled members in Toronto and Montreal.[210] When the Fenians began to plan the invasion and conquest of Canada, however, they lost the sympathy hitherto felt for their cause.

As time went on and the news of Fenian activities accumulated, the populace of Upper Canada in particular became more and more hostile. It also became nervous. The most grotesque and lurid rumors were given credence,[211] and the Canadian militia was kept constantly on the alert from Manitoba to New Brunswick.[212] Trade through the Welland Canal, and even on the Great Lakes, was interrupted during May, 1866,[213] and the Canadian government began to make active preparations for defense.

D. *The Raids.*—The first raid against Canada was launched on June 1, 1866.[214] In view of the time and energy spent in prepara-

[208] *Ibid.*

[209] McGee estimated this at one million. Skelton, *op. cit.*, p. 441.

[210] *Idem*, p. 445. See also Cumberland, "The Fenian Raid of 1866 and Events on the Border," *Publications of the Royal Society of Canada,* series 3, vol. IV, sec. 2, 1910, pp. 85–108.

[211] Skelton, *op. cit.*, pp. 443 ff.

[212] Shortt and Doughty, *op. cit.*, vol. VII, p. 420; Dafoe, "The Fenian Invasion of Quebec, 1866," *Canadian Magazine*, February, 1898, vol. X, no. 4.

[213] Cumberland, *op. cit.*, pp. 85–108.

[214] This is omitting the abortive attack on Campo Bello Island, New Brunswick, which was of slight importance. See Rutherford, *op. cit.*, pp.

tion, the whole affair was incredibly mismanaged. It had been intended to thrust across the border at a number of points simultaneously; but only one attack actually materialized at the appointed time. A party some eight hundred strong, under the leadership of a certain John O'Neil, had concentrated at Buffalo. On the night of May 31st they moved without interference to Black Rock, and in the morning, having crossed the Niagara River, they captured the moss-grown Fort Erie.[215] The Canadian authorities had, of course, known of the coming attack, and on May 31st the Adjutant-General had issued a call for 14,000 volunteers. This appeal was responded to enthusiastically, and by June 3rd the province had more than 20,000 men under arms.[216] The Canadian troops, however, had little save their enthusiasm, and as a result of poor equipment and bad leadership, the party which tried to stop the raiders at Ridgeway was forced to retire.[217] But this was the limit of Fenian success. Including reinforcements, it is probable that O'Neil's force did not at any time exceed 1200 men, while the Canadians were concentrating ten times that number.[218] In spite of their grandiloquent proclamation, which offered freedom to the Canadian people, the Fenians gained little or no support from the local inhabitants, and by June 3rd they were in full retreat.[219] On their way back to Buffalo O'Neil and many of his followers were arrested by the commander of the United States gunboat *Michigan* which had been patrolling the Niagara River.[220]

244–245. Shortt and Doughty, *op. cit.,* vol. VII, p. 420; Macdonald, *op. cit.,* p. 23.

[215] Dent, *op. cit.,* vol. II, pp. 457–464; Somerville, *op. cit.,* pp. 9–14.

[216] Shortt and Doughty, *op. cit.,* vol. VII, pp. 408–411.

[217] *Ibid.* The skirmish at Ridgeway is described in Ascher, "Number One Company Niagara," *Niagara Historical Society Publication,* no. 7, pp. 60–73.

[218] Shortt and Doughty, *op. cit.,* p. 410; Macdonald, *op. cit.,* p. 28 places the number of Fenians at 2000. The Fenians, moreover, were very poorly equipped, and in no condition to carry on a vigorous campaign. Cumberland, *op. cit.*

[219] Macdonald, *op. cit.,* p. 88; Buffalo *Express,* June 3, 1866.

[220] "Report to Privy Council," *Sessional Papers, 1872.*

In a few days, however, they were released and their arms were returned to them.[221]

On June 4th a second incursion into Canadian territory took place on the Vermont border. With a peculiar fitness St. Albans had been selected as one of the Fenian concentration centers, and three days after O'Neil's attack at Fort Erie, 1800 Irish-Americans crossed into Lower Canada. Headquarters were set at Pidgeon Hill, but the invaders finally retired without giving battle to the Canadian troops who were advancing against them.[222]

During these raids some eighty Fenians were captured by the Canadian authorities and a number of these were condemned to death; the sentences were later commuted.[223] On June 6th President Johnson, urged on by the British Ambassador, issued a proclamation ordering the strict enforcement of the neutrality laws.[224] This tardy action led Governor-General Monck to write to Secretary of State Seward, stating that the United States government "is entitled to my thanks, which I beg that you will convey to them, for vigorously and faithfully putting their laws into force against the Fenians after the invasion of Canada had actually taken place."[225] Sarcasm is not usually a characteristic of diplomatic correspondence, and its presence here is significant of the anger felt by Canadians in regard to what they considered to be the criminal negligence of the American officials. Once taken, however, the action of the American government was temporarily effective, and for this the British minister made suitable and even cordial acknowledgment.[226] The Fenian leaders were enraged at this hampering of their activities, and asserted that they had been

[221] *Ibid;* Rutherford, *op. cit.,* vol. II, p. 263; Macdonald, *op. cit.,* p. 91.
[222] Shortt and Doughty, *op. cit.,* p. 411; Macdonald, *op. cit.,* pp. 111–113.
[223] *Canadian Archives, 1867,* vol. XX, sec. 6, nos. 22, 23. The American government made representations on their behalf through Sir Frederick Bruce, British Minister at Washington. Macdonald, *op. cit.,* p. 123.
[224] Richardson (editor), *Messages and Papers of the Presidents, 1789–1907,* vol. VI, p. 433; Dent,, *op. cit.,* pp. 457–464.
[225] *Canadian Archives,* June 13, 1866, vol. XX, sec. 6, no. 7.
[226] Bruce to Seward, July 13, 1866. *Diplomatic Correspondence, 1866,* vol. I, p. 245.

cheated by the American government, which "had given them to understand that it would not interfere." [227]

In September, 1866, three months after this first assault upon Canada, a Fenian convention was held, and at this meeting announcement was made of preparations for another invasion of the British Dominion. To raise funds for this enterprise balls, picnics, and meetings were held; Irish bonds were sold, and contributions were accepted from American sympathizers. Military displays were arranged, until the Fenian uniform became a well-known sight in all northern cities. In the Fall of the same year, Speaker Colfax of the House of Representatives announced at a Fenian picnic that he "was humiliated when our army was sent to do the dirty work of spies and detectives against the Fenians." At the same meeting Governor Oglesby and General Logan made fiery addresses. General Barry, who had punished some of his soldiers for assisting the Fenians, was dismissed from his command and the soldiers were pardoned. The Fenian headquarters stated publicly that they had assurance on "highest authority" that Federal aid would appear but "slowly" if requested by state authorities for the purpose of checking the Fenians.[228]

In December, 1867, John O'Neil became President of the Fenian Brotherhood,[229] and at a great convention held in Philadelphia early the following year more than 6000 Fenian soldiers, in uniform and carrying the Fenian flag, paraded the streets on several successive days.[230] It was two years later, however, before all of the arrangements for the invasion of Canada were completed; the delay was due to internal strife between various factions of the brotherhood. The money chests again were the cause of fratricidal strife. The raid finally took place in May, 1870, but it was an even more dismal failure than the first attempt. The Ca-

[227] "General" Heffernan, quoted in Macdonald, *op. cit.,* p. 118.

[228] "Report of the Privy Council," *Sessional Papers, 1872.*

[229] O'Neil not only indulged in graft and malfeasance, but murder and arson were laid at his door. The assassination of Thomas D'Arcy McGee, the Irish-Canadian statesman, made the Fenian brotherhood even more loathsome to Canadians. Rutherford, *op. cit.,* vol. II, pp. 307, 310; Rutland *Herald,* April 9, 1868.

[230] McNeill, *op. cit.,* p. 255.

nadian authorities had full information regarding the contemplated attack, at a number of points the American officials intervened, and the Fenians, disorganized and disheartened, were easily defeated.[231] President Grant ordered the arrest of O'Neil, who was accordingly taken, "as he had been in 1866, to be again tried, convicted, and again pardoned unconditionally." [232]

After his second release O'Neil was still enthusiastic and determined. He now turned his attention to what was then the far west—the Minnesota-Manitoba district. In Manitoba British authority was represented by a mere handful of soldiers and fewer officials.[233] The Anglo-Saxon population was just beginning to enter the province and the half-breed Metis were already suspicious of their designs.[234] O'Neil planned to take advantage of the unsettled situation in western Canada and turn it to his own uses.[235] An expedition of about forty men was organized in Minnesota, crossed the border on October 5, 1871, and captured the Hudson's Bay Company's fort at Pembina.[236] They had been followed, however, by a squad of American troops, who arrested and marched them back to the United States.[237] The expected rising of the Metis did not take place. The attack ended as a farce.[238]

This ended the activities of the Fenian Brotherhood against the Dominion of Canada, and their real importance is to be found, not in the raids themselves, but in the way in which they renewed the old Canadian hostility toward the United States, and in their influence in helping on the cause of federation. The general feeling in Canada was that American newspapers had urged on the Irish bands; that minor officials had assisted them, and that the

231 Macdonald, *op. cit.*, pp. 153–180 gives a detailed account of the preparation and the various attacks.

232 "Report of the Privy Council," *Sessional Papers, 1872;* Rutherford, *op. cit.*, vol. II, p. 210.

233 McMicken, "The Abortive Fenian Raid on Manitoba," *Transactions of the Historical and Scientific Society of Manitoba*, no. 32.

234 Shortt and Doughty, *op. cit.*, vol. II, pp. 158–159.

235 Macdonald, *op. cit.*, p. 182.

236 Shortt and Doughty, *op. cit.*, p. 101; Macdonald, *op. cit.*, p. 182.

237 Dent, *op. cit.*, p. 514.

238 Shortt and Doughty, *op. cit.*, p. 158; Dent, *op. cit.*, p. 514.

leaders of the country had failed to display reasonable care in guarding against violations of Canadian territory. Canada's anger was later enhanced by the refusal of the American government to consider Canadian claims for damages arising from the Fenian raids, at the time of the Alabama arbitrations in 1871. Canadians felt that the new principle of "due diligence," first enunciated there,[239] applied with particular nicety to this problem.[240] In their reaction upon Canadian life, however, and in particular upon the problem of federation, the Fenian raids had a distinctly unique importance.[241] As one student of Canadian affairs has well written, they "transmuted much more rapidly than was in any other way possible, into a steady Canadian spirit, the various opposing elements of the West and the East." [242]

In the United States the raids have long since been forgotten, even by historians.[243] The majority of Canadians also have now come to realize that these raids were but the natural outcome of conditions in the United States of the period. National hostility to Great Britain as a result of the real and imagined wrongs of the Civil War period, the ambitions of selfish and dishonest politicians, and the unsettled conditions arising from demobilization, all contributed to make the raids possible. Irish enthusiasm and hatred of England made them inevitable. As a formative factor in the growth of Canadian nationalism, the raids may well be remembered, but as unpleasant episodes between neighboring nations, each of which was in a state of considerable excitement, they may well be relegated to the realm of unremembered facts.

[239] "The *Alabama* Case," Hershey, *International Law,* New York, 1927.

[240] Griffith, *The Dominion of Canada,* London, 1911, p. 115. The Americans, of course, opposed these claims and pointed to the Confederate raids which had originated in Canada.

[241] Particularly affected the vote on confederation in New Brunswick. See Vroom, "The Fenians on the St. Croix," *Canadian Magazine,* March, 1898, vol. X, no. 5.

[242] Peter H. Bryce, *The Illumination of Joseph Keeler, Esq.,* Boston, 1915, p. 46.

[243] While Rhodes, Schouler, Hosmer and others dedicate several pages to the minor affair at St. Albans, they omit all mention of the Fenian raids.

5. BRITISH COLUMBIA—ANNEXATION OR CONFEDERATION?[244]

By the treaty which settled the Oregon Boundary in 1846, the Pacific coast of North America between 49° and 54° 40′ north latitude, and including Vancouver Island,[245] was definitely declared to be part of the British domain. In all of the standard and conventional histories of the continent the struggles, intrigues, and arguments which preceded the signing of this treaty are considered at length, and the justice of the ultimate compromise is discussed. Yet these histories pass over in silence a period some twenty years later when the destiny of the same region again became uncertain.[246] In 1846 there was but a slight possibility of the surrender of this district by Great Britain; in 1868 it was almost questionable whether the Crown either desired, or would be able, to retain it.

Due to a multiplicity of circumstances in the years before confederation, the annexation of British Columbia to the United States appeared to be the almost inevitable solution of what was, from the British point of view, a very unfortunate situation. An insignificant incident might easily have altered the whole course of western history and have given the status of American territory to a region that is today the richest section of the Canadian Dominion. Had this event occurred, Canada would in the twentieth century have been barred from the Pacific, her development would have been delayed, her future growth retarded. Vancouver, already the largest port in the Dominion,[247] would now be on Amer-

[244] Adapted from a paper read before the Canadian Historical Association, Winnipeg, June, 1928.

[245] The definition of the boundary was so inexact that it later brought about two disputes, resulting in the San Juan and Alaskan affairs. See Chapters V and VI.

[246] For valuable information on the annexation movement in British Columbia see Sage, "The Annexationist Movement in British Columbia," in *The Transactions of the Royal Society of Canada*, 1927, sec. 2, pp. 97–110.

[247] According to figures supplied by the Dominion Bureau of Statistics, Vancouver leads all Canadian ports in the number of vessels entering and clearing, and in coastal as well as ocean tonnage.

ican soil, and Canadian trade with the Orient would be practically non-existent. On the other hand, the United States would have gained a territory rich in timber, minerals, and fish; a region of almost unlimited water power, and of scenic beauty unsurpassed. All this was at stake in the crucial years between 1866 and 1870, yet little interest was displayed at the time, and historians have ignored it since.

Eliminating the anthropological and ethnographical significance of the Pacific Coast Indians,[248] the early history of British Columbia is synonymous with that of the various fur-trading companies. The fur business was a thriving industry and save for an occasional traveler or explorer the officers of the North West Company or the Hudson's Bay Company were the only Europeans in the region.[249] Gradually, however, settlers appeared and in 1849 the Colony of Vancouver Island was founded with Richard Blanshard as Governor. He was shortly succeeded by the famous James Douglas, chief factor of the Hudson's Bay Company.[250]

The fur trade remained the economic backbone of the colony, however, until, in 1858, gold was discovered on the Fraser River, and, in 1860, in the Cariboo. Immediately the character of the colony changed, and Victoria, being the only settlement of any size, became the headquarters of adventurers and prospectors of every type.[251] In three months it is estimated that twenty thousand immigrants entered through this port.[252] The vast majority of these men were Americans, mainly from the deteriorating mines of California.[253] There were many, however, from the eastern

[248] By 1863 there were only about 8000 Indians in the province. Cf. R. C. L. Brown, *British Columbia,* New Westminster, 1863, p. 3.

[249] These companies united in 1821.

[250] See Sage, *Life of Douglas; Biographical Dictionary of Well-known British Columbians,* Vancouver, 1890. An almost universal mistake derives the name of the Douglas Fir from Sir James. This famous tree was not named for the Governor but for a naturalist of the same name.

[251] Ballantyne, *Handbook to the New Gold Fields,* Edinburgh 1858; Sage, "The Gold Colony," *Canadian Historical Review,* June, 1922; Howay, *The Early History of the Fraser River Mines,* Victoria, 1926.

[252] Brown, *op. cit.,* p. 52; Sage, *The Annexationist Movement in British Columbia,* p. 97.

[253] Downie, *Hunting for Gold,* San Francisco, 1893.

states and from England, and Victoria shortly achieved a distinctly cosmopolitan aspect.[254]

The newcomers were an extraordinary aggregation of men; the majority of them hardy, courageous, enterprising, and self-reliant. With these virtues, however, was coupled an unusual proficiency in the vices common to such men in such an environment.[255] The quiet villages of Victoria and New Westminster were soon following the lead of the godless San Francisco.

The economic and social results of this sudden influx caused a great increase in the difficulties of government, and Douglas soon found it necessary to exceed his powers in order to control the situation which developed on the mainland. Realizing the need of action, in August, 1858, the imperial government passed an "Act to provide for the government of British Columbia," which formed the mainland region into an Imperial Colony, and Douglas was here also appointed Governor.[256] Vancouver Island was allowed to remain a separate colony, but the two could unite at the will of the colonial legislators and on the acquiescence of the Queen.[257]

At first it appeared as though the American immigrants would soon outnumber the British to such an extent that the colonies would of necessity become a part of the American Union. As the initial excitement died down, however, and as many of the miners, disappointed in their hopes of midatic wealth, left the colony, the balance became restored, and in 1862 an increased British immigration tightened the imperial bonds.[258] But with the working out of the placer-mines and the practical collapse of the "rush", the two Pacific colonies became involved in ever-increasing difficulties. The imperial government was prodigal of advice, but did little in the way of offering the financial assistance which the colonies so badly needed. In an effort to improve conditions Van-

[254] Cornwallis, *The New El Dorado,* London, 1858.

[255] Howay, *op. cit.;* Sage, *The Gold Colony.*

[256] Howay, *British Columbia from the Earliest Times to the Present.* Vancouver, 1914, vol. II, pp. 48–49.

[257] *Idem.* p. 50.

[258] Brown, *op. cit.,* p. 52.

couver Island and British Columbia united in 1866, pooling resources and debts, and endeavoring by the reduction of administrative offices to alleviate the economic stringency.[259]

Although the population of the new colony of British Columbia
totaled only 10,000 souls, the public debt in 1866 was $1,-
300,000, and one quarter of the annual income was needed to
meet the interest charges.[260] To understand fully the deplor-
able situation which now faced the colony, it is necessary to
appreciate its complete isolation from other parts of the British realm. The inhabited regions of Canada were two thousand miles away, and separated from British Columbia by
almost impassable mountains, by desolate prairies, and the
barren northern shores of the rockbound Lake Superior. A boat
to England must round Cape Horn, or at best the passengers must
cross the Isthmus of Darien and embark again upon the Atlantic.
The only foreign intercourse easily available was with the American settlers in Washington, Oregon, and California, and upon
these British Columbia depended for supplies of every description.
Even here there was no proper system of postal communication,
and letters to Portland or San Francisco had to be prepaid in
cash or else bear the American stamps which were sold in the
post offices of New Westminster and Victoria.[261] There was little
industrial life in the colony, and the products of agriculture were
insufficient to supply the local demand.[262]

The physical barriers, however, were not the only obstacles to
a firm union between the colony and the mother country. English
opinion was far from unanimous as to the value or expediency
of giving further support to the outposts of empire. The *Times*
did no more than express the common opinion in the following editorial comments:

> "British Columbia is a long way off. . . . With the exception of
> a limited official class it receives few immigrants from England,
> and a large proportion of its inhabitants consists of citizens of the

259 Howay, *op. cit.,* vol. II, p. 227.
260 *British Columbian,* April 29, 1868.
261 Sage, *The Annexation Movement in British Columbia,* p. 98.
262 Howay, *op. cit.,* vol. II, p. 278.

United States who have entered it from the south. Suppose that the colonists met together and came to the conclusion that every natural motive of contiguity, similarity of interests, and facility of adminis- tration induced them to think it more convenient to slip into the Union than into the Dominion. . . . We all know that we should not attempt to withstand them." [263]

Lord Granville,[263] Secretary of State for the Colonies, went even further and "expressed a wish that the British possessions in North America 'would propose to be independent and annex themselves.'" [264]

Here English colonizing spirit is seen at a low ebb. The Whigs immersed in the philosophy of Richard Cobden, had grave doubts concerning the ethical and the pragmatic value of a strong colonial policy. The Tories, prevented from exploiting the colonies for the good of the mother country, were inclined to cast them off as a hindrance and an expense. On the whole, English opinion was adverse, rather than favorable, to any strong effort to retain British Columbia, and no very grave obstacles would have been opposed to a peaceful transfer to the United States, had this been urged by the colonials themselves.

Many considerations of local pride and immediate advantage urged British Columbia toward American annexation. Local au- tonomy could be more fully exercised as a state of the Union [265] than as a province of the newly-formed Dominion of Canada. With the elimination of all trade barriers between British Colum- bia and the United States, the necessities of life could be ob- tained more cheaply, trade would be stimulated, and intercourse facilitated. With a population almost equally divided between Americans and British; with Canada far off and little known; with the English homeland unresponsive and apathetic; with a tremendous financial burden and inadequate political institutions; in a physical situation impossible of defense and isolated from

---

[263] London *Times,* quoted in *British Colonist,* January 26, 1870.

[264] Sage, *op. cit.,* p. 101.

[265] British Columbia would probably have been admitted as a territory at first (see below, "Banks Bill"), but would soon have achieved state- hood in accordance with the tradition of American expansion in the West.

the British world—with all of these factors urging her forward, the logical solution of the difficulties of British Columbia appeared to be found in annexation with her only neighbors, the western states of the American Union.

It should be noted here that while Vancouver Island tended to favor annexation, the mainland was practically unanimous in support of federation with the Dominion of Canada. This situation was the result of a number of factors, outstanding among them being the fact that in the Union of 1866 the "Islanders" felt that they had been somewhat unfairly treated. They had been forced to accept the tariff laws of the mainland and even the seat of government was for some time removed from Victoria to New Westminster.[266]

That many Americans fully expected annexation to result from the situation on the North Pacific Coast is amply verified by a study of the legislative debates, forensic utterances, and editorial comments of the period. The New York *News* anathematized the Whig party which during Polk's administration had lost to the United States "a territory more valuable than all the wealth of all the Indies," but added that the existing conditions pointed to an early annexation of British Columbia.[267] On July 2, 1866, one amiable but rather optimistic individual even went so far as to introduce into the House of Representatives a bill "for the admission of the States of New Brunswick, Nova Scotia, Canada East and Canada West, and for the organization of the territories of Selkirk, Saskatchewan and Columbia." [268] Another suggestion was that British Columbia should be accepted in liquidation of the *Alabama* claims.[269] As early as 1858 *Harper's Weekly* had declared that "many months cannot elapse before the Stars and Stripes float over the Fort (Victoria)." [270]

[266] Sage, *op. cit.*, p. 100.

[267] Quoted in the Jacksonville (Oregon) *Herald,* July 17, 1858.

[268] Introduced by Major Banks, July 2, 1866. Sir E. W. Watkins, *Canada and the United States*, pp. 128 ff.

[269] *Report of the United States Senate Committee on Pacific Railroads, 1869.* Cf. *British Columbian,* May 18, 1869.

[270] Quoted in the Victoria *Gazette,* October 1, 1858.

At the close of the Civil War, the "Manifest Destiny" convictions of the American people were held with peculiar intensity, and *any* destiny which involved the taking over of British territory was viewed with particular satisfaction. Few expositions of this visualization of the American people as the chosen race have the clarity and directness of the following portion of an address on the subject of British Columbia, delivered before a Washington state society by the Hon. Elwood Evans in 1870.[271] (The sentiment expressed was not unique but was held by the speaker in common with many Americans; the grammar, however, was peculiarly his own.)

> "That it is the destiny of the United States to possess the whole of the northern continent I fully believe. . . . Our destiny, which must not, cannot be altered—a fiat which has the potency of irrevocable law—the forward march of Americanization until the whole continent shall be but one nation, with one sovereign government, one flag, one people." [272]

Great Britain had won British Columbia at the time of the Oregon boundary dispute by graft, chicanery, and deceit; therefore it is

> "commendable patriotic pride,—not covetousness, or ambition for territorial expansion nor lust for power which justifies—commands the effort" to regain it.[273]

Not all of the settlers in British Columbia, however, were willing to forego their British allegiance, and many there were who preferred union with the Canadian Dominion—could suitable terms be arranged. "No union on account of love need be looked for," wrote one British Columbian. "The only bond of union . . . will be the material advantage of the country, and the pecuniary benefits of the inhabitants. Love for Canada has to be acquired by the prosperity of the country and from our children." [274] In

271 Delivered before the Tacoma Library Association, January 25, 1870. Published as *The Reannexation of British Columbia to the United States: Right, Proper and Desirable*, p. 3.

272 *Ibid.*

273 *Idem*, p. 11.

274 Quoted in H. J. Bram (compiler), *British Columbia*, London, 1912, p. 44.

other words, many of the colonists were willing to remain, or desirous of remaining, within the empire if some solution could be found for their economic and political problems. It is an interesting fact that throughout this period the strongest advocates of confederation were also the most sturdy opponents of the existing government in British Columbia.[275] Discontent was rampant in the colony. It was felt that England had given little but advice, that the government was arbitrary and wasteful, and that prosperity could not return while the colony remained in the empire—unless connection by road and rail were formed with Canada.[276] In 1867 a petition had been sent to the home government by a group of citizens of Victoria, which asked that in view of the exigencies of the situation the colony be allowed to join the United States.[277] Although this plea was heartily denounced by many other British Columbians, a second petition was circulated in 1869. On this occasion the document was addressed to President Grant, and requested him to intercede with the British government, and to arrange for the transfer of the colony to the United States. A report that the leaders in this movement were to be arrested led the Olympia *Tribune* to publish the following statement which gives an incidental sidelight upon conditions in the Washington territory:

"We understand that the ruling powers of British Columbia . . . will arrest and punish the leaders of the annexation movement if it cannot be otherwise suppressed. We warn the rulers against such folly. The incarceration of a few men longing for American citizenship would fan into flame a fire long smouldering in our midst, and bring upon the people of that country a force of filibusterers who under the pretext of releasing the prisoners would really seek the overthrow of the British Dominion upon this coast." [278]

[275] The Governor and his officials feared to lose their positions under Confederation and therefore delayed and hindered the movement. Some of them even favored annexation—as did Dr. J. S. Helmcken, first speaker of the Legislative Assembly of Vancouver Island and son-in-law of Douglas. Dr. Helmcken was later sent to Ottawa as one of three commissioners to negotiate terms of union. See Sage, *op. cit.*, p. 106 ff.

[276] *British Colonist*, August 15, 1868.

[277] Howay, *op. cit.*, vol. II, p. 280.

[278] Olympia *Tribune*, November 20, 1869.

To this the Victoria *Colonist* aptly replied that at the time the abortive movement was abandoned the document bore considerably less than fifty signatures.[279] Whatever the number of signatures, President Grant ignored the petition, and its only effects were to assist in crystallizing opinion in British Columbia, and in providing an argument for American expansionist orators. The petition did, however, reach the United States Senate, and the Committee on Pacific Railways quoted from it in its report in 1869. The committee at that time felt that the construction of an American line to the north Pacific would almost inevitably result in the annexation of British Columbia.[280]

In January, 1868, a great meeting had been held in Victoria, at which Amor de Cosmos, one of the most picturesque figures in Canadian history, argued eloquently in favor of confederation, and in opposition to union with the United States.[281] As a result of his efforts a committee was selected to urge upon Governor Seymour, and upon the Dominion government, the desirability of uniting the Dominion and the colony. On March 25th Ottawa replied to the representatives of this committee in the following terms: "The Canadian Government desires union with British Columbia and has opened communication with the Imperial government on the subject of the resolutions, and suggests immediate action by your legislature and passage of an address to Her Majesty regarding union with Canada. Keep us advised of Progress." [282] The Legislative Council of British Columbia, however, was controlled by the annexationists, and the supine governor was too weak to support either cause.[283]

[279] Victoria *British Colonist,* November 24, 1869.

[280] Sage, *op. cit.,* pp. 103–104.

[281] This interesting figure was born at Windsor, N. S., with the prosaic name of William Alexander Smith. He emigrated to California, changed his name, came to Victoria in the gold rush of 1858 and established the *British Colonist.* Later he became Prime Minister of British Columbia, and then member of the Dominion House. He died from the effects of an overlong oration (himself the orator).

[282] Hon. S. L. Tilley to H. S. Seeley, March 25, 1868, given in Begg, *History of British Columbia,* Toronto, 1894, p. 377.

[283] *British Columbian,* April 29, 1868.

In May, 1868, the Confederation League was organized. As expressed in its title, the object of this body was to secure the entry of British Columbia into the Dominion of Canada. On September 14th a convention was held at Yale—the head of navigation on the Fraser River—at which the Governor and the Legislative Council were severely criticized for their failure to forward the case of confederation, and for misgovernment in general.[284] But in spite of the interest aroused by the League, the elections of December, 1868, went against its leaders, and the Legislative Council by a vote of eleven to five condemned the taking of any action at that time.[285]

During the summer of 1869 one of the great obstacles to confederation was removed when the Dominion government took over the rights of the Hudson's Bay Company to the territory between British Columbia and Canada proper. Thus the way for the transcontinental railway was opened—and such a railway was the *sine qua non* of all schemes of confederation. This cannot be too strongly emphasized. Without the prospect of railroad communication with Canada, British Columbia would certainly have joined the American Union. The patriotic *British Colonist* warned the Canadian government that if the enterprise stopped at the east of the Rockies "it may stop there for good as far as British Columbia is concerned. Whatever may be the pecuniary interests and necessities of Canada, we know ours to demand immediate consolidation by the only bond strong enough to retain British Columbia." [286] The same paper again wrote that "of all the conditions usually attached to a union of this colony with Canada, that of early establishment of railroad communication from sea to sea is the most important. If the railroad scheme is utopian, so is confederation. The two must stand or fall together." [287]

Governor Seymour died in May, 1869—an event of great good fortune for the Loyalists of the colony. At a time when British

[284] *Confederation Papers*, pp. 18–26; Gosnell and Coats, *Sir James Douglas (The Makers of Canada* Series), London, 1908, pp. 311–312.
[285] *British Columbian*, February 20, 1869.
[286] *British Colonist*, January 19, 1870.
[287] *Idem*, February 2, 1870.

Columbia had needed a leader, it had been ruled by a man whose strongest attitude was a tentative negation.

The Imperial government was now enabled to appoint Mr. Anthony Musgrave, whose energetic personality was the precise antithesis of that of the willowy Seymour.[288] The processes of government, however, were slow, and due to an accident the new Governor was not able at once to attend to the vital problem of annexation or confederation. As a result, during the winter of 1869–1870 a resurgence of annexation sentiment was evident. "Annexation may now be said to be rampant in this community" wrote the editor of the *Colonist*. "It no longer lurks in secret places and shuns publicity. It may be said, and doubtless with much truth, that the Annexationists are for the most part American citizens who, having adopted this colony as their home, are naturally anxious that the institutions and the flag of the Fatherland should extend over it. But the party is not solely composed of such." [289] Two of the Victoria papers vigorously supported annexation, and it was obvious that a crisis was approaching. The American people were again interested in the question by the introduction of the Corbett Resolution in the Senate. This resolution contained instructions to the Secretary of State to "inquire into expediency of . . . the transfer of British Columbia to the United States." [290] It was not, however, acted upon.

The crisis came in British Columbia with the meeting of the Council in February, 1870. Governor Musgrave had prepared for this meeting a statement urging immediate consideration of terms of confederation. The insistent character of the Governor's demand bore down the opposition, and in spite of the protests of Dr. Helmcken and a few other staunch Annexationists, the desired resolution was passed. This was the turning point of the contest, and, when on April 13th a great meeting was held in Victoria, the *Colonist* was able to report that "the most ardent

[288] See Howay, "Governor Seymour and Confederation," and "Governor Musgrave and Confederation" in *Transactions of the Royal Society of Canada*, Third Series.

[289] *British Colonist*, January 28, 1870.

[290] Quoted in *British Colonist*, February 9, 1870.

advocate of confederation with responsible government must have felt satisfied with the result. The most intense enthusiasm pervaded the assemblage. The most vague hint in the direction of annexation was met with a howl of execration." [291] Thus rapidly did conditions change under the hand of an adroit and determined leader.

All that then remained was to decide upon the terms of union and this was done with mutual satisfaction. On July 20th, 1871, British Columbia became an integral part of the Dominion.

In the carrying out of the terms of the union, the railroad agreement was the first in importance, and the long delays in construction resulted in much ill-feeling in British Columbia. The union had not been born primarily of love, and any failure on the part of the Dominion government might easily have resulted in the withdrawal of the western province.[292] In 1878 the British Columbia legislature went so far as to threaten separation, but a change of ministry at Ottawa, and a more energetic railway policy soon cleared the atmosphere.[293] With the completion of the Canadian Pacific Railway in 1885, "Manifest Destiny" was finally cheated of this prey.

[291] *British Colonist,* April 19, 1870.
[292] Bram, *op. cit.,* p. 44.
[293] Gosnell and Coats, *op. cit.,* p. 323.

CHAPTER V

Major Boundary Disputes

I. INTRODUCTION

THE British and American negotiators who wrote the Treaty of Paris (1783) left to their descendants a legacy of ambiguous phrases. In attempting to decide the boundaries which should divide the new nation from the remnants of the old empire, these diplomats undertook the task of defining in exact language geographical boundaries of which they had a very inexact knowledge. As a result the treaty became a very Pandora's box, whence issued problems and perplexities which more than once led Britain and America to the verge of war, and which were for many years a constant source of irritation to the peoples of the United States and Canada.

The Treaty of Paris, however, was not alone as a cause of boundary disputes. As the American and the British settlers pushed westward over the continent, it became necessary to settle again and again the old question of division and demarcation. The Great Lakes; the Lake of the Woods; the central plains; the Oregon territory; and finally, turning north, the deeply wooded coast of Alaska—each provided a new problem for dispute and disagreement.

Three of the controversies which strained the peaceful relations of the claimant countries may well be classified as of major importance in the history of British-American relations on the continent of North America. Maine, Oregon, and Alaska were on different occasions words potent in their threat of war. Now finally settled, they may be discussed with a candor and an understanding which was not possible during the heat of the struggle, while bitter passions still endured.

2. THE NORTHEASTERN BOUNDARY

A. The Significance of this Dispute.—The most persistent Canadian criticism of British diplomacy has, for three-quarters of a century, centered on the imperial conduct of Canadian-United States boundary disputes—and particularly upon the negotiation of the clauses of the Ashburton Treaty dealing with the Maine-New Brunswick line. The burden of this complaint has been that British statesmen sacrificed Canadian interests in order to advance the cause of Anglo-American friendship. That there has been some general justification of this dissatisfaction can hardly be denied, but to an objective observer the Canadian case appears weakest just where it has been most strongly urged —that is, in the case of the Ashburton negotiations. The fact that the American Senate and the Legislature of Maine each had to be intimidated by Webster's threat of disclosing concealed information favorable to Canada before these two bodies would agree to the Treaty of 1842 proves that Americans did not feel that Lord Ashburton had unduly favored their case. Nevertheless, Canadian public opinion was persistent in the belief that British complacency and American sharp practice resulted in 1842 in a surrender of Canadian rights.[1]

The explanation of this long-continued feeling of dissatisfaction is found in the vital importance which the northern portion of the territory in dispute possessed from a Canadian standpoint. Direct railroad connection between Canada proper and the maritime provinces was a necessity, and such a connection, under the settlement of 1842, has necessarily to pass through Maine. Thus every Canadian who travels by rail from Montreal to Halifax [2] is reminded of the treaty in which "Canadian rights" were "sacrificed" on the altar of Anglo-American friendship. More than

[1] This is discussed by Col. Dudley A. Mills, R. A., in *The United Empire Magazine,* October, 1911, p. 684. In *Canada, 1760–1900,* Cambridge, 1900, chapter 5, J. G. Bourinot insists that Canada did not receive equitable treatment in this matter.

[2] The main line of the Canadian Pacific Railway runs through the State of Maine; that of the Canadian National swings north in order to stay on Canadian soil.

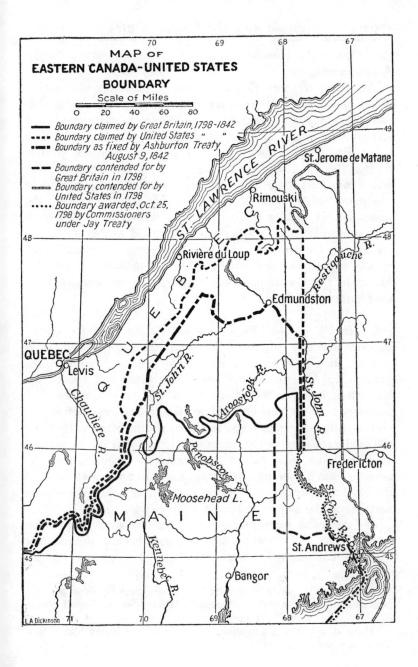

MAP OF
**EASTERN CANADA-UNITED STATES
BOUNDARY**

Scale of Miles

0   20   40   60   80

━━━━ Boundary claimed by Great Britain, 1798-1842
━ ━ ━ Boundary claimed by United States "   "
━ ▪ ━ Boundary as fixed by Ashburton Treaty
         August 9, 1842
━ ━ Boundary contended for by
         Great Britain in 1798
══════ Boundary contended for by
         United States in 1798
• • • • • Boundary awarded, Oct. 25,
         1798 by Commissioners
         under Jay Treaty

ST. LAWRENCE RIVER

St. Jerome de Matane

Rimouski

Rivière du Loup

Restigouche R.

Edmundston

QUEBEC

Levis

Chaudiere R.

St. John R.

Aroostook R.

St. John R.

Fredericton

Penobscot

Moosehead L.

M A I N E

St. Croix R.

Kennebec R.

St. Andrews

Bangor

L.A. Dickinson

once Canada has been described as the "shuttlecock" of Anglo-American relations.[3]

The actual territory involved in this controversy was not of prime importance; as compared with Oregon, for example, it was practically valueless. In 1840, however, northern Maine seemed more important and Oregon infinitely less important than today. From the Canadian point of view, the retention of this territory by the United States was an annoyance because it cut across the direct route to the Atlantic coast. Its commercial value was more highly appraised than it is today, but, above all, the contestants in 1842 were actuated by a sentimental antipathy to any derogation of their sovereign rights; and in this they were not unique, for exactly similar emotions would be aroused today by any suggestion that Canada be allowed to purchase northern Maine, or that the United States arrange for the annexation of the maritime provinces.[4]

B. History of the Dispute.—The difficulty over the north-eastern boundary was a product of the American Revolution and the Treaty of 1783. Even before that time, however, the problem had been recognized, and Great Britain and France had been struggling for the possession of this very territory. The boundary between New England and Acadia had ever been in dispute, and this uncertainty was particularly acute between 1713 and the final expulsion of the French in 1763. After the Treaty of Paris, with the whole Atlantic coast under the British Crown, the boundary was rather vaguely located as the southern watershed of the St. Lawrence River, and, on the east, as a line drawn due north from the source of the St. Croix River.[5]

The American representatives in Paris during the negotiation of the Treaty of 1783 were among the most brilliant men of their day, but unfortunately their knowledge of geography was in-

[3] Bourinot, *op. cit.,* p. 291.

[4] Yet, judged by purely geographic or economic factors, either of these proposals would be probably a sound procedure. See J. Russell Smith, *North America,* New York, 1925, chap. 5.

[5] Mills, *op. cit.,* p. 683. Channing, A History of the United States, New York, 1921, vol. V, p. 639.

adequate for the successful completion of the task to which they were assigned: the definition of the boundaries of the United States and the British dominions in North America. Moreover, the maps of the period were faulty, and place-names varied at the whim of the cartographer. The British commissioners in Paris were unwilling to accept the New England-Nova Scotia boundary as the international line of the future, and advanced claims to territory west of the St. Croix as far as the Piscataqua—claims which were subsequently reduced by successive steps to the Kennebec, the Penobscot, and finally the St. Croix itself.[6] The claims were based upon old French pretensions which Great Britain had heretofore combated.[7] It is interesting to note that France still supported this view as late as 1778, in spite of her close relations with the revolting colonies.[8] The Americans, on their part, at first contended for the St. John, but agreement was finally reached in a return to the St. Croix.[9] Regardless of the method by which the agreement was reached, and without attempting to evaluate the personal or national motives involved or the relative dexterity of the British and American commissioners, the fact remains that a decision was made, and that it then became the foundation upon which all subsequent argument was based. The agreement was expressed in the Treaty of 1783, as follows:

"From the northwest angle of Nova Scotia, viz., that angle which is formed by a line drawn due north from the source of the St. Croix River to the Highlands; along the Highlands which divide those rivers that empty themselves into the River St. Lawrence, from those which fall into the Atlantic Ocean, to the north-

[6] John Adams, *Works,* vol. I, p. 665. Gannett, *Boundaries of the United States,* U. S. Geological Survey. Bulletin No. 6. Washington, 1904, pp. 9–19.
[7] Ganong, *Proceedings of the Royal Society of Canada,* 1901, vol. VII, sec. 2, pts. 3, 4.
[8] D'Ansille, *Partis Orientale du Canada,* Venice, 1776; Philippeaux, *Carte générale des colonies Anglaises,* Paris, 1778.
[9] Winsor, *Narrative and Critical History of America,* vol. VII, p. 171. Oswald, the British commissioner, had first agreed to the St. John, but the British government sent Strachey to insist upon a more favorable line. Fitzmaurice, *Shelbourne,* vol. III, p. 294. John Adams later admitted that the American claim was unjust. John Adams, *Works,* vol. VIII, p. 210.

westernmost head of the Connecticut River. . . . East, by a line to be drawn along the middle of the River St. Croix, from its mouth in the Bay of Fundy to its source, and from its source directly north to the aforesaid Highlands." [10]

The treaty further provided that any islands which had heretofore been included in Nova Scotia, should so remain.

Almost at once difficulties arose, and the first of these was in regard to the identity of the St. Croix River. On the map used by Oswald, Franklin, and their compatriots at Paris, two rivers were shown as emptying into Passamaquoddy Bay, and the most easterly of these was agreed upon as the boundary river. In reality, three rivers reached the sea in this bay, the third being to the west of those known to the negotiators, and all three rivers were sometimes known as "St. Croix," according to the whim of individual cartographers. The difficulty was further accentuated by the fact that the true situation of the boundary river (the present Magaquadavic) was not as it was depicted on Mitchell's map.[11] Canadian settlers in the newly-formed province of New Brunswick thus had an excuse to push on and to proclaim the more westerly river the true St. Croix. Mr. Jay said that the fault in Mitchell's map had been discussed in the Paris negotiations, and that the decision had been made with this mistake in mind, but Adams declared that the negotiators knew nothing of the ambiguity.[12] Jay and Adams agreed, however, that the Magaquadavic was the river selected.[13] Investigations and surveys were made by individuals, and by the Massachusetts and federal governments.[14] After some years of uncertainty, the Jay Treaty of 1794 made a temporary and partial settlement. (As John Bassett Moore has

[10] Malloy, *op. cit.,* vol I, p. 581.

[11] The famous Mitchell's map of 1755. Cf. D. A. Mills, *op. cit.,* p. 683. A discussion of the identity of the St. Croix is to be found in Ganong, *op. cit.,* p. 5.

[12] Winsor, *op. cit.,* vol. VII, p. 172.

[13] This is probably wrong. The negotiators would naturally intend to select the St. Croix used by Great Britain after 1763; they merely mistook its position on Mitchell's map. Cf. Ganong, *op. cit.,* pt. 5.

[14] *American State Papers: Foreign Relations,* vol. I, pp. 91–97, October 21, 1784.

pointed out in recent addresses, this treaty was the result of the first modern recourse to arbitration, a procedure known in classical times and then forgotten for fifteen centuries.) The commissioners were agreed that the river claimed as the St. Croix by the Americans should be accepted, and not the more westerly stream designated on Mitchell's map.[15] Thus, in a contest between the validity of a faulty map and a questionable local appellation, the name rather than the cartographical definition was accepted.

Under the Treaty of 1794 a commission was appointed to discover the "source" of the St. Croix, and here Great Britain lost its contention. The more northerly branch was chosen, and at its headwaters was erected a monument. This solution was agreed to in 1798.

With the boundary agreed upon to this point, the real difficulty then became apparent. How far north should the "due north" line extend? The line was to run as far as "the Highlands . . . which divide those rivers that empty themselves into the River St. Lawrence, from those which fall into the Atlantic Ocean." Now the St. John River empties into the Bay of Fundy, and the United States insisted that this was, in fact, emptying into the "Atlantic Ocean." Great Britain disputed this, insisting that the words "Atlantic Ocean" had been intended in a strictly literal sense, and the St. John did not fulfil the requirements.[16] The importance of the controversy arose from the fact that the highlands which separate the headwaters of the St. John from the headwaters of the St. Lawrence tributaries are very near the great river itself; while the highlands separating the Maine rivers (which surely emptied into the ocean) from the tributaries of the St. Lawrence, would be crossed at Mar's Hill, only 40 miles "due north" of the monument erected on the St. Croix. Great Britain insisted that the intention had been to divide the river basins, and that the words "Atlantic Ocean" had been used to assure the St.

[15] Amory, *Life of James Sullivan,* vol. I, chapter 14. See also Judge Burson's statement of the grounds for this decision in the library of the Massachusetts Historical Society.

[16] C. Buller in *The Westminster Review,* 1840, supports the distinction between the Bay of Fundy and the Atlantic Ocean. See also *Quarterly Review,* March 1841, pp. 501–541, and March, 1843, pp. 560–595.

John valley to the British domain.[17] The Americans replied that
the intention had been to define the southern boundary of Quebec
as it had been proclaimed in 1763; and in that proclamation the
highlands had been mentioned as running to the Bay of Chaleur
—undoubtedly the northern range.[18] The fact that an old French
grant, known as Madawaska, was situated in the middle of the
territory claimed by the United States, and that the United States
had never exercised jurisdiction over this district, seemed to support the British contention.[19] So also did various French maps,
though Great Britain had previously contended against the French
for the very region which she now attempted to retain. The testimony of the maps, however, was inconsequential, for ample cartographical proof could have been adduced to support almost any
claim by either side.[20] In general, the French and English maps
were opposed to those produced by the United States. Each state
could find scientists to support its politicians.

The War of 1812 demonstrated very forcibly the necessity of
a direct and uninterrupted line of communication between Canada
and the maritime provinces. The result was an added insistence
from the side of Great Britain upon the validity of her claim.

The Treaty of Ghent, December 24, 1814, provided for a
number of joint commissions to settle various boundary problems.
The first of these, that to decide the ownership of certain islands
in Passamaquoddy Bay, reported an equitable settlement on
November 14, 1817.[21] The commission on the main problems

[17] Col. Joseph Bouchette, *Topographical Description of Lower Canada,
1815,* contains a full statement of the British case.

[18] The American claim was put forward by Nathan Hale in *The North
American Review* for April, 1828, pp. 421–444; *idem* for July, 1831, pp.
262–286; and *idem* for October, 1836, pp. 431–44. It was also supported by
Jared Sparks in *The North American Review* for April, 1843, pp. 452–
496, and by C. S. Davies, *idem*, April, 1832, pp. 514–564. In the *American
Almanac, 1840,* p. 91, Nathan Hale counters the Bay of Fundy argument.

[19] Fish, *American Diplomacy,* New York, 1915, p. 230.

[20] Winsor, *op. cit.,* p. 175.

[21] In *The Aspinwall Papers,* of the Massachusetts Historical Society, G.
Chalmers supports the British claim, which was successful. The support of
the unsuccessful American case is to be found in Amory, *op. cit.,* vol. II,
p. 399, while Ganong gives a more objective view in *op. cit.,* pt. 5, pp. 278–
295.

connected with the northeast boundary continued its deliberations until April, 1822, when the two sides drew up *ex parte* reports, and the arbitration broke down.

In 1820 Maine separated from Massachusetts and was admitted to the Union as a sovereign state. From that time on, the contest bore a more threatening aspect, for the legislature of Maine was more vitally interested in a successful solution than had been Massachusetts, and violent measures appeared more excusable to those who felt more deeply.

In January, 1825, Maine protested that Canadians were trespassing upon American soil and cutting timber in the forests of that state.[22] Great Britain, in reply, pointed out that the Madawaska and Aroostook settlements had been founded many years before, and that heretofore the United States had registered no objection.[23] The British government further declared that certain American officials had been attempting to exert their jurisdiction in these regions, and the United States, in reply, asked that Maine and New Brunswick display a mutual forbearance until some definitive agreement could be reached.[24] Such an arrangement was made, but frequent clashes of state and provincial representatives continued to take place.[25]

In 1826 Mr. Gallatin was sent to England to attempt to effect a settlement. Great Britain insisted upon neutral arbitration, for joint commissions had already proven a failure, and to this Mr. Gallatin was finally forced to accede. An agreement to this effect was drawn up and with the consent of the American Senate and the signature of the President it became operative.[26] The King of the Netherlands was agreed upon as arbiter.[27] For his use and assistance a general map of the region was jointly prepared, and this was submitted together with the British and American arguments.[28]

[22] *British and Foreign State Papers,* vol. XV, p. 469.
[23] *Idem,* p. 474.
[24] *Idem,* pp. 476, 478, 487.
[25] *American State Papers: Foreign Relations,* vol. VI, p. 626.
[26] Adams, *Writings of Gallatin,* vol. II, pp. 398, 544–545.
[27] *American State Papers: Foreign Relations,* vol. VI, p. 643.
[28] Adams, *Writings of Gallatin,* vol. II, pp. 308–309, 331, 363, 369, 388.

The difficulty encountered in the ensuing arbitration was the difficulty invariably attending international discussions. Each nation, through its accredited representatives, had made a claim; the people, therefore, accepted this as their own and became insistent upon receiving "justice"; the diplomats were driven by the pressure of public opinion to defend and win their case (defeat might mean the unhonored end of a public career). To the aid of the diplomats were called the scientists, who prostituted their learning to the support of a diplomatic brief. Thus the case was prepared, and it was presented with an accompaniment of forensic eloquence which tended further to obscure the truth. No attempt was made to do justice, no search was prosecuted to discover the truth. Public opinion, diplomats, scientists, and orators joined to advance the cause of the nation, and truth, justice, and sincerity were lost in the excitement of winning the case.

Albert Gallatin prefaced the American case, simply restating at great length, and with careful attention to every detail, the claim outlined above.[29]

There can now be little doubt that the American claim was justified by the intentions of the commissioners of 1783. It is morally certain that the intention then was to reënact the boundary line of the Proclamation of 1763, and that the British argument based on the difference between the Bay of Fundy and the Atlantic Ocean was simply an ingenious quibble.[30] Unfortunately, the Treaty of 1783 was so badly worded that it could not be translated into a practical topographical boundary.[31] The British

[29] *Statement on the Part of the United States*, Washington, 1829; A *Definitive Statement*, Washington, 1829; *An Appendix*, Washington, 1829; *The Right of the United States, Etc.*, New York, 1840. These have also been published under Gallatin's name. See also "A Memoir," read by Gallatin before, and to be found in *The Proceedings of The New York Historical Society*, 1843.

[30] "On the merits it is difficult to avoid the conclusion that 'the British claim had no foundation of any sort or kind' in law." Morison, *History of the United States*, vol. II, p. 42; John Bassett Moore, *Digest of International Arbitrations*, Washington, 1898, vol. I, pp. 157–160.

[31] See statement of the two cases in Moore, *op. cit.*, vol. I, pp. 1–161.

case was not a sound one,[32] and a decision based solely upon justice would, in all probability, have given Maine more than was ultimately received.

The King of the Netherlands was so impressed by the topographical difficulties which obstructed the running of a boundary line in accordance with the wording of the treaty, that he entirely gave up the attempt. On January 20, 1831, he declared that the treaty was "inexplicable and impracticable," [33] and he designated an arbitrary compromise line as the most feasible solution.[34] This decision gave 7908 square miles to the United States, and 4119 square miles to Great Britain. It was based largely upon the line of the St. John, as the United States had desired, but met the British claim in regard to certain other details.[35] The State of Maine violently protested against acceptance of such a decision,[36] and, although President Jackson was ready to join the British government in assenting to the award, the Senate refused to give its consent. The President was forced to acquiesce.

American feeling against the King's award was crystallized and made vocal largely through the efforts of W. P. Preble, American Minister of The Hague, and himself a citizen of Maine. He returned to the United States and wrote and spoke against acceptance with intensity and vigor.[37]

The King's decision was not in accordance with the terms upon which the problem had been submitted to him. He had been asked for a judicial decision: he had replied with a political compromise. Yet from both a practical and an ethical standpoint, it would have

[32] For the British case see *Remarks upon the Disputed Points of the Boundary,* St. Johns, New Brunswick, 1838; see also a volume published by the British government entitled *The North American Boundary,* London, 1838, sec. A.

[33] *Quarterly Review,* vol. LXVII, p. 507.

[34] See "The Award of January 10, 1831" in *State Papers,* vol. XVIII, pp. 1249 ff.

[35] For example, in regard to the headwaters of the Connecticut River. See Moore, *op. cit.,* vol. I, pp. 119–127.

[36] *Resolve of the Legislature of Maine,* Portland, 1831.

[37] Preble, *The Decision of the King of the Netherlands,* Portland, 1831.

been better if the United States had accepted his decision. To
refuse was to give the impression, however unjustified, of bad
sportsmanship. President Jackson later recognized this, and wrote
in reference to this event:

> "The only occasion of importance in my life, in which I allowed
> myself to be overruled by my friends, was the one of all others in
> which I ought to have adhered to my own opinions." [38]

The arbitration agreement had invited the arbiter to "make a
decision on the points of difference," and this was to be final
and conclusive.[39] From the practical standpoint, the failure to
agree to this award ultimately cost the United States 900 square
miles of the territory in dispute, and it cost her much more than
that in the favorable judgment and esteem of the world. The award
was unjust, but it should have been accepted.[40]

Between 1831 and 1841 the portfolio of Foreign Affairs in
the British Cabinet was held, with one short interruption, by
Lord Palmerston, and his far from subtle diplomacy produced
a reaction in the United States that did not promote a peaceful
settlement of the outstanding differences at issue between the
two governments. Throughout the period popular feeling in the
United States, as well as in Nova Scotia and New Brunswick, was
gradually intensifying, and on several occasions war appeared to
offer the most probable solution. Overt acts on the part of nationals
of one country or the other were of frequent occurrence. In 1831

---

[38] Everett, *The Life of Daniel Webster,* quoted in Mills, *op. cit.,* p. 688.
Jackson might have declared the award in force without reference to the
Senate.

[39] Malloy, *op. cit.,* vol. I, p. 646.

[40] Technically, the United States defended its action on the basis of Preble's argument that the King had failed to interpret the treaty, that he had
entirely ignored it, and that he had decided independently of it. The whole
difficulty was centered in Maine, whose inhabitants were united behind the
energetic and intransigeant Preble. For a clear exposition of the state's attitude see article by Israel Washburn, Jr., *Collections of the Maine Historical Society,* vol. VIII; *Benton's Debates,* vol. XIV, pp. 574, 595; *Document of the House of Representatives,* no. 2, 27th Cong., 3rd sess. On
Preble see L. Q. Deane, *Biographical Sketch of John G. Deane,* Washington, 1887.

the New Brunswick authorities arrested, tried, and convicted certain officers of Maine for attempting to hold an American election in the Madawaska district.[41] In 1836 a Canadian justice was arrested for executing process on American soil.[42] In 1837 a certain Greeley was arrested with some others for attempting to take a census in Madawaska for the American government,[43] and in the same year British engineers began survey operations on a proposed railway, designed to pass through the disputed region.[44]

On December 28, 1835, the British also withdrew their acceptance of the Dutch award, and they then offered another compromise boundary, which the United States refused.[45] In return, the President offered to request Maine to accept the line of the St. John River from its source to its mouth as the boundary, but this Great Britain, in its turn, refused.[46] In March, 1838, Maine again entered the lists, demanded that a survey be made in accordance with the American interpretation, and insisted upon the enforcement of this boundary.[47] The federal government refused to accede to these requests, but it did authorize a survey of the region with a view to erecting fortifications.[48]

Throughout this period the population was increasing in both Maine and New Brunswick, and the disputed area was constantly increasing in value. The people of the maritime provinces were largely Loyalist in derivation, and their natural anti-American sentiment was accentuated by every hostile act and word in Maine or the United States.

In 1838 the Legislature of Maine gave Governor Fairfield $800,-

[41] *Senate Executive Documents*, no. 3, 22nd Cong., 1st sess.

[42] *British and Foreign State Papers*, vol. XXII, p. 1030; *idem*, vol. XXIII, pp. 404, 426.

[43] *House Executive Documents*, no. 126, 25th Cong., 2nd sess. They were indemnified by Congress.

[44] *British and Foreign State Papers*, vol. XXV, pp. 938, 943.

[45] *Idem*, vol. XXIV, p. 1179.

[46] *Idem*, vol. XXII, p. 1184; *idem*, vol. XXV, p. 903; *Senate Executive Documents*, no. 319, 25th Cong., 2nd sess.

[47] *Senate Reports*, no. 502, 25th Cong. 2nd sess.

[48] *Senate Executive Documents*, no. 35, 25th Cong. 3rd. sess.

ooo for military defense, and, thus supported, the Governor called
out the militia and took forcible possession of the greater part
of the disputed area. Forts were erected throughout the region
to prevent a successful counter-action.[49] At the same time, Congress authorized the President to call forth the militia for a six
months' term, and placed at his disposal the sum of ten million
dollars.[50] The province of New Brunswick was now thoroughly
aroused, and the bellicose attitude of Governor Fairfield seemed
to presage further difficulties. Nova Scotia, aroused for the safety
of her sister province, and actuated by the same Loyalist antipathy
toward the Americans, called a special session of its Legislature
and voted $100,000 for the immediate support of New Bruns-
wick, and amid scenes of great popular enthusiasm promised to
place at the disposal of the junior province every dollar and every
man in Nova Scotia, should war become an actuality.[51] War
appeared to be not only a possible, but even a probable, result.[52]

In an attempt to avert such a calamity, General Winfield Scott
was dispatched to Maine, where he succeeded in persuading Governor Fairfield to withdraw his troops and to await the outcome
of the newly-resumed diplomatic negotiations.[53] New surveys were
made by each country [54] and negotiations continued through 1840

[49] Webster, *Works,* vol. V, p. 93. A few local encounters did take place,
but these were chiefly between Canadian lumbermen and American settlers.
This whole movement is known as the Arostook War.

[50] 5 *Statutes at Large,* 355.

[51] Chisholm, *Speeches and Public Letters of Joseph Howe,* p. 399. Feeling on each side of the line was further intensified in 1836–1837 by events
attending the contemporary Canadian revolutions and particularly by the
burning of the *Caroline.* Kingsford, *History of Canada,* London, 1888–1898,
vol. X, pp. 430–45; *House Executive Documents,* no. 74, 25th Cong., 2nd
sess.

[52] "Presidential Message of May 19, 1838" in Richardson (editor), *Messages and Papers of the Presidents, 1789–1907,* vol. III, pp. 470–475.

[53] Webster, *Works,* vol. VI, pp. 89–98; *North American Boundary Blue
Book,* London, 1840, pt. 1. A temporary division of the territory was agreed
upon without prejudice to either claim. Scott, *Autobiography,* vol. II, pp.
331–351.

[54] 5 *Statutes at Large,* 402; *House Executive Documents,* no. 102, 26th
Cong, 2nd sess.

and 1841.[55] In the latter year Lord Palmerston was succeeded as Secretary of State for Foreign Affairs by Lord Aberdeen, and Anglo-American relations at once took a more favorable course. Aberdeen, apparently, believed in the justice of the British contentions regarding the northeastern boundary, but he also realized that the Americans were equally convinced of the validity of their case, and consequently he decided that a compromise was the only possible solution. He realized, moreover, that an early decision was imperative if war was to be avoided. Neither Great Britain nor the United States really wanted war: indeed, such a struggle would have been commercially disastrous for both countries.[56]

In March, 1841, Daniel Webster became American Secretary of State, and he too was desirous of finding a "shorter way" to the settlement of this old and serious conflict.[57] As a result of Webster's expressed willingness to accept a decision by direct negotiation, and to agree if necessary to a compromise boundary,[58] Lord Aberdeen, passing over certain senior but "die-hard" diplomats, commissioned Lord Ashburton to proceed to America, at the same time investing him with full powers to arrange a definitive settlement.[59]

The appointment of Lord Ashburton was a real concession to the United States. In 1808, as Alexander Baring, he had vigorously attacked the British Orders-in-Council, and in 1816 he had told John Quincy Adams that he wished Great Britain would give all Canada to the United States immediately.[60] Ashburton's wife was an American, and he was well and favorably known in the United States. This, then, was the man who arrived in Washing-

---

[55] This correspondence is to be found in *Senate Documents,* no. 274, 29th Cong., 1st sess; *idem,* no. 107, 26th Cong., 1st sess; *idem,* no. 382, 26th Cong., 1st sess.

[56] Morison, *op. cit.,* vol. II, pp. 36–38.

[57] *Webster's Private Correspondence,* vol. II, p. 102.

[58] Webster, *Works,* vol. I, pp. 124–125; *idem,* vol. VI. p. 270.

[59] *Webster's Private Correspondence,* vol. II, pp. 113–114, 120; *British Sessional Papers, 1843,* vol. LXI; Adams, *History of the Foreign Policy of the United States,* New York, 1924, p. 220.

[60] Dunning, *op. cit.,* pp. 12, 101, note; Adams, "Lord Ashburton and the Treaty of Washington," *American Historical Review,* vol. XVII, p. 765.

ton, "authorized to treat for a conventional line, or line by agreement, on such terms and conditions, and with such mutual consideration and equivalents as might be thought just and equitable." [61]

After a great deal of persuasion, Mr. Webster succeeded in getting Maine to appoint delegates equipped with full powers to negotiate a final agreement.[62] Massachusetts was also included. Lord Ashburton formally opened the discussions on June 13, 1843. The arbiters at once concurred "in the opinion that no advantage would be gained by reverting to the interminable discussions on the general grounds on which each party considers their claims respectively to rest." [63] These claims had been thoroughly canvassed with no prospect of a mutual agreement.

Lord Ashburton began by asserting the British right to the whole territory, but indicated his willingness to compromise on a line which would give Great Britain some two-thirds of the territory in dispute. This proposal so enraged the Maine delegation that their leader (the ubiquitous Preble) advocated an immediate adjournment. On Webster's insistence, however, this plan was abandoned, and on June 29th the Maine commissioners offered a counter-proposal,[64] which Ashburton in turn declared impossible of acceptance. Personal conferences between Ashburton and Webster were initiated by the former on July 13th, and by July 15th tentative terms were arranged and submitted to the state representatives for approval.[65] Without covering the intricate details, suffice it to say that the United States received seven-twelfths of the disputed territory, the right to navigate the St. John River, and, according to Mr. Webster, four-fifths of the

[61] Webster to Ashburton, June 17, 1842. *Canadian Archives,* vol. XLIV. sec. 2, no. 2.

[62] From the beginning, Maine demanded compensation for any territory yielded. *Webster's Private Correspondence,* vol. II, pp. 128, 131.

[63] Ashburton to Webster, June 13, 1842. *Canadian Archives,* vol. XLIV, sec. 2, no. 1.

[64] For the proceedings see Webster, *Works,* pp. 270 ff.; *House Executive Documents,* no. 2, 27th Cong., 3rd sess.; E. D. Adams, in *American Historical Review* (1912), vol. XVII, pp. 764–782.

[65] *Webster's Private Correspondence,* vol. II, pp. 120–121.

value at stake.[66] Great Britain further agreed to allow the United States to retain the land at Rouse's Point, Lake Champlain, upon which an American fort had been erected.[67] Webster gained further concessions in Lake Huron and in the Lake of the Woods.[68] On July 22nd, the Maine delegation with protests and lamentations agreed to this boundary, and Mr. Preble departed "as sulky as a bear." [69] On August 9th the treaty was signed by Ashburton and Webster [70] and on the 11th of the same month it was communicated to the Senate.[71]

A recital of the events leading to the ratification of this treaty would be far from complete without mention of the part played by the famous "red-line map." This map was discovered in the Paris Archives by Jared Sparks, who was carrying on an investigation there to obtain material in support of the American case.[72] This map was supposed to be the one used by Franklin, and upon which that astute diplomat had drawn a red line designating the boundary substantially in accordance with the claims of Great Britain as later presented.[73] Webster, realizing the damaging nature of this évidence, at once impounded the map and ordered the search discontinued.[74] The true significance of this document appears in its later use by the Secretary of State. Using the threat of publication as a club, he was able to force the Legislature of Maine and the United States Senate to agree to the Webster-Ashburton Treaty.[75] Webster was subsequently assailed

---

[66] Moore, *op. cit.*, p. 150.

[67] Bouchette; *British Dominions in North America*, vol. I, p. 420; Bouchette, *The Topography of Lower Canada*, p. 279.

[68] Winsor, *op. cit.*, p. 180.

[69] Ashburton's description, in Mills, *op. cit.*, p. 693.

[70] *House Executive Documents*, no. 2, 27th Cong., 3rd sess.

[71] Webster, *Works*, vol. VI, p. 347; *Webster's Private Correspondence*, vol. II, p. 146.

[72] Sparks, *North American Review* (1843), vol. LVI, pp. 470–471; for Sparks' letter to Webster see *Collections of the Maine Historical Society*, vol. VIII, p. 96.

[73] *Idem,* vol. LVI, p. 468.

[74] Curtis, *The Life of Daniel Webster*, New York, 1893, vol. II, p. 103.

[75] *Burton's Debates*, vol. XIV, p. 546; Grenville, *Memoirs*, pt. 2, vol. I, p. 147.

by American, British, and Canadian opponents with the charge of dishonesty because he failed to make public the map during the negotiations.[76] But, wrote Webster in reply, "I did not think it a very urgent duty to go to Lord Ashburton and tell him that I had found a bit of doubtful evidence in Paris." [77] That Webster's action was not contrary to the "rules of the game" was verified by Lord Ashburton who said, "My own opinion is that in this respect no reproach can fairly be made." [78] Great Britain, moreover, was involved in a very similar transaction, for with the opening of negotiations the foreign office went to the trouble of concealing the famous Mitchell's map, which tended to support the American case. Even Ashburton was not apprised of its existence,[79] until it was produced in Parliament to silence the violent criticism levelled against the treaty by Lord Palmerston and his irate friends.[80]

The Webster-Ashburton Treaty was ratified by the Senate on August 20, 1842.[81] In homage to clarity it may be summarized thus: [82]

Maine and Massachusetts surrendered five-twelfths of their territorial claim, and received in return the privilege of navigating the St. John River, and $300,000 as general compensation.

Great Britain surrendered seven-twelfths of its territorial claim, made various concessions at other doubtful points on the international boundary, and received approximately 5000 square miles of the disputed region.

The United States received the right of navigation on the St.

[76] Curtis, *op. cit.*, vol. II, pp. 132, 134, 149, 154, 155, 159–162, 167.

[77] Webster, *Works*, vol. II, p. 149.

[78] *Croker Papers*, vol. II, p. 200.

[79] Fitzmaurice, *Shelbourne*, vol. III, p. 324.

[80] *The Cambridge History of British Foreign Policy*, vol. II, pp. 24, 26, 27.

[81] *Webster's Private Correspondence*, vol. II, p. 146. Webster's great defense of the treaty was made after his return to the Senate in 1846. Webster, *Works*, vol. V, pp. 78–150.

[82] Malloy, *op. cit.*, vol. I, pp. 650–656. For further information on this treaty see Benton, *Thirty Years in the United States Senate*, New York, 1856, vol. II, pp. 422–455; H. Brougham, *Speech on the Ashburton Treaty*, London, 1843.

John; 40 square miles at Rouse's Point, where an American fort had been raised; 40 square miles at the head of the Connecticut River, and an island of about the same size between Lakes Huron and Superior; 7000 square miles of the disputed territory; and in return abandoned a weak claim to 6000 square miles on the west of Lake Superior, and the 5000 square miles on the Maine-New Brunswick border.

C. The Reception of the Treaty.—Mingled sentiments greeted the treaty when its terms were made public in Great Britain. The Tories under Lord Palmerston vituperated against the "Ashburton Capitulations," [83] and a series of scathing articles by Palmerston was published in a London paper and did much to arouse popular dissatisfaction.[84] On the other hand, the Liberal leaders greeted the solution with satisfaction, and in Parliament Peel, Brougham, Aberdeen, Hume, Douglas, and even Disraeli joined in the defense and praise of Lord Ashburton. Great Britain, after all, was not vitally interested, and popular feeling soon died down with a growing appreciation of the peace which followed the settlement.[85] Lord Ashburton, writing on the subject, wisely declared:

> "It is a subject upon which little enthusiasm can be expected. The truth is that our cousin Jonathan is an aggressive, arrogant fellow in his manner . . . by nearly all our people he is therefore hated and a treaty of conciliation with such a fellow, however considered by prudence or policy to be necessary, can in no case be very popular with the multitude. Even my own friends and masters who employed me are somewhat afraid of showing too much satisfaction with what they do not hesitate to approve." [86]

In the United States a feeling of gratitude was generally expressed at the termination of this long and profitless struggle. Maine and Massachusetts grumbled, but the financial compensa-

[83] *Webster's Private Correspondence,* vol. II, p. 146.
[84] London *Morning Chronicle,* September 19th to October 3rd, 1842.
[85] Curtis, *op. cit.,* vol. II, pp. 180 ff.
[86] Ashburton to Croker, November 25, 1842, quoted in Adams, *op. cit.,* in *Proceedings of the American Historical Society,* p. 782.

tion proved an excellent sedative. The country as a whole rapidly forgot the incident, and this in spite of the fact that the United States was the country which had the most right to complain, for as has now been generally admitted by the better type of historian, the American case was founded upon a much surer basis than that of Great Britain, and pure justice would have given to the United States an even larger percentage of the territory in dispute.[87]

Far different was the reception of the treaty in Canada. The old Loyalist sentiment was still strong, and to these men the attempt of the United States to seize a portion of New Brunswick was simply another act in a long series of hostile operations which included the expedition of 1775, the War of 1812, the overt incidents during the Canadian rebellion of 1837, and the generally antagonistic, threatening, and bombastic attitude of the American press and people. Now, with the supine assent of Great Britain, the United States had succeeded in driving a wedge between Canada and the British possessions in the maritime provinces. Canadian interests had been "sacrificed" to feed the insatiable appetite of American imperialism, and Britain had not defended her own. The legend of "the sacrifice of Canadian interests" here had its start, and it has been propagated in school texts, in serious histories, and on platform and forum, almost to the present hour.[88] Mr. Kingsford, whose copious volumes are still read by some Canadians, speaks of Lord Ashburton, "whose name to this day is never uttered in Canada without contempt and shame." [89] Unjust as such accusations are, it is, nevertheless, a fact that many Canadians still consider the Ashburton Treaty of 1842 to be the first and most important instance of the loss of Canadian rights

[87] This view is found expressed in: Sir Francis Hincks, *The Boundary Formerly in Dispute Between Great Britain and the United States,* Montreal, 1885; Ganong, *op. cit.;* Mills, *op. cit.;* Morison, *op. cit.,* pp. 42–45; J. B. Moore, *op. cit.,* vol. I, pp. 157–160

[88] Coffin, "How Treaty Making Unmade Canada," *Canadian Monthly Magazine,* 1876; Dent, *op. cit.,* chapter 10; Bourinot, *Canada and the United States.*

[89] Quoted in Mills, *op. cit.,* p. 696.

due to the complacency of Great Britain and the crooked diplomacy of the United States. And, in this way, the Maine-New Brunswick boundary dispute has held, in Canada, an importance that would be totally inexplicable judged solely by the value of the geographical prize involved.

3. THE OREGON BOUNDARY

A. The Point at Issue.—The nineteenth century, on the continent of North America, was a period of political and military expansion, and with the United States, Russia, Spain, and Britain all taking part in this movement, a conflict of interests became inevitable. Of the many territorial disputes which thus arose, that concerning the "Oregon" [90] boundary involved the largest, and incomparably the richest, domain. The territory in dispute included not only the modern and beautiful state of Oregon, but Washington, the lower portion of British Columbia, and all that section of the United States north of the 42nd parallel of north latitude and west of the Rocky Mountain divide. In short, the Oregon Territory was bounded by 42° and 54° 40′ north latitude, on the east by the crest of the Rockies, and on the west by the Pacific Ocean. An approximate width of 550 miles, and a length of 650 miles, made the total area some 360,000 square miles: no mean prize, even on this most bountiful of continents. When the respective territorial rights of the United States and Great Britain in this region were defined, the long boundary that began in the waters of the Atlantic reached its destination on the shores of the Pacific. The partition that began in 1783 was then complete.[91]

[90] The origin of the name *Oregon* has now been satisfactorily explained, as being derived from the Indian name for the Columbia River. For theories see Bancroft, *History of Oregon,* vol. I, pp. 17–25.

[91] This was not entirely true, because the work done in 1846 was badly bungled, and because the United States in 1867 purchased Alaska. See Chapter V, sec. C, and Chapter VI, sec. I.

Not only was the Oregon Territory extensive geographically, but it contained immensely rich resources in timber, fisheries, and minerals. When to these advantages are added the excellent agricultural, ranching, and fruit lands of the interior valleys, the fur trade of British Columbia, the admirable harbors of Prince Rupert, Vancouver, and Seattle, and finally (on the coast at least), a delightful climate, some idea is obtained of the reward for which diplomatic battles were waged in the first half of the nineteenth century. Fortunately, the true value of the region was not suspected in 1845, for, had the governments of the day fully realized the worth of the prize for which they were contending, "54° 40' or Fight" might well have become more than an election cry, and Great Britain would have maintained with more determination her claim to the territory lying between the 49th parallel and the Columbia River. The common attitude of the day, however, was well expressed in the scornful words of a British author, who mentions "Vancouver's Island, which, if we are absurd enough to plant a colony in the Northern Pacific, is the least objectionable seat." [92] Until a few years before the final settlement of the dispute, Oregon was thought of—in England, at least—only as the home of the fur trader and his prey, a region to be visited by the adventurous; to be fought for if "national honor" demanded it, but of no real importance. Even the closer view obtained from the American States failed to indicate the potentialities which are so obvious today.

Spain and Russia, as well as the United States and Great Britain, were involved in the contest for this last and greatest of the frontier regions. In the earliest days of Pacific exploration Spanish and British seamen had fought for gold and glory; in later years the Chancellories of Great Britain and America strove for territory and power. As the days of treasure ships and authorized piracy passed away, the contest changed its nature, and British, American, and Russian fur companies carried on an economic and political, as well as semi-military, battle for control. Even this unacknowledged warfare did not force a solution of

[92] *Edinburgh Review*, July, 1845, contains an editorial summary and review of a number of books on the Oregon question.

the problem, and it was not until farmers began to force their way across the mountain barriers, and to settle in the fertile valleys of the coast, that the logic and the dangers of the situation became sufficiently powerful to force a compromise—in 1846.

B. Discovery and Occupation.—As rights of sovereignty, gained by discovery, were claimed by both Great Britain and the United States, some knowledge of the history of the exploration of the Pacific Coast is an essential prerequisite to a just appreciation of their conflicting claims. Yet an accurate knowledge of the history of Pacific exploration did not exist in 1846, and indeed, even at the present time, the name of the first European to visit the western coast of North America cannot be stated with assurance. It is known that, within thirty years of the discovery of the Pacific Ocean, Spanish captains were sailing on its waters, and it is generally supposed that one Fenelo was the first to follow the coast to a point above the 42nd parallel of north latitude.[93] This trip was made in 1543, and apparently it was not until 1602 that another Spaniard reached the region that was to become the Oregon Territory. In that year Aguilar, a lieutenant of Vizcaino, sailed as far as the 34th parallel, discovering and naming Cape Blanco.[94] In 1774 Perez and Martinez sailed as far north as 55°, and on their return anchored off Point Esteven, taking possession in the name of the Viceroy of Mexico, whose commission they bore.[95] In the following year, three adventurers—Hecata, Ayala and Quadra—explored the coast from the 27th to the 58th parallels, the former entering and naming the San Roque (Columbia) River.

The earliest British claim was based on the voyage of Sir Francis Drake (1580), but the latitude reached by this patriotic adventurer has never been accurately determined, although most authorities agree that he at least reached 43° north latitude, and

[93] De Mofras, *Exploration du territoire de l'Oregon*, Paris, 1844, vol. I, pp. 96–97.
[94] de Mofras, *op. cit.*, vol. I, p. 97.
[95] Humboldt, *New Spain* (translated by Black), vol. II, pp. 316–318; de Mofras, *op. cit.*, vol. I, pp. 107–108.

some even insist on 48°.[96] In 1778 the famous Captain Cook, who shortly afterwards lost his life on the Sandwich Islands, explored the coast from the 44th to the 59th parallels, and proceeded even farther north.[97]

Captain Robert Gray, a New England trader, was the first American to reach the Oregon coast, and the record of his trips, from 1787 on, formed the foundation on which the American claim to discovery principally rested. He claimed to have first discovered, and certainly he named, the Columbia River, but in view of the well-authenticated record of Hecata's trip, Gray's claim cannot be substantiated.[98]

Starting in 1788, Captain Meares, an Englishman, made frequent trading voyages to the west coast, using Nootka as a base. Many, if not all, of these trips were made under the Portuguese flag because of the existing British monopoly regulations.[99] In the same year that Meares made his first trip, Martinez and Lopez, two Spanish captains, explored the whole coast even as far as the Aleutian Islands.[100]

The first man actually known to have crossed the continent from the Atlantic to the Pacific was Alexander Mackenzie, a partner in the North-West Company. In 1793 he crossed the Rockies at about 54° north latitude, descended the Fraser to 52° 20′, and thence, passing the Coast Range, ultimately reached the ocean.[101] In 1805 the famous Lewis and Clark expedition passed the moun-

[96] de Mofras, *op. cit.*, p. 98; Howay and Scholefield, *op. cit.*, vol. I, pp. 39 ff.; *Edinburgh Review*, July, 1845, p. 252.

[97] de Mofras, *op. cit.*, vol. I, chapter 3.

[98] "Oregon," *Encyclopaedia Britannica* (11th edition), vol. XX, pp. 247–248. The first mention of the Columbia River is to be found in Carver, *Travels*, London, 1776, chapter 11, but there is considerable doubt as to the knowledge of the author (see Simpson, *The Oregon Territory*, London, 1846, p. 14), and he himself never traveled on the Oregon, or River of the West, as he called it.

[99] Meares, *Voyages*, London, 1790. Lack of space makes it necessary to omit reference to many voyages, such as those of Herrera, Barkley, and others.

[100] de Mofras, *op. cit.*, vol. I, p. 110.

[101] Davidson, *The North-West Company*, Berkeley, 1920; Mackenzie, *Voyages from London*, London, 1801.

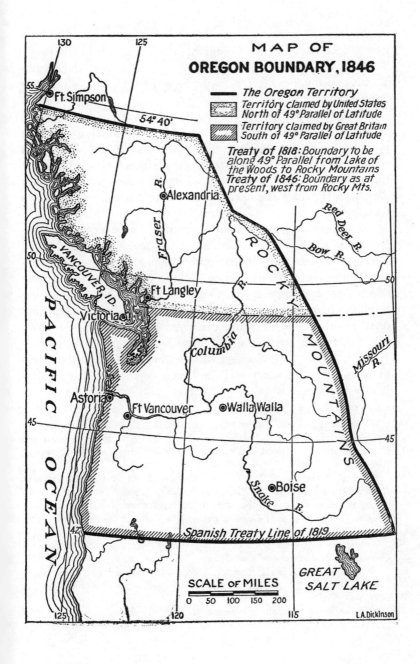

MAP OF
OREGON BOUNDARY, 1846

—— The Oregon Territory
Territory claimed by United States
North of 49° Parallel of Latitude
Territory claimed by Great Britain
South of 49° Parallel of Latitude

Treaty of 1818: Boundary to be
along 49° Parallel from Lake of
the Woods to Rocky Mountains
Treaty of 1846: Boundary as at
present, west from Rocky Mts.

Ft. Simpson

54° 40'

Alexandria

Fraser R.

Red Deer R.

Bow R.

VANCOUVER ID.

ROCKY

Ft Langley

Victoria

Columbia

MOUNTAINS

Missouri R.

PACIFIC

Astoria

Ft Vancouver

Walla Walla

OCEAN

Snake R.

Boise

Spanish Treaty Line of 1819

GREAT
SALT LAKE

SCALE OF MILES
0   50   100   150   200

L.A. Dickinson

tain barriers, reached the Columbia, and followed it to the sea.[102] The following year Simon Fraser, another officer of the North-West Company, reached the Pacific by way of the river which now bears his name.[103]

From this time forward visits to the Pacific Coast were of frequent occurrence, both by land and by sea, and the trading posts of the American, British, and Russian fur companies were soon established in the territory.[104] The Hudson's Bay Company rapidly outdistanced or absorbed all its competitors, and only the American Trading Company was able to maintain any serious opposition.[105]

These exploring and trading expeditions were not always attended by peace. Captain Meares, after 1788, had made Nootka a semi-permanent base—a proceeding to which Spain voiced strenuous opposition. Without waiting for the end of the negotiations which were in progress, the Viceroy of Mexico outfitted an expedition under Captain Martinez, who proceeded to Nootka, captured most of Meares' ships, destroyed his buildings, and drove him out.[106] The Spaniards took formal possession of Nootka on June 24, 1789.[107] The Spanish King again laid claim to the whole of the Oregon Territory and the Count de Florida attempted to justify this claim when he wrote that "although Spain may not

[102] Lewis and Clark, *Travels,* London, 1817.

[103] Davidson, *op. cit.* The original manuscript of Fraser's Journal is in the Toronto Reference Library. Records of many of these western explorations are to be found in Thwaites, *Early Western Travels,* Cleveland, 1904–1907.

[104] In 1808 the North-West Company opened its first posts. In 1811 Astoria was founded on the Columbia by John Jacob Astor and his associates. Incidentally, six of the original partners were British. Twiss, *The Oregon Territory,* p. 191; Lee and Frost, *Ten Years in Oregon,* New York, 1844, p. 17.

[105] For the best description of the activities of the American traders see Chittenden, *The American Fur Trade of the Far West,* New York, 1902.

[106] *Idem,* p. 13; *Annual Register, 1790,* p. 295; Manning, "The Nootka Sound Controversy," *Report of the American Historical Association for 1904,* pp. 388 ff.

[107] "The First Spanish Settlement at Nootka," *Second Annual Report of the British Columbia Historical Association, 1925;* Howay and Scholefield, *op. cit.,* vol. I, chapter 6.

have establishments or colonies planted upon the coasts, or in the
ports in dispute, it does not follow that such coasts or ports do
not belong to her." [108] To this Great Britain replied that "British
subjects had an indisputable right to the enjoyment of a free and
uninterrupted navigation, commerce, and fishing; and to the possession of such establishments as they should form with the consent of the natives of the country not previously *occupied* by any
European nation." [109] The capture of Nootka nearly precipitated
a war, but Spain was deserted by her ally, France, and could not
undertake such a conflict alone. As a result she agreed by the
Escurial of October 28, 1790, to pay an indemnity, and to allow
British subjects equal rights as to trade and settlement, north of
the 38th parallel of north latitude. South of that parallel, Spain
claimed exclusive jurisdiction.[110] This Nootka Convention was
the first public withdrawal by Spain from her long-established
attitude—that of the possessor of exclusive sovereignty over the
American shores of the Pacific Ocean, south of Alaska.[111]

After the outbreak of the War of 1812 Astoria, the American
trading post on the Columbia River, founded by John Jacob Astor,
was sold by the Pacific Fur Company to the British North-West
Company to prevent its falling into the hands of the British as
a prize of war.[112] A month later a Royal man-of-war appeared,
and its captain took formal possession in the name of King George.
But the Treaty of Ghent (1815) authorized a return to the
status quo and the American government demanded the resti-
tution of Astoria.[113] Great Britain insisted, naturally, that the
post had been purchased and was not included in the spoils of
war. The difficulty was settled and the United States was again
given possession in 1818. In the convention of that year, a *modus
vivendi* covering the whole "Oregon Question" was agreed to,
and this compact remained legally in force until 1846, though

[108] Quoted in Falconer, *The Oregon Question*, London, 1845, p. 17.
[109] Quoted in *idem*, p. 17.
[110] The Nootka Convention of October 28, 1890.
[111] Manning, *The Nootka Convention*, p. 462.
[112] Davidson, *op. cit.*, pp. 138–139.
[113] *American State Papers:Foreign Relations*, vol. III, p. 731.

primarily signed only for ten years.[114] By this convention the
two nations agreed

> "that any country that may be claimed by either party on the
> north-west coast of America, westward of the Stony Mountains,
> shall, together with its harbors, bays and creeks, and the navigation
> of all rivers within the same, be free and open for the term of ten
> years from the date of the signature of the present Convention,
> to the vessels, citizens and subjects of the two powers; it being well
> understood that this agreement is not to be construed to the prejudice
> of any claim which either of the two high contracting parties may
> have to any part of the said country, nor shall it be taken to affect
> the claims of any other power or state."

The following year a treaty was signed by Spain and the United
States, in which the Spanish King "ceded to the said United States
all his rights, claims and pretentions to any territory east and
north of the said line (42nd parallel), and . . . renounces all
claim to the said territory forever." [115] Thus the United States became heir to the Spanish claims, which, so far as discovery was
concerned, were unimpeachable. Spain had, however, agreed to
Britain's assertion of equal rights to commerce and settlement.
There was, moreover, great doubt as to the validity of the Spanish claim because occupation had failed to follow discovery within
a reasonable time.[116] This lack was in part supplied by the priority

---

[114] Convention of October 20, 1818, Malloy, *op. cit.*, vol. I, article III,
pp. 631–633; Reeves, *American Diplomacy under Tyler and Polk*, Baltimore, 1907, pp. 224 ff.

[115] February 22, 1819. Malloy, *op. cit.*, vol. II, p. 1652. By 1819, Spain
had lost practically all her possessions in the new world as the result of
a decade of revolutionary activity on the part of the Spanish colonists in
America. See Robertson, *Rise of the Spanish-American Republics*, New
York, 1921; Paxon, *Independence of the South American Republics*,
Philadelphia, 1916.

[116] Under the rules of international law, discovery alone gives only a
tentative or inchoate title, and this does not become legally valid unless
followed within a reasonable time by settlement. See Scaife, "The Development of International Law as to Newly Discovered Territory," *Papers of
the American Historical Association*, vol. IV, p. 269; John Bassett Moore.
op. cit., vol. I, p. 258.

of the establishment of Astoria which had been founded by the American Fur Company in 1811.

In 1821 another complication arose. By an imperial ukase of that year, the Czar of Russia claimed the whole of the west coast of North America from the Aleutian Islands to the 42nd parallel.[117] The United States and Great Britain immediately protested (this Russian threat was one of the major factors leading to the promulgation of the Monroe Doctrine), and the result is seen in the Treaty of 1824 with the United States,[118] and the Treaty of 1825 with Britain,[119] in which Russia agreed to 54° 40′ as the southern boundary of her North American domains.

In 1824 Fort Vancouver was established on the north bank of the Columbia River, not far from its mouth, by the Hudson's Bay Company (which had absorbed the North-West Company in 1821). Here "a Scots factor, Dr. John McLaughlin, ruled the community with wisdom and humanity, preserved the peace between whites and Indians, upheld civilized standards of social life, and later received American missionaries so hospitably that the school children of the American North-West today are taught to regard him as 'the Father of Oregon.' "[120]

In 1818, 1824, and again in 1826 attempts were made by the British and American governments to find a mutually acceptable line of division. As Britain, however, insisted on the line of the Columbia, and as the United States refused to consider any division south of the 49th parallel, these attempts were doomed to failure. In 1826 Great Britain disclaimed any pretensions to an exclusive title, merely insisting that her title was good as against

[117] *American State Papers: Foreign Relations,* vol. V, p. 436; Reddaway, *The Monroe Doctrine,* Cambridge, 1898; Ford, "John Quincy Adams and the Monroe Doctrine," *American Historical Review,* vols. VII, VIII.

[118] April 17, 1824. Malloy, *op. cit.,* vol. II, p. 1512.

[119] Foster, *op. cit.,* p. 305.

[120] Morison, *History of the United States,* vol. II, p. 47. This felicitous description of "the Father of Oregon" is too good to omit despite the fact that Dr. McLaughlin's father was Irish and that he himself was born in Quebec. His mother was a Scotch-Canadian, which will partially justify Professor Morison in referring to him as "a Scots factor."

the United States. The American government, on the contrary, asserted an exclusive sovereignty from the 42nd to the 52nd parallels—this being the territory drained by the Columbia, and also claimed the whole Oregon Territory by right of discovery and occupation.[121] The greatest concession that the Americans would make was outlined in a letter from Clay to Gallatin:

> "As by the Convention of 1818 the 49th parallel of north latitude has been agreed to as the line of boundary between the United States and Great Britain east of the Stony Mountains, there would seem to arise . . . a strong consideration for the extension of the line along the same parallel west of them to the Pacific Ocean. . . . This is our ultimatum. . . . We can consent to no other line more favorable to Great Britain." [122]

This offer was refused by the British, who in turn proposed the Columbia River, guaranteeing freedom of navigation to American citizens. On August 6, 1827, the Convention of 1818, as regards the Oregon Territory, was indefinitely renewed, subject to denunciation by either nation on one year's notice. It remained in force until 1846.[123]

From 1827 to 1838 little interest was manifested in the Oregon Territory, except by those engaged in trading or missionary enterprises.[124] The Hudson's Bay Company had rapidly gained control, and in 1838 Mr. Pelly of that company was able to report as follows: "We have compelled the American adventurers, one by one, to withdraw from the contest, and are now pursuing the Russian Fur Company so closely that we hope at no very distant period to confine them to their own proper territory." [125] The Hudson's Bay Company officials acted not only as commercial agents, but filled the offices of legislator, executive, and judiciary

[121] Twiss, *op. cit.*, pp. 105 ff.; also *Edinburgh Review*, July, 1845, pp. 259 ff.

[122] Clay to Gallatin, quoted in Falconer, *op. cit.*, p. 13; Reeves, *op. cit.*, pp. 240 ff.

[123] For these negotiations see Twiss, *op. cit.*, pp. 105 ff, which contains an excellent statement; see also *Correspondence Relative to the Negotiations Concerning Oregon Territory*, London, Houses of Parliament, 1846.

[124] Bashford, *The Oregon Missions*, New York, 1918.

[125] Pelly to Lord Glenelg. *House of Commons Papers*, no. 547 (1842).

throughout the whole region. In 1821 they had absorbed their ancient rival, the North-West Company, and by 1845 they had eight permanent posts on the Columbia, six on the Fraser, and a great number of smaller stations scattered throughout the territory— many of them in the disputed region between 49th parallel and the Columbia River. Communication was almost entirely by company vessels, and Indians and settlers alike depended on the company for supplies.[126] Greenhow, who compiled the official case for the American government in 1846, said that "from 1813 to 1823 few if any American citizens were employed in the country west of the Rocky Mountains; and ten years more elapsed before any settlement was formed or even attempted by them in that part of the world. The Americans had no settlements of any kind and their government exercised no jurisdiction west of the Rockies." [127] Thus, until 1823 at the earliest, the United States could advance little claim to sovereignty in Oregon based on occupation, and even in 1839 it was estimated that there were only one hundred and fifty-one citizens of the United States in the territory.[128] In that year it was reported to Congress that:

"A few years will make the country west of the Rockies as completely English as they can desire. Already the Americans are unknown as a nation, and as individuals their power is despised by the natives of the land. A population is growing out of the occupancy of the country whose prejudices are not with us, and before many years they shall decide to whom the country shall belong, unless in the meantime the American government make their powers felt and seen to a greater degree than has yet been the case." [129]

[126] Wallace, *The Oregon Question,* London, 1846, pp. 21 ff.

[127] Greenhow, *History of Oregon and California,* Washington, 1846, p. 34; this book is based on the same author's *Memoir, Historical and Political, on the North-West Coast of America,* New York, 1840, which was the official American statement. See also Merk, "Oregon Pioneers and the Boundary," *American Historical Review,* vol. XXIX, pp. 681–699.

[128] *Reports of the House of Representatives,* no. 101, 25th Cong., 3rd sess.

[129] Mr. Wyeth to the Hon. Caleb Cushing, *idem,* p. 22.

The Oregon Provisional Emigration Society was founded in 1838, and due to its endeavors and the energy of certain pioneer settlers, a considerable increase in population occurred after 1840.[130] Time was on the side of the Americans, for the fur trade in the Columbia valley was gradually waning in importance, while hard times among eastern farmers were making the fertile fields of Oregon seem more and more attractive.[131]

The Maine-New Brunswick boundary dispute was ended by the Ashburton Treaty of 1842. This being out of the way, Mr. Fox suggested to Secretary of State Webster that an early and final settlement of the Oregon Question would still further cement the international friendship that they both desired.[132] To this Mr. Webster heartily consented.[133] Conversations then started, which continuing to 1846, resulted in a definite resolution of the difficulty. Before tracing this development, however, it might be well to examine the bases upon which the two nations founded their claims to possession.

C. *The American Case.*[134]—By the Treaty of 1819 Spain had ceded all her title to the Oregon Territory to the United States. What legal title, then, did Spain enjoy? Sovereignty may be obtained over unoccupied territory, according to the law of nations, by *discovery, occupation, treaty, prescription* or *contiguity.* Spain's claims were based on discovery, treaty, and a Papal decree. The fact that Spanish officers, duly commissioned by the Spanish government, had been the first to discover the Oregon Territory, cannot be contradicted. But a summary of opinion shows that international law does not give a clear title to sovereignty based on discovery alone—to make such a title valid, occupation must follow within "a reasonable time." Grotius, the father of international law, said that "in order to enjoy the domain there should be a corporeal possession." [135] Puffendorf

[130] Mr. Tracy to the Hon. Caleb Cushing, *idem,* p. 25.
[131] Reeves, *op. cit.,* pp. 250 ff.
[132] Fox to Webster, November 18, 1842. *State Papers,* vol. XXXIV, p. 49.
[133] November 25, 1842. *Canadian Archives,* vol. XLIV, sec. 9, no. 1.
[134] Greenhow, *Memoir,* op. cit.
[135] Grotius, *De Jure Belli ac Pacis,* Book 2, chapter 2, sec. 5.

was more explicit: "The title to the territory shall rest in him who is first to occupy it, and not in him who happens first to come in sight of it." [136] Burlamaqui wrote that "the dominion over vacant countries is to be acquired by taking possession of them," [137] while Vattel, the greatest lawyer of his day, said, "All mankind have an equal right to the things that have not yet fallen into the separate possession of anyone; such things belong to the first occupant." [138] The same author again states that any nation can claim a territory "in which it has formed some settlement, or of which it makes some actual use." [139] Sovereignty is given "by occupation, not by mere discovery," wrote a more modern lawyer.[140] At best, discovery alone could give only an inchoate title, or, as Gallatin himself admitted, "Discovery gives an *incipient* claim." [141] Again this American diplomat declared, "Prior discovery gives a right to occupy, provided that occupancy takes place within a reasonable time, and is followed by permanent settlements, and by cultivation of the soil." [142] As was to be expected, Great Britain also took this view, and Rush reported to Adams that "Great Britain could never admit that the mere fact of Spanish navigators having first seen the coast at a particular point . . . without any subsequent or efficient acts of sovereignty or settlement following on the part of Spain, was sufficient to exclude all other nations from that portion of the globe." [143] Therefore, it appears that although Spain had gained an incipient or tentative title to Oregon by discovery, the fact that no attempts at settlement or occupation were made during the 280 years between 1543 and 1819 rendered the Spanish title invalid.

By the Nootka Convention of 1790, Spain and Great Britain

---

[136] Puffendorf, *De Jure Naturæ et Gentium,* Book 4, chapter 4, sec. 5.
[137] Burlamaqui, *Principles,* pt. 4, chapter 9, sec. 6.
[138] Vattel, *Droit des Gens,* Book 1, chapter 9, sec. 6.
[139] *Idem,* div. 208.
[140] Oppenheim, *International Law,* chapter 7, sec. 8.
[141] Gallatin, *The Oregon Question,* New York, 1846, p. 11.
[142] Document no. 199, pp. 63–69, 20th Cong., 5th sess.
[143] Rush to Adams, August 24, 1824. *State Papers,* 1825–1826; Document no. 65, p. 512.

were declared to enjoy equal rights on the Pacific coast, and thus the Spanish title to exclusive possession was again invalidated.

The only other basis of the Spanish claim was that founded on the bull of Pope Alexander VI in which the new world was divided between the monarchs of Portugal and Spain.[144] This claim was not seriously considered by either Spain or Great Britain, after the first few years of westward expansion, but Secretary Buchanan later went so far as again to introduce it, as he "had never seen (it) seriously questioned by any European nation." [145] Mr. Gallatin, however, treated this argument in a summary fashion, when he wrote: "The claim of the United States to absolute sovereignty over the whole Oregon Territory, in virtue of the ancient exclusive Spanish claim, is wholly unfounded." [146]

Thus the Spanish title, based on discovery, or treaty, or on Papal decree, in reality amounted only to a right of joint occupation shared in its entirety with Great Britain. The rights and pretensions ceded to the United States in 1819 were practically worthless, for the United States gained nothing that she did not already possess by the Convention of 1818. Nevertheless, many American lawyers contended that the Spanish right by discovery, combined with the American right by settlement, gave the American government a just title to exclusive control. Considering, however, that it was not until 1840 (300 years after the discovery) that occupation on any measurable scale occurred, this contention is not particularly convincing.

The American case, however, did not rest solely on the rights derived from Spain. On the basis of discovery, occupation, treaty rights, and contiguity, Washington asserted its own claim.

The trips of Captain Robert Gray, who, it was asserted, discovered the Columbia River,[147] and the overland explorations of Lewis and Clark, formed the foundation of the American claim

[144] Fiske, *Discovery of America*, Boston, 1892, vol. I, appendix.

[145] Buchanan to Pakenham, quoted in a pamphlet, by "A Friend of the Anglo-Saxon," entitled *The Oregon Controversy Reviewed*, New York, 1846, p. 12.

[146] Gallatin, *op. cit.*, p. 14.

[147] The Columbia River was in reality discovered by Hecata in 1775.

based on discovery. The United States also advanced a peculiar claim to the basin of the Columbia.[148] "The rights of the United States," wrote Secretary Adams to Rush, "to the Columbia River rest upon its discovery from the sea and nomination by a citizen of the United States; upon its exploration to the sea by Captains Lewis and Clark." [149] And as further amplified by Calhoun this claim included the whole valley of the Columbia and its tributaries, extending from the 42nd to the 52nd parallels.[150] This interpretation of international law was, of course, combated by Great Britain, and the British argument, moreover, questioned the right of Gray, a private commercial adventurer, to give any claim whatever. He had not been officially commissioned by the American government, and that government could not rely on any title derived from his travels; this view was upheld by the international lawyers of the day.[151] Lewis and Clark were properly commissioned and, had they been the first to discover Oregon, the "incipient" rights thus attained would then have been impregnable. Both Drake and Cook, however, had antedated Captain Gray. To have had any validity whatever, the explorations of Gray and of Lewis and Clark should have been followed within a reasonable time by occupation or settlement, and this, according to the American government, had actually occurred. Astoria was founded in 1811, and was restored to the United States at the close of the War of 1812, at which time an American garrison had taken formal possession of the post. This was the only official act performed in the Oregon Territory by the United States government.[152] But Astoria had been shortly afterwards abandoned, and was subsequently sold to and occupied by the North-West Company. Between 1818 and 1839 almost the only Americans living in Oregon were the missionaries, and, although after 1840

[148] Twiss, *op. cit.,* in *Edinburgh Review,* July, 1845, pp. 254–255.

[149] Adams to Rush, July 22, 1823. *Documents of the House of Representatives,* no. 65, 19th Cong., 1st sess.

[150] Calhoun, August 23, 1844. *Canadian Archives,* vol. XLIV, sec. 9, no. 17.

[151] Twiss, *op. cit.,* p. 184; G. J. Wallace, *The Oregon Question Determined by the Rules of International Law,* London, 1846.

[152] *Documents of the House of Representatives,* no. 65, 19th Cong., 1st sess.

a large number of settlers did come in,[153] they did so simply as private individuals, and were not authorized or assisted by the federal government.[154] Consequently, they could give no valid claim to sovereignty, although their presence did undoubtedly affect the decisions of the political negotiators who ultimately settled the dispute.[155] Finally, these migrations took place after the signing of the Convention of 1818, and according to the terms of agreement the question of sovereignty was left in abeyance, and no act performed while it was in operation could affect the respective claims of Britain or America.[156]

Thus, by discovery and by occupation, the American title was dubious at best, and certainly could not support any pretensions to complete and exclusive control.

The treaties affecting the validity of the American case were the Treaty of Ghent, by which Astoria was handed back; the Convention of 1818, authorizing joint occupation with Great Britain; the Treaty of 1819, by which Spain's claims were transferred to the United States; and the Treaty of 1824, in which Russia agreed to remain north of $54° 40'$. By no interpretation could these treaties be logically considered a basis upon which to build an exclusive American right to the sovereignty of Oregon.

Prescriptive rights, obviously, could not apply to a region so recently discovered.

Only the claim based on contiguity remains. As a result of the Lousiana Purchase and the Convention of 1818, the territory

[153] In 1843, 900 settlers arrived at one time, acknowledged allegiance to a provisional government and chose a governor in 1845. This had a vital influence on the home governments, for it was impossible not to recognize the actual presence of the settlers.

[154] Greenhow, *op. cit.*, p. 34 The romantic story of Whitman's ride, which pictured the famous missionary rushing across the continent just in time to prevent Webster from giving the whole of Oregon to Great Britain, is now recognized as a myth. He did cross the continent, but largely on personal business, and Webster was certainly contemplating no such plan. Bourne, "The Legend of Marcus Whitman" in *Essays in Historical Criticism*, New York, 1911; Johnson, *America's Foreign Relations*, New York, 1916.

[155] Merk, *op. cit.*

[156] Twiss, *op. cit.*, in *Edinburgh Review*, July 1845, p. 258.

of the United States was contiguous with that of Oregon between the 42nd and the 49th parallels. Viewed from an objective standpoint, this appears to be the only truly valid claim that could be advanced in support of the American case.[157]

To sum up, even accepting Gallatin's unification of the Spanish claim by discovery with the American claim by occupation [158] (a questionable procedure, for the Spanish claim, apart from its inherent weakness, was not acquired until after the Convention of 1818 which left the question of sovereignty in abeyance), the argument of the United States does not appear valid. A very long time elapsed after discovery before any attempt was made at colonization, and when the settlers did arrive, they were unsupported and unauthorized by the government at Washington.[159] By treaty and by prescription, the United States enjoyed no right that was not shared with Great Britain, and the slight though valid claim by contiguity applied only to that section of Oregon south of 49°.

D. The British Case.—The British government, differing from that of the United States, made no claim to exclusive sovereignty over the whole of the Oregon Territory. What Great Britain did claim was a title as valid as that of the United States, and a better title to the region north of the Columbia River. The British case was based on the following arguments:

(*1*) *Discovery.* The voyages of both Drake and Cook had antedated those of Gray, and each of these adventurers had been a duly commissioned representative of the British Crown. Meares, Vancouver, Mackenzie, Fraser, and Thompson had all carried on this work, and Vancouver in particular had made a very careful survey of the west coast, even sending a cutter one hundred miles up the Columbia River.[160] The English claim is vitiated, however, by the fact that only Drake, Cook, and Vancouver had

[157] *Idem,* p. 264.

[158] Gallatin, *op. cit.,* pp. 16 ff.

[159] The American government refused to assist Astor, and likewise refused aid to the later settlers. See Bourne, "Aspects of Oregon History Previous to 1840," *Oregon Historical Society Quarterly,* vol. IV, p. 255.

[160] Twiss, *op. cit.,* in *Edinburgh Review,* July 1845, p. 245.

been commissioned, and by the fact that Spanish explorers had preceded them all.

(*2*) *Occupation.* The first attempt to found anything in the nature of a permanent settlement in Oregon was the establishment of Meares at Nootka Sound. This post, started in 1788, was considered so important by the Spanish Viceroy in Mexico that he sent an expedition to destroy it—an act for which Spain was forced to make compensation, at the same time admitting Britain's right to the enjoyment of all privileges on the west coast.[161] The first official act of occupation in the Oregon Territory was performed by a British officer in the War of 1812, when he took command of Fort George (Astoria). This settlement, however, was later returned to the United States and finally passed to the North-West Company. Consequently, neither country could use its connection with Astoria as a basis of a legal claim. The North-West Company and the Hudson's Bay Company each made many small settlements, but these were of a temporary character only, and were not the official colonizing action of a sovereign state. Thus the British claim to jurisdiction based on exploration followed by occupation was quite as untenable as that of the United States.

(*3*) *Treaties.* The Nootka Convention of 1790 gave Britain equal rights with Spain to carry on trade or colonization; the Convention of 1818 was a similar agreement with the United States; and in 1825 Russia agreed to refrain from disputing Britain's title south of 54° 40′. Thus Great Britain gained by treaty only the privileges of trade and settlement—privileges also held under similar conventions by the United States.

(*4*) *Contiguity.* The Convention of 1818 extended the British-American boundary from the Lake of the Woods to the crest of the Rocky Mountains, along the 49th parallel. All to the north of this line and east of the Rocky Mountains was British territory, and thus by contiguity Great Britain had a claim to Oregon north of 49°, just as valid as that of the United States from 42° to 49°.

[161] Escurial of 1790; see above, p. 193.

It may thus be seen that neither nation had a perfect, or even a strong, case. The United States, through the Spanish cession (even if Spain had not forfeited her rights by non-use), gained only an incipient right, which her failure to colonize rendered nugatory. Britain's title by discovery and occupation was equally invalid. No exclusive right was given either nation by treaty, and no right at all could be urged by prescription. The only possible claim which either nation could justly advance was that gained by contiguity, and this favored the United States below 49° and Great Britain above that parallel.[162]

E. Negotiating the Treaty.—An involved dispute in which neither litigant can prove his case easily leads to grave excesses of partisan exaggeration. The very weakness of a national cause is sometimes responsible for the most violent outbursts in its defense. In the matter of Oregon this condition was particularly true of the United States, for the American people had a better appreciation of the value of the prize for which their government was contending. To the average Englishman, Oregon appeared to be "a costly, unprofitable encumbrance,"[163] but being involved in the dispute he had the natural and human dislike of admitting defeat. To the Americans, with a better knowledge of the country and imaginations heated by the contest, Oregon appeared to be "our land of promise—and England must and will take herself off."[164] A further incentive to American interest was the "isolation complex" which had been created by Monroe's enunciation of his famous doctrine. Thus in 1840 it seemed to be "the true policy of the United States by all lawful means to resist the inclusion of European dominion in America and to

[162] "No nation now possesses any title perfect or imperfect by discovery, by settlement, by treaty, or by Prescription. . . . No nation possesses a perfect title by contiguity—an imperfect title by contiguity to that portion which lies north of the 49th parallel in England—and to that part which lies south of that parallel in America." Twiss, *op. cit.,* in *Edinburgh Review,* July, 1845, p. 264.

[163] *Idem,* p. 265.

[164] McOwen, quoted in London *Times,* February 24, 1844.

confine its limits and abridge its duration wherever it may actually exist." [165] This attitude has been generally overlooked in appraising the forces at work in the Oregon question. Yet it was stated with crystal clearness by President Polk himself—to whom, incidentally, much of the bitterness of the controversy was due. "The fixed policy of the American Government," he wrote, "should be not to permit Great Britain or any foreign power to plant a colony or hold dominion over any portion of the people or territory . . . of Oregon." [166] General Cass was even less diplomatic. "We must have no red lines traversing Oregon—the whole is ours and we must have it." [167]

Fox and Webster reopened the discussion of the Oregon question in November, 1842.[168] Increasing difficulties in the territory, where the new settlers were beginning to object to the rule of the Hudson's Bay Company, made both parties anxious for a settlement. On December 7, 1842, President Harrison nearly caused an international crisis when he spoke of the "territory of the United States generally called the Oregon Territory." [169] A week later, however, Mr. Fox was able to write to Lord Aberdeen that it was "satisfactory to observe that . . . no rash or irrevocable assertion is hazarded of the intentions of the United States to persist in their entire claim." [170]

In the presidential campaign of 1844 the Oregon controversy played an important part. James K. Polk, floating the vessel of his political ambitions on the high tide of expansionist sentiment, stirred his fellow-Americans to enthusiasm with his insistence upon "the whole of Oregon," the annexation of Texas, and the popular catchwords "Fifty-four forty or fight." The success of this campaign surprised even the most ardent Democrats, and it sheds an illuminating light on the feelings and ambitions of the American people in the "Roaring Forties."

[165] Greenhow, *op. cit.,* p. 355, note.
[166] Quoted in Falconer, *op. cit.,* p. 44.
[167] Quoted in Simpson, *The Oregon Territory,* London, 1844, p. 10.
[168] *State Papers,* vol. XXXIV, p. 49.
[169] *Canadian Archives,* vol. XLIV, sec. 9, no. 4.
[170] Fox to Aberdeen, December 13, 1843. *Canadian Archives,* vol. XLIV, sec. 9, no. 9.

On January 15, 1845, Sir Richard Pakenham, the British Minister at Washington, suggested arbitration, but Calhoun refused to consider this so long as any possibility of reaching a decision by direct negotiation remained.[171]

In his inaugural address President Polk reiterated his campaign pledges in regard to Oregon, and again declared that the American "title to the whole of Oregon is clear and unquestionable." [172] The new President's actions, however, were not as extreme as his words. He had hardly recovered from the trials of the inauguration ceremony when he offered, through Secretary of State Buchanan, to compromise the dispute at the 49th parallel.[173] This proposal was addressed to Sir Richard Pakenham, and that official refused the offer without even referring it to London.[174] This forced Polk to take more strenuous measures, and he asked Congress to give the required notice to terminate the joint occupation of Oregon, to extend the laws of the United States over that territory, and to erect forts there.[175] He again asserted the rights of the United States to the whole region,[176] and still later declared "that the British contentions of title could not be entertained to any portion of the Oregon Territory." [177] On December 27th the British proposed arbitration, but by this time American feeling had risen too high for such pacific measures, and the proposal was refused.[178]

President Polk's campaign had aroused a real interest in Oregon among the American people—an interest that had been prepared for by the migrations into the territory during the early

---

[171] *Idem,* nos. 22, 23.

[172] Richardson (editor), *A Compilation of the Messages and Papers of the Presidents,* Washington, 1897.

[173] Buchanan had stated that he hoped to adopt "the principle of giving and taking." *Canadian Archives,* vol. XLIV, sec. 9, no. 25.

[174] *Idem,* no. 28, enc. 2; Bassett, *A Short History of the United States,* New York, 1921, p. 415.

[175] *Ibid.*

[176] Buchanan to Pakenham, August 30, 1845. *Canadian Archives,* vol. XLIV, sec. 9, no. 29.

[177] December 2, 1845. *Idem,* no. 31.

[178] December 27, 1845, January 3, 1846. *Idem.* nos. 32, 33.

'forties. Countless pamphlets and scores of books were written and published in support of the American claims, and extraordinary productions some of them were.[179] Voices were not lacking, however, to proclaim the idiocy of a war over this question, and to remind the legislators of the bad light which such a war would cast upon the United States, in view of her refusal to arbitrate.[180] The popular and perfectly safe sport of "twisting the Lion's tail" was carried to such an extreme by some Congressmen that Senator Haywood of North Carolina was led to quote from George Washington that "the nation which indulges toward another habitual hatred, is, in some degree, a slave." [181]

Neither country, however, actually wanted war. Britain was not vitally interested in Oregon, and few Canadians were thinking of the Pacific. The British Foreign Office, as Professor Merk has pointed out, was no longer obsessed by the idea that the Columbia River was another St. Lawrence or Mississippi and a vital link in the trade route to China.[182] Great Britain was more ready to compromise because the Hudson's Bay Company had now withdrawn, or was preparing to withdraw,[183] from Fort Vancouver on

[179] For example: "If this pamphlet shall serve to convince my countrymen of the insolent selfishness of Great Britain—her grasping injustice, her destitution of political honesty—and serve to show a necessity for the people to act for themselves and to expect from their government at Washington the maintenance of the rights and honors of their country; the author will feel richly rewarded for the labor he has bestowed in collecting and arranging 'the evidence of their rights to the Oregon territory—the whole of it and nothing less.'" T. J. Farnham, *History of the Oregon Territory*, New York, 1844.

[180] "A Friend of the Anglo-Saxon," *op. cit.*, pp. 8–9.

[181] "I confess that I did feel mortified in reading the news by the last steamer, at the necessity of conceding to the debates of the British Parliament a decided superiority over those of ourselves in dignity and moderation; and it would be quite a satisfaction to me to get news by the next packet of an outrageous debate in the British Parliament at least sufficient to put us even with them on that score." Haywood, *Senate Address*, 1846, pp. 4, 18.

[182] Merk, *op. cit.*, pp. 695 ff.

[183] Both Howay and Sage are convinced that actual withdrawal did not take place until 1849.

the Columbia, and had established its headquarters at Fort Victoria on the southern point of Vancouver Island. The fur trade in the Columbia valley was dying out.[184] The British, moreover, were involved in an exceptionally acute domestic problem as a result of the crop failures of 1845. In Scotland and Ireland a large percentage of the population was threatened with starvation, and in the Houses of Parliament the repeal of the Corn Laws was absorbing the attention of all the party leaders.[185] In the United States, on the other hand, the struggle over slavery was already casting its ominous shadows over the land,[186] and President Polk, having succeeded in annexing Texas, was now preparing for war with Mexico.[187] It was quite evident that the responsible officials of each country would support a sensible compromise proposal. Britain certainly did not want a war (even Salisbury and Pakenham would have hesitated before taking that plunge), and the United States, although it would not have surrendered any territory south of the 49th parallel, equally certainly was not prepared to fight for 54° 40′ [188] This was now realized by Great Britain.

On May 18, 1846, Lord Aberdeen initiated the conversations which ultimately led to a settlement of the question at issue. On that date he wrote to Pakenham, "You will . . . propose to the American Secretary of State that the line of demarcation should be continued along the 49th parallel from the Rocky Mountains to the sea-coast, and thence in a southerly direction through King George's Channel and the Straits of Fuca to the Pacific Ocean, leaving the whole of Vancouver's Island with its ports and harbors in the possession of Great Britain." [189] This was the line

[184] *Ibid.*
[185] Adams, *History of the Foreign Policy of the United States,* p. 228.
[186] Many southern Congressmen were opposed to a war that would, if successful, add immensely to the "free" territory of the United States. Bassett, *op. cit.,* p. 445.
[187] Adams, *op. cit.,* p. 229.
[188] *Ibid;* Reeves, *op. cit.,* pp. 261 ff.
[189] *The Case of His Britannic Majesty, etc.,* London, Houses of Parliament, 1873, no. 3.

for which the United States had in reality been contending, and in spite of the opposition of Buchanan, the proposal was submitted to the Senate by President Polk, and the consent of that body was quickly obtained.[190] The treaty was signed on June 15, 1846. It drew the line of division along the 49th parallel "to the middle of the channel which separates the continent from Vancouver's Island, and then southerly through the middle of the said channel, and of Fuca's Straits, to the Pacific Ocean." [191] Provision was also made for free navigation of the Columbia River, and for the confirmation of the rights and titles of the Hudson's Bay Company and the Puget Sound Agricultural Company.

The treaty was, under the existing conditions, just and equitable. *Neither nation had a clear title to any of the territory* and the result was practically an equal division. Great Britain was given the better harbors, and greater resources in minerals, timber and fish; the United States received much more agricultural land, and a district which has, on the whole, a better climate. This decision is, moreover, almost unique among the solutions of American boundary troubles, in that it has been accepted with reasonable satisfaction by both nations.[192] A better proof of its justice could hardly be demanded.

4. THE ALASKAN BOUNDARY

A. The History of the Problem.—Although the dispute over the Alaskan Boundary did not become serious until after the discovery of gold in the Yukon in 1897, and was not perma-

---

[190] Pakenham to Palmerston, August 13, 1846, *idem,* no. 106, Historical Note.

[191] Malloy, *op. cit.,* vol. I, p. 657.

[192] This does not apply to such extreme imperialists as Benton, or, at a later time, Theodore Roosevelt. The latter in his *Life of Benton,* shows both subject and author as devoid of any sense of proportion so far as American expansion is concerned. See Roosevelt, *Thomas H. Benton,* New York. 1886, pp. 260-273.

nently settled until 1903, it is necessary to go back almost one hundred years in order to understand the facts upon which Canada and the United States based their respective contentions.

During the early years of the nineteenth century the ownership of the northwestern corner of the continent was in dispute. Explorers, fur traders, and merchants of Russia, the United States, and Great Britain were all pursuing their vocations by sea or land along the island-sheltered coasts of the Alaskan peninsula.[193] Under the circumstances it was inevitable that conflicts should arise, and the vigorous policy of Russia in particular aroused some anxiety in the United States.[194] By a ukase of 1821, Russia asserted her exclusive sovereignty as far south as the 51st parallel of north latitude: a claim that was at once combated by Washington and London.[195] It is now generally recognized that the fear of Russian aggression in Alaska played a large part in convincing Adams and Monroe of the necessity of stating and defending the policy which was soon enunciated in a presidential message, and has since been known as the Monroe Doctrine.[196]

The threat of force as implied in the Monroe Doctrine was not an altogether satisfactory solution of the Alaskan problem, and negotiations between the American and Russian governments were instituted, to culminate in the Convention of 1824. Under the terms of this convention the United States agreed to establish no posts north of 54° 40', and in return was assured of unrestricted opportunities in the fishing industry, and of permission to trade for ten years in the interior seas, gulfs, harbors, and

[193] de Mofras, *Exploration du Territoire de l'Oregon*, Paris, 1844, vol. II, chaps. 6, 7, 9, 10.

[194] In 1806 Russia had actually claimed the whole west coast down to the Golden Gate and for some time garrisoned a post near Bodega Bay in California. *The Cambridge History of British Foreign Policy*, vol. II, p. 229.

[195] *Fur Seal Arbitration Papers* (1893), vol. IV, p. 370; *The Cambridge History of British Foreign Policy*, vol. II, p. 66.

[196] *American State Papers: Foreign Relations*, vol. V. p. 436. The Monroe Doctrine was enunciated on December 2, 1823.

creeks of the Alexander Archipelago—as the whole coastal region north of the 54th parallel was known.[197]

Meanwhile Great Britain was not idle. After some delay, Canning succeeded in negotiating a similar treaty, which was signed on February 28, 1825.[198] It was on the wording of this Anglo-Russian Treaty that all the subsequent debate over the exact boundary of Alaska was based. Articles III and IV contain the passages which were so variously interpreted. Their importance justifies quotation in full:

Article III. "Commencing from the southernmost part of the Island called Prince of Wales Island, which point lies in the parallel 54° 40′, and between the 131st and 133rd degrees of west longitude (meridian of Greenwich) the said line shall ascend to the north along the channel called Portland Channel, as far as the point of the continent where it strikes the 56th degree of north latitude. From this last mentioned point the line of demarkation shall follow the summit of the mountains situated parallel to the coast as far as the point of intersection of the 141st degree of west longitude (of the same meridian), and, finally, from the said point of intersection, the said meridian line of the 141st degree in its prolongation as far as the Frozen Ocean, shall form the limit between the Russian and British posssessions on the continent of America to the North-west.

Article IV. With reference to the line of demarkation laid down in the previous article it is understood: *1st*. That the Island called Prince of Wales Island shall belong wholly to Russia. *2nd*. That whenever the summit of the mountains which extend in the direction parallel to the coast from the 56th degree of north latitude to the point of intersection of the 141st degree of west longitude shall prove to be at a distance of more than 10 marine leagues from the ocean the limit between the British possessions and the line of the coast which is to belong to Russia, as above mentioned shall

[197] de Mofras, *op. cit.,* vol. II, pp. 273–274; *Treaties and Conventions,* Washington, 1873, p. 733. The convention was signed April 24, 1824. Davidson, *The Alaskan Boundary,* San Francisco, 1903, p. 23. Russia relinquished her claims to exclusive ownership south of 54 ° 40′ on April 17, 1824, and not in 1826 as stated in one account in *The Cambridge History of British Foreign Policy,* vol. II, p. 66.

[198] *The Case of His Britannic Majesty Before the Alaska Boundary Tribunal,* London, 1903, appendix I, p. 37.

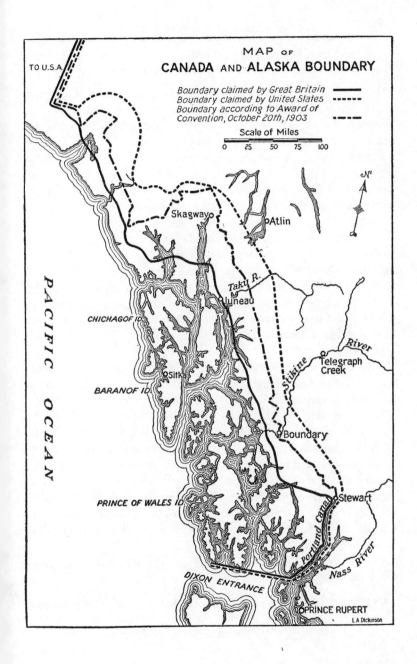

MAP OF
CANADA AND ALASKA BOUNDARY

Boundary claimed by Great Britain ————
Boundary claimed by United States ---------
Boundary according to Award of
Convention, October 20th, 1903 —·—·—

Scale of Miles
0   25   50   75   100

N°

TO U.S.A.

PACIFIC OCEAN

Skagway   Atlin

Taku R.
Juneau

CHICHAGOF ID.

River

Stikine
Telegraph
Creek

Sitka

BARANOF ID.

Boundary

PRINCE OF WALES ID.

Stewart

Portland Canal

Nass River

DIXON ENTRANCE

PRINCE RUPERT

L A Dickinson

be formed by a line parallel to the windings of the coast, and shall never exceed the distance of ten marine leagues therefrom." [199]

In these two articles are found the definitions which, by partisan interpretation, became the basis of the Alaskan boundary controversy. Article III was written under the supposition that an orderly range of mountains paralleled the north Pacific coast—a supposition later proven alogether erroneous.[200] Mountains there were in great profusion; but of order there was none. To one who has traveled through the famous "inside passage" of the British Columbian and Alaskan coast the utter impossibility of drawing "a line parallel to the windings of the coast," is at once evident.

Due to a meager knowledge of the country, and to a general lack of interest, no disputes arose concerning this boundary between 1825 and 1867, with the single exception of a trivial altercation over the right of navigation on the Stikine River. In the year 1867, however, the Dominion of Canada was formed, and the United States purchased Alaska from the Czar.[201] Four years later British Columbia entered the Dominion. Thus the stage was prepared.

The Lieutenant-Governor of the new Canadian province soon requested the federal authorities to take steps to bring about a final and definitive elucidation and settlement of the national rights in northwestern America.[202] On the 11th of July, 1872, Canada requested the British Foreign Office to approach the United States on this subject. As a result of the efforts of Edward Thornton, British Ambassador at Washington, the President, on December 2, 1872, recommended to Congress the appointment of a joint commission "to determine the line between the territory of Alaska and the co-terminous possessions of Great Britain." [203] Unfortunately for the future good relations of the two countries,

[199] *Ibid.*

[200] *Ibid.* See also maps in the appendix. See also Mr. Dall to Mr. Dawson, p. 245, and *Argument of the United States Government,* Washington, 1903.

[201] July 1, 1867, October 11, 1867. Bassett, *A Short History of the United States* New York, 1920, pp. 643–644.

[202] *The Case of His Britannic Majesty, etc.,* appendix 1, p. 103

[203] *Idem,* p. 166.

this suggestion was not well received. Mr. Fish, Secretary of State, announced publicly that such a commission would take ten years to do the work and would cost a million and a half dollars. This expense the United States was unwilling to bear.[204]

Matters soon became more complicated. American and Canadian settlers and trappers in the region of the Stikine River were in a constant state of commotion. In 1877 the case of Peter Martin, an American citizen, arrested and convicted by Canadian officials for an offense committed on disputed territory, aroused international interest.[205] In the same year the Dominion government sent Joseph Hunter to the Stikine to determine, if possible, the line of demarcation. Hunter's instructions from the office of the Surveyor-General were to locate the line at a distance of ten marine leagues from the coast, "on a course at right angles *to the general bearing* thereof, opposite." [206]

Thus Canada stated her belief that "the line of the Coast" should be taken to mean the "general bearing" or "general trend" of the coast, an interpretation that the United States was later to reject indignantly, for a settlement based on such a premise would give Canada a number of the finest harbors in Alaska. Twice during 1877 Thornton pressed on Secretary Evarts the desirability of an early agreement, but a *modus vivendi* by which Hunter's line on the Stikine would be temporarily recognized was the most that Washington would do. This temporary acceptance was to be "without prejudice to the rights of the parties when the permanent boundary came to be fixed." [207]

On April 24, 1884, Mr. Dall of the United States Survey wrote to Mr. Dawson of the Division of Geological Survey of Canada, stating that the line of the Treaty of 1825 was impossible of location, as there was "no natural boundary, and the continuous range of mountains, parallel to the Coast, shown on Vancouver's charts, having no existence as such, the United States would un-

[204] *Idem,* p. 168.
[205] *Canadian Sessional Papers,* no. 125, vol. XI, pp. 37–59, 143, 152, 155. *United States Diplomatic Correspondence,* 1877, pp. 268–271.
[206] *The Case of His Britannic Majesty, etc.,* appendix I, p. 224.
[207] *Idem,* p. 33; *United States Foreign Relations, 1878,* pp. 339, 346.

doubtedly wish to fall back upon the line parallel to the windings of the coast. It would, of course, be impracticable to trace any such winding line over the sea of mountains." [208] Secretary Bayard wrote to Lord Salisbury that, in view of the erroneous ideas of those who drew up the treaty, the document "really gave no boundary at all" [209]—a statement that was completely and obviously true. This presented an ideal opening for the discussion of a compromise line, but no steps were taken to that end. During 1887–1888 Dall and Dawson continued their discussions at Washington and the divergent views became ever more pronounced. Was the boundary to cross over inlets which projected 40, 50 or even 100 miles into the interior, or was the American *lisière* to remain intact? Each of these eminent scientists decided in favor of the contentions of his own country, and no agreement could be reached. [210]

In 1897 gold was found in the Yukon and Alaska, and the boundary question immediately took on a new importance. Sir Julian Pauncefote suggested that a commission of three, one American, one Briton, and one neutral, be selected to adjust the difficulty, and that in the meantime an arbitrary line should be agreed upon. [211] This suggestion was not accepted by the United States, but in June, 1898, a joint commission met at Quebec to discuss a number of international difficulties. Canada made two proposals to this body in relation to the Alaskan boundary; *1st.* that a conventional line be drawn giving the Dominion Pyramid Harbor on Lynn Canal, [212] and ceding the remainder to the United States; or *2nd.* that the whole matter be left to arbitration in accordance with the terms of the Venezuelan arbitration. [213] Both of these plans were rejected by the United States. The American commissioners in turn offered their suggestion, namely, that a

[208] *The Case of His Britannic Majesty, etc.,* appendix 1, p. 245.

[209] January 18, 1886. *Idem,* p. 254.

[210] *Senate Documents,* no. 146, 50th Cong. 2nd sess.

[211] *The Case of His Britannic Majesty, etc.,* appendix 1, p. 305.

[212] The longest inlet in the disputed territory, and the natural doorway to the British Yukon.

[213] *Protocol LXIII of the Joint High Commission, Fourth Session, Eighth Parliament,* 62 Victoria, 1899.

judicial body of three eminent jurists from each country be convened and instructed to interpret the treaty. This scheme was vetoed by Great Britain.[214] The matter was then referred back to the national governments for further discussion through diplomatic channels.[215]

An agreement was at length reached, and on January 24, 1903, the United States and Great Britain agreed to the formation of a joint tribunal, composed of three "impartial jurists of repute" from each nation. The duties of this body were to adjudicate on the provisions of the treaty. It was not an arbitral commission; [216] it was a judicial board. It was appointed, not to arrange a practical and reasonable solution of the difficulty, but to interpret legally a document that was geographically absurd.

B. The Members of the Tribunal.—The composition of this judicial body was of great moment, for only as the people of the two countries were assured of the impartiality of the judges would they be satisfied with the results. The British government in response to the demand of Canadian sentiment nominated Louis A. Jette [217] and Allen B. Aylesworth,[218] two eminent members of the Canadian bar. The third member nominated by Great Britain was Lord Alverstone, who held the highest position in the Judiciary of the United Kingdom.[219] Few exceptions were taken to these appointments by the American press or people. Americans in general, however, felt that Canada was engaged in "trying to put something over" on the United States. From the President down, it was believed that the Dominion had trumped

[214] Foster, *op. cit.*, p. 456.

[215] Feeling was running high in the United States, for many thought that England wanted to build a "Gibraltar of the North" on the Lynn Canal. See letter of F. W. Seward in the New York *Tribune* for November 14, 1902; Balch, *The Alaska Frontier*, p. 175.

[216] *Alaska Boundary Correspondence*, p. 45, summarized in the Manitoba *Free Press*, October 23, 1903.

[217] He was Lieutenant-Governor of Quebec, and therefore not engaged in politics.

[218] Mr. Aylesworth took the place of Mr. Armour, who was nominated but died before the tribunal met; he later became Chief Justice of Canada.

[219] Lord Alverstone was Lord Chief Justice.

up a spurious claim only after the territory had been suddenly and unexpectedly proven of value. This criticism was not entirely just, as an examination of the previous negotiations will prove, but it is of course true that the Canadian claim was urged much more vigorously after 1897 than before, and that many of the Canadian arguments were exceedingly feeble.

On February 18, 1903, President Roosevelt made public announcement of the names of the American nominees—Secretary of War Root, Senator Lodge of Massachusetts, and Senator Turner of Washington. A storm of protest swept over Canada, and the Dominion government took the unusual step of formally objecting to the appointment of the two Senators.[220] Elihu Root had then, as now, the confidence and respect of the whole English-speaking world. He was, and is, a man of the most scrupulous honesty: honorable, able, and conscientious. Senator Turner was little known even in his own country—but was a politician from Washington, the state most vitally interested in the retention of Alaska. The political career of Henry Cabot Lodge, on the other hand, had been characterized by an excessive devotion to partisan and nationalistic ends. It is not too much to say that for a quarter of a century he had been recognized as a mischievous force in international relations, and that in relation to things British in particular he had displayed a complete lack of objectivity. He had been the incarnation of bigoted nationalism and jingoistic imperialism, and his nomination as an "impartial jurist of repute" was bitterly resented in Canada.[221]

Whatever may be said of the final decisions of the tribunal (and they were probably quite justified), it must be agreed that "in making these selections the United States Government dishonored its own Treaty." [222] Every member of the trio was a politician, and while Root might have been willing to sacrifice his political future in order to deal fairly in the matter of the

[220] *Alaskan Boundary Correspondence,* March 6, 1903, summarized in the Manitoba *Free Press,* October 23, 1903.

[221] On Lodge see White, "Henry Cabot Lodge and the Alaskan Boundary Award," *Canadian Historical Review,* December, 1925, pp. 332–347.

[222] Manitoba *Free Press,* February 24, 1903. President Roosevelt was, of course, responsible.

Alaskan boundary, no such illusions could be held in regard to Senators Lodge and Turner.[223] The former, moreover, had already committed himself in regard to the matter to be settled. In a speech at Northampton, Massachusetts, delivered on October 16, 1902, Senator Lodge had said that "no nation with any self-respect could have admitted" the Canadian claims, and went on to link the "national honor" with the American contentions regarding the Alaskan boundary.[224]

With the announcement of the choice of American delegates public opinion in Canada at once became pessimistic. If Lodge and Turner are to represent the United States, declared the Toronto *Globe,* "it makes little difference how ably the Canadian case is presented." [225] The Montreal *Gazette* agreed that "the representatives of the United States were hardly open to conviction," [226] while the Toronto *News* summed it up thus: "Mr. Root is a lawyer of real eminence. Senator Lodge is a well-known jingo. Senator Turner comes from the State in which Seattle is situated." [227]

But the Canadian papers were not alone in recognizing the inappropriateness of President Roosevelt's selections. The famous Springfield *Republican* (an American journal that for liberal independence deserves to be linked with the Manchester *Guardian* in Great Britain or the Manitoba *Free Press* in Canada) stated editorially:

"If the President were to seek the country over for men who were entirely without the judicial quality on this question, he could not find persons whose minds are more set than Messrs. Lodge, Turner

[223] "Neither of them is an impartial jurist in any sense of the word. Both of them are extreme partisans. . . . Senator Lodge, a fiery jingo, has delivered characteristic intemperate speeches on this very subject which he is supposed to view now with objective eyes, speeches in which he has assailed Britain and sneered at Canada. . . . Turner represents the State in which are centered the interests which will derive most benefit from a settlement in harmony with American contentions." Ottawa *Citizen,* February 23, 1903.

[224] Quoted in the Manitoba *Free Press,* February 24, 1903.

[225] Quoted in the Victoria *Colonist,* February 28, 1903.

[226] Montreal *Gazette,* October 19, 1903.

[227] Toronto *News,* February 29, 1903.

and Root. Their selection cannot be interpreted in any other way than that the President intends to block the slightest chance of a decision in the least favorable to Canada." [228]

Unfortunately, however, the famous Massachusetts paper did not express the sentiments of a majority of Americans. The Seattle *Post-Intelligencer,* having previously argued that "there was nothing to arbitrate," [229] now relied upon and was proud of the fact that "none of the American commissioners will yield a single point." [230] The State House of Representatives at Olympia passed a resolution denouncing England in violent terms and demanding of the American representatives a firm adherence to every American claim.[231]

Placed on the defensive as a result of his appointments, President Roosevelt wrote to Judge Holmes of the Supreme Court explaining his choice by the statement that "no three men fit for the position could be found in all the United States who had not already come to some conclusion" on this subject, and that the American delegates were "anxious to do justice to the British claim on all points." [232] The first statement of the President was probably true, but the inference was absurd. Had Mr. Roosevelt appointed three judges of the United States Supreme Court, there could have been no possible occasion for Canadian objection; but in order to pacify the Senate, to assure himself of its support, and because he honestly felt that Canada was making a consciously unjust claim to American territory, he had appointed the men named. This, of course, is an explanation, and is not an excuse. There can, furthermore, be no possible justification for the President's bombastic method of informing Britain (through Judge Holmes) "that if there is any disagreement—not only will there be no arbitration of the matter but in my message to Congress I shall take a position which will prevent any possibility of arbitration hereafter . . . and which will give me the authority to run

[228] Springfield *Republican,* February 23, 1903.

[229] Quoted in the Victoria *Times,* February 11, 1903.

[230] Seattle *Post-Intelligencer,* March 1, 1903.

[231] Biggs, *A Review of the Alaskan Boundary Question,* pp. 20–21.

[232] Roosevelt to Holmes, July 25, 1903. Bishop, *Theodore Roosevelt and His Times,* New York, 1920, vol. I, pp. 259–261.

the line as we claim it without any further regard to the attitude of England and Canada." [233] His letter to Judge Holmes demonstrated the great failing of President Roosevelt—his complete inability to see more than one side of any given question; but it also shows the existing attitude of the United States. Americans generally felt that Canada was trumping up an unjustifiable claim. It was this sentiment, as well as the real need for greater police protection, that led the President to dispatch a large body of troops to Alaska at this time,[234] and few people who understood his attitude could doubt that he fully intended to use them in case the tribunal decided against the American claims.[235] Here was "shirt-sleeve" diplomacy in its crudest form.

It was distinctly creditable to the Canadian people that they did not demand at this time that the King appoint "impartial jurists" of the same type as those representing the United States.[236] Though realizing that the decision of the tribunal would probably be against them,[237] and that it could not be for them. The Canadian authorities carried out the treaty stipulations in spirit and in letter.

C. The Problems before the Tribunal.—In summary, the questions before the tribunal, which met in London on September 3rd, 1903, may be stated as follows:

[233] *Idem*, p. 260.

[234] *Idem*, p. 261.

[235] *Ibid.*

[236] Some suggestions were made by Vancouver papers that a commissioner be chosen from the Pacific Coast province, but these were not strongly pressed.

[237] The British Foreign Office was attempting to cement the good relations with the United States which had been inaugurated during the Spanish-American War. Canadians feared that political influence would be exerted on Alverstone to make him agree to the American case. Thus Canada's "rights" would "again" be sacrificed to the United States by action of the mother country. As has already been pointed out, this feeling that Canada's rights had been sacrificed for the sake of Anglo-American friendship in the Northeastern and Oregon boundary disputes was almost, if not quite, without justification in fact. Had Canada been left to press her case alone in either instance, she would probably have emerged with much less territory than she did actually obtain. See above.

(*1*). *The Point of Commencement of the Boundary.* On this particular matter there was little discussion. At first the American counsel argued that Wales Island (considerably south of the island now known as Prince of Wales Island) was the one intended in the definition. Inasmuch as this island was not named until long after 1825, the contention was dropped, and Cape Muzon was declared to be the correct point of departure.

(*2*). *What was meant by Portland Channel?* The only inlet of that name was discovered, named and charted by Captain Vancouver. The difficulty arose from the fact that the channel divided in its upper reaches and where united it was studded with islands, making many small channels. The two great inland branches of Portland Channel were known as Portland Canal and Observatory Inlet. Both sides agreed that Portland Canal was the branch mentioned in the treaty, but the difficulty arose in drawing the line through Portland Channel itself. Did the name Observatory Inlet include that part of Portland Channel between the 55th degree of north latitude and the ocean, to the south of the larger islands? The British claimed that the line should follow the northern bank leaving all the islands to Canada; that Observatory Inlet extended all the way to the Ocean and that "Portland Channel" was the passage between the islands and the northern coast. The Americans claimed that the line should, on emerging from Portland Canal, cross to the Observatory Inlet side of Portland Channel, and thus to the ocean. By this method the United States would take all four islands. The American counsel pointed out that the lower part of Observatory Inlet had usually been mentioned as "Portland Channel," [238] while the British attempted by quoting Vancouver to prove that "Portland Channel" *did not* include the lower part of the inlet.[239]

(*3*). *The line from "the southermost point of Prince of Wales Island to Portland Channel."* This depended upon the decision in the second problem, and was adjusted in accordance with that award.

[238] *The Case of the United States,* Washington, 1903, p. 104.
[239] *The Case of His Britannic Majesty, etc.,* appendix 1, p. 94; for maps see appendix 2, nos. 1, 2, 3, 37.

(4). *The line from Portland Canal to the 56th Parallel.* The United States claimed that the line should be drawn straight, entirely disregarding the contour of the coast.

(5). *The Width of the Lisière.* This was the real problem. The British claimed that the words "coast" and "ocean" had been used indiscriminately and with identical meaning, but the Americans replied that the treaty specifically stated that the line should be drawn parallel to the sinuosities of the coast. It being impracticable to draw a line parallel to such a coast in such a country, the Americans claimed that it should be laid out at a distance of ten marine leagues from a line following the general trend of the headwaters of the many inlets.[240] Britain claimed that the boundary should parallel a line joining the headlands of the coast—the outlets of the fiords. Under this interpretation Britain would have access to the headwaters of certain inlets, for many of these narrow lanes extended more than 30 miles inland. Equally authentic maps were produced to support each case.

(6). *How the Lisière Should be Measured.* This was the same as question five. There were three possible alternatives. The boundary might be drawn (a) parallel to the general direction of the mainland coast, as the British contended; (b) parallel to the line separating Russian territorial waters from the Ocean; (c) parallel to a line joining the heads of the inlets, as the Americans desired.

(7). *Did Mountain Ranges exist?* The United States claimed that no ranges, upon which measurements could be based, existed;[241] Great Britain maintained that individual mountains joined by imaginary lines might be considered a range. This contention was not strongly urged, and thus Article III of the Treaty of 1825 was declared inapplicable.

---

[240] The United States had not invariably claimed this. In 1893 Dr. Mendenthal, surveying under the terms of the Convention of 1892, had directed that the line be drawn "not less than 30 nautical miles from the coast of the mainland, in a direction at right angles to its general trend." *The Case of His Britannic Majesty,* etc., appendix 1, p. 274. Dr. McGrath, surveying Taku Inlet, had issued a similar order. *Idem,* p. 276.

[241] *The Case of the United States,* p. 106: "Such mountains do not exist within ten marine leagues of the Coast."

D. The Decision of the Tribunal.—The difficulties which confronted the tribunal arose, primarily, from the fact that the boundary definition which these judges were to interpret was written by men who had but a scant knowledge of the physiographic conditions of the country they were dividing. Thus it was necessary to go behind the phraseology and find the motives of the negotiators of a treaty signed almost one hundred years before. The objects which the Russian and British diplomats of 1825 had attempted to accomplish had to be explored, and to be interpreted in the light of a scientific knowledge of the geographic conditions.

The tribunal met in London on September 3rd, and on October 20th the results of its deliberation were announced.[242]

From the first Canadians had feared that Lord Alverstone would be influenced by the exigencies of British foreign policy —a policy at this time primarily directed toward the establishment of better relations with the United States.[243] Whether or not the famous British jurist was, in fact, influenced by political motives is, and probably will remain, an open question. The fact is that on every question of importance he voted with the American representatives, and that thus, by a vote of four to two, the contentions of the United States were upheld; but it should also be noted that the Americans had the stronger case.

The point of departure of the boundary line was, as stated above, decided by agreement and with little discussion.

The question of how the boundary should be drawn through Portland Channel was one of the most difficult tasks before the tribunal, and, by Canadian authors, the decision in this instance is considered positive proof of the potency of political considerations over the actions of the tribunal. In truth, no other explanation seems adequate; there can be little doubt that the tribunal

[242] Bassett, *op. cit.*, p. 825.

[243] The Victoria *Colonist* of February 24, 1903 stated: "The tone of the British press toward the Boundary Commission foreshadows a surrender to the United States." The London *Saturday Review* of February 21, 1903 stated: "The directors of our policy are throwing our premier colony to the able diplomacy of the United States as a small pledge of our determination to be friends at all hazards."

in this instance accepted a compromise, which, however justified by the political considerations involved, was a direct violation of the judicial character of the court. Instead of accepting either the American or British claim *in toto,* the line was drawn through Tongas Passage, thus giving each country a portion of its claim, but entirely disregarding the real problem involved. The original negotiators might, logically, have intended the line to be drawn either as the British claimed or as the Americans claimed; certainly they had no intention of dividing the channel islands between the two. Alverstone urged that "Vancouver may have intended to include Tongas Passage in that name (Portland Channel) and . . . I think that the negotiators may well have thought that Portland Channel . . . issued into the sea by the two passages." [244] But this was a direct contradiction of Alverstone's own words on a previous occasion, when he had stated the Canadian contention to be "absolutely unanswerable." [245] Moreover, this compromise was not suggested until a deadlock seemed imminent.[246] There can be scarcely any doubt that Lord Alverstone's final pronouncement was merely an attempt to rationalize a political expedient, and that Mr. Aylesworth spoke the truth when he said: "There is not the slightest evidence anywhere . . . that either Vancouver or any subsequent explorer ever considered or so much as spoke of Portland Channel having two entrances to the Ocean or as including the Passage through which this Boundary line is now made to run." [247]

This particular decision cannot be viewed except as an immense mistake, for it cast doubt upon the judicial quality of the whole award. Such doubts do not seem justified by the other decisions, which all have ample basis in the arguments presented.

The third problem, regarding the course of the line from Cape Muzon to Portland Channel, was dependent upon the second, and the decision was made to accord with the boundary in the channel.

---

[244] *Alaska Boundary Tribunal Award,* London (Foreign Office), 1903, p. 994.
[245] Toronto *Globe,* October 21, 1903.
[246] *Ibid.*
[247] *Alaska Boundary Tribunal Award,* p. 949.

The fourth question was settled when the line was drawn directly from the head of the Portland Canal to the 56th parallel, disregarding the coast entirely, and thus favoring the American contention.

The fifth and sixth points were so closely allied that they may be treated as one. This was the most important of all the problems before the tribunal, and here again the American case won by a vote of 4 to 2. A careful study of the documents on either side seems to confirm the justice of this conclusion. The American counsel claimed that in the negotiation of the Treaty of 1825 the Russian diplomats had intended "to create an unbroken barrier along the entire waterfront of the continent." [248] Thus the boundary must be drawn parallel to a line joining the headwaters of all the larger inlets, for otherwise this *lisière* would not be intact. This view seems to be supported by a perusal of the records of the negotiations of 1824–1825.[249]

The British claim that individual mountains might be joined to form a chain was so weak that it easily succumbed to argument.

These, in summary, are the decisions of the tribunal.[250] In all but one case they seem justified by the facts, and yet that one case of political compromise tarnished the whole award. The two Canadian judges took the almost unprecedented and unfortunate action of refusing to sign the award.[251] This did not affect the validity of the findings, but it did crystallize public sentiment in Canada against the "political agreement." Sir Louis Jetté and Mr. Aylesworth issued a minority report in which they stated that they had refused to sign the award because they could "not

---

[248] *Case of the United States*, p. 52.

[249] *Fur Seal Arbitration Papers*, 1893, vol. IV. An *ex parte* but clear statement of the American case by the Hon. J. W. Foster may be found in *The National Geographic Magazine* for November, 1899.

[250] For text of the award see *Alaska Boundary Tribunal Award*.

[251] The best known precedent was the action of Lord Chief Cockburn at the Geneva Arbitration Tribunal of 1872. Scott, *Cases on International Law*, St. Paul, 1906, p. 718.

consider the finding of the tribunal as to the islands, entrance to Portland Channel, or as to the mountain line, a judicial one." [252]

E. Effect of the Decisions.—As was to be expected, the decisions of the tribunal were received with rejoicing in the United States. Lord Alverstone was praised for his impartiality evidenced in voting against his country, and the whole adjudication was looked upon as a triumph of American diplomacy.[253]

In Canada the award was almost universally condemned. This censure was directed not so much against the details of the award itself as against the methods employed in reaching these decisions. Two main lines of criticism were evidenced in the national press; first, the betrayal of Canadian interests by the mother country, for political reasons; and second, the American disregard of the convention stipulations in the selection of jurists.

With reference to the first point, the Vancouver *Province,* one of Canada's leading journals but published on the Pacific Coast where feeling was most intense, declared: "It shows that we cannot depend upon the Mother Country to protect our interests; it shows that we cannot depend on her to see common justice done us, when, by sacrificing us, she has an opportunity of catering to a sentiment which does her much less credit than she imagines." [254] The Victoria *Colonist* summarized the Canadian feeling thus: "About the decision we do not care. Our main consideration is the means by which it was arrived at. . . . The prevailing tone of the British Press has not been the necessity of maintaining Imperial rights, but the necessity of cultivating the friendship of the United States." [255] *Le Journal,* an influential French paper of Montreal, stated that "we find ourselves contemplating, not the decisions of an Arbitration Commission, but a diplomatic ar-

[252] *Canadian Associated Press,* October 20, 1903.

[253] Chicago *Tribune,* October 21, 1903; New York *Times,* October 21, 1903.

[254] Vancouver *Province,* October 21, 1903.

[255] Victoria *Colonist,* October 18, 1903.

rangement." [256] In a bitter mood the Rossland *Miner* exclaimed: "Perhaps we should be thankful that there is no territory left which grasping Americans can reach for, and complaisant British Commissioners give away." [257] This sentiment was again voiced as follows: "This is not the first time that British diplomacy has proven costly to Canada. Canada, however, accepted a 'loaded' Tribunal as a means of effecting settlements. The negotiations have gone against us and it is our duty to submit. . . . What Canada should do to protect herself in the future is a question which deserves and will undoubtedly receive deep consideration." [258]

Perhaps the most exact summary of the Canadian viewpoint is to be found in the editorial of the Manitoba *Free Press*, from which the following is quoted:

"We recognize, of course, that the Canadian case may have been the weaker of the two. If this were the case it is doubly unfortunate that the decision should have been reached by means that have left one of the parties to the dispute convinced that it has not been justly dealt with. . . . The merits of the case, to the satisfaction of one of the parties, can never be decided now. If Canada was right, the decision was lamentable; if she was wrong, it is calamitous that an impartial tribunal could not have made this clear. As it is, the damage is irreparable. Canadians, with very few exceptions, will accept without question the statements of their representatives that their interests were sacrificed; and the resulting resentment is certain to affect the attitude of Canada towards the United States, and, in a still greater degree, towards the Motherland." [259]

Such, unfortunately, was the reaction of Canada to the award of the Alaskan boundary tribunal. Had the United States been willing to submit her case to The Hague, or to an impartial juridical body, as Canada had desired,[260] the result would have been,

[256] *Le Journal* (Montreal), October 19, 1903.

[257] Rossland *Miner*, October 22, 1903.

[258] Toronto *World*, October 19, 1903. It may well be pointed out again that Canada alone certainly could not have made a better bargain with the United States.

[259] Manitoba *Free Press*, October 21, 1903.

[260] See above, p. 216.

in all probability, substantially the same, except that Canadians could not feel that they had been unfairly treated. The United States had the better case, and it is unfortunate that President Roosevelt should have taken such means to assure himself of victory. Had justices of the United States Supreme Court been appointed in the place of the two Senators, Canadian criticism of the award would not have been audible.[261] Under the circumstances, when faced with what they considered to be a "loaded" bench; when they saw what appeared to be incontrovertible proofs of political influence being used against their case; and when every decision of importance was decided against them, the chagrin of the Canadian people can be readily understood and appreciated.

That justice was done under the circumstances cannot but be regarded as a fortuitous circumstance; for once right was on the side of might. The United States gained her just deserts, but by means of which she cannot be proud; while many Canadians do not yet feel that a case supported in such a manner could have been sound.

The decision is still a matter of heated comment in certain parts of the Dominion, particularly in British Columbia and the Yukon, for the American *lisière* adds considerably to the difficulty of communication and shipment between British Columbia ports and Yukon mines. Unless, however, Alaska and the Yukon experience a very great revival of industry and trade, it is probable that this matter will gradually sink into the oblivion of the forgotten past.

It might perhaps be noted that suggestions have recently been made in British Columbia looking toward the purchase by Canada of part or all of the Alaskan panhandle. Even one port would perhaps satisfy this ambition and meet the very real needs of the case. With Alaska steadily depreciating in value (and population) it is possible that the United States will yet grant this concession —for a suitable consideration.

[261] This was suggested by Great Britain. *Alaskan Boundary Correspondence,* summarized in the Manitoba *Free Press,* October 23, 1903.

CHAPTER VI.

Minor Boundary Disputes

ALTHOUGH the problems of Maine, Oregon, and Alaska were the most important boundary questions to arise between the United States and Canada, they were not the only difficulties which developed in the demarcation of the territorial possessions of the two nations. The San Juan boundary dispute resulted from the carelessness or the lack of geographical knowledge of the negotiators of the Oregon treaty. The Lake of the Woods boundary was of very slight importance, but the question of jurisdiction over Bering Sea, and the seal herds which frequented it, was of a more vital import. This problem, though dealing with more than boundary definitions, has been included in this chapter for the sake of convenience.

I. THE SAN JUAN BOUNDARY

A. The Genesis of the Question.—The Treaty of 1846 settled the Oregon boundary question in its major details. The treaty was not, however, specific and exact in its delineations of the respective rights of the United States and Great Britain in regard to the islands situated between Vancouver Island and the mainland. Whether this lack of detailed specification was due to carelessness on the part of the negotiators, or was simply a result of the meager knowledge of the geography of the Pacific Coast current at the time, is immaterial. Article I of the treaty traces the boundary along the 49th parallel of north latitude "to the middle of the channel which separates the continent from Vancouver's Island, and thence southerly through the middle of the said channel, and of Fuca's straits to the Pacific Ocean: provided, however,

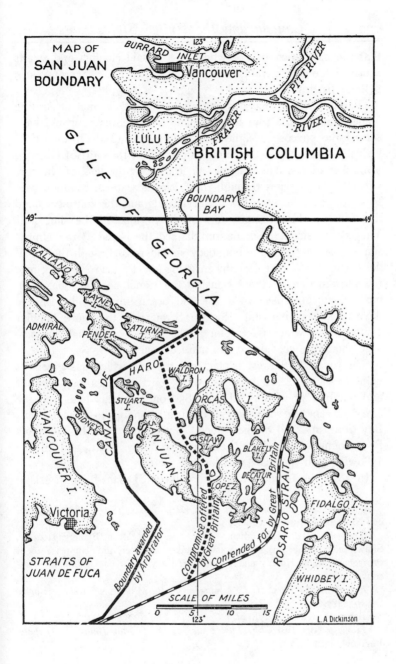

MAP OF
**SAN JUAN
BOUNDARY**

BURRARD INLET
123°
Vancouver
PITT RIVER

GULF
LULU I.
FRASER RIVER
BRITISH COLUMBIA

OF
BOUNDARY BAY
49°   49°

GEORGIA
GALIANO I.
MAYNE I.
ADMIRAL I.
PENDER I.
SATURNA I.
HARO
WALDRON I.
CANAL DE
STUART I.
ORCAS I.
SIDNEY I.
SAN JUAN I.
SHAW I.
BLAKELY I.
DECATUR I.
LOPEZ I.
ROSARIO STRAIT
FIDALGO I.

VANCOUVER I.

Victoria

Compromise offered by Great Britain
Contended for by Great Britain
Boundary awarded by Arbitrator

STRAITS OF
JUAN DE FUCA
WHIDBEY I.

SCALE OF MILES
0   5   10   15
123°

L. A. Dickinson

that the navigation of the whole of the said channel and straits south of the 49th parallel of north latitude remain free and open to both parties." [1]

Had there been one obvious and coherent channel separating Vancouver Island from the mainland, this definition would have served the purpose designed. Due, however, to the presence of a cluster of islands in the southern portion of the Gulf of Georgia, a number of possible channels made difficult the task of the surveyor. Two passages through these islands were in common use: Rosario Strait between the major islands and the continent; and the Canal de Haro, the waters of which touched the shores of Vancouver Island. Each nation claimed the islands, [2] the United States asserting that the boundary should pass through the Canal de Haro, and Great Britain insisting on Rosario Strait. Since the introduction of the steamship the Canal de Haro has been more frequently used by coast and ocean shipping, but in the days of the sailing ship Rosario Strait was the more popular route—a fact which gave color to the British claim that this passage should be considered the main channel.

San Juan, the largest island, and the one which has given its name to the whole controversy, was "fourteen miles long by four and one-half in width." [3] Until 1850 only Indians had used the island, except for some herds of cattle belonging to the Hudson's Bay Company, and the herdsmen. [4] But in that year the Hudson's Bay Company established a salmon-canning plant, and in the following year a "post" was located there. [5]

In 1852 the Oregon Legislature included San Juan in Island

---

[1] *Treaties and Conventions of the United States,* 1889, p. 375; *Federal and State Constitutions,* vol. II, p. 1484.

[2] These consisted of San Juan, Orcas, Lopez, Waldron, Blakely, Decatur, Shaw, and a number of smaller islets; taken together, they comprise about 170 square miles. Howay and Scofield, *History of British Columbia,* Vancouver, p. 301.

[3] *Report of the Hon. H. L. Langevin, C. B., Minister of Public Works,* Ottawa, 1872.

[4] Bancroft, *History of British Columbia,* San Francisco, 1887, p. 612.

[5] *Idem,* p. 607; Fish, *The Last Phase of the Oregon Boundary Dispute,* Portland, 1921, p. 27.

County, and when Washington Territory was created in 1853, the island became a part of Whatcom County. The sheriff of the county appeared on the island in 1854 when the company refused to pay the American taxes, seized a number of sheep and sold them at auction. He was driven off and pursued in the S. S. *Beaver* (the first steamer on the North Pacific Ocean) by company officials, but escaped.[6] Governor Douglas of Vancouver Island immediately sent a letter of harsh protest to Governor Stevens of Washington Territory, stating that he had orders from the home government "to treat those islands as part of the British Dominions." [7]

Relations became so unpleasant that in 1856 the American and British governments appointed commissioners in an attempt to solve the difficulty in a mutually satisfactory manner. Mr. Archibald Campbell, on behalf of the United States, and Captain James C. Prevost for Great Britain, met at Esquimalt on June 27, 1857.[8] After a careful study of the treaty and a survey of the hydrographic conditions, Prevost decided that Rosario Strait was the one intended by the negotiators of the Treaty of 1846; after an equally careful investigation, Mr. Campbell decided in favor of the Canal de Haro. From these conclusions neither commissioner would move. Mr. Crampton, British Ambassador at Washington, suggested to President Pierce that a compromise line be selected,[9] but this request was refused, as was also the proposal that the decision be left to the arbitration of representatives of Belgium, Switzerland, and Denmark.[10]

Pending a solution of the difficulty, matters had become peaceful on the island, when, suddenly, on June 27, 1859, Captain

[6] *British Colonist,* August 15, 1868.

[7] Douglas to Stevens, in *Washington Historical Quarterly,* vol. II, pp. 352–353.

[8] "Report of Archibald Campbell, February 22, 1868," *Senate Documents,* no. 20, 40th Cong., 2nd sess.

[9] Considering the conflicting claims, this would seem to have been the fairest settlement. Great Britain would have kept San Juan, but the Americans would have taken over half the total area in dispute. Fish, *op. cit.,* p. 58.

[10] Bancroft, *op. cit.,* p. 635.

George Pickett, acting under the orders of Brigadier-General
Harney, commandant of the Oregon Department, descended upon
the island with D Company of the 9th Infantry. Harney had taken
this action on his own initiative for the purpose of protecting
American settlers from Indian attacks, and "to resist all attempts
at interference by the British authorities." [11] The entire control
of the island was vested in Pickett's force. This action was a
breach of faith, and although applauded by the citizens of Washington, Harney was a source of considerable anxiety to his home
government.[12] Governor Douglas was ready to plunge the two
great nations into war, but fortunately Admiral Baynes, in charge
at Esquimalt, was a man of cooler mind, and he vetoed any pre-
cipitate action. The American Secretary of War sent General Winfield Scott to take temporary control in Oregon—an admirable
appointment, as General Scott was a man of clear understanding
and excellent judgment. He removed the American troops from
San Juan; arranged with Admiral Baynes for a joint occupation
to commence on March 30, 1860; and tried (though in this he
was unsuccessful) to persuade General Harney to accept a command in another field.[13]

Matters having been thus settled, General Scott departed for
the East. Scarcely had he left the Territory when General Harney
again proclaimed San Juan Island a part of Washington. Thereupon he was recalled to Washington and lightly reprimanded;
the legislature of the territory at the same time passed a resolution
of praise and gratitude, and nominated General Harney for the
Presidency of the Union.[14]

The people of Washington and Oregon Territories were, more-

---

[11] *Idem*, p. 618.

[12] The United States government considered his action "rash and impetuous," but he escaped censure because of his great popularity. *Puget
Sound Herald*, October 28, 1859.

[13] *Executive Documents*, no. 65, 36th Cong. 1st sess., pp. 28 ff.

[14] Bancroft, *op. cit.*, p. 633. Scott wondered "Whether it is safe in respect to our foreign relations, or just to the gallant officers and men of the
Oregon Department, to leave them longer at so great a distance subject to
the ignorance, passion and caprice of the headquarters of that department."
American State Papers: Executive Documents, no. 65, pp. 190–191. "I

over, deeply enraged against General Scott. Writing a short time
after this, a western editor declared: "When the result of General Scott's negotiations with the British authorities in regard to
the island of San Juan became known to the people of the Pacific
Coast there was an almost universal surprise and indignation in
regard to it. There were none to defend the action of the American commissioner"; an action "so disgraceful to the flag of his
country and so unworthy the commission he bore." [15]

During the Civil War the question of San Juan was forgotten
and it was not until 1871 that final action was taken to effect
a settlement. By the Treaty of Washington of that year, Great
Britain and the United States mutually agreed to leave the question to the decision of the Emperor of Germany.[16]

B. The Claims.—The British case rested on a very literal interpretation of the wording of the treaty.[17] The channel which
"separates the continent from Vancouver's Island," according to
the proponents of the imperial view, could apply only to Rosario
Strait, the strait nearest to the mainland. The Canal de Haro
did not divide "the continent from Vancouver's Island," because
it was already separated to the east by Rosario Strait. Again, the
Canal de Haro in part of its course took a westerly direction,
while Rosario Strait bore "southerly" in accordance with the
treaty terms. A more potent argument for the British claim was

found General Harney and Captain Pickett proud of their conquest of the
island and quite jealous of any interference therewith on the part of higher
authority." *Idem*, p. 212.

[15] Portland *Daily Advertiser*, Jan. 24, 1860. The editor went on to explain that Gen. Scott was really angling for a Presidential nomination, and
that "his unworthy concessions to the insolent demands of the British officials were intended to conciliate the commercial interests of the eastern
cities, to which a war with England must prove exceedingly injurious, if
not fatal."

[16] Cushing, *The Treaty of Washington*, New York, 1873; *Executive
Documents*, no. 1, pt. 2, 42nd Cong., 3rd sess.

[17] *The Case of Her Britannic Majesty Submitted to the Arbitration and
Award of His Majesty the Emperor of Germany*, London, 1871. The
British argument is to be found also in the *Edinburgh Review* for April,
1864.

found in the fact that Rosario Strait was used almost invariably by the mariners of the time. This strait was, moreover, the one marked on Vancouver's maps,[18] and certain official American charts showed the boundary passing through Rosario Strait.[19]

The most valid claim of the United States was founded upon the acknowledged fact that the only reason which led the negotiators of the Oregon Treaty to depart from the 49th parallel was to give all of Vancouver Island to Great Britain.[20] The greater width and depth of the Canal de Haro was also urged in an attempt to prove it the logical channel, and evidence seemed to indicate that some, at least, of the original negotiators had the Canal de Haro in mind. Mr. McLane, American minister in London, had, in 1846, reported to his home government the outline of a proposal about to be made by the British government, in which the Canal de Haro was specifically mentioned.[21] In an address to the Senate, Benton spoke of the line passing through this channel—a statement to which the British authorities took no exception.[22] In refutation of the arguments favoring Rosario Strait, the American case enumerated maps of both countries in which the boundary was drawn through the Canal de Haro.[23] Bancroft contended that "southerly" was intended only in contradistinction to "northerly"; and he further pointed out that the

[18] Crampton wrote to the United States State Department on January 13, 1848: "It is believed that only one channel—that, namely, laid down by Vancouver in his chart—has, in this part of the gulf, been surveyed and used; and it seems natural to suppose that the negotiators of the Oregon convention, in employing the word 'channel,' had that particular channel in view." Quoted in Viscount Milton, *The San Juan Boundary Question,* London, 1869, p. 47.

[19] Such as Preston's map, issued by the Surveyor-General's office in Oregon City on October 21, 1852.

[20] See G. Bancroft, "Memorial on the Canal de Haro, Presented to the German Emperor," *British Columbia Archives; Senate Documents,* no. 29, 40th Cong., 2nd sess. A summary of this memorial may be found in *Putnam's Magazine* for September, 1870.

[21] *Senate Documents,* no. 29, 40th Cong., 2nd sess, appendix 42, p. 47.

[22] *Idem,* appendix 43, p. 50.

[23] *Senate Documents,* no. 29, 40th Cong., 2nd sess.

Canal de Haro had been surveyed and used by the Spanish and the Americans.[24]

It is probable that the truth of the case was most clearly expressed by Ambassador Pakenham when he said: "It is my belief that neither Lord Aberdeen nor Mr. McLane nor Mr. Buchanan possessed at that time a sufficiently accurate knowledge of the geography or hydrography of the region in question to enable them to define more accurately what was the intended line of boundary than is expressed in the words of the treaty." [25] He added further that neither of the lines suggested could "exactly fulfill the conditions of the treaty which, according to their literal tenor, would require the line to be traced along the middle of the channel (meaning the whole intervening space) which separates the continent from Vancouver's Island." [26] Finally, a modern scholar has summarized the matter thus: "If the British diplomats had in mind the Rosario channel along which Vancouver had sailed, as traced on his chart, they kept it securely secret: and if the Americans had Haro Strait in mind they refrained from saying so. The terms of the treaty fitted either strait, or perhaps it would be more nearly correct to say, fitted neither strait." [27]

C. The Decision.—The United States was fortunate in having as Ambassador to Berlin a gentleman of the reputation and wide learning of George Bancroft. When the problem of San Juan was left to the arbitration of the German Emperor, Mr. Bancroft prepared and presented the American case. Admiral Prevost, who as Captain Prevost had negotiated with Mr. Campbell some twelve years before, presented the British argument. Due to the insistence of the United States, the Emperor was requested to deliver a decision designating either the Canal de Haro or Rosario Strait— no compromise was admissible.

On October 21, 1872, Emperor William delivered his verdict in the following terms:

[24] Bancroft, *op. cit.;* Fish, *op. cit.,* p. 57.
[25] Quoted in Milton, *op. cit.,* p. 44.
[26] *Idem,* p. 43.
[27] Howay and Schofield, *op. cit.,* vol. I, p. 324.

"The claim of the Government of the United States,—viz., that the line of boundary between the dominions of His Britannic Majesty and the United States should be through the Canal de Haro—is most in accordance with the true interpretation of the Treaty concluded between the Government of His Britannic Majesty and that of the United States of America, dated at Washington, June 15, 1846.

William." [28]

Thus was finally settled as fairly and satisfactorily as might be, the final westward link of the boundary between the United States and the British Dominions on the continent of North America. The islands have proven of little real value, and the memory of the contest for sovereignty is fast fading. Residents of the city of Victoria may still sigh as they view San Juan Island lying almost at their doors, but even they are resigned and the rest of Canada has forgotten.

2. THE LAKE OF THE WOODS BOUNDARY

The Treaty of 1783, which ended the American War of Independence, outlined the boundary which was to separate the revolted colonies from British North America, but, as has been pointed out before, this treaty was drawn up by men who possessed only the most elementary and inadequate knowledge of the geographical conditions with which they dealt so confidently. The result was a long succession of disputes which for many years endangered the peace, and disturbed the relations, of Britain and America. One of the smallest and least momentous of these disputes was that connected with the Lake of the Woods.

A glance at a map of the boundary between Minnesota and Manitoba shows the line running due east along the 49th parallel of north latitude well into the center of the Lake of the Woods, It then takes a sharp turn to the north, crossing a broad penin-

[28] *Correspondence Respecting the Award of the Emperor of Germany*, London. 1873, p. 3.

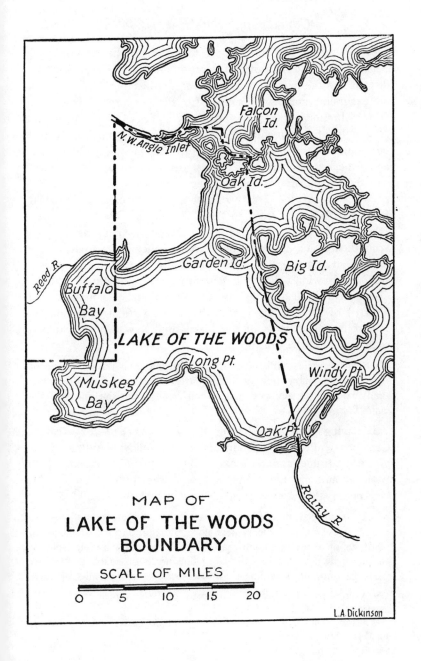

MAP OF
LAKE OF THE WOODS
BOUNDARY

SCALE OF MILES

0   5   10   15   20

L.A. Dickinson

sula to meet a narrow inlet of the lake on the northern side. Thence it proceeds through the center of the lake in a southerly direction to the head of Rainy River. Thus, the line seems to take an excursion northward simply for the purpose of cutting off from Manitoba this wide peninsula. The explanation of this seemingly unaccountable divergence from the straight line is to be found in the inadequate geographical knowledge of British and American diplomats of the last two decades of the eighteenth and the early years of the nineteenth centuries.

Article II of the Treaty of 1783, after tracing the boundary from the Atlantic Ocean to the Lake of the Woods, proceeded, "through the said Lake to the northwestern point thereof, and from thence on a due west course to the River Mississippi. . . ." [29] Doubts shortly arose as to the possibility of meeting the Mississippi by drawing a line due west from the point thus designated. Consequently, in the Treaty of Amity and Commerce (Jay Treaty) of 1794, it was agreed that if, as a result of a joint survey of the headwaters of the Mississippi it was proven that no such line could be drawn, then

"the two parties will proceed by amicable negotiation to regulate the boundary line in that quarter . . . according to justice and material convenience, and in conformity with the intent of the said Treaty." [30]

It having been agreed after the War of 1812–1815 that the Canadian-United States boundary should follow the 49th parallel of north latitude from the Lake of the Woods to the summit of the Stony mountains, the following article was approved in the Convention of 1818 between Great Britain and the United States:

"It is agreed that a line drawn from the most northwestern point of the Lake of the Woods along the 49th parallel of the north latitude, or, if the said point shall not be in the 49th parallel, then that a line drawn from the said point due north or south as the case may be until the said line shall intersect the said parallel of north

[29] A provision of the Definitive Treaty of Peace signed at Paris, September 5, 1783, Malloy, *op. cit.,* vol. I, p. 587.

[30] A provision of the Treaty of Amity and Commerce, signed November 19, 1794. Malloy, *op. cit.,* p. 593.

latitude, and from the point of such intersection due west along and with the said parallel, shall be the line of demarkation between the territories of the United States and those of His Britannic Majesty." [31]

It was the wording of this article which ultimately caused the idiosyncrasy of the modern boundary.

In the same year a joint boundary commission was appointed and by 1826 the line had been traced through the Great Lakes, and the "most northwestern" corner of the Lake of the Woods had been decided upon and marked.[32]

It was not until April, 1870, that difficulties arose over the boundary defined in 1818. In that month, however, a party of American engineers reported that a Hudson Bay Company's post to the north of Pembina was, in fact, on American soil. This report led President Grant to insert in his annual message a plea for the final settlement and demarcation of this part of the international boundary.[33] Congress and the British government having agreed, a joint commission was appointed. Archibald Campbell, who represented the United States in the San Juan boundary dispute, was the American commissioner, and Captain D. R. Cameron, R.A., was associated with him on behalf of Great Britain.

The first meeting was held on September 16, 1871, at Pembina, and here the methods of procedure were agreed upon.[34] After a careful search the monument raised in 1826 to mark the northwestern point of the Lake of the Woods was discovered, and although the British commissioner at first refused to agree, this point was ultimately accepted as correct.[35] The temporary refusal of Captain Cameron was made in the hope that some political arrangement might be made by the home governments by which Canada could retain the peninsula which jutted out into the lake just south of the "most northwestern" point. On this peninsula

[31] Article 2 of the Convention of 1818, signed October 20, 1818. Malloy, *op. cit.*, p. 632.

[32] Begg, *History of the North-West*, Toronto, 1894, vol. II, p. 152.

[33] Annual message of the President, 41st Cong., 1st sess, December 5, 1870.

[34] *Report of the United States Commissioner*, Washington, 1878, p. 22.

[35] *Idem*, pp. 23 ff.

the Canadians already had a primitive post, and a wagon road joining it to Fort Garry—afterwards Winnipeg. As the home governments could not reach any agreement, Captain Cameron complied with his instructions and agreed to the American contention.

This matter settled, the remainder of the problem was purely scientific, and on May 29, 1876, the reports were certified and duly attested in London.[36]

Although comparatively unimportant, the final demarcation of this section of the boundary was unnecessarily exact, and the peninsula in dispute might well have been surrendered by the United States. The result would have been a minute financial and territorial loss, and in view of the Canadian post established on the peninsula, such an action would have been very well received in the Dominion. Legally, however, the United States was only maintaining her rights, and the territory was properly allotted.

3. THE BERING SEA ARBITRATION

A. The Problem.—By an imperial ukase issued on the 7th of September, 1821, Alexander I, Emperor of Russia, granted to the Russian-American Company exclusive rights in commerce and fishing on the west coast of North America above the 51st degree of north latitude.[37] He further asserted the sole jurisdiction of Russia over Bering Sea to a distance of one hundred Italian miles from the coast. Foreign vessels violating this edict would be liable to capture and confiscation.[38] John Quincy Adams, American Secretary of State, joined with the British government in a strong protest against these pretensions, and, as a result, in the Treaties of 1824 and 1825, negotiated respectively with the United States and Great Britain, Russia formally agreed

[36] *Idem.* p. 27.
[37] See Chapter V.
[38] de Martens, *Traité du Droit International*, Paris, 1883, p. 500.; Scott, *Cases on International Law*, St. Paul, 1906, p. 446; *American State Papers; Foreign Relations, 1890*, p. 439.

to restrict her claim of exclusive jurisdiction "to the reach of a cannon-shot from shore." [39]

The Emperor of Russia, in a convention signed at Washington on March 30, 1867, transferred to the United States the Russian title to "all the territory and dominion now possessed on the continent of North America and in the adjacent islands." [40] The eastern boundary of the territory thus ceded was defined in the Treaty of 1825 with Great Britain.[41] The western boundary commencing in Bering Straits proceeded "due north without limitation." South of the Straits the line ran through Bering Sea "to the meridian of 172° west longitude : thence from the intersection of that meridian in a southwesterly direction . . . to the meridian of 193° west longitude so as to include in the territory conveyed the whole of the Aleutian Islands east of that meridian." [42]

The particular value of Alaska at this time was due to the abundance of fur-bearing animals, and the presence of the extensive seal-fisheries which were centered about the Pribiloff Islands. The sealing industry had commenced as early as 1706 when the Russian ship *Vladimir* had taken two thousand pelts to an Asiatic port.[43] The business as carried on by the Russian-American Company was purely a land enterprise, and it was not until 1866 that a certain Captain Hugh McKay perceived the possibilities of pelagic sealing. This gentleman was a British sailing master using Victoria as his base, and by 1890 that picturesque port had become the center of a considerable sealing industry. At its height, more than fifty ships were employed annually in the sealing business for Canadian firms.

So successful were the efforts of these companies that the number of seals annually reaching the breeding grounds on the Pribiloff Islands rapidly decreased, and the danger of total extermination became serious.[44] The American firm of Hutchinson, Kobel

[39] Hershey, *op. cit.,* pp. 321 ff. This was the original basis of the three-mile limit. Malloy, *op. cit.,* vol. II, pp. 1512–1514.

[40] Malloy, *op. cit.,* vol. II, p. 1521.

[41] *American State Papers: Foreign Relations, 1890,* p. 503.

[42] Malloy, *op. cit.,* vol. II, p. 1521. article I.

[43] Howay and Scofield, *History of British Columbia,* vol. I, p. 458 ff.

[44] Stanley-Brown, "Bering Sea Controversy," *Yale Review,* vol. II, p. 196 ff.

and Company had leased the Pribiloff rookeries from the United States government in 1869, but their lease was shortly transferred to the Alaska Commercial Company. This company, like its predecessors, confined its activities to the capture of the seals during the breeding season when the animals were helpless on the rocks of St. Paul, St. George, and other islands. The profits of the company soon began to suffer serious depreciation, due to the diminished size of the herds, which in turn resulted largely from the pelagic activities of Canadian ships (a few Americans, Russians, and Japanese also engaged in this business), and to the reduced price received in the world markets as a result of this competition.

A number of regulatory statutes were enacted by the American government with a view to the conservation of the seal herds, but it was not until 1881 that, as a result of repeated solicitations made by the Alaska Company, any drastic action was taken. In that year a United States Treasury order was issued which, inferentially at least, proclaimed the greater portion of Bering Sea as a *mare clausum*.[45] This ruling was confirmed in 1886 by Mr. Manning, then Secretary of the Treasury,[46] and in August of that year three Canadian vessels were seized in Bering Sea. Although these vessels had been captured at a distance of over sixty miles from the nearest land, they were confiscated, condemned and sold,[47] their masters were found guilty of killing seals "within the limits of the Alaska Territory or the waters thereof," [48] and were fined. Judge Dawson of Sitka, in condemning these vessels, had acted under direct instructions from the Attorney-General of the United States, and there could be no mistaking the issue,[49] although Secretary Blaine later denied that

[45] Acting Secretary of the Treasury French to Collector of the Port of San Francisco, March 12, 1881, in Henderson, *American Diplomatic Questions*, New York, 1901, p. 15.

[46] *Idem*, p. 16. See also, "Fur Seal Question," in *American Journal of International Law*, vol. I, p. 742.

[47] "Report of the Canadian Privy Council, May 16, 1887," *State Papers*, vol. LXXIX, p. 1266.

[48] *Revised Statutes*, sec. 1956.

[49] Admiral Seymour to the Admiralty, August 24, 1886, in *State Papers*, vol. LXXIX, p. 1241; Moore, *op. cit.*, vol. I, p. 773.

a claim to Bering Sea as a *mare clausum* had ever been made. At that time he declared that the Canadians were arrested because engaged in a traffic that was *contra bonos mores*.[50] The British government entered an immediate and formal protest.[51] In the following year five more Canadian vessels were captured, and the British government, actuated by the intense feeling aroused in the Dominion, again vigorously protested. During 1888 Secretary Bayard attempted to arrange an international conference, but at the request of the Canadian government, which was preparing a monograph on the problem, Great Britain withdrew and the projected conference was never convened.[52]

Throughout this period popular resentment had been rising in Canada against what were considered to be the arbitrary actions of the American authorities. The sealing industry in Victoria was threatened with disaster. "It is monstrous," wrote the editor of the Ottawa *Journal*, "that a vessel should be seized on the open sea, its contents rifled, itself confiscated, mayhap its owners jailed, all on the strength of a single nation's self-authorized legislation." [53] The Victoria *Colonist* was no less emphatic: "The idea of cutting off a part of the ocean by a line in great part purely imaginary, and then calling the part so cut off a closed sea, is an act for which there is neither law nor reason." [54] The same paper expressed its opinion of the motives actuating the Washington government when it stated that "the cruiser *Rush* was the Alaska Fur Company's scarecrow—nothing else." [55] The matter aroused in Canada a feeling decidedly hostile to the United States, but it must be recognized that the Canadian methods of sealing were rapidly destroying the herds and that a few years more would have ended the industry entirely. The methods employed and

[50] Hershey, *op. cit.*, p. 322, note.

[51] Sackville-West to Bayard, October 19, 1886, in *State Papers*, vol. LXXIX, p. 1285. Also Browning, "Bering Sea Controversy," *Law Quarterly Review*, vol. VII, p. 128.

[52] The negotiations from September 1, 1866, to December 12, 1888, are to be found in *American State Papers*, vol. LXXIX, pp. 1240–1306.

[53] Ottawa *Journal*, July 31, 1889.

[54] Victoria *Colonist*, August 2, 1889.

[55] *Idem*, August 22, 1889.

arguments used by the United States were unfortunate, but some serious action was necessary.

During the years 1888 and 1889 the problem of the Bering Sea fisheries was canvassed in all of its phases by American legislators and press.[56] In the latter year five more Canadian ships were seized, while three others were warned to leave the sea. As one American historian has phrased it, "in Great Britain public opinion became much aroused, and in Canada it was still more excited. In the United States Republicans and Democrats vied with each other in 'twisting the Lion's tail.' "[57] Nor was international friendship increased by the imperious tones of Lord Salisbury, or the crude and prejudiced bluntness of Secretary Blaine.[58] Ultimately, however, the practical commonsense of the two nations prevailed, a *modus vivendi* was agreed upon as a temporary expedient,[59] and after many fruitless attempts the diplomatic obstructions were overcome, and a treaty of arbitration was signed on February 29, 1892. By this treaty the signatory powers agreed to refer the problem for settlement to a judicial tribunal composed as follows: two members were to be appointed by the President of the United States; two by the Queen of Great Britain; and one each by the President of the French Republic, the King of Italy, and the King of Sweden. The gentlemen appointed were required to be "jurists of distinguished reputation in their respective countries," and the fourteenth article provided that "the high contracting parties agree to consider the result of the proceedings of the Tribunal of Arbitration as a full, perfect, and final settlement of all the questions referred to it by the arbitrators."[60]

B. The Tribunal and the Five Points.—The first session of the tribunal was held in Paris on February 23, 1893. The judges

[56] Foster in *The North American Review* for December, 1895.

[57] Johnson, *America's Foreign Relations*, New York, 1916, vol. I, p. 102.

[58] *Ibid; American State Papers*, vol. LXXXII, pp. 202–291; *idem*, vol. LXXXIII, pp. 306–357; *idem*, vol. LXXXIV, pp. 453–589.

[59] *State Papers*, vol. LXXXIV, pp. 482–488; *Senate Executive Documents*, no. 55; 52nd Cong., 1st sess.

[60] Malloy, *op. cit.*, p. 744–747.

appointed by the President of the United States were, the Hon. John M. Harlan of the Supreme Court and Senator John T. Morgan. The Right Hon. Lord Hannan, of the High Court of Appeal, and the Hon. Sir John Thompson, Minister of Justice and Attorney-General of Canada, were appointed by the British Crown. The neutral arbitrators were: Baron Alphonse de Courcel of France; the Marquis Emilio Visconti Venosta of Italy; and Mr. Gregers Gram, a minister of state of Norway and Sweden.[61]

The questions to be decided were summarized in five articles, as follows: [62]

"I. What exclusive jurisdiction in the sea now known as the Bering's Sea, and what exclusive rights in the seal fisheries therein, did Russia assert, and exercise prior and up to the time of the transfer of Alaska to the Uited States?

"II. How far were these claims of jurisdiction as to the seal fisheries recognized and conceded by Great Britain?

"III. Was the body of water now known as the Bering's Sea included in the phrase 'Pacific Ocean,' as used in the Treaty of 1825 between Great Britain and Russia; and what rights, if any, in the Bering's Sea were held and exclusively exercised by Russia after the said Treaty?

"IV. Did not all the rights of Russia as to jurisdiction, and as to the seal fisheries in Bering Sea east of the water boundary in the Treaty between the United States and Russia of the 30th of March, 1867, pass unimpaired to the United States under that Treaty?

"V. Has the United States any right, and, if so, what right, of protection of property in the fur seals frequenting the Islands of the United States in Bering Sea, when such seals are found outside the ordinary three-mile limit?"

The two nations further agreed that if the foregoing questions were settled in such a way that "the concurrence of Great Britain is necessary to the establishment of regulations for the proper protection and preservation of the fur seal . . . the Aribtrators shall then determine what concurrent regulations . . . are neces-

[61] Johnson, *op. cit.*, vol. I, p. 102.
[62] Moore, *op. cit.*, p. 801.

sary." [63] Provision was also made for the determination of an indemnity if the tribunal found that the United States had exceeded its legal right in confiscating Canadian vessels.

C. The American Case.—The case of the United States government was carefully prepared, and was presented by attorneys of outstanding ability.[64] Although Mr. Blaine had distinctly stated that the United States did not regard Bering Sea as a *mare clausum*, it seems impossible to interpret otherwise the claims of the American case. In the argument the United States declared that Russia had acquired a proscriptive right to sovereignty in Bering Sea through immemorial use. Alexander I had claimed this right in the ukase of 1821, and Russia had enjoyed it undisturbed until 1867 [65] when it was transferred inviolate to the government of the United States. The case declared emphatically that Russia had ceded all her rights to land and sea in North America to the United States in 1867. In support of this claim the American case cited the various acts of Congress; the letters of the Treasury Department; and the judicial decisions in connection with the confiscated vessels. It was further argued that the term "Pacific Ocean," as used in the treaties of 1824 and 1825, did not apply to Bering Sea, and that various actions taken by Russia between 1825 and 1867 confirmed her title to undisputed sovereignty in Bering Sea. On the fifth question before the tribunal, the American contention was susceptible of more logical and more plausible support. The United States claimed "a right of protection and property in the fur seals frequenting the Pribiloff Islands when found outside the ordinary three mile limit, based upon the established principles of the common and the civil law, upon the practice of nations, upon the laws of natural history, and upon the common interests of mankind." [66] A long description of the life and habits of the fur seal was detailed, and the fact that the

[63] Article 7. Malloy, *op. cit.*, vol. I, p. 746.

[64] Moore, *op. cit.*, p. 805.

[65] This was, of course, absurd, as Russia had specifically given up her claim in the Convention of 1824. See above, p. 195.

[66] *American Case, Fur Seal Arbitration Tribunal,* Washington, 1892, pt. 2, p. 295 ff.

seal herds regularly resorted to the Pribiloff Islands was stressed. The herds spent every breeding season on this American territory, they left only in search of food, and they were, in fact, domestic animals in which the United States claimed an exclusive property right. Argument by analogy in support of the claim to supervision and protection beyond the three mile limit was based upon the British defense of the Irish oyster fisheries, the Scotch herring fisheries, and the pearl beds of Australia and Ceylon. Finally, the case demonstrated that if pelagic sealing continued without restriction, in a very few years the whole seal herd would be exterminated, resulting in an irreparable loss to mankind as a whole.

D. The British Case.[67]—Having pointed out that Bering Sea was the common highway to and from the Arctic Ocean, the northern part of the Yukon territory, and the Mackenzie River, the British case maintained that it must be "an open sea in which all nations of the world have a right to navigate and fish. The British case demonstrated by a series of historical notes that Russia had never before 1821 "asserted or exercised" any rights in the north Pacific to the exclusion of other nations. This claim was supported by an overwhelming mass of historical data including the works of almost every noted authority on the region.[68] The imperial ukase of 1821 was the only attempt on the part of Russia to claim sovereign rights in Bering Sea, and this claim "was made the subject of immediate and emphatic protest by Great Britain and the United States of America." Russia, then, "unequivocally withdrew her claims." The treaties of 1824 and 1825 declared and recognized the right of subjects of the United States and Great Britain to navigate and fish in all parts of the sea beyond the territorial limit of three statute miles.[69] Between 1825 and 1867 these rights were freely exercised by the vessels of many nations. The Treaty of 1867 drew a water boundary merely for

[67] *The Case of Her Britannic Majesty, Fur Seal Arbitration Tribunal,* London, 1892.

[68] For references see Moore, *op. cit.,* p. 317.

[69] See above.

the purpose of dividing the Russian from the American islands, and no intention of giving dominion over the open sea was implied or expressed. In correspondence with the Russian government in 1882, the American Department of State had been told that the Imperial government had claimed no jurisdiction beyond the recognized limit of three miles.

In regard to the claim of the United States to possess property rights in, and protectional jurisdiction over, the seals when beyond the generally recognized limit of territorial waters, the British case maintained that this protection was entirely without precedent; that American citizens had engaged in pelagic sealing; and that protective rights extended only to the boundary of territorial jurisdiction.

Each nation presented a rebuttal of the opening arguments in a counter case. These counter cases presented elaborate and lengthy contentions, but they altered in no material sense the fundamental claims of the two nations.

E. The Decision.[70]—Argument having been completed by the 10th of July, the tribunal thenceforth met behind closed doors to discuss the nature and wording of the award. These secret discussions continued until August 14th, and on the following day the decision was made public.

The first question, as to the "exclusive jurisdiction" and "exclusive rights in the seal fisheries," was decided as follows, by a vote of five to two (the American justices dissenting):

"By the Ukase of 1821 Russia claimed jurisdiction in the sea now known as 'the Bering's sea' to the extent of 100 Italian miles from the coasts and islands belonging to her; but in the course of the negotiations which led to the conclusion of the Treaties of 1824 with the United States, and of 1825 with Great Britain, Russia admitted that her jurisdiction in the said sea should be restricted to the reach of cannon-shot from the shore; and it appears that from that time up to the time of the cession of Alaska to the United States, Russia never asserted in fact, or exercised,

[70] See Malloy, *op. cit.*, vol. I, p. 751.

any exclusive rights in the seal-fisheries therein, beyond the ordinary limit of territorial waters."

On a similar division the tribunal declared that "Great Britain did not recognize or concede any claim upon the part of Russia to exclusive jurisdiction as to the seal fisheries in Bering Sea outside of the ordinary territorial waters."

Regarding the application of the term "Pacific Ocean" as used in the Treaty of 1825, the arbitrators unanimously decided: "The body of water now known as Bering Sea was included in the phrase 'Pacific Ocean' as used in the Treaty of 1825 between Great Britain and Russia." Further, the award declared that "no exclusive rights of jurisdiction in Bering Sea and no exclusive rights as to the seal fisheries therein were held or exercised by Russia outside of the ordinary territorial waters after the Treaty of 1825." Senator Morgan alone voted against this decision.

The tribunal decided unanimously that all rights previously held by Russia passed unimpaired to the United States by the treaty of March 30, 1867.

As to the rights of property and protection enjoyed in and over the seal herd by the United States, the Tribunal declared: "The United States has not any right of protection or property in the fur seals frequenting the islands of the United States in Bering Sea when such seals are found outside the ordinary three mile limit." Here again the two American judges voted against the remainder of the tribunal.

The legal points at issue having been very definitely decided against the United States, the arbitrators proceeded, in accordance with the terms of the treaty, to draw up regulations for the control of the sealing industry. A set of nine regulations was approved which decided the time, method, and place of legal sealing "outside the jurisdictional limits of the respective governments." No seals were to be taken within 60 miles of the Pribiloff Islands. East of longitude 180° and north of the 35th parallel of north latitude there was to be a closed season each year from May 1st to July 31st. Only sailing vessels bearing special licenses could engage in the industry. Indians hunting for their personal benefit were exempt, but all others engaged in sealing were to be subject to supervision by either government. No use was to be made of firearms, nets, or explosives. These regulations were to remain in force for five years, but could be abolished or modified by common agreement. They were to be examined every five years with a view to revision.

The tribunal further urged: (1) the desirability of supplementary legislation by the governments of Canada and the United States; (2) a closed season everywhere for two years; and (3) the enactment of municipal measures to give effect to the regulations determined upon by the tribunal.

As the seizures of Canadian vessels had been declared illegal, the question of a financial indemnity now arose. The British claims amounted to $542,169.26 with interest at seven per cent.[71] On August 21, 1894, Mr. Gresham offered a lump sum of $425,-000 in full payment—an offer at once accepted by Great Britain. But the American Congress was at that moment in an uncompromising mood and it refused to pass the appropriation.[72] Thereupon a joint commission was appointed by the two governments, and after discussions lasting until December, 1897,[73] Great Britain was awarded the sum of $473,151.26—the money being duly voted by Congress.

There can be no reasonable doubt that, on questions of international law, the contentions of the United States were ill-founded. The arguments presented by the counsel, and the dissenting opinions of the American members of the tribunal do not carry conviction, and in the opinion of all modern and reputable authorities the American case was not legally tenable. It was unfortunate that America, who had ever prided herself upon being the foremost nation in declaring the inviolability of property at sea, should thus flagrantly and illegally violate the very principles for which she had so long and bravely contended.

F. *The Reception of the Award and Further Developments.*—
Public opinion in Canada was gratified by the legal justification

[71] Johnson, *op. cit.*, vol. II, pp. 104–105.
[72] *State Papers*, vol. LXXXVII, p. 1134.
[73] *Idem*, vol. XXVIII, pp. 8 ff.

of the British case. But this gratification was tempered with doubt in regard to the probable effect that the regulations would exert upon the Canadian sealing industry. The Ottawa *Citizen* stated that "while the Arbitrators had solemnly recorded their judgment that the United States' contentions were untenable, they had, nevertheless, adopted provisions for the future government, of the industry which practically handed it over to the Americans." [74] The editor of the Victoria *Colonist* wrote: "These Regulations as effectively close the sea as if there had been an actual recognition of the claims of the Americans to jurisdiction." [75] These typical quotations fairly voice the opinion of the majority of the Canadian people, who, being unaware of, or refusing to credit, the terrible destruction consequent upon pelagic sealing, could not appreciate the imperative necessity of such strict control. Although not always accepted with the best of grace, the regulations were, in almost every case, scrupulously obeyed.[76]

In the United States the award was viewed in a different light. Chagrined at the summary treatment meted out to the American case, the people of the United States, nevertheless, soon realized that in securing the regulations they had in fact won their case.[77] "The decision," said the New York *World,* "seems to be against the United States. Really it gives the government and its lessee, the fur company, all that was rightly asked." [78] Mr. Phelps, one of the American counsel before the tribunal of arbitration, declared that "the stringent regulations propounded on the restriction of pelagic sealing will amount . . . to a substantial prohibition of it, and give the United States all the fruits they would have obtained by a decree in favor of the claim of right." [79]

At the end of the five-year period during which the regulations were to be operative, matters tended to return to their previous lawless state—a condition that was intensified by the growing

[74] Ottawa *Citizen,* August 16, 1893.
[75] Victoria *Colonist,* August 16, 1893.
[76] Henderson, *op. cit.,* pp. 41–42.
[77] *Ibid.*
[78] New Work *World,* August 18, 1893.
[79] *The Empire,* August 17, 1893.

competition of Japanese sealing vessels.[80] Although the United
States forbade its citizens to engage in pelagic sealing, the Canadian government took no such action, and general dissatisfaction
was expressed in the United States.[81] After a great deal of discussion the matter was referred, with many other Canadian-American problems, to a joint tribunal composed of six representatives
of each country. This tribunal began its sessions at Quebec on
August 23, 1898, but, owing to trouble over the Alaskan Boundary
question, it dissolved with nothing material accomplished. In 1897
a provisional treaty was signed by Russia, Japan, and the United
States, but as the British government refused to acquiesce in its
terms, it was never enforced.[82]

After more than a decade of futile attempts at agreement and
regulation, a fifteen-year agreement was signed by Russia, Japan,
Canada, and the United States. By this agreement of July 7, 1912,
there was to be no pelagic sealing north of the 35th parallel of
north latitude. The United States was to divide its catch as follows: 70% for herself; 15% to Canada; 15% to Japan. Japan
was to give Canada 10% of her total catch, and the same amount
to Russia and the United States. Finally, Russia was to divide 30%
of her catch equally between Canada and Japan. By these terms
the United States received a practical monopoly, but agreed to
apportion her gains among those who had been her competitors.
By 1912 the annual catch of Canada, Russia, and Japan was quite
insignificant.[83]

The award of the Paris Tribunal ended the halcyon days of
the Canadian sealing fleet, but had the indiscriminate slaughter
of pregnant and nursing animals continued, as in the years from
1865 to 1890, the whole herd would shortly have been exterminated. Even under present conditions the industry is of no primary
importance, and the future does not appear to offer prospects of
material improvement, unless some more effectual method of international control and conservation is developed.

[80] Hershey, *op. cit.*, p. 323, note.
[81] Johnson, *op. cit.*, p. 105.
[82] *Idem*, pp. 54–55.
[83] Moore, *op. cit.*, pp. 155 ff.

CHAPTER VII

The Fisheries Controversy

I. A CENTURY OF CONTENTION

THE fishing banks of Newfoundland and Labrador provided the incentive for the first industrial activity undertaken by Europeans on the continent of North America.[1] The Breton sailors who followed Jacques Cartier developed a flourishing and dependable trade based upon the unlimited supply of marine food discovered in the northwestern Atlantic. So productive did this undertaking become that other nations soon turned covetous eyes upon the shores of Newfoundland, and English fishermen began to invade the waters hitherto monopolized by France. By virtue of the voyage of Sir Humphrey Gilbert, England claimed the island as her own —an assertion of title vigorously opposed by the French. After many years of strife France gave up the battle and, in the disastrous Treaty of Utrecht (1713), admitted the sovereignty of Great Britain, and received in return certain carefully restricted privileges pertaining to the fisheries which her citizens had so largely developed.

With France practically eliminated, sixty years passed in an uneventful manner, but with the success of the American Revolution the controversy again started, involving not alone the right of fishing in the waters of Newfoundland and Labrador, but certain vested interests in the Gulf of St. Lawrence, the Atlantic coast of Nova Scotia and the Bay of Fundy. The whole problem

[1] Strictly speaking, of course, these fisheries were off the coast of Newfoundland. There is some evidence to support the idea that French fishermen were acquainted with the "banks" even before the time of Columbus. See Payne, *Discovery of the New World Called America;* Channing, *History of the United States*, vol. I.

became known as the North Atlantic Coast Fisheries Dispute, and down to the present day it has been an almost constant, and a most irritating, factor in the international relations of the United States, Great Britain, Newfoundland, and Canada. Arbitrary actions by local authorities, disregard of essential restrictions by fishing vessels, and the completely divergent and contradictory claims of two great nations, produced a series of exasperating incidents which on a few occasions threatened serious consequences, and which always acted as a disturbing factor by the prevention of complete understanding and international harmony.

As with so many other problems on this continent, the fisheries dispute was a product of the American Revolution. Before 1776 British subjects in Boston, New York, or Charlestown had enjoyed precisely the same rights of participation in the Atlantic fisheries as had their fellow-citizens in Halifax, Quebec, or London. They were equally subjects of the British Crown, in which reposed the title of ownership. With the enunciation of the Declaration of Independence, however, and in its subsquent recognition by Great Britain, the rights of the citizens of the United States in regard to the fisheries of Nova Scotia, Newfoundland, and the Gulf of St. Lawrence became obscured. During the negotiations in Paris which ended the Revolutionary War, a clear distinction became apparent between the "shore" fisheries and the "bank" fisheries. Great Britain had previously claimed the right to exclude foreign vessels not only from fishing within territorial waters, but even from fishing on the "banks," which in many cases were thirty or forty miles from the shore. This claim had been agreed to by both France [2] and Spain.[3] With the strange complacency which marked the British conduct during the Paris negotiations, it was shortly agreed that "the people of the United States shall *continue to enjoy* unmolested the right" to indulge

[2] Article V of the Paris Treaty of 1783.
[3] Article XVIII of the Paris Treaty of 1783. For the British case see *Proceedings in the North Atlantic Coast Fisheries Arbitration before the Permanent Court of Arbitration at The Hague,* Washington, 1912, vol. IV, appendix, sec. 8.

in the bank fisheries, and that they should *"have the liberty to take fish"* in territorial or coast waters.[4] Of this distinction in wording much was to be said later.

The American negotiators at Paris, especially Franklin, Jay, and Adams, adhered to the statement that prior to independence the right of fishing was vested equally in the mother country and the colonies, and that when these separated equal rights accrued to each. In later years the British government asserted that it had agreed to no such proposal, and the wording of Article III of the Treaty of 1783 at least gives room for doubt:

"It is agreed that the people of the United States *shall continue to enjoy unmolested, the right to take fish of any kind on the Grand Bank and on all the other banks of Newfoundland:* also in the Gulf of St. Lawrence and at all other places in the sea where the inhabitants of both countries used at any time heretofore to fish: and also, that *they shall have the liberty to take fish of every kind on such part of the coast* of Newfoundland as British fishermen shall use, but not to dry or cure the same on that island: and also on the coasts, bays, and creeks of all other of His Britannic Majesty's dominions in America: and that the American fishermen shall have liberty to dry and cure fish in any of the unsettled bays, harbors, and creeks of Nova Scotia, Magdalen Islands and Labrador, so so long as the same shall remain unsettled, and so soon as the same or either of them shall be settled it shall not be lawful for the said fishermen to dry or cure fish at such settlements without a previous agreement for that purpose with the inhabitants, proprietors or possessors of the ground." [5]

The conflict of definitions embodied in the use of the words "right" and "liberty" formed the basis for all subsequent disputes in regard to the Atlantic fisheries. The United States claimed that its nationals enjoyed the advantages here enumerated as inalienable "rights" which could not be affected by any future decision of Great Britain, nor be abrogated by war. The British leaders, however, disputed this interpretation and, while admitting

[4] Article III of the Paris Treaty of 1783. Malloy, *op. cit.,* vol. I, p. 558.

[5] *Idem, ibid.*

the right of Americans to take fish on the banks which were outside the territorial waters, insisted that the "liberty" of engaging
in the "shore" fisheries was simply a treaty right, and therefore,
by the rules of international law, subject to cancellation in the
event of war between the signatory states. A right thus given
might also be withdrawn by the King, who enjoyed the full perquisites of sovereignty within his territorial domains. (This insistence upon complete and inalienable sovereignty has ever been
a characterstic of American political philosophy.) John Adams, a
member of the American delegation at Paris, stated that the
word "liberty" was used in this article merely as a sop to the
feelings of the British who would have become incensed at a
too frequent use of "right." "It amounted to the same thing for
liberty was right, and privilege was right: but the word *right* was
more unpleasing to the people of England than *liberty,* and we
did not think it necessary to contend for a word." [6] The American
negotiators considered that the treaty embodied merely a legal
division of the British Empire, and that the fisheries, like the
territory, should be subject to partition. The treaty was "nothing
more than a mutual acknowledgment of antecedent rights." [7] But,
whatever the moral justification for such a contention, it certainly was legally untenable,[8] and the testimony of Adams is
contradicted by the evidence of the draft treaties drawn up by
the British negotiators which showed that the imperial delegates
did not consider the American claims to be irrefragible.[9] In fact,
a careful consideration of the negotiations would tend to support
the later contention of Great Britain, namely, that the Treaty of
1783 combined a recognition of the American "right" to fish on
the "banks" (in the open sea), and a "liberty" or license to take

[6] Case of the United States, p. 31. James Brown Scott, strangely enough,
takes this statement at its full face value despite the many evidences tending to a contrary interpretation. Scott, *Introduction to Argument of the
Hon. Elihu Root. . . . Before the North Atlantic Coast Fisheries Arbitration,* 1912, p. 31.

[7] Case of the United States, sec. 7. From *Proceedings . . . at The
Hague, op. cit.*

[8] Scott, *op. cit.,* p. 27.

[9] Case of the United States, sec. 7.

fish in British territorial waters, given for political reasons.[10] This statement seems consonant with the character and details of the negotiations, with the political conditions of the time, and with the wording of the treaty itself.

It is quite possible that Adams believed his statement to be true, and that the Americans may have considered that their "rights" were recognized, while at the same time the British diplomats were equally convinced that they were simply bestowing a privilege with a view to the promotion of American good will toward Great Britain.

Difficulties did not immediately arise. Neither Jay's Treaty of 1794 nor the unratified Pinckney Treaty of 1806 even mentioned the fisheries—a good proof that no grave problem was as yet recognized. The germ of dissension, however, had been planted, and it was brought to maturity in the period after the War of 1812. The Treaty of Ghent [11] which closed this struggle did not mention the subject, but shortly afterwards a real difference of opinion developed. The British felt that there was here "no exception to the rule that all treaties are put to an end by a subsequent war." [12] Therefore, the privilege of engaging in the North Atlantic fisheries, given by the Treaty of 1783, was annulled, and it was not to be renewed unless purchased by some commensurate advantage. The Americans in reply argued that "since the division of territory survived the war, so the division of fisheries survived." [13] This difference of interpretation was irreconcilable, and when in July, 1815, American fishing vessels were ordered away from the waters in which they had been accustomed to pursue their occupation, the Department of State was flooded with complaints; and these complaints, translated into official protests, were forwarded to London. After a lengthy diplomatic exchange, two American commissioners, Gallatin and Rush, repaired to the British capital, where they entered into conference with Mr. Goul-

[10] British Case, p. 8. From *Proceedings . . . at The Hague, op. cit.*
[11] Dec. 14, 1814.
[12] Bathurst to Adams. *American State Papers: Foreign Relations.* vol. IV, p. 354.
[13] American Case, sect. 9.

bourn and Mr. Robinson, representing the Imperial government. Three months of consultation followed before a convention was signed—October 20, 1818—which played a prominent part in all subsequent British-American history. This convention dealt not alone with fisheries, but included questions of boundaries and slavery.[14] Article I of this convention dealt with the fisheries problem, and it was upon the interpretation of this article that all the succeeding controversy rested. The section was signed in the following form:

"Whereas differences have arisen respecting the Liberty claimed by the United States for the Inhabitants thereof, to take, dry, and cure Fish on Certain Coasts, Bays, Harbors and Creeks of His Britannic Majesty's Dominions in America, it is agreed between the high contracting Parties, that the Inhabitants of the said United States shall have forever, in common with the subjects of His Britannic Majesty, the Liberty to take Fish of every kind on that part of the southern Coast of Newfoundland which extends from Cape Ray to the Ramean Islands, on the Western and Northern Coast of Newfoundland, from the said Cape Ray to the Guerpon Islands, on the shores of the Magdalen Islands, and also on the Coasts, Bays, Harbors and Creeks from Mt. Joly on the southern Coast of Labrador, to and through the straits of Belle Isle, and thence northwardly indefinitely along the Coast, without prejudice however, to any of the exclusive Rights of the Hudson Bay Company; and that the American Fishermen shall also have the liberty forever to dry and cure Fish in any of the unsettled Bays, Harbors and Creeks, of the southern part of the Coast of Newfoundland hereabove described, and of the Coast of Labrador; but, so soon as the same or any portion thereof shall be settled, it shall not be lawful for the said Fishermen to dry or cure Fish at such portion so settled, without previous agreement for such purpose with the Inhabitants, Proprietors, or Possessors of the ground, and the United States hereby denounces forever, any Liberty heretofore enjoyed or claimed by the Inhabitants thereof to take, dry or cure Fish, on, or within, three marine miles of any of the Coasts, Bays, Creeks or Harbors of His Britannic Majesty's Dominions in America not included within the above mentioned limits: provided, however, that the American Fishermen shall be admitted to enter such Bays

[14] Malloy, *op. cit.,* vol. I, pp. 631–633.

or Harbours for the purpose of shelter and of repairing Damages therein, of purchasing wood, and of obtaining Water, and for no other purpose whatsoever. But they shall be under such restrictions as may be necessary to prevent their taking, drying or curing Fish therein, or in any other manner whatever abusing the Privileges hereby reserved to them." [15]

The wording of this article apparently supported the British contention as regards the interpretation of the Treaty of 1783, for in regard to the privileges guaranteed to American fishermen the word *liberty* rather than *right* is again employed. The convention, moreover, gravely restricted the *liberty* to be enjoyed by the United States. In return for the privilege of drying and curing fish in certain uninhabited regions, the American commissioners specifically renounced all claim to the enjoyment of the fisheries outside the limits definitely prescribed. Although American vessels were permitted, under stress of weather or other circumstances, to enter any harbor or bay in the North Atlantic, they were in so doing to be subject to British supervision. The rights here acquired, or, as Gallatin and Rush claimed, reasserted, were given in perpetuity, and were not subject to abrogation by war. Thus viewed, the convention of 1818 was a compromise; the United States gained certain perpetual rights, but Great Britain succeeded in greatly restricting the area over which any American claim could be asserted.[16]

There were two outstanding defects in the convention as finally signed, and it was these two points which formed the basis of the dispute which later developed. According to this agreement, American fishermen were to have the liberty of taking fish "in common with the subjects of His Britannic Majesty." Now, did this signify that the Americans were to enjoy complete national autonomy in all places frequented by British fishermen (within the pre-

[15] Malloy, *op. cit.,* vol. I, pp. 631, 632.
[16] It is interesting to note that the American commissioners were authorized to accept an even greater restriction in regard to the territory to be covered by a perpetual grant of fishing liberty. Cf. Adams' instructions to Gallatin and Rush of July 28, 1818: Case of the United States, appendix, sec. 304: British case, appendix, sec. 83.

scribed limits), or did the words "in common" mean that the
American vessels and crews were to be subject to the same restrictions as their British competitors? In other words, were the
fishing regulations imposed by Great Britain (later Canada and
Newfoundland) to be binding upon American as well as British
and colonial fishermen? The convention definitely stated that,
when taking refuge in harbors and bays not included in the treaty
coast, American vessels were to be subject to British regulations.
Did the failure to include such a specific statement mean that on
the treaty coast the British authorities could legislate only for
their own nationals? The British contention was that the Americans
had equal rights on the treaty coast, and that they, like the British,
were subject to the rules of the territorial authorities. The United
States argued that the treaty would have included a specific statement to this effect, if it had been intended.[17]

The second point upon which differences developed was found
in the renunciatory clause. The United States gave up all rights
to fish within three miles of "the coasts, bays, creeks or harbors
of His Britannic Majesty's dominions in America" not included
in the treaty coast. The problem arose in regard to the line from
which the three-mile limit was to be measured. Should this line
of demarcation follow the sinuosities of the coast, or should it
parallel a line drawn from headland to headland across the open-
ings of each harbor or bay?[18] Was every expanse of water de-
nominated a "bay" to be closed to American vessels, even though
it might be twenty miles wide? This was the claim of Great
Britain, while the United States demanded that the boundary parallel every twist or turn of the coast, thus opening to
American vessels every bay whose mouth was over six miles

[17] Under similar circumstances France had contended that "liberty"
meant that they could keep out the British. The Americans claimed that
the words "in common" had been inserted to prevent any such claim by the
United States, but that they did not mean that the Imperial authorities
could impose their regulations upon American vessels. Elihu Root (Bacon
and Scott, editors), *The North Atlantic Fisheries Arbitration*, Cambridge,
1917, p. xvi.

[18] See above, Chapter V, arguments on this point in the Alaskan
boundary case.

(three miles from each shore being territorial water) in width.

These two issues were discussed and debated for more than eighty years by the leading statesmen, politicians, and lawyers of two great nations, and more than once the threat of war was brought into the argument. Ultimately, by a somewhat unusual coincidence, the management of the foreign affairs of the British Empire and of the United States fell at the same time into the hands of reasonable, pacific, and intelligent men. The major issues involved were then settled in a very few months.

Although the faults of the Convention of 1818 were apparent and although the various methods of interpretation were obvious to all, the document was signed, and in the following year, by Parliamentary enactment [19] and by Orders-in-Council, Great Britain instructed the Governor of Newfoundland to carry out the new arrangement to the best of his ability.[20]

For some little time after the signing of the Convention of 1818 no matters of great moment disturbed the international harmony. It is interesting to note, however, that in correspondence with France in regard to the Gallic claim of exclusive rights in certain fishing waters off the Newfoundland coast, the United States accepted and urged the British case.[21]

In 1836 the government of Nova Scotia, aroused by undoubted infringements [22] of the treaty stipulations by American fishermen, passed more stringent regulatory statutes calculated to end these violations. Between 1820 and 1830 a few seizures had been made,[23] but the extended coast line of British North America had offered an alluring prospect to unscrupulous American fishermen and traders, and, in consequence, a great deal of illicit fishing and trading had been accomplished with very little danger of interruption. The law now passed by Nova Scotia, and later

[19] 59 George III, C. 38.
[20] British case, p. 11.
[21] *Idem,* pp. 11–12; *idem,* appendix, secs. 102–108.
[22] These infringements were (1) fishing within territorial waters; (2) employing illegal methods; and (3) using the Nova Scotia coast as a base, contrary to the existing regulations.
[23] British case, sec. 12.

embodied in the imperial statute of 1919,[24] permitted customs officers, members of the Import and Excise Service, sheriffs and magistrates, to board any suspicious vessel found within territorial waters, and to seize and confiscate it, upon failure to comply with an order to leave within twenty-four hours. A fine of $200 was to be collected from any person who attempted to hinder the officers of the Crown in carrying out this duty.[25] A similar law was enacted in Prince Edward Island.[26]

2. THE *WASHINGTON* INCIDENT

In 1843 a real issue developed. In that year the American ship *Washington* was seized in the Bay of Fundy, though at a distance of ten miles from the shore, and condemned in a Canadian court. This seizure was made under the British construction of the Convention of 1818, by which all "bays" were closed to American vessels, except on the treaty coast.[27] As a result of the excitement caused by this event, Mr. Everett and Lord Aberdeen [28] carried on a protracted correspondence, in which each set forth again and again their conflicting views as to the interpretation of the convention of 1818 in regard to the meaning of "bays." [29]

As was to be expected, the controversy over the *Washington* aroused no little feeling in the United States, particularly in the sections of New England which relied to a great extent upon the Atlantic fishing trade for their existence. This high tension was reflected in a letter sent to his Secretary of State by President Fillmore, in which he expressed the hope that there might be found "some line of proceeding that will allay the present excitement and prevent any bloodshed." [30] The advisability of send-

[24] *Ibid.*

[25] 6 *William* IV, cap. 8.

[26] 6 *Victoria,* cap. 14.

[27] British case, sec. 12.

[28] Respectively, the American Secretary of State and British Secretary of State for Foreign Affairs.

[29] British case, appendix, sec. 131 h.

[30] Fillmore to Webster, July 30, 1852. *Idem,* sec. 156.

ing an American warship to protect the citizens of the United States engaged in the fishing trade was discussed,[31] and Great Britain countered with the promise of a fleet of small armed patrol vessels to assist in guarding the colonial waters.[32] A heated discussion was carried on in the United States Senate, during which it was plainly stated that the object of the British enforcement laws was to compel the United States to enter into a reciprocity agreement with the colonies.[33] Feeling among the fishing population was becoming more and more intense, and during 1853 many fishing vessels left Gloucester and Boston equipped with arms and ammunition for protection against any action by British vessels. The danger involved in such a proceeding was apparent, and Mr. Marcy, then Secretary of State, sent a circular to all port directors warning them against all acts of hostility.[34] At the same time an American naval force was dispatched to the fishing grounds for the protection of the national rights.

The point at issue was settled, though the principle was not established, by the declaration of the British government that, so far as the Bay of Fundy was concerned, American vessels would be allowed to sail and fish therein without molestation, as an act of grace, though the United States could assert no legal right.[35] It was immediately made apparent that similar treatment was not to be accorded American vessels in other large bays. In 1852 Mr. Webster, American Secretary of State, had practically admitted that the British contention in this regard was justified by the Treaty of 1818.[36] His statement, which was officially given to the press, declared in part:

"It would appear that by a strict and rigid construction of this Article (Article I, Convention of 1818) fishing vessels of the

[31] *Ibid.*

[32] British case, appendix, sec. 153.

[33] Extracts from speeches in the United States Senate. British case, appendix, secs. 152–168.

[34] British case, appendix, sec. 201.

[35] October 9, 1844, Mr. Everett to Lord Aberdeen: British case, sec. 12. March 10, 1845, Lord Aberdeen to Mr. Everett: British case, appendix, sec. 141, 142.

[36] British case, appendix, secs. 152–153.

United States are precluded from entering into bays or harbors of the British Provinces . . . A bay, as is usually understood, is an arm or recess of the sea, entering from the ocean between capes or headlands; and the term is applied equally to small and large tracts of water thus situated . . . The British authorities insist that England has a right to draw a line from headland to headland, and to capture all American fishermen who may follow their pursuits inside that line. It was undoubtedly an oversight in the Convention of 1818 to make so large a concession to England. . . ." [37]

Shortly after this Mr. Webster went further and admitted that Great Britain was "undoubtedly right," [38] a concession that was used with effect in the British case presented at The Hague in 1909.

On the 5th of June, 1854, was signed the famous Reciprocity Treaty, which was to endure until destroyed by the bad feeling incidental to the American Civil War. This treaty gave to American fishermen the enjoyment of all the British fisheries in North America, the privilege of purchasing bait and supplies in Canadian and Newfoundland ports, and exemption from all taxes except lighthouse dues. In return, the United States granted to British fishermen the right to pursue their occupation in American waters north of 39° north latitude, and there was a mutual reduction in customs dues. The treaty could be abrogated by either party on one year's notice, and this was given by the United States on March 17, 1865. [39]

In 1856 the last act in the drama of the *Washington* was staged, when by a vote of two to one the arbitration tribunal organized for the purpose declared the owner's claim for damages to be valid. The tribunal decided that the treaty of 1818 gave Great Britain no right to exclude American vessels from the Bay of

[37] Official statement by Daniel Webster. Boston *Courier,* July 6, 1852.
[38] Crampton to Malmsbury, August 2, 1852. British case, appendix, sec. 157.
[39] Malloy, *op. cit.,* vol. I, p. 672; British case, appendix, sec. 36 ff. The clauses of the reciprocity treaty which related to the fisheries had worked with reasonable satisfaction during the years they were in force.

Fundy, and that the United States had never renounced their right to fish in that bay.[40]

The reciprocity treaty terminated in 1866, and during the negotiations for its renewal American fishermen were issued licenses which assured them of the same privileges that they had enjoyed under the treaty.[41] On July 1, 1867, the Dominion of Canada was formed, and on January 8, 1870, all efforts at renewing the reciprocity treaty having failed because of the hostility of the United States, by an Order-in-Council the Dominion ended the system of issuing licenses to American fishing vessels, and provision was made to prevent illegal encroachments upon Canadian waters.[42]

On the 9th of June, 1870, Mr. Boutwell, then American Secretary of State, issued a circular of instructions which was important in its bearing on one of the main points later to be at issue between Great Britain and the United States. In this dispatch the Secretary said: "Fishermen of the United States are bound to respect the laws and regulations for the regulation and preservation of the Fisheries *to the same extent to which they are applicable to British* or Canadian fishermen." [43]

This statement was frequently quoted in the subsequent controversy concerning the jurisdiction of the British legislative bodies over American fishermen.

3. THE TREATY OF WASHINGTON

The many-sided Treaty of Washington, concluded on May 8, 1871, dealt with the fisheries problem in Articles 18 to 25 inclusive. These articles provided for the annulment of all duties upon fish; American citizens were given the right to participate in all Canadian sea fisheries; Canadians received similar concessions in American waters north of the 39th degree of north latitude, and,

[40] British case, appendix, secs. 212 ff.
[41] British case, sec. 13; 31 Victoria, C. 61.
[42] British case, appendix, sec. 230.
[43] British case, sec. 13.

finally, provision was made for the establishment of an arbitration board to decide the justice of the British claim that in this treaty the empire had surrendered more rights than it had received in return.[44] The board met at Halifax in 1877 and, conceding the validity of Britain's claim, awarded damages to the sum of $5,500,000.[45] This amount has generally been considered, and justly, to have been excessive.[46]

The next incident of international importance occurred in 1878 at Fortune Bay, Newfoundland.[47] The inhabitants of this, Great Britain's oldest colony, were noted then, as they are today, for a sincere and somewhat unusual interest in matters of religion. As a result of this characteristic, there was among the laws of the colony a statute forbidding the pursuit of the fishing industry on the Sabbath Day. There was also a law designating certain closed seasons for particular methods sometimes employed in herring fishing. Many of the New England fishermen had so far forgotten their Puritan heritage as to be greatly annoyed at this restriction on the seventh day, and in many cases completely ignored the regulation. Moreover, they did not see the necessity of obeying a law which fixed an arbitrary closed season at the very time that they most desired to fish. Naturally, this attitude caused an unfavorable reaction among the subjects of the Queen in Newfoundland, and on a certain January Sabbath morning in 1878 a body of indignant citizens put off their habitual calm and descending upon a party of American fishermen who were pursuing their vocation in Fortune Bay, drove them off,[48] declaring that they had violated the laws cited above, and that they had also made an illegal use of a seine.[49] Again a sharp discus-

[44] Malloy, *op. cit.*, vol. I, pp. 707-709.

[45] British case, appendix, sec. 254.

[46] This fact is usually attributed to a desire on the part of the American government to make some amends for accepting $15,000,000—an enormous sum—in settlement of the *Alabama* claims.

[47] Henderson, *American Diplomatic Questions*, New York, 1901, pp. 518, 519.

[48] *House Executive Documents*, no. 84, 46th Cong. 2nd sess.

[49] British case, appendix, secs. 280 ff; *Report of the United States Secretary of State, May 17, 1880.*

sion arose between the British and American governments respecting the amenability of the American fishermen to the laws of Newfoundland. Great Britain supported the claim of the colony that American fishermen were subject to local laws while in the territorial waters, but the Department of State replied that the Treaty of Washington, and the Convention of 1818 before it, had given citizens of the United States full rights to regulate their own conduct while engaged in the North Atlantic fisheries. To settle the matter temporarily and to remove the danger inhering in the existing situation, Great Britain agreed to pay compensation for the occurrence at Fortune Bay, on the ground that the individual citizens of Newfoundland had no authorization to take matters of control into their own hands. The Foreign Office stated, however, that it had no intention of giving up its contention in regard to the applicability of colonial laws to American fishermen within territorial waters.[50]

The strict regulations imposed by the colonial governments upon their own and American fishing vessels, and the far-reaching measures taken to prevent illicit trade, were a continual source of annoyance to the American fishermen. In December, 1884, delegates from nearly every fishing center in New England met at Gloucester, and passed a rather violent resolution urging the government of the United States to repudiate the fishery clauses of the Treaty of Washington, and "restore to our fishermen the rights taken from them by the Treaty of 1818." [51]

At this time the industries of the United States were shielded by a very high tariff (though not so high as the tariffs since that date) and the New England delegation to Congress was insistent in its demand that similar protection be given the important fishery interests of New England. As a result, in 1885 the American government terminated the application of the fishery clauses of the treaty of Washington.[52]

In 1886 Canada countered with a law which specifically for-

[50] British case, sec. 14.
[51] *Bulletin of the United States Fish Commission,* vol. 5 (1885), pp. 447–448.
[52] British case, section 14.

bade the purchase of bait by American fishermen in Canadian
ports, and provided for the seizure of any foreign vessel which
entered Canadian waters "for any purpose not permitted by
treaty or convention of the United Kingdom or Canada for the
time being in force." [53] Numerous seizures of American vessels
charged with illegal fishing, smuggling or breaches of the regulations of the Convention of 1818, brought about an acrimonious
discussion in legislature and press. Americans charged that Canada was trying to force the United States into renewing the reciprocity agreement of 1854–1866. On the other hand, Canadians
denounced the actions of the United States as an attempt of
"big business" to break down Canadian tariff walls. There was,
obviously, more truth than imagination in each of these charges.
Feeling in the United States became so strong that a retaliatory
statute was enacted by Congress, which forbade all Canadian and
Newfoundland fishing vessels to use American ports except as
a measure of safety.[54] Fortunately, this law was never put into
effect.[55]

In the same and following years Newfoundland passed laws
increasing the restrictions on the catch and sale of bait fishes,
and demanding that all who wished to take part in this trade
first acquire licenses. In 1893, by the Foreign Fishing Vessels
Act, these regulations were strengthened and enlarged to include
the prohibition of recruiting crews for American vessels within
Newfoundland waters.[56]

A treaty was concluded on February 15, 1888, which provided
for a complete and just settlement of all the points in dispute,
but owing to the political situation in the United States, the Senate refused its ratification. Pending such action, a *modus vivendi*
was agreed upon between Canada and the United States, by
which American fishermen who had purchased licenses were relieved of all other restrictions. This was originally intended to

[53] 49 Victoria, cap. 114, (1886).
[54] British case, sec. 15.
[55] *Ibid.; idem*, appendix, sec. 30.
[56] Dunning, *The British Empire and United States*, New York, 1914, p.
280.

operate for two years only, but at the end of that time it was continued in force, under statutory authority,[57] until January 1, 1924.[58]

Although the feeling aroused in the United States by the renewal of the fisheries troubles was at first directed against Canada and Newfoundland, the incidence of this ill-will was soon transferred to Great Britain because of the activities of the Irish and other American groups afflicted with Anglophobia. As a recent author has said, "every frictional episode was systematically exaggerated and the permanent diplomatic settlement of all the controversies prevented." [59] The accession, at this time, of Salisbury to the British premiership was only exceeded as a calamity by the appointment of Mr. Blaine to the office of Secretary of State at Washington. Salisbury was uncouth in his blunt use of the imperative, while Blaine, in many of his actions, adequately represented the hyphenated Americans whose enthusiastic support he received. From such men no possible solution could be expected—unless it were war. In spite of these obstacles, however, comparative calm reigned over this field of controversy between 1886 and 1905. This was due to the policy of Newfoundland in issuing licenses, and the practical good sense of the American fishermen in accepting this method of regulation rather than in trying to force a hasty settlement more in accord with their desires.

In 1902 an effort had been made by Secretary Hay to negotiate with Newfoundland. The Bond-Hay agreement,[60] which was then drawn up, gave reciprocal freedom from customs duties on certain articles, and permitted the American fishermen to purchase bait and supplies in Newfoundland.[61] There was a good deal of opposition to this agreement in Canada, as it would have

[57] Falconer, *op. cit.*, p. 92.
[58] Dunning, *op. cit.*, p. 280.
[59] This failure does not mean that Canadian fishing vessels had free access to American ports.
[60] Drawn up between Sir Robert Bond of Newfoundland and Secretary of State John Hay.
[61] British case, sec. 16.

deprived the Dominion of the lever that it had been using in its
constant effort to force the United States to agree to reciprocity.[62]
This convention would have been an excellent arrangement for
both Newfoundland and the American fishermen, though it would
have hurt the business of the big canning and fish-products concerns of New England, as Newfoundland competition would not
be hindered by a protective tariff. Henry Cabot Lodge, Senator
from Massachusetts, led the forces of opposition in the United
States,[63] and as an election was approaching, and these fishing
companies were expected to contribute heavily to the Republican cause, it was found impossible to gain a favorable vote in
the Senate. In 1904 all hope of ratification of the Bond-Hay convention was abandoned.[64] The measure was also vetoed by the
Imperial Parliament at the insistence of Canada.[65]

The conflict now was really three-sided, rather than two-sided.
Canada wanted free entry for her fish into American ports, and
wished to gain a general reciprocity agreement. In return, she was
prepared to allow American fishermen to have access to the disputed waters. She also hoped that the imbroglio might result in
the union of Newfoundland with the Dominion.[66]

Newfoundland was obtaining about $15,000 a year from license
fees. The island colony realized that in its control of the supply
of bait it had the strongest of all levers, and in return for
freedom of purchase it demanded access to the American markets.[67]

The United States was not greatly averse to the admission of
Newfoundland fish, but did seriously object to the proposed ad-

[62] McGrath, "The Bond-Hay Treaty," *The Nineteenth Century*, vol. 53
(1903).

[63] Sykes, *The Rt. Hon. Sir Mortimer Durand*, London, 1926, pp. 293 ff.

[64] Shortt and Doughty, *op. cit.*, vol. VIII, p. 705: White, *The North
Atlantic Fisheries Dispute*, Ottawa, 1911, p. 75.

[65] McFarland, *A History of the New England Fisheries* (University
of Pennsylvania Publications in Political Economy and Public Law),
1911.

[66] McGrath, *op. cit.*; McFarland, *op. cit.*, pp. 321 ff.

[67] *Idem.*

mission of the immensely larger Canadian catch. This would have crippled the New England industry.[68]

In 1905 the fishing industry was again thrown into confusion. Newfoundland repealed the Foreign Fishing Vessels Act, and enacted a new law forbidding Americans to purchase or to recruit crews in Newfoundland waters.[69] Proving ineffective, this law was also repealed, and in 1906 a new bill, forbidding American captains to hire Newfoundland crews, was drawn up. As a result of earnest diplomatic representations from the United States and Great Britain, however, this law never went into effect,[70] and after a great deal of discussion the following rules were agreed to as a temporary expedient,[71] until some final settlement could be arranged:

(1) American fishermen were allowed the use of purse seines.
(2) Newfoundland sailors could be hired outside the three-mile limit.
(3) Americans agreed to refrain from fishing on Sundays.
(4) Americans agreed to make entries at customs-houses.
(5) Americans agreed to pay light-house dues.
(6) Statute of 1906 was not to become effective.

In the following year this agreement was amended to forbid the use of purse seines.[72] In 1908 Canadian representatives appeared in Washington to discuss the possibility of a general treaty to regulate the whole fisheries situation, as far as these two countries were concerned. A tentative agreement was prepared, but it was not signed.

By a coincidence as fortunate as the conjuncture of Salisbury

[68] *Idem.*
[69] British case, appendix, sec. 757. American fishermen overcame this obstacle by employing Newfoundlanders on their vessels. Shortt and Doughty, *op. cit.,* vol. VIII, p. 705.
[70] British case, appendix, sec. 758.
[71] *Idem,* secs. 504–506.
[72] British case, secs. 508–509. A summary of the history of the fisheries dispute in tabular form is to be found in Shortt and Doughty, *op. cit.,* vol. IX, p. 126. See also White, *op. cit.,* p. 75.

and Blaine had been unfortunate, there were in Washington at this time two men of unusual intellectual attainments and actuated by a sincere desire for international understanding. These men held the responsible positions of American Secretary of State and British Ambassador to the United States, and were, respectively, Elihu Root and James Bryce. A further excellent indication of the probability of an era of good will and accommodation was found in the person of the British Minister of Foreign Affairs, Sir Edward Grey. The results produced by these three men in the promotion of international amity are a striking proof of the ability of honest and intelligent men to use even the prevailing methods of diplomacy to produce a salutary result.

On April, 14, 1908, there was signed at Washington by Mr. Root and Mr. Bryce an arbitration convention under which these two great world powers agreed henceforth to submit to arbitration at The Hague those differences "of a legal nature or relating to the interpretation of treaties" which had arisen or which might in the future arise.[73] It at once became obvious that the northeastern fisheries question came within the scope of this convention, and on January 27, 1909, the two powers agreed to submit the legal aspects of this problem to The Hague for final and definitive settlement.[74] This agreement provided for the selection of a tribunal under Rule 45 of the Hague Conventions; it outlined the methods of presentation and argument to be adopted; agreed that the Hague decision was to be subject to revision by the two parties; and specifically stated the seven questions to be submitted for decision.[75]

4. THE HAGUE TRIBUNAL

Article 45 of the Hague Conventions was used as the basis for selecting the panel of judges who were to adjudicate the mat-

[73] Malloy, *op. cit.,* vol. I, p. 814.

[74] The suggestion on this occasion came from the United States. Shortt and Doughty, *op. cit.,* vol. VIII, p. 706; Richards, "The North Atlantic Coast Fisheries Arbitration," *Journal of the Society of Comparative Legislation,* vol. II (1910–1911).

[75] *Treaties and Agreements affecting Canada in force between His Majesty and the United States of America,* Ottawa, 1927, p. 319.

ter at issue. It was agreed that there should be one American member of the tribunal and one subject of the King, and these offices were filled by the Hon. George Grey, judge of the United States Circuit Court of Appeals, and Sir Charles Fitzpatrick, chief justice of Canada. There were also three neutral members, A. F. de Savornin Lohman, Minister of State in the Netherlands; Luis Maria Drago, former Minister of Foreign Affairs in the Argentine Republic, and author of the famous "Drago Doctrine"; and Dr. Heinrich Lammasch, Professor of International Law in the University of Vienna, and member of the Upper House of the Austrian Parliament. Dr. Lammasch was to act as umpire, and to preside over the sessions of the tribunal. Both he and Dr. Lohman had had previous experience in important international arbitrations, and their selection was most satisfactory.[76] In fact, the whole court was composed of men of the highest judicial character, and to this is due, in a large measure, the success of its work and the universally favorable reception everywhere accorded its decisions.

The proceedings of the court of arbitration in this matter have been collected and published in twelve large volumes. Necessarily, then, all that can be attempted here is a statement of the problems, a brief and condensed summary of the leading arguments of either side, and an outline of the decision of the court. As previously indicated, the points at issue were summarized in seven questions, and these will be separately considered.[77]

The first question submitted to the tribunal, and also perhaps the most important, was as follows:[78]

Can Great Britain impose reasonable regulations,

(1) As to hours, days and seasons, when fish may be taken on the treaty coast, without the consent of the United States?

(2) as to the methods, means and implements to be used in taking fish, or in carrying on fishing operations upon such coast, and

[76] "Introduction," Root, *op. cit.,* p. 26.

[77] John Bassett Moore, *Principles of American Diplomacy,* New York, 1918, pp. 146, 147.

[78] Summary of James Brown Scott, *op. cit.,* p. 50.

(3) as to any other matters of similiar character relating to the fishing industry?

The matter here at issue rested primarily upon the interpretation of the words "liberty" and "in common" as used in the Convention of 1818. Great Britain insisted that the "liberty" accorded the United States by that document was simply a privilege —"equivalent merely to permission." [79] In support of this the British lawyers pointed to the phraseology of the treaty whereby Great Britain acknowledged the "right" of the Americans to the bank fisheries (which were outside territorial waters), but used the word "liberty" in regard to the shore fisheries.[80] The United States, however, argued that "liberty" and "right" were here used with the same meaning or intent. The American counsel further contended that the Convention of 1818 was simply a restatement of the inalienable rights which the United States had always claimed, and which had been acknowledged in the treaty of 1783, except insofar as these rights were specifically renounced in the convention itself.[81]

Again, Great Britain argued that the words "in common" definitely limited the American sailors to such rights as were possessed by their British rivals. "Now there can be no pretence that British fishermen are not subject to the sovereign power of His Majesty and these words show that American fishermen are to have the same liberty as British fishermen, but no more." [82] And again, "It was merely permission to fish, in common with British fishermen, and was necessarily subject to the right of regulation by the government of the country." [83] The American lawyers replied, however, that the words "in common" had been inserted for a particular purpose. In a previous argument between Britain and France, in which the former had granted fishing privileges to French vessels, the government at Paris had attempted to inter-

---

[79] British case, sec. 47.
[80] British argument, p. 15.
[81] American argument, p. 35.
[82] British case, sec. 46.
[83] *Idem*, sec. 47.

pret this action as a transfer of exclusive rights. They had then refused to share the fisheries with the British. It was to obviate the possibility of the recurrence of such a situation that Great Britain had insisted on the insertion of the words "in common" in the Anglo-American convention.[84] The United States insisted that it was on a parity with Newfoundland insofar as the right to formulate regulations was concerned. For reasons of expediency, the American government could not make these regulations, but it claimed the right to approve or disapprove laws enacted by the island authorities.[85] The United States agreed that some form of control was necessary and reserved the right to decide whether or not the fishery statutes from time to time enacted by Canada and Newfoundland were reasonable. Regulations might very easily be enforced which were discriminatory and unfair.[86]

Great Britain replied that, since the United States admitted the necessity of regulations, since the Newfoundland government was the logical body to enact such rules, and since the Convention of 1818 did not hint at any restriction upon the right of Great Britain in this regard, American fishermen were obliged to obey such laws in common with those of Great Britain.[87] The Americans insisted, however, that the Convention of 1818 had definitely limited British sovereignty by granting certain perpetual liberties to the United States, and further, "that the government of the United States fails to find in the treaty any grant of right to the makers of the colonial law to interfere at all, whether reasonably or unreasonably, with the exercise of the American rights of fishery."[88]

Finally, Great Britain contended that the Convention of 1818 bestowed a new and unrelated liberty upon American citizens, that the circumstances surrounding the negotiation and the wording of the Treaty of 1783 no longer had any bearing upon the

[84] A discussion of this may be found in Scott's introduction to Root, *op. cit.*, pp. 64–65.

[85] American case, appendix, sec. 500.

[86] American argument, p. 43.

[87] British argument, p. 18.

[88] American case, appendix, sec. 980–983.

problem of fishing rights.[89] This the United States denied, arguing that the War of 1812 had not abrogated the inalienable rights resident in the American government, and that the Convention of 1818 confirmed in favor of the United States, as against Great Britain, an international servitude.[90]

In view of the obvious and fundamental divergence of the two interpretations—a divergence that had apparently existed in the minds of the framers of the convention, as well as in those of the men who now sought to explain it—a decision in the nature of a compromise was to be expected. Such a decision was given. The award upheld the right of Great Britain to make laws without the consent of the United States—this being an inalienable attribute of sovereignty—but such laws were not to violate the convention; they must be appropriate or necessary for the protection of the fisheries, or desirable on the grounds of public morality, and must apply without discrimination to American and British alike. Furthermore, all laws relating to these matters must be published, two months before enforcement, in the London, Canada, and Newfoundland gazettes. If the United States should consider any such law to be unreasonable, it might appeal to a permanent mixed commission, which was to be composed of one national of each country, and if necessary, a neutral referee. Finally, in regard to anterior actions of the two states, the tribunal decided that they should be subject to review by a joint commission, which would decide upon a satisfactory settlement. The tribunal itself agreed to appoint the third member of such a commission.[91] This decision was later revised by mutual agreement, and in accordance with the provisions of the Root-Bryce agreement.

The second problem proposed to the Hague Tribunal for arbitration was as follows:

"Have the inhabitants of the United States, while exercising the liberties referred to in the said Article, a right to employ, as

[89] British argument, p. 21.

[90] American argument, pp. 30, 31.

[91] *Official Report of the Bureau of the Permanent Court of Arbitration in the North Atlantic Coast Fisheries Case, Arbitrated at The Hague,* 1910, pp. 104 ff.

members of the fishing crews of their vessels, persons not inhabitants of the United States?"

Here the issue was less involved than in the first question.
Great Britain claimed that the convention meant exactly what
it said—that liberty to fish on the treaty coast was given to "the
inhabitants of the United States." The American government
maintained, on the contrary, that the intent of the treaty was to
confer this privilege upon American vessels, or vessels owned by
Americans, and that the nationality of the crew was immaterial.[92]
The difficulty which necessitated the insertion of this question had
arisen from the practice of certain American owners who had
annually sent vessels north under a very small crew, and had
relied upon the services of hired Newfoundlanders to fill their
holds with fish. A long diplomatic correspondence had centered
about this practice, but no solution had been achieved. The British
argument was logical and clear. Vessels, as such, can have no
right: the American negotiators of the Convention of 1818 had
been interested in supplying occupation for New Englanders, not
for the residents of Newfoundland: and finally, Secretary Evarts
had admitted these facts (May 17, 1880) in regard to the similar
Washington treaty.[93] The American counsel denied that Rush and
Gallatin had been actuated by such motives in 1818; they criticized
the British interpretation of Secretary Evart's report; and contended that the hiring of men to fish for American owners was,
in reality, the same thing as the Americans fishing themselves.
Great Britain had simply admitted an American right, and had
made no stipulations as to how the inhabitants of the United States
should profit from this right; and, in conclusion, it was contended
that the term "inhabitants of the United States" was used only
for the purpose of eliminating other foreign nationals.[94] The decision of The Hague was ingenious. The right of the United
States to hire fishermen of other nationalities was admitted, but
foreigners "employed as members of the fishing crews of Ameri-

[92] American case, sec. 41; *idem*, appendix, sec. 492.
[93] British case, secs. 56–57.
[94] American argument, pp. 87–96.

can vessels" were to "derive no benefit or immunity from the Treaty." [95] In other words, Americans were given the privilege of hiring whom they liked, but Great Britain was assured at the same time of a perfect right to refuse access to her waters to any foreigners or British citizens serving on American vessels. These rights were, of course, inherent in each nation as a sovereign state, and the Hague decision did no more than reiterate a platitude of international law.

The third question was defined thus:

"Can the exercise by the inhabitants of the United States of the liberties referred to in the said article be subjected without the consent of the United States to the requirements of entry or report at customs-houses, or the payment of light, or harbor, or other dues, or to any other similar requirement, or condition or exaction?"

As interpreted by the British case, the question was, whether or not "American fishing vessels were entitled to frequent the British coasts, bays, creeks, and even harbors, to land upon British territory, and to exercise all the privileges accorded to trading vessels, and yet to be exempt from the supervision which all nations exercise over all vessels (not only foreign, but their own) coming into their harbors and discharging upon their territory: and exempt also from contribution to the upkeep of lights necessary to the navigating of the waters." [96]

The United States here admitted that it had not contended that the Convention of 1818 had given American fishing vessels the right to carry on commercial or trading activities in British ports. But, after Great Brtain had thrown open her colonial trade to the nations of the world, it then rested with the United States government as to whether or not American fishing vessels were to be allowed also to trade. The United States admitted, however, that when engaged in commercial ventures, her ships should pay harbor and light dues. When the vessels were engaged solely in fishing, no such obligation existed. [97] British fishing vessels were not com-

[95] "Award of the Tribunal," *Proceedings of the North America Coast Fisheries Arbitration,* Washington, 1919, vol. I, p. 89.

[96] British case, sec. 61.

[97] American argument, pp. 97–99.

pelled to pay these taxes, and Americans were supposed to enjoy equal rights and immunities.[98] Finally, both Lord Elgin and Sir Edward Grey had admitted that any such discrimination was unjust.[99]

The British reply to these arguments was based on practical and geographical conditions. In a country such as Newfoundland it was quite impossible to prevent illicit trade by vessels which claimed to be engaged only in fishing.[100] In view of this fact, the Newfoundland government announced that American vessels must report at customs-houses that their character might be determined.[101] It was also held to be logical that ships which were assisted by lights and flag signals should contribute to the maintenance of these necessities.[102]

Taking cognizance of the fact that the necessity of reporting at customs-houses might frequently cause unnecessary hardship and delay, the Hague Tribunal decided that American fishing vessels should report "if proper conveniences for doing so were provided." The obligation, moreover, was simply to report, and did not necessitate the obtaining of formal clearance papers. In regard to light and harbor taxes, "American vessels were not to be subject to dues not imposed upon Newfoundland fishermen." [103]

The fourth question presented to the tribunal was somewhat different in character. Questions One, Two, and Three had dealt with American rights on the treaty coast: Question Four was concerned with certain special privileges extended to American vessels in other British waters. It was proposed as follows:

"Under the provision of the said Article, that the American fishermen shall be admitted to enter certain bays, or harbors, for shelter, repairs, wood, or water, and for no other purpose whatever, but that they shall be under such restrictions as may be necessary

[98] American case, appendix, sec. 1007.
[99] *Idem,* secs. 989, 1007.
[100] British case, sec. 70.
[101] *Idem,* sec. 62.
[102] *Idem,* sec. 71.
[103] "Award of the Tribunal," *loc. cit.,* p. 91.

to prevent their taking, drying, or curing fish therein, or in any other manner whatever abusing the privileges thereby extended to them, is it permissible to impose restrictions making the exercise of such privileges conditional upon the payment of light, or harbor, or other dues, or entering or reporting at customs-houses or any similar conditions?" [104]

The British case here reiterated the arguments used in Question Three, and pointed out that every vessel entering a harbor, whether under legal right or merely by privilege, was obliged, unless especially exempted, to pay all customary dues, and to observe the regular formalities suitable to that act.[104] The convention gave no special exemption to American craft, but on the contrary exposed them "to such restrictions as may be necessary to prevent . . . their abusing the privileges . . . extended to them." [105] And, in fact, it was not until 1905 that any objection had been raised to the imposition of such restrictions.[106]

The American reply was practical and conclusive. Due to the extended coastline of Newfoundland, and the few customs-houses in operation, the necessity of reporting every time that an American vessel was driven in for shelter, would cause a great deal of inconvenience—frequently necessitating a detour of fifty or one hundred miles to reach the nearest customs-house.[107] Moreover, such a regulation would not "be necessary" to prevent "the taking, drying or curing of fish . . ." within the prohibited area.[108]

Here it appears that the right of the British authorities to issue regulations was undeniable, but these regulations should not be of such a character as to destroy the value of the privilege given to American ships. The local authorities were undoubtedly entitled to the knowledge of the presence of foreign vessels in their territorial waters, but care should be taken not to impose such rules as would unnecessarily hinder American fishermen engaged in the honest pursuit of their calling. On these grounds

[104] British case, sec. 79.
[105] From the Convention of 1818, quoted in British case, sec. 80.
[106] British case, sec. 81.
[107] American argument, p. 114.
[108] *Idem*, p. 115.

of commonsense and humanity the tribunal decided that the imposition of restrictions making compulsory a report at a customshouse was not permissible. Nor was the levying of light and harbor dues. On the other hand, if an American vessel remained in British waters for forty-eight hours, the captain must report in person or by telegraph to a customs official "if reasonably convenient opportunity therefore is provided." [109]

Question Five ranks with Question One as one of the two most important problems before the tribunal.

"From where must be measured 'the three marine miles off any of the coasts, bays, creeks, or harbors' referred to in the said article?"

The primary importance of the division involved resulted in a great expenditure of time, argument, and oratory. Fortunately, the matter lends itself to concise analysis.

The question was one of definition. The United States claimed that the expanse of territorial water was to be measured at three marine miles from a line which followed the sinuosities of the coast, with the exception of those bays and harbors which were less than six miles wide at the mouth (thus being entirely territorial).[110] Great Britain argued for a literal interpretation of the treaty. To the British lawyers a bay was a bay, regardless of size or particular configuration.[111] According to this definition, the line separating territorial waters from the open sea should be drawn parallel to another line joining the headlands of the coast.[112] An exact interpretation of the wording of the convention undoubtedly upheld the British case, and so the tribunal awarded. "In the case of bays the three miles are to be measured from a straight line drawn across the body of water, at the place where it ceases to have the characteristics and configuration of a bay. At all other places the three marine miles are to be measured following the sinuosities of the coast." Realizing, however, the imprac-

[109] American case, appendix, sec. 217 H.
[110] British case, sec. 83.
[111] *Idem*, sec. 16.
[112] *Award of the Tribunal, op. cit.,* p. 92.

ticability of this decision, the tribunal, through a doubtful interpretation of Article IV of the Root-Bryce agreement, advised the
adoption of the rule heretofore used—particularly in the case of
Conception Bay. This plan was that all partially enclosed bodies
of water measuring ten miles or less from headland to headland
should be considered to be territorial waters, or, for the purpose of
this decision, bays.[113] Certain other bays [114] which were even larger
were also recognized (apparently on historical grounds) as territorial waters.

This decision was not assented to by Judge Drago, who contributed a lengthy dissenting opinion.[115]

Question Six was submitted as follows:

> "Have the inhabitants of the United States the liberty under
> the said Article or otherwise to take fish in the bays, harbors and
> creeks of that part of the southern coast of Newfoundland which
> extends from Cape Ray to the Ramean Islands, or on the western
> and northern coasts of Newfoundland from Cape Ray to the Guis-
> pon Islands, or on the Magdalen Islands?"

This problem arose from a discovery of Sir Robert Bond in
1905, which had apparently never been considered before that
time,[116] and was from the British standpoint the weakest of the
cases prepared. By a careful analysis of the wording of the convention, Sir Robert Bond had found that whereas American
fishermen were given the liberty to fish "on the coast, bays, harbors and creeks from Mount Joly on the southern coast of Labrador . . ." they were given similar privileges only on the "coast"
of Newfoundland and on the "shores" of the Magdalen Islands.
Here, argued the British case, was a clear distinction,[117] and under
the liberty to fish on the "coast" and "shores," American fisher-

---

[113] *Idem*, pp. 102–112.

[114] *Idem*, pp. 97–98.

[115] Scott's introduction to Root, *op. cit.*, p. 145.

[116] Chaleur Bay, Egmont Bay, and Miramichi Bay, for example. This
sets an important precedent and was drawn to the attention of the author
by Mr. William A. Found, Director of Fisheries, Ottawa.

[117] British case, secs. 123, 124.

men could not enter the bays, harbors, and creeks behind. In other words, they must confine themselves to the British territorial water outside the shore line, which, by the decision in Question Five, was to be drawn from headland to headland.[118] A weak attempt was made to prove that this distinction had been undisturbed by negotiators in 1818.[119]

Inasmuch as the American fishermen depended upon these bays for bait fish, the decision was distinctly important,[120] and the argument of the United States was sufficiently clear to convince the tribunal of its justice.[121] Mr. Root and his assistants proved conclusively that no such distinction had been thought of in 1818, and that no just basis could be found for the British claim. As one eminent American scholar has written, "the question was political rather than legal, and seems to rest on no substantial basis of law or fact." [122]

The tribunal ruled, very briefly, thus: "American inhabitants are entitled to fish in the bays, creeks and harbors of the Treaty coasts of Newfoundland, and the Magdalen Islands." [123]

Another section of Question Six follows:

"Are the inhabitants of the United States whose vessels went to the Treaty coast for the purpose of exercising the liberties referred to in Article I of the Treaty of 1818 entitled to have for those vessels when duly authorized by the United States in that behalf, the commercial privileges of the Treaty coast accorded by agreement or otherwise to United States trading vessels generally?"

Stated in other terms, do American fishing vessels command the privileges generally accorded commercial craft? Can a single ship be at once a fishing vessel and a trader? Had Great Britain the right to close her ports to fishing schooners which sought to engage in commercial enterprises?

---

[118] *Idem*, sec. 124.
[119] *Ibid.*
[120] American argument, p. 225.
[121] *Idem*, p. 226.
[122] Scott, *op. cit.*, p. 146.
[123] *Award of the Tribunal. op. cit.*, p. 100.

Great Britain contended that American fishermen could claim no liberties in British waters except those conferred by the Convention of 1818; that no commercial privileges were then granted; and that the treaty did not give rights to vessels, as vessels.[124]

The United States replied that the treaty did not deny commercial privileges—that it did not concern itself with commerce at all.[125] By other and later decrees Americans were given the right to carry on trade with the British colonies,[126] and the United States, being a sovereign power, had the right to permit any of its subjects to act in a commercial capacity, even though that person were at the same time a fisherman.[127] No stipulation in the treaty forbade inhabitants of the United States to act as traders and fishermen at one and the same time.[128] American fishing vessels had American registry and were therefore entitled to trade under the American flag, and this was not forbidden by any existing agreement.[129] All this of course, entirely overlooked the right of Great Britain, also a sovereign nation, to close her ports to any vessels except fishing craft as agreed to in the convention of 1818.

The British case was chiefly concerned with the practical problem involved. If an American vessel were allowed to trade and fish at the same time, all of the safeguards insisted upon in the treaty of 1818 would be useless. The Americans would be able to establish their headquarters on British soil and fish or trade as occasion suited. Endless confusion would ensue. A fishing vessel was a fishing vessel, and apart from the liberties granted in 1818 it had no rights in British waters. Moreover, by international law, Great Britain (or any other state) could close its ports to foreign ships or any particular class of foreign ships, and consequently the imperial government (or the government of

[124] British case, sec. 127.
[125] American argument, p. 257.
[126] American case, appendix, sec. 764.
[127] *Idem*, sec. 974.
[128] American argument, p. 264.
[129] American oral argument, sec. 1457; American case, appendix, sec. 514.

Newfoundland) could forbid all American trading vessels, which also engaged in fishing, to enter her harbors. American fishing vessels could use them only in accordance with the treaty of 1818.

The decision of The Hague recognized the right of American vessels to fish, or to trade, but stated that these rights could not be used concurrently.[130] This decision was, beyond all doubt, legally sound, and practically sensible. Any other award would have resulted in constant discord and endless confusion.

This ended the duty of the Hague Tribunal. As can be seen, the decisions handed down were, in almost every case, based upon a compromise, which found some justification in each case. The chief end in view was to settle the problems in a practical and workable manner, in order to obviate further collisions. Although this award was, on the whole, satisfactory to both parties, it was decided, as had been provided for in Article X of the Root-Bryce Agreement, to revise the Hague decisions. For this purpose a joint commission [131] met at Washington, and on July 20, 1912, announced a final and definite settlement. The modifications agreed upon by this commission were not of vital import, but were designed to eliminate all possible charges of injustice, and to provide machinery to deal with any further trouble that might arise in the future.

The final agreement may be summarized as follows: [132]

Article 1. All future laws for the regulation of fisheries passed by Canada, Great Britain, or Newfoundland shall be promulgated and come into operation within the first 15 days of November each year, unless intended to apply to the conduct of fishing between the period from November to February, when it shall be promulgated at least six months before the first of February. These laws shall be published in the London *Gazette,* the Canada *Gazette,* and the Newfoundland *Gazette.* The dates fixed here, for promul-

---

[130] *Award of the Tribunal, op. cit.,* p. 101.

[131] This commission was composed of Chandler P. Anderson of the United States Department of State and Alfred Mitchell Innes, *Chargé d'Affaires* of His Majesty's Embassy at Washington.

[132] 37 *Statutes at Large,* pt. 2, p. 1634.

gation, may be altered after ten years, on the agreement of the Permanent Mixed Fishery Commission. If the government of the United States should object to any such laws, as inconsistent with the Treaty of 1818, it may notify the government of Great Britain within forty-five days and may request that the said law be submitted to the Permanent Mixed Fishery Commission for decision. If the law is not contested, or if it is contested, but declared to be reasonable, it shall come into force: if declared unreasonable it shall not be applicable to the inhabitants of the United States. A Permanent Mixed Fishery Commission shall be established for Canada and another for Newfoundland. The United States shall appoint one member to each, and all shall be appointed for five years. The third member in each case shall be agreed upon by the two national members, or failing such agreement, shall be appointed by the Queen of Holland. The two national members must be summoned by Great Britain within thirty days from the date of the protest by the United States. If they are unable to agree, a third member shall be added, and a majority decision shall be final and binding.

Article 2. In the matter of bays it is agreed that "the limits of exclusion shall be drawn three miles seaward from a straight line across the bay in the part nearest the entrance at the first point where the width does not exceed ten miles." Here follows a definite settlement in regard to certain well-known bays, specifically excluding from this agreement any connection with Hudson Bay.[133]

Article 3. It was agreed that the declaration of any or all the bays on the coast of Newfoundland, does not require consideration at present.

Article 4. This agreement to be ratified by the President and Senate of the United States and by His Britannic Majesty.

This final settlement was received with approbation in the four countries involved, and the whole course of the arbitration formed a most pleasing example of the possibilities of international adjudication, when each side is willing to make concessions and to agree upon a just decision. The fisheries question had been a

[133] The author has in his possession letters from the State Department at Washington, and the office of the Minister of Justice of Canada, which set forth diametrically opposed views on the question of the neutrality of Hudson Bay. See Chapter X.

cancerous growth in the international relations of the English-speaking peoples, and at times had threatened to become malignant: yet, by a few months of earnest and peaceful endeavor, the danger was eliminated.[134] To Lord Bryce, Elihu Root, and Sir Edward Grey belong primarily the credit of this splendid achievement—assuredly a proof of the pragmatic value of interesting men of character in the conduct of international affairs.

The legal aspects of the fisheries problem were settled by the adjudication of the Hague Tribunal. The practical regulations to govern the conduct of the industry, however, were still somewhat uncertain. For the time being, Canada was content to allow the *modus vivendi* which had been effective since 1888 (see p. 270) to remain in effect. This was satisfactory also to the United States, and when the Underwood Tariff Bill of 1913 was enacted it appeared as though a real era of good feeling were about to be inaugurated.[135]

For some years after 1912 the problem of the northeastern fisheries remained quiescent, and the representatives of the two countries were able to devote some much-needed attention to the minor problems of the protection of sockeye salmon on the Fraser River, the threatened extermination of the halibut off the coast of Alaska and northern British Columbia, the fisheries of Lake Champlain, the protection of the sturgeon fisheries in the Great Lakes, rules for the lobster industry of Nova Scotia, and the international protection of whales.[136]

Under the pressure of war conditions, an agreement was reached early in 1918, by which the fishing vessels of each country were to be accorded in the ports of the other all the privileges enjoyed by domestic vessels.[137]

[134] The Reciprocity Treaty of 1911 placed fish and its by-products on the free list, and practically returned to the conditions of 1854-66. This treaty, however, was defeated in Canada. See Chapter VIII.

[135] This tariff greatly reduced the duties on Canadian goods entering the United States. In effect, it gave to Canada many of the concessions that had been provided for in the abortive Reciprocity Bill of 1911.

[136] *Report of the United States Commissioner of Fisheries for 1918*, Washington, 1920, p. 94.

[137] *Ibid.*

On September 2, 1919, a treaty was signed at Washington providing for the protection of the sockeye salmon of the Fraser River. This industry had been steadily losing ground for many years, very largely as a result of the methods employed by American fishermen in taking the salmon before they entered the river. The treaty was received with great pleasure in British Columbia.[138]

During the Washington Conference of 1921, Sir Robert Borden, the leader of the Canadian representatives, took up with the American officials the question of a new treaty to regulate the international fisheries. A conference was arranged to consider the situation. On July 15th the United States cancelled its war legislation, which had allowed Canadian vessels free access to American ports. This proved to be a signal for the renewal of some of the old difficulties. Within a week nine American vessels were seized by Canadian patrol boats for poaching in forbidden waters.[139] The situation was further complicated by the enactment of the Fordney Tariff Bill, which raised an almost prohibitive wall against the importation of Canadian fish.

On July 26th the conference arranged by Sir Robert Borden reported and, although its recommendations were not adopted, they are worthy of serious consideration, as they undoubtedly point the way to the only really satisfactory solution of this most involved problem. The recommendations may be summarized as follows:

(1) The markets of both countries should be made available to the fishermen of both, on equal terms.

(2) The Treaty of 1818 should be so amended as to allow the fishing vessels of either country to enter and clear from the ports of either country.

(3) The fishing vessels of either country should be allowed to dispose of their catches, and purchase bait, ice, coal, nets, lines, oil, provisions, and all other supplies in the ports of either country.

138 *Canadian Annual Review for 1919,* Toronto, 1920.
139 *Ibid.*

(4) A treaty for the more adequate protection of the Fraser River sockeyes should be enacted.

(5) A close season for Pacific halibut should be enforced, between November 16 and February 15, each year for at least ten years.

Canada would, of course, gain more from such an agreement than would the United States, but it would, in the long run, prove beneficial to the fishing industries of each country. The embattled cannery industries of Washington and New England, however, were unwilling to endorse such proposals, and in this attitude they were supported by the ultra-protectionist administration of President Harding.[140]

Although irritated by the American cancellation of the wartime privileges, and the enactment of the Fordney tariff, the Canadian government continued to apply the rules of the *modus vivendi* in the hope that the American policy might soon be modified. During 1922 and 1923, however, opposition to this one-sided condition developed in the Dominion. During the session of the House of Commons in the latter year, vigorous expression was given to the Canadian feelings on this matter. Mr. Duff (Nova Scotia), speaking on this subject, declared:

"The Fordney Bill, as I have said, was very injurious to the people of Nova Scotia. For instance, the business in which I am most interested, fish, is hard hit, a duty of $1.60 per hundred pounds having been imposed on salt, dry fish . . . and on fresh fish, herring, mackerel, and so on a prohibitive duty of two cents a pound . . . It is no wonder that all over Nova Scotia and the other two Maritime Provinces the fishermen are leaving for the United States, because they find that under the Fordney Tariff they cannot make a living." [141]

Mr. Martell voiced the common sentiment when he pointed to the following solution:

[140] *Ibid.*
[141] *Debates of the House of Commons,* vol. CLV (Session of 1923), vol. I, p. 112.

"We have a weapon, I believe, in our hands . . . (American vessels) are enabled by means of this licensing system [142] to come into Canadian ports and use our ports to transship their catch, take bait, buy their nets, twine and all their other supplies and outfit and ship their goods through to the United States in bond . . . whereas when our own fishermen come in from the banks, if they wish to sell to the United States, which in days gone by took 40% of their catch, they are obliged to pay two cents a pound duty on fresh fish, which is practically a prohibitive rate. The United States vessels, I believe, would not be able to successfully prosecute the catching of fresh fish if they were not allowed the use of our Canadian ports. . . . If they were denied that privilege I really believe that it would be conducive to the United States authorities negotiating with the Dominion government for reciprocity, at least on fish." [143]

As a result of continued protests, the Dominion government finally notified the United States that after December 31, 1923, the privileges heretofore extended to the United States fishing vessels in Canadian ports would be discontinued.[144] At the same time Ottawa issued a statement explaining that for upwards of thirty years Canada had granted these privileges to the United States, but that except for a brief period (1918–1921) during which American war legislation had made the privileges reciprocal, the United States had done nothing to assist the Canadian fishermen. Canada had waited for over two years after the repeal of the American war legislation in the hope that the United States might again enact the rules of that time. "In this hope Canada has been disappointed. The government of the United States has not only not made provision for the restoration of the arrangements of 1918, but has by tariff provisions imposed additional duties upon Canadian fish. . . ."

"From the action of the United States authorities the obvious conclusion was reached that little or no value was attached by the people of the United States to the privileges that Canada had

[142] Under the *modus vivendi.*

[143] *Debates of the House of Commons,* vol. III (Session of 1923), p. 2906.

[144] *Canadian Annual Review for 1923.*

been voluntarily extending for so long a period." [145] These privileges in consequence were now to be withdrawn.

There, unfortunately, the matter still rests. A number of attempts have been made to evolve a satisfactory solution of the problem, but so far without result. The fact is that Canada insists on using the fisheries situation as a make-weight in her bargaining for better tariff relations with the United States. To this Washington will not agree, and this century-old problem is still far from being solved. A determined effort will probably be made through the new legations at Washington and Ottawa to reach a mutually satisfactory solution. It was to handle such problems as this that they were established.

It seems altogether likely that when the final settlement is achieved, it will be based on mutual freedom on the banks, and equal access to the markets.

[145] *Ibid;* Falconer, *op. cit.,* p. 92.

CHAPTER VIII

Commercial Intercourse Since 1845

I. ECONOMIC INTERESTS

IT is an obvious fact that economic interests form the backbone of international relations. At least nine-tenths of the work of ambassadors, ministers, and other diplomatic officials has to do with commercial, industrial, or financial problems. Perhaps it was with this fact in mind that Dr. Johnson described an ambassador as "a man who lies abroad for the good of his country."

In the history of the relations of the United States and Canada the part played by economic factors is a most important one. Not only did material considerations influence such events as the American Revolution, the War of 1812, and the various boundary disputes, but in more modern times as well they have been preeminent in conditioning the intercourse of the two countries. The fact that the industrial output of these neighbors has been in part complementary and in part competing has produced a complex but extremely interesting situation—a situation that may be summarized as follows: *First,* the desire of American industrial and manufacturing interests to gain control of the vast storehouse of raw materials known as the Canadian Dominion. *Second,* the attempts of these same interests to break down the Canadian tariff against manufactured articles, to the end that American goods may capture the Canadian market. *Third,* the bitter opposition of the western and southern states to any lowering of the American duties on raw materials—an event that would bring Canadian grain, minerals, dairy products, and fish into serious competition with the commodities of the American farmer, miner, and fisherman. *Fourth,* the desire of the Canadian farmer to gain unrestricted access to the American market, and to purchase his supplies at the lowest figure regardless of the place of manufacture. *Fifth,* the fear of the Canadian industrial interests that any lowering of the tariff on finished products will result in their extermination by the more powerful and highly developed manufacturing organizations of the United States.[1] In the United States the high tariff interests have won an almost complete victory, with the result that the American customs wall is the admiration of protectionists the world over. Even the Democratic Party favors a tariff that would seem colossal in any other state. Canadian opinion, on the other hand, has not surrendered so completely to the protectionist philosophy; Liberals and Conservatives alike defend a situation in which manufacturers are accorded only a moderate degree of protection.[2] The result has been that Canadian goods, whether manufactured or in the raw, have been very largely barred from access to the American consumer, with resulting economic distress to those Canadian producers who, like the fishermen of the maritime provinces, look to the United States as their logical market. American manufacturers, on the contrary, have had much less opposition in gaining entrance to the Canadian field.

The history of independent commercial intercourse between Canada and the United States goes back only to the middle of the nineteenth century. It was between the years 1840 and 1849 that

---

[1] To obviate the necessity of surrendering to the American trusts, and at the same time to gain a form of reciprocity in raw materials, has always been the object of the Canadian government, and to this end the fisheries situation has been used consistently as a make-weight. Sir John A. MacDonald declared that "the Treaty of 1854 was obtained chiefly by the vigorous protection of the fisheries which preceded it" and objected because a similar bargain was not made in the Washington Treaty of 1871. *Canadian Sessional Papers, 1872,* no. 18.

[2] It must be noted, however, that Canadian legislatures are prone to extend aid to industries in the form of bounties, loans, or special assessment rates. This is, in reality, a form of protection. See Porritt, *Sixty Years of Protection in Canada,* London, 1908. Canada is the only country in the world that has reduced its tariff schedules since the end of the World War.

Canada first took over the active control of her own economic life.[3] During this decade the last remnants of the Navigation Laws were abolished, and Great Britain, whose adoption of the policy of free trade had seriously injured Canadian commerce, was henceforth treated in the matter of tariffs as a foreign state.[4] Having lost its tariff preference in the British markets, Canadian trade came almost to a standstill, and the United Provinces were forced to turn to the United States for aid. The desire for reciprocity was more insistent and vigorous than ever, and during the great depression of 1849 a strong movement in favor of annexation was centered in Montreal.[5] But Canadians preferred reciprocity to annexation, and they even went so far as to lower the Canadian tariff on American goods in the hope that the United States would follow suit. This example of homeopathic magic, however, was not effective.[6] During this period of financial stringency, Lord Elgin reported that

"If things remain on their present footing . . . there is nothing before us but violent agitation ending in convulsion or annexation. No measure but the establishment of reciprocal trade between Canada and the United States, or the imposition of a duty on the produce of the States when imported into England, will remove it."[7]

England, however, would not modify the application of her new economic philosophy even for the benefit of her premier colony, and all Canadian efforts were soon directed toward the achievement of a reciprocal agreement with the United States.

[3] Davidson, *Commercial Federation and Colonial Trade Policy*, London, 1909, p. 15; Galt, *Canada, 1849–1859*, Quebec, 1860.

[4] Until the Laurier government granted a preference in 1897. See "Memorial to the Queen from the Montreal Board of Trade," Quebec *Gazette*, January 8, 1849; Hansard, *Colonial Correspondence, 1846*, vol. LXXX, p. 562; Haynes, *The Reciprocity Treaty with Canada, 1854*, London, 1892, p. 9.

[5] See Chapter IV.

[6] *United States Executive Documents*, no. 64, 31st Cong., 1st sess.

[7] Walrond, *op. cit.*, pp. 101–102. See also Porritt, *op. cit.*, pp. 44–65; Tansill, *The Canadian Reciprocity Treaty of 1854* (Johns Hopkins University Studies, series XL, no. 2), chapter I.

Congress was not enthusiastic. Southern delegates felt that such an agreement would lead to the annexation of Canada—the admission of many "free" states.[8] The Representatives and Senators from the North, on the other hand, believed that the commercial pressure resulting from the refusal of the United States to grant reciprocity would lead most surely to the political union which the North desired. For six years negotiations were continued without success,[9] until in 1854, as a result of the realistic and highly efficient diplomatic methods of the Governor-General of British North America, the Elgin-Marcy Treaty was drawn up and ratified.[10] It is generally believed that the avenues of approach which finally led to this goal were social rather than economic or political. The treaty was described by a contemporary observer as having been "floated through on a sea of champagne."[11]

It must now be noted, however, that the United States government, having decided to support the reciprocity agreement, did some "floating" on its own account. A special agent was sent into those parts of the maritime provinces and Newfoundland which were opposed to, or lukewarm concerning, reciprocity. He subsidized newspapers and individuals with funds supplied by Washington and did a great deal to produce the unanimously favorable attitude with which the various provinces greeted the treaty. This episode is so little known that it is worth particular attention. Most of the documents relating to this early venture in dollar diplo-

[8] Skelton, *The Canadian Dominion,* pp. 122–123.

[9] Tansill, *op. cit.,* chapter 2, discusses these negotiations in great detail. As he shows, all American opinion was not hostile to the idea of freer trade relations with British North America. President Van Buren and Henry Clay had been outspoken in its favor.

[10] It was proclaimed on September 11, 1854; for its terms, see Malloy, *op. cit.,* vol. I, pp. 668–672. The influence of the anti-protectionist forces of the South and West should not be minimized. Protection, as a political theory, was less in favor at this time than at any subsequent period of American history. Cf. Stanwood, *American Tariff Controversies in the Nineteenth Century,* 1903, vol. II, p. 136.

[11] Sir Francis Hincks, *Reminiscences,* Montreal, 1884, pp. 233 ff; Oliphant, *Episodes in a Life of Adventure,* New York, 1887, p. 45.

macy are kept under lock and key in Washington, and are not available, even for historians. Enough is known, however, to justify the statements made above.[12]

The Elgin-Marcy Treaty was made acceptable to the United States by the inclusion of certain stipulations giving to American fishermen full privileges in the Atlantic Coast fisheries. Lord Elgin, moreover, succeeded in convincing the southern Congressmen that failure to enact such an agreement would result in the annexation of Canada,[13] and the natural tendency towards freer trade inherent in the agricultural South was gratified. The products of forest, farm, and mine were placed on the free list by both countries; American vessels were allowed to use the St. Lawrence River, and Canadians were given similar privileges in Lake Michigan. The treaty was designed to run for ten years, and subsequently was to be subject to abrogation by either party on one year's notice.[14]

The result of this treaty was an immense stimulus to trade in both Canada and the United States.[15] The economic life of the two countries became closely integrated. Commodities were imported by the United States from Canada at one point in the long boundary line, and goods of the same type were exported to Canada at another point. Canadian fish, lumber, and farm products found a ready market in the large cities of the eastern states; American manufacturers had access to greatly expanded sources of raw materials and the cost of living was perceptibly lowered in both countries. In 1854 the total value of Canadian-United States trade was $3,480,000, while in 1856, the first com-

---

[12] Tansill, *op. cit.*, pp. 66–74.

[13] Skelton, *op. cit.*, p. 123; Porritt, *op. cit.*, p. 116.

[14] Malloy, *op. cit.*, vol. I, pp. 668–672. This treaty was ratified by the United States, Great Britain, Canada, Prince Edward Island, Nova Scotia, New Brunswick, and Newfoundland.

[15] Cf. *Canadian Annual Review for 1911*, p. 18: Harvey, *The Reciprocity Treaty—Its Advantages to the United States and Canada*, Quebec, 1865. For the complaints voiced by the textile manufacturers of New England when the treaty was abrogated see *Memorial from the National Association of Wool Manufacturers in the United States*, Boston, 1866.

plete year after the signing of the treaty, this total was raised to $57,000,000.[16]

As the result of notice given a year earlier, the reciprocity treaty was terminated by the United States on March 17, 1866.[17]

It cannot be doubted that the primary factor in bringing to an end this mutually advantageous agreement was the hostility aroused in the United States by the attitude (real or supposed) of Canada during the American Civil War.[18] The tone of many Canadian papers, the Confederate raids from Canadian soil, and the sudden raising of the Canadian tariff on manufactured articles, all tended to estrange American friendship and to make the people of the United States anxious to terminate the existing commercial arrangements which so greatly benefited Canada. As Charles Francis Adams declared, the abrogation of this treaty was "the result rather of a strong political feeling than of any commercial consideration." [19] The argument most frequently used by opponents of the treaty in the United States was that Canada had violated the spirit of the agreement by raising her duties on manufactured articles, thereby hurting American trade.[20] What had really happened was that Canadian manufacturers had been slowly growing, and, fearful of extermination unless protected against their larger American rivals, they had demanded and, in 1858 and 1859, received tariff assistance.[21] This action had so frequently occurred in the United States that American politicians should have recognized it in another country. Indeed, dur-

[16] Haynes, *op. cit.*, p. 31.

[17] Malloy, *op. cit.*, vol. I, p. 668.

[18] Goldwyn Smith, *Canada and the Canadian Question*, p. 141.

[19] *House Executive Documents,* 39th Cong., 1st sess., vol. I, pt. 1, p. 111.

[20] Dr. Skelton summarizes the reasons for the American action as follows: "In 1864 the cumulative effect of anger at British and Canadian sympathy with the South; rising protectionist sentiment, pressure of internal taxation, aggrieved sectional interests, and the absence from Congress of the low-tariff southerners led the United States to give notice of the abrogation of the Treaty of 1854." *General Economic History, 1867–1912,* p. 127.

[21] Dent, *The Last Forty Years.* Toronto, 1881, vol. II, pp. 427 ff.; Porritt, *op. cit.,* chapter 8. Both English and American explorers protested against this increase.

ing this same war period the American tariff rates had also under-
gone a process of elevation.[22] These increases, however, did not
affect the commodities in which Canada was most interested. The
Canadian action was certainly a violation of the spirit of the
treaty, although legally justifiable.[23] Two other motives were to
be found for the American action: the first was retaliation for
Canada's action in making American vessels pay tolls on the Canadian canals,[24] and the second was the frequently expressed desire
to force Canada, by depriving her of all trading privileges, to
agree to annexation.[25] The American House of Representatives
protested in 1867 against the formation of the Dominion of Canada which occurred in that year. Their contention was that this
organization of a new state was a violation of the Monroe Doctrine.[26]

Canada, however, was still anxious to continue the agreement,[27]
and to this end the Confederate Council on Commercial Treaties,
composed of representatives of all the British colonies in North
America, sent a commission to Washington early in 1866. This
delegation received a distinctly hostile reception, and, their mission failing, the treaty expired on March 17th.[28]

The termination of the reciprocity treaty dealt a heavy blow
to American-Canadian trade which fell from $60,500,000 in 1865

[22] Taussig, *Tariff History of the United States* (5th edition), New York,
1910, pp. 155 ff.

[23] Porritt, *op. cit.*, pp. 140 ff.

[24] *Congressional Globe,* 36th Cong., 1st sess., pt. 2, p. 1357. The Canadian
government answered this in *Report of the Minister of Finance upon the
Report of the Commission of Commerce of the House of Representatives,*
Ottawa, 1862.

[25] Joseph Howe, *The Reciprocity Treaty, Hamilton,* 1865, p. 14.

[26] Fish, *American Diplomacy,* New York, 1919, p. 334.

[27] It is an interesting fact that, under the treaty, the United States
exported more goods to Canada than Canada sent to the United States.
Skelton, *The Canadian Dominion,* p. 124.

[28] The Hon. George Brown, famous Liberal leader and editor of the
Toronto *Globe,* denounced this mission as truckling to an unfriendly neighbor and as beneath the dignity of Canada. Dent, *op. cit.*, vol. II, pp. 455–
457; Haynes, *op. cit.*, p. 30.

to $50,200,000 in 1867 and $48,900,000 in 1868; and this in spite of the tremendous expansion then going on throughout the continent.[29] The constant demands of westward expansion shortly led to an improvement in conditions in the United States, but in Canada this movement came later and the effects of the American tariff policy were really serious. For some time after the termination of the reciprocity treaty, Canadian tariffs were allowed to remain at the old level. Canadians "assumed that there were matters existing in 1865 –1866 to trouble the spirit of American statesmen for the moment, and they waited patiently for the sober second thought which was sure ere long to put all things right." [30] The great majority of Americans, also, expected that the high rates imposed during the war would be lowered on its conclusion. The vested interests that had been built up during the war years, however, proved to be too strong, and session after session of Congress passed without any serious attempt to lower the tariff walls.[31]

Meanwhile negotiations were continued. In 1869 Sir John Rose, Minister of Finance in the Macdonald cabinet, proposed at Washington a treaty which would have practically unified the economic life of the two nations, and which embodied discrimination against Great Britain itself.[32] This proposal was almost immediately denounced in the Canadian House. Hope was aroused, when it was announced in Canada that Premier Macdonald was to be one of the five British commissioners charged with the negotiation of the Treaty of Washington in 1871. Despite his most earnest endeavors, however, this treaty included no provision for reciprocal trading relations. The British delegates wanted a treaty at any cost and were little anxious to assist the Canadian Premier in bartering fishery rights for trading privileges. The fishery question was

[29] Prices were raised in both countries. *House Executive Documents*, no. 240, 40th Cong., 2nd sess.

[30] The Hon. George Brown, *Memoir on the Proposed Reciprocity Treaty, 1884.*

[31] Taussig, *op. cit.*, pp. 173 ff.

[32] *Annual Register for 1910*, p. 458.

treated by itself; Canada's claim for indemnity for the Fenian raids was disregarded;[33] and reciprocity was not mentioned.[34] Indeed, Senator Sumner, having drawn up a bill for 2½ billion dollars against Great Britain (on account of the *Alabama* and other British activities which, he claimed, had prolonged the war), proposed to buy Canada with a part of this sum. His offer was not accepted.[35] The treaty was received with protests by Canada, to be accepted finally as a sacrifice borne by the Dominion for the good of the empire.

In 1874 there was made a most notable attempt to secure the enactment of a just and mutually beneficial agreement. At the instigation of the Canadian government, Sir Edward Thornton, British Minister at Washington, and the Hon. George Brown were empowered to enter into negotiations with the Americans with a view to improving Canadian trade;[36] the resulting agreement (largely the product of Brown's peculiar ability) was received with considerable favor even in the protectionist press of the United States. The Brown-Fish Agreement, as it was known, settled the problem of the fisheries and raw materials as they had been settled in the Treaty of 1854; the canals and rivers were thrown open as agreed upon in the Treaty of Washington, and Canada agreed to further enlarge her waterways; the coasting trade of the Great Lakes was to be free to ships of either nation; and finally, a considerable list of manufactured articles was made exempt from tariff dues. The treaty was to run for twenty-one years, and subsequently, subject to three years' notice of abrogation.[37] Advantageous as this agreement would undoubtedly have proved to both participants, and in spite of an unusually favorable reception in the American press, the United States Senate, controlled by industrial and commercial interests which felt that

[33] These claims were not included in the original terms of reference and in consequence were not properly subject to discussion.
[34] Skelton, *General Economic History, 1867–1912,* p. 130.
[35] Fish, *op. cit.,* pp. 341, 344, 347.
[36] Porritt, *op. cit.,* pp. 165–174.
[37] For its terms see Dent, *op. cit.,* p. 547.

the concessions made by Canada were not sufficient, at first post-poned a decision, and finally refused to act favorably.[38]

Throughout this period, and until the Taft-Fielding Agreement was enacted in 1911, the motivating force urging closer commercial relations came from Canada.[39] To Washington, the Dominion was of small importance—a colony which would one day break with England, and inevitably become a part of the all-powerful United States. Why, then, should American legislators take the trouble of ameliorating the conditions of Canada while she retained her colonial status? Let her progress as best she could, that she might enter the Union the more readily when the ordained time arrived. When Canada was ready to enter a complete *zollverein,* Congress would be ready to receive her; but the bargaining for and limited profits of restricted reciprocity were not worth the trouble. For Canada, however, access to the American market was of vital importance. Isolated from the other markets of the world, and unassisted by preferential treatment in Great Britain, the economic life of the country was dependent to a large extent upon the American demand for Canadian raw materials. Thus it was that Canada was ever ready to urge reciprocal trade agreements, while the United States was never truly enthusiastic.

The years of depression following 1873[40] resulted in Canada in the adoption of a high protective tariff.[41] The "National Policy" of Sir John A. Macdonald was promulgated in 1879, and although he made an offer of reciprocity, the underlying principle of his policy was a determination to "go it alone."[42] If the United States

[38] Skelton, *op. cit.,* p. 132; Johnson and others (editors), *History of the Domestic and Foreign Commerce of the United States,* Washington, 1915, vol. II, p. 341; *Annual Register for 1910,* p. 458.

[39] Breckinridge, *History of the Canadian Banking System,* Washington, 1910, pp. 264–268.

[40] Frost (editor), *Report of the House of Commons Committee on Depression,* Ottawa, 1876, p. 120.

[41] *Canada Year Book,* Ottawa, 1926, p. 436.

[42] Cf. "Report of the Select Committee on Manufacturing Interests," appendix to *Journals of the House of Commons,* 1874, no. 3; *Proceedings of the Dominion Board of Trade,* 1876.

was not willing to agree to "reciprocity of trade," it must encounter a "reciprocity of tariffs." [43]

In 1883 the United States gave the required two years' notice of termination of the fisheries agreement negotiated by Hon. A. T. Galt in 1874, and consequently in 1885 this century-old problem again became a matter of dispute.[44] The resulting dissatisfaction made some form of agreement necessary, and Canada once more suggested reciprocity, pointing to the satisfactory conditions in the fishing industry during the period of reciprocity from 1854 to 1866. A rather more liberal Democratic administration was now in power at Washington, and a reciprocity agreement was actually prepared, but President Cleveland was unable either to persuade or coerce the Senate into giving its consent, and this attempt to better conditions failed as had its predecessors.[45] The protectionists were becoming more and more strongly entrenched in the Capitol at Washington.[46] Even the power of the White House could not dislodge them.

As the depression of 1873–1878 had led Canada to demand tariff protection as a sovereign remedy, so the stringency of 1884–1889 induced the demand for commercial union. This term meant exactly what it denoted: the complete union of Canada and the United States in all matters pertaining to commerce and to trade.[47] Identical tariffs were to be imposed on all foreign goods, while free trade was to exist between the two countries. Customs and excise duties were to be pooled and distributed on the basis of population. The leaders in this movement were Erastus Wiman, a Canadian, resident in the United States, and S. J. Ritchie, an American capitalist with large interests in Canada.[48] Starting in

[43] These were campaign slogans in 1878. The tariff after 1879 averaged approximately 35 per cent *ad valorem.*

[44] See Chapter VII; Lodge, *Reciprocity with Canada,* Boston, 1903, p. 15.

[45] *Canadian Sessional Papers, 1888,* no. 36.

[46] Taussig, *op. cit.,* pt. 2, chapter 3.

[47] Skelton, *op. cit.,* p. 167; Bourassa, *The Reciprocity Agreement,* Montreal, 1911, p. 20.

[48] Hopkins, *Canada, An Encyclopaedia,* vol. I, pp. 412 ff. An interesting

1887, the campaign for commercial union shortly brought to its standard such papers as the Montreal *Witness,* and the Toronto *Globe,* and although its advocates were disheartened by the triumph of high protection in the American elections of 1888,[49] in the modified form of "unrestricted reciprocity"[50] it became the platform upon which the Liberals fought the election of 1891. The Conservative leaders, though at first tending to favor the proposed union, gradually turned against it as disloyal to the imperial ties, and on the eve of election they announced that plans were under way for a settlement of all outstanding grievances between the United States and Canada, [51] including the reënactment, with necessary modifications, of the reciprocity agreement of 1854.[52] The disclosure that several leading proponents of commercial union were also favorable to annexation practically nullified the chances of a Liberal victory,[53] and a Conservative majority was returned.

The years 1892 to 1895 were characterized in both the United States and Canada by an acute financial depression,[54] and in consequence the Canadian desire for reciprocity became more and more insistent. A delegation had been sent to Washington in 1891, but Secretary Blaine had refused to receive it. In the following year another commission was sent, but as the American Secretary of State insisted upon the assimilation of the Canadian

sidelight on the methods employed by Wiman and his compatriots is given in the recently published memoirs of Walt McDougall, *This Is the Life,* New York, 1927.

[49] Taussig, *op. cit.,* p. 255.

[50] Each country was to maintain its own customs service. Skelton, *op. cit.,* p. 167.

[51] Lodge, *op. cit.,* pp. 15–16; Porritt, *op cit.,* p. 176.

[52] *Canadian Sessional Papers, 1891,* no. 38, sec. 4. Conservative leaders declared that the United States had instigated these discussions, a statement which Secretary Blaine angrily denied. Porritt, *op. cit.,* pp. 176 ff.

[53] Denison, "The Influence of the United Empire Loyalists upon American-Canadian Relations," President's Address in *Proceedings of the Royal Society of Canada,* vol. X; Bourassa, *op. cit.,* p. 21.

[54] Viner, *Canada's Balance of International Indebtedness, 1900–1913,* Harvard, 1924, p. 37.

to the American tariff, and discrimination against Great Britain, the discussions were unproductive.[55]

It should be noted that during this period (1866–1897) the political power of the manufacturing interests of Canada was steadily increasing. The Conservative Party, which preëminently represented these interests in Parliament, was frequently (and flatly) accused by the Liberals of making only half-hearted attempts to gain reciprocity with the United States. Indeed, the Conservative leaders were finally forced to admit that they were prepared to grant free entry only to *raw products*. This, of course, was of little value to the United States, which desired a market for its *manufactured* goods.[56]

In 1897 President McKinley, taking cognizance of the many matters disturbing the harmony of the two nations, proposed the appointment of a Joint High Commission to discuss and settle the Alaskan boundary; the question of Bering Sea; the fisheries problems; and reciprocity. This commission first met in August, 1898, and its discussions continued until February, 1899, when, unable to agree on the Alaskan problem, it disbanded with but little accomplished on any of the issues that had been raised.[57]

Dr. Skelton has well characterized the difficulties of this period:

"The conditions were not favorable for a broad and statesman-like settlement of the outstanding issues, consistent with the economic advantage and political independence of both countries. The United States, throughout this period, was still dogmatically protectionist, still prosperous, still provincial, still prodigal of resources; the 'muck-raker' and foreign complications and wealthy malefactors had not yet disturbed her complacency. The organized anarchy of the check and balance system, carried to its illogical extreme in a Constitution which kept executive, Senate and Representatives normally at loggerheads, still made negotiation difficult and ratification a gamble." [58]

[55] Skelton, *op. cit.*, p. 169; Porritt, *op. cit.*, p. 182.
[56] See the extended discussions of this matter in Porritt, *op. cit.*, pp. 177 ff.
[57] Skelton, *The Life of Laurier*, vol. I, pp. 133 ff.; Lodge, *op. cit.*, pp. 15–16.
[58] Skelton, *General Economic History*, p. 170.

With the opening of the twentieth century, American-Canadian relations underwent a surprising metamorphosis. The disappearance of the American frontier, the opening of the Canadian West, the rapid reduction of American resources as the result of the activities of wasteful and unscrupulous exploiters, the growing American demand for markets and for raw materials, the adoption by the Canadian government of modern advertising methods in their campaign for immigrants—these and other factors tended to increase the importance of Canada in the view of American manufacturers, farmers, and financiers. Within the Dominion itself a new spirit was manifested. The increased demand for Canadian goods, the growth of local industry, a realization of the immense potential wealth of the western provinces, combined to develop among Canadians a new buoyancy and optimism, a determination to justify the oft-repeated words of Sir Wilfrid Laurier: "The nineteenth century belonged to the United States, the twentieth century belongs to Canada." [59]

Canada had grown from a weak and puny infant to a strong and lusty youth. Feeling more confidence in its own ability and more assurance of its future success, the Dominion ceased its practice of organizing political pilgrimages to Washington. The vast emigration of young Canadians to the United States was gradually ceasing, and, in contrast, Canada was beginning to provide homes for the more adventurous of American farmers and to give employment and residence to American engineers and promoters. More rapid and convenient methods of transportation were opening ever wider markets to the Canadian producer, and the importance of the United States in this respect was correspondingly lessened. A feeling of confidence pervaded the whole country; every branch of national life was expanding; Canadians were thrilling with pride in their new-found strength. The Dominion became less sensitive to the slights of the United States, and less interested in the actions of her mighty neighbor. At the same time, however, trade with the United States was rapidly increasing. (See Chart No. 1.)

[59] Speech delivered in Massey Hall, Toronto, on May 20, 1902.

The great accumulation of capital resulting from the extraordinary industrial development of the nineteenth century made it inevitable that American financiers should look beyond the boundaries of the United States for opportunities for investment. Canada, possessing almost unlimited resources but seriously handicapped for lack of capital, was the logical field of exploitation.

As Canadian self-confidence increased, so American interest in Canada developed; pilgrimages to Ottawa succeeded the pilgrimages to Washington. Nor were reasons for this change difficult to find. The tremendous immigration into the United States since the Civil War had resulted in the rapid occupation of the West; the best farm lands were taken, the forests and mines had come into the power of unscrupulous corporations, and were being rapidly destroyed. So great had been the industrial development that new and increasing supplies of raw materials were becoming ever more necessary; and foreign markets must be developed for the finished product, or American industry would be seriously affected. Both as a depository of raw materials and as a market for manufactured articles, Canada was taking a more prominent place. American industrialists suddenly realized that no nation in the world was better supplied than Canada with the resources of nature, while only Germany and Great Britain exceeded Canada in the amount of imports from the United States.[60]

As corollary to the increased industrial preoccupation of the Republic, the manufacturing interests had established a firmer control over the legislative and executive departments of the government. It was, then, only logical to expect, when the industrial leaders of the country should demand the negotiation of a reciprocity agreement with Canada (on the basis of American manufactures for Canadian raw materials), that Congress should accede to the request. For once the consumers' interests ran parallel to those of the capitalistic promoter, for reciprocity with Canada would mean cheaper food for the American public.

Thus, as the United States began to look more favorably upon closer trade relations with the Dominion, Canada was undergo-

[60] *Canadian Annual Review for 1911*, pp. 22 ff.

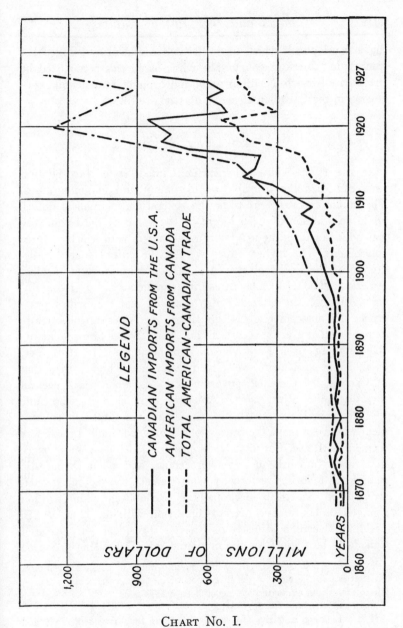

CHART No. I.

The Development of United States-Canadian Trade, 1868-1927

ing a development which made her self-confident and dulled her interest in American policy. The whole issue was crystallized by the Payne-Aldrich Tariff of 1909 and brought to a definite conclusion in the Canadian elections of 1911.

2. RECIPROCITY IN 1911

In the Payne-Aldrich Tariff the United States for the first time embodied the principle of maximum and minimum rates. The minimum rates were to be the general and permanent duties, while an addition of 25 per cent of the value of the commodity was added to form the maximum rate—a club with which to force concessions. The higher duties were to be enforced at the discretion of the President against all nations discriminating against American goods. In Canada this threat was considered grossly unfair. Although the United States admitted that the British preference did not comprise discrimination, the American negotiators demanded that Canada accord to the United States terms as favorable as those given France in an agreement made in 1910. Yet, as the American tariff was already very much higher than that of Canada, the Canadian government looked upon the American threat as quite unjustifiable.[61] American commissioners who came to Ottawa in March, 1910, were told that the Canadian government would not make the concessions demanded,[62] and a tariff war seemed inevitable. Fortunately the people of neither country were in a mood for such an insane procedure, and when Democratic candidates favoring reciprocity with Canada showed unexpected strength in American elections, the Republican administration changed its course and after a discussion with the Hon. W. S. Fielding, Canadian Minister of Finance, President Taft declared Canada to be eligible for the minimum rates.[63] Fielding promised

[61] As remarked by Skelton, *op. cit.*, p. 221, this is "A sound criticism . . . but not to the point in the discussion of modern protectionist warfare, where ethics and etiquette have never been conspicuous."

[62] *Annual Register for 1910*, p. 455.

[63] Mr. Fielding told the House of Commons that President Taft and Secretary Knox had taken the initiative in suggesting reciprocity. Com-

certain minor reductions and agreed to enter negotiations for a general discussion of reciprocity.[64]

In November, 1910, President Taft sent Messrs. Pepper, Hoyt, and Foster to Ottawa to discuss the tariff problem with Mr. Fielding. The American representatives were "authorized to take such steps for formulating a reciprocal arrangement as might be necessary and to receive and consider any proposition which the Canadian government might care to submit." [65] These discussions were adjourned to Washington in January, 1911, and on the 26th of that month agreement was reached.[66] Products of the farm, dairy, sawmill, and mine were in most cases placed on the free list, as also were fish and their by-products. Substantial reductions were to be made in the tariffs on meat, flour, coal, agricultural implements, and many manufactured articles. The agreement was to be made effective by concurrent legislation, not by treaty.[67]

These proposals met with strong opposition from many members of the Republican Party in Congress. They could not easily forget the protectionist doctrine they had so frequently upheld. The western farmers and lumbermen objected to the admission of Canadian cereals and forest products. The fishing interests of the United States feared Canadian competition in the markets of Boston, Seattle, and San Francisco. On the other hand, the "regular" Republicans voted with the administration as they had been trained, and the Democrats, delighted at the division in their opponents' ranks, and naturally tending toward freer trade, supported the proposals of the President. The powerful financial interests of the East, feeling that reciprocity would facilitate their endeavors to obtain control of the Canadian market, liberally as-

plete free trade was refused by the Canadian commissioners. *Canadian Hansard,* March 30, 1910, pp. 5942–5873; *Canadian Annual Review for 1910,* p. 623.

[64] Skelton, *op. cit.,* pp. 222–223.

[65] "The President's Annual Message to Congress," *Congressional Record,* December 6, 1910.

[66] Walker, *The Reciprocity of William Howard Taft,* New York, 1912, p. 2.

[67] *Congressional Record,* January 26, 1911, pp. 1516–1519.

sisted in the campaign—indeed their campaign had started long before.[68] The border states sent delegations to Secretary Knox protesting vigorously against a tariff war with Canada, and favoring reciprocity.[69] An attempt was made in some quarters to convince the American public that reciprocity would ultimately lead to the annexation of Canada. This idea was particularly stressed by the Hearst publications,[70] and unfortunately the statements of many responsible Americans, who should have been better acquainted with the situation, followed the same line. President Taft himself made an incredible blunder while in the process of outlining one of the strongest arguments from the American point of view, for reciprocity. "The amount of Canadian products that we would take," he declared, *"would make Canada only an adjunct of the United States.* It would transfer all their important business to Chicago and New York, with their bank credits and everything else; and it would increase greatly the demand of Canada for our manufactures." [71] Largely true, but surely an impolitic statement to make in regard to American relations with a proud and sensitive neighbor.

The Reciprocity Bill was passed by the House of Representatives, but the Senate failed to act before adjournment on March 4th. President Taft immediately called a special session and, assisted by the Democrats and the weather, the bill was passed on July 22d.[72]

Almost half a century had passed since the abrogation of the first reciprocity treaty between the United States and Canada.

[68] The following are typical subsidized publications: Sargent, *Free Raw Materials,* Boston, 1902; Whitman, *The Tariff Revisionist,* Boston, 1906; Farquhar, *The Need of Reciprocity,* Boston, 1902.

[69] *Canadian Annual Review for 1910,* p. 622.

[70] The papers were shipped in great quantities for free distribution in eastern Canada; they served as one of the primary factors causing the defeat of reciprocity. The Point Grey *Gazette* for September 23, 1911, declared: "The Hearst papers meddled too much in Canadian affairs for the good of the Liberal Party."

[71] Quoted in Walker, *op. cit.,* p. 15.

[72] *Congressional Record,* July 22, 1911; Skelton, *op. cit.,* p. 225.

During that time the renewal of the agreement of 1854–1866 had been a cardinal principle of Canadian policy. Time after time Canadian proposals of reciprocity had been refused by the United States, but now, at long last, the objective of Canadian diplomacy seemed about to be achieved. The United States had expressed its readiness to engage in a mutual reduction of tariffs; all that remained was for Canada to implement the agreement she had tried so long and so vainly to achieve.

At first glance the result of the Canadian general election of 1911 seems to be an inexplicable phenomenon. Why should a country turn so suddenly and so completely against a policy that had been advocated by both its political parties and by practically every class of its citizens for over fifty years? It is true that for a decade or more Canada had been less dependent than formerly upon American trade for her prosperity; and it is also true that certain Conservative leaders who were in close touch with the manufacturing interests of Montreal and Toronto had been somewhat lukewarm in their advocacy of reciprocity; but the great majority of the Canadian people, regardless of party or class, had been educated in the belief that reciprocity with the United States would mean prosperity in Canada. Yet in the election of September 21, 1911, the Conservative Party, whose whole campaign was based on opposition to reciprocity, won 133 seats to 88 for the Liberals.

The real explanation of this apparently sudden alteration in Canadian policy is to be found in two facts: the hostility of the manufacturing and financial interests of Ontario and Quebec, and the latent hostility of Canadians to the United States. Opposition to the agreement was organized, advertised, and subsidized by the great railroad, manufacturing, and banking interests of eastern Canada. All their propaganda would have been useless, however, had it not been for the anti-American sentiment which characterized the Canadian people in much the same way that hostility toward Great Britain had been during the nineteenth century a national characteristic of the people of the United States. However regrettable the revival of anti-American feeling may have been, and however unjustified by contemporary conditions, yet it is beyond dispute that this prejudice was the vital factor in the defeat of the Taft-Fielding agreement of 1911.

Because of its importance as marking the end of an era in Canadian-American relations, and because of the insight that it gives into the modern Canadian attitude toward the United States, a somewhat extended consideration of this election is clearly demanded.

The attitude of the United States can be stated very briefly. American opinion was obviously divided, but the subject was not then an issue of paramount and extreme importance. Canada, after all, was a comparatively small neighbor, and in letting down the bars to the north the manufacturers, or even the primary producers of the United States, were not running a very serious risk. The former at least would gain much more than they would lose. But in either event it was not a problem of life and death.

Nevertheless, President Taft was faced by the prospect of a rupture within the ranks of his own party, and it had taken all of his forensic ability, and all the influence of his office, to force the bill through the Senate. In his determination to crown a mediocre administration with at least one real achievement, he toured many sections of the country, pointing out "the peculiar relations existing between Canada and the United States" which "justify a different policy as to imports and exports from that which obtains in regard to European and Oriental countries." He further declared that "if, by reciprocal arangements we can make the commercial bond closer, it will be for the benefit of both nations." [73] Eugene R. Foss, seeking Congressional honors in Massachusetts, stated the attitude of American advocates of reciprocity thus succinctly: "We need Canada more than she needs us. In a few years we shall have to beg for favors that now she might willingly grant." [74]

The political argument based on loyalty to the empire largely overshadowed the economic phases of the reciprocity question in

[73] Address delivered at Pittsburgh, May 2, 1910. New York *Times,* May 3, 1910. See also *Canadian Annual Review for 1910,* pp. 623 ff.

[74] *Canadian Annual Review for 1910,* p. 621.

Canada. Nevertheless, the latter aspect was not completely slighted. As might be expected, Canadian farmers[75] and producers of raw materials generally favored the bill, for it promised them a wider market and higher prices.[76] This applied to the mine owners in the British Columbia coal region, although the Nova Scotia miners did not profit because of the close relation between the railroads and coal producers of the eastern United States. Canadian millers, packers, brewers, and canners were opposed to the agreement because they would have to raise their payments for raw materials to the level of the American industries of the same class. Canadian manufacturing interests greatly feared, and with justice, the competition of American firms, and the banks of Canada were too closely involved in Canadian industrial life to oppose the manufacturers. The railroads of the Dominion, particularly the all-powerful Canadian Pacific, feared the substitution of north-and-south for the existing east-and-west lines of shipment,[77] and joined in the opposition.

Proponents of the agreement argued logically that reciprocity would allow greater specialization in each country; that the complementary seasons would result in a greater variety of cheap fruits and vegetables; that transportation charges would be lighter because of the possibility of utilizing the nearest source of supply regardless of its geographic situation in relation to the boundary; and, finally, that it would result simply in an enormous expansion of the home market.[78]

Conservation became a magic word in Conservative circles during the campaign. Reciprocity, declared the followers of R. L. Borden, would result in denuding Canada of its natural resources to feed the hungry maw of American industry. The United States

[75] A great delegation from the National Council of Agriculture went to Ottawa to urge reciprocity on December 16, 1910. *Annual Register for 1910*, p. 455.

[76] American prices for grain, meat, and other products averaged slightly higher than did the Canadian. Skelton, *op. cit.*, p. 225.

[77] Pepper, *American Foreign Trade*, New York, 1919, p. 262.

[78] For a summary of the Liberal Party's arguments in favor of reciprocity, see the Toronto *Globe* and the Manitoba *Free Press* for September 20, 1911.

had wasted and destroyed her own timber; had taken only the best from her own mines; and had exterminated the fish which once had thronged her waters. Now she was preparing the way to exploit the resources of Canada. Under reciprocity Canada would become "a mere feeder to the Hill system—the back yard and lumber camp of New England." [79]

Important as were the arguments to be made against reciprocity on the basis of commercial inexpediency, the Conservative Party early chose a different method of attack. Spending little time on a discussion of the economic factors involved, they declared in unequivocal terms that reciprocity was but the first step to annexation; that a vote for Laurier was a vote against the King; and that a ballot cast for the Conservative Party was a ballot cast against union with the United States. This issue became the center of the campaign, and in spite of the repeated denials of any such tendency by all Liberal leaders, tens of thousands of Canadians voters went to the polls on September 21st firmly convinced that the fate of the empire rested upon their ballots.

Too much stress can hardly be laid upon the assistance given the anti-reciprocity forces of Canada by the more vocal expansionists of the United States. Conservative editors searched the pages of the *Congressional Record,* and delved in the files of the more bombastic section of the American press, and their gleanings made excellent irritants to disturb the minds of an already excited public. "Canadian annexation," said Senator McCumber, "is the logical conclusion of reciprocity with Canada." [80] "We are preparing to annex Canada," declared the Speaker of the House of Representatives.[81] The New York *American* represented the attitude typical of all Hearst publications: "Eventually, of course, Canada will come in," said the editor. "That will be when we want her." [82] To this assertion a Canadian editor made

[79] *Senate Documents,* no. 80, vol. XV, 62nd Cong., 1st sess., pp. 2202–2205; Victoria *Colonist,* September 19, 1911; Toronto *Mail and Empire,* September 20, 1911.

[80] Quoted in Nanaimo *Free Press,* September 14, 1911.

[81] Quoted in *op. cit.,* p. 230.

[82] Quoted in Nanaimo *Free Press,* September 14, 1911.

the obvious reply that Canada was "united in a bond that extends from England around the world and back again to England . . . the answer from the Canadian people is that Canada is, and intends to remain, British." [83] The Hon. Samuel McCall of Massachusetts declared himself of the opinion that under reciprocity "the inevitable day will be more quickly reached when the two countries will be politically one." [84] Congressman Prince of Illinois was unusually frank: "Be not deceived," he advised his northern neighbors. "When we go into a country and get control of it, we take it." Senator Cummins was even more brief, stating, "I am for the annexation of Canada." The hope of Representative Madden of Illinois was that Canada "may become part of us, as it should be," while the famous railroad magnate James J. Hill rejoiced that "reciprocity will stop the union of the British Empire." [85] Champ Clark's expressed desire to see the Stars and Stripes float over the whole continent, and the famous "adjunct" speech of President Taft, made splendid fuel for the fires of hostility lighted in the Canadian Dominion.[86]

When American political leaders began to understand the damage which these declarations were doing the cause of reciprocity, an attempt was made to minimize the issue. Secretary Knox stated that

"The United States recognize that the Dominion of Canada is a permanent North American political unit and that her autonomy is secure. . . . There is not the slightest probability that their racial and moral union will involve any political change, or annexation, or absorption." [87]

[83] Quoted in a collection of similar speeches in the Regina *Standard*, September 15, 1911.

[84] *Idem.*

[85] *Idem.*

[86] The Point Grey *Gazette* for September 23, 1911 stated: "Champ Clark blames Taft and Taft blames Champ Clark for voicing the annexation question. . . . There is little doubt that the talk of both these gentlemen helped to swell the majority." Skelton, in *The Canadian Dominion*, declares that Clark's statement was worth tens of thousands of votes to the Conservative Party.

[87] *House Documents*, no. 1418, 61st Cong., 3rd sess.

President Taft in his message urging ratification took pains to make clear that the agreement "in its intent and terms was purely economical." [88] The Liberal Party of Canada, and all who favored closer economic relations between the two countries joined in the same chorus. They declared it an insult to Canadians to argue that a mere commercial agreement would make them false to their imperial obligations, and their fealty to the Crown. They "scouted all ideas of political or commercial annexation by the United States and protested their entire and whole-hearted loyalty to the empire." [89]

These assurances from the United States and from Canadian Liberals did not, however, satisfy the voting public. The Conservative Party, well supplied with campaign funds by the financial interests, was able to carry on a propaganda that thoroughly convinced a majority of Canadians that the election offered only a choice between "the Union Jack or Old Glory." [90] Sir James Whitney, Premier of Ontario, expressed the current Canadian opinion of the American designs when he said,

> "There is not an American who does not hope away down in his heart that Canada will some day be a part of the United States and feel that reciprocity is the first step in this direction. It is the means by which annexation will be reached most quickly." [91]

Commenting on this statement, a western paper expressed another conviction commonly held by the Canadian people, namely, that reciprocity was a method employed by the United States to secure "control of Canada's vast natural resources, and of dominating the Dominion at first commercially, and then, afterwards, politically." [92] The Hon. George E. Foster saw in reciprocity "a

[88] *The United Empire Review,* February, 1911.
[89] *Ibid.*
[90] Grand Forks *Gazette,* September 16, 1911. One humorous aspect of the election lay in the fact that the capitalists who financed the loyalty campaign of the Conservative Party were themselves the strongest opponents of the British preference started by Sir Wilfrid Laurier.
[91] Grand Forks *Gazette,* September 16, 1911.
[92] *Ibid.*

menace to national solidarity," [93] and the Conservative Party declared its platform to be "the historic policy of high protection," and "loyalty toward England." [94] "Commercial Union is another name for commercial control," wrote a Conservative pamphleteer. "Commercial control means the reduction of Canadian ports to mere subsidiaries of Boston and New York. Permit that and Canadian nationality is hopelessly emasculated; and the partnership in the empire becomes a subsidiary affair also. When that point is reached there is no need to talk of annexation. It will take care of itself." [95] "The adoption of the Reciprocity pact," wrote a western editor, "means the disruption of the Empire." [96]

Although a large majority of the leading statesmen of Great Britain favored any movement toward freer trade on the part of the Dominion,[97] there were prominent Englishmen whose fears were identical with those of the Canadian Conservatives. Preeminent among the latter was that ardent imperialist, Rudyard Kipling, and his widely-circulated appeals had no little effect upon Canadian opinion.[98] The final appeal of R. L. Borden, leader of

[93] *North American Review,* May, 1911.

[94] *The Forum,* December 10, 1910, p. 656; Montreal *Gazette,* September 20, 1911.

[95] Hawkins, *The Road to Washington,* Toronto, 1911.

[96] Regina *Standard,* September 18, 1911. In *The Spectator* for the same date Andrew McPhail said: "Reciprocity binds both parties by an economic tie which will eventually grow into political bonds."

[97] Asquith, Lloyd George, Haldane, Chamberlain, Balfour, and Bryce all declared their sympathy with the movement for reciprocity. Regina *Leader,* September 19, 1911. Lord Bryce reported that political union was not involved and that British interests would be fully preserved. *State Papers,* vol. CIV, p. 291.

[98] Kipling wrote as follows: "I do not understand how nine million people can enter into such arrangements with ninety million strangers . . . and at the same time preserve their national integrity. It is her own soul that Canada risks today. Once that soul is pawned for any consideration, Canada must inevitably conform to the commercial, legal, financial, social, and ethical standards which will be imposed upon her by the sheer admitted weight of the United States. Whatever the United States may gain, and I assume that the United States proposals are not wholly altruistic, I see nothing for Canada in Reciprocity except a little ready money that she does not need, and a very long repentance." Victoria *Colonist,* September 20, 1911.

the Conservative Party, to the Canadian electors struck again the note of national and imperial patriotism:

"I beg Canadians to cast a soberly considered and serious vote for the preservation of our heritage, for the maintenance of our commercial and political freedom, for the permanence of Canada as an autonomous nation of the British Empire." [99]

It would be erroneous to suggest that reciprocity was the only issue in the election of 1911. No government can stay in power for fifteen years, as that of Sir Wilfrid Laurier had done, without making enemies and without stains upon its record. The Laurier administration had not escaped, and during the campaign the Liberal failures and mistakes were not overlooked. The plan of organizing a Canadian navy was also attacked: by the Conservatives who wished to make a direct contribution to the British Admiralty, and by the Nationalists in Quebec who wanted no naval expenditure of any sort. For the first time Sir Wilfrid Laurier was faced by real opposition in his own province, and the activities of Henri Bourassa and his Nationalist followers contributed in no small measure to the defeat of the government.[100] But, making every allowance for these issues, the vital question in the minds of the majority of the Canadian people was the question of reciprocity.

The election was held on September 21st, and resulted in an overwhelming victory for the Conservative Party. A Liberal majority of forty-four in a House of 221 members was converted into a Conservative majority of forty-five. Eight cabinet ministers were defeated.[101] "The Ghosts of the United Empire Loyalists stalked triumphant through the corridors of Ottawa." [102] Reciprocity was no longer an issue. ·

[99] Toronto *Star,* September 20, 1911.

[100] On almost every point except opposition to a Canadian navy the Nationalists and the Conservatives were diametrically opposed. Their "Unholy Alliance," as it was termed by the Liberals, caused much of the bitterness that marked the campaign in eastern Canada. See Bourassa, *op. cit.*

[101] Montreal *Star,* September 22, 1911.

[102] F. H. Soward, quoted in Keenleyside, "American Economic Penetration of Canada," *Canadian Historical Review,* March, 1927, p. 36.

In commenting on the election Canadian journals, while admitting the strength of the anti-administration sentiment which had been accumulating for fifteen years, and while laying full stress upon the French-Canadian opposition to the Laurier navy policy, yet were practically unanimous in declaring that fear of American encroachment had been the determining factor in the Liberal defeat. The election was "Canada's decided Declaration of Independence." [103] One of the most influential and, at that time, comparatively independent papers in Canada declared that the choice was between "Imperialism and ultimate Continentalism, and the realization of this had an immense influence on the result. Unmistakably the country had decided against Continentalism in trade or politics." [104] The economic value of reciprocity was invariably questioned by Conservative journals, but "even these practical considerations counted for less in the contest than the determination of the people to permit nothing to be done which would weaken the bonds of Empire." [105] The Toronto *Globe,* for nearly a century the leading organ of Liberalism in Canada, stated: "The people of Ontario do not like their neighbors to the south. That is emphatically the lesson of yesterday's election. Liberals in tens of thousands . . . joined the Conservatives . . . to show their objection to having any 'truck or trade with the Yankees.' The campaign orators of the Conservative Party builded better than they knew when . . . they appealed to the people of this province to save Canada from the Americans." [106]

In the United States much less interest naturally was taken in the defeat of reciprocity. After all, Canada was only one country, and while important to American trade, the failure of the reciprocal agreement was not by any means a fatal, or even a very serious, blow. Sorrow and some perplexity were expressed over the reasons that led Canada to take such action, but in gen-

[103] Kamloops *Standard,* September 22, 1911.
[104] Vancouver *Province,* September 22, 1911.
[105] Vancouver *News-Advertiser,* September 22, 1911.
[106] Toronto *Globe,* September 22, 1911. Yet the popular vote was only 669,000 to 625,000.

eral the issue was minimized, and the result explained by local political conditions in the Dominion.[107]

As recent discussions in Parliament have shown, the election of 1911 did not permanently settle the question of reciprocity between Canada and the United States. It is inevitable that it should arise again, and it is reasonably certain that it will receive a good measure of support from the Conservative as well as from the Liberal, Progressive and Labor Parties. The Canadian people will hardly be fooled twice by the tactics employed in 1911.[108]

3. THE EXCHANGE OF MONEY AND POPULATION

The election of 1911 marked the end of an era in the trade relations of Canada and the United States, but its actual effect upon the economic life of the two countries can easily be exaggerated. It was a dramatic gesture by which the people of the Dominion renounced a profitable bargain in order to prove to the United States—and perhaps to themselves as well—that the Dominion no longer needed to beg for economic favors. While Canada had been weak, undeveloped, and suppliant, the United States had viewed the Dominion with careless, indifferent, or impatient eyes; but at the very time when the Republic was awakening to its need of Canadian markets and supplies, the Dominion found itself "sufficiently prosperous to sacrifice a further gain . . . in

[107] The American attitude may be found represented in the following newspapers, all of the date of September 22, 1911: New York *Times,* Seattle *Post-Intelligencer,* Kansas City *Star,* Springfield *Republican.* See also Pepper, *op. cit.,* p. 262.

[108] The newly-chosen leader of the Conservative Party, the Hon. R. B. Bennett, recently caused astonishment by the declaration that the Conservatives had opposed reciprocity in 1911 *because it did not go far enough!* A study of the literature of the period does not support this bizarre interpretation. The Conservative Party is most unlikely to oppose reciprocity should the question again arise, and it is improbable that it will again be submitted to the Canadian people as an election issue.

order to show its resentment of long years of American hostility and condescension." [109] Increased trade with the United States was no longer a fundamental necessity, and Canada was in a position to make her southern neighbor pay for every concession. With the memory of the real or fancied slights and injuries of other years, the Dominion delighted in this opportunity partially to "even up the score."

The defeat of reciprocity, however, did not seriously affect the steadily growing trade between the United States and Canada. Both imports and exports were rapidly increasing, as an examination of the table on page 309 will demonstrate. At the same time, an even more vital form of economic intercourse was becoming increasingly important. This was the investment of American funds in Canada.

The Canadian economic renaissance began about 1896, but in spite of the new optimism, the influx of settlers, and the rapidly increasing trade, the Dominion was still financially dependent; it lacked the capital which was necessary for its industrial and social development. English investors had already discovered Canada, but their investments had been limited in amount and confined very largely to government and railroad bonds.[110] This was vital to Canadian progress, but capital for industrial and speculative purposes was also needed, and in progressively increasing amounts

---

[109] Skelton, *General Economic History,* p. 232; Skelton, "Canada's Rejection of Reciprocity," *Journal of Political Science,* vol. XIX, 1911, p. 730. In *The Canadian Annual Review for 1911,* pp. 22–23, J. Castell Hopkins wrote as follows: "There was in the national sense the further complication represented by a sort of subconscious resentment in many Canadian minds as to the United States' treatment of the provinces and the Dominion in many and varied matters. Of these the abrogation of the 1854 treaty was only one; the invasions of 1774 and 1812, the raids of 1837, and the sharp, shrewd treaty negotiations of other dates were too far distant to be more than unpleasant and occasional memories: the Fenian raids, the Atlantic fisheries, and the Bering Sea and Alaska boundary disputes were more recent and more irritating matters."

[110] C. K. Hobson, "British Overseas Investments—Their Growth and Importance," *Annals of the American Academy of Political and Social Science,* vol. LXVIII, p. 218.

this was supplied from American sources.[111] American industry, the greatest economic and technical organization that the world has seen, was in need of raw materials, and of these Canada was a veritable storehouse. The logic of the situation made it inevitable that American capital and American technicians should soon be employed in the process of extraction.

During the first decade of the present century American investments in the Dominion steadily increased, and even the election of 1911 did little, if anything, to lessen the flow of gold across the border. In spite of that dramatic incident, the industrialization of Canada continued.[112] It is estimated that, as early as 1914, American investments in Canada had reached a total of $700,000,000.[113] At the same date British investments, still largely in railroad securities and government bonds, totaled some $2,000,-000,000 to $2,500,000,000.[114] Canadian dependence upon the United States was shown even more clearly in the annual trade returns, which were still mounting. In 1900 Canada had imported from the United States goods valued at $102,000,000; in 1910 this had increased to $218,000,000; and in 1914 to $396,000,000.[115] Canadian exports to the United States fell far short of these totals,[116] and the situation developed to the point where Canada was bor-

[111] "American investors desired profits, the British investors interest." *Ibid.* By 1921 British investments in stocks exceeded British bond holdings, but the American discrepancy was very much greater.

[112] On the growth of Canadian industry as evidenced in urban increases see H. L. Keenleyside, *Notes on the History of Canada,* Vancouver, 1926, p. 28.

[113] C. K. Hobson, *op. cit.,* p. 217. See also *Monetary Times Annual for 1914.* It must be understood that all figures used in dealing with this particular field of investigation are approximate and subject to revision. No complete and final figures are available, and it would probably be impossible to devise any adequate technique to obtain them. See letter from Prof. K. W. Taylor in *The Canadian Historical Review* for June, 1927, p. 137.

[114] Taylor, "Canadians Control Two-Thirds of all Canadian Securities," *Financial Post,* January 13, 1928; C. K. Hobson, *op. cit.,* p. 29; Viner, *Canada's Balance of International Indebtedness,* Cambridge, 1924.

[115] *Canada Year Book, 1926,* p. 461.

[116] The exports for these three years totalled respectively $57,000,000, $104,000,000, and $163,000,000.

rowing money from Great Britain to pay for purchases in the United States.[117] These facts were viewed with apprehension by certain groups in Canada, who tended to see in American financial investments so many golden bars to thwart the national or imperial destiny of the Dominion.

Another cause of uneasiness to those who feared American encroachment was the influx of settlers from the United States to the middle western provinces.[118] In 1901, somewhat less than 18,000 American settlers moved to the Dominion, but for five years before the outbreak of the World War over 100,000 annually crossed the border. The result gave a distinctly republican tinge to many of the settlements on the Canadian prairie. Between the years 1901 and 1911 (the census in Canada is taken in the years ending in 1) the American-born population of Canada increased by almost exactly one hundred and seventy-five thousand. Of this increase more than one hundred and six thousand was provided by the returns from the three Prairie Provinces. In the latter year the American-born formed 3½ % of the population of Manitoba, over 14% of the population of Saskatchewan, and almost 22% of the population of Alberta.[119] This trend grew even more pronounced between the census year 1911 and the outbreak of the World War in 1914. It is not surprising, therefore, to find ex-Americans playing an important part in all the activities of life in the Canadian middle west.

[117] C. K. Hobson, *op. cit.*, p. 219.

[118] Speaking in Brandon, Manitoba, in 1908, William Jennings Bryan declared that Canada was the only country in the world that could draw population away from the United States.

[119] *Sixth Census of Canada.* Ottawa 1925, Vol. II, p. 239. The population problem in these Provinces has caused acrimonious discussion in Canada during the past year (1928). There has been little opposition to the influx of American settlers, but a few of the more fanatical exponents of the "Nordic" idea (led, as is too often the case, by a nominal follower of the man who came to bring "peace on earth, goodwill to men") have complained against the introduction of immigrants from Europe. Bishop Lloyd of Saskatchewan, leader of this opposition, might be asked to reflect that the proposed regulations would exclude Christ, if at His Second Coming He should choose to be reborn at the eastern end of the Mediterranean. The spirit actuating the Bishop is also reflected in Saskatchewan by the growth there of a Canadian branch of the Ku Klux Klan.

DEPARTMENT OF TRADE AND COMMERCE
OTTAWA, 1920 *

Summary of the Trade of Canada with the United States, 1868–1920

Fiscal Years	Merchandise Imports	Merchandise Exports
1868	$22,660,132	$25,349,568
1869	21,497,380	26,717,656
1870	21,697,237	30,361,328
1871	27,185,586	29,164,358
1872	33,741,995	32,871,496
1873	45,189,110	36,714,144
1874	51,706,906	33,195,805
1875	48,930,358	27,902,748
1876	44,099,880	30,080,738
1877	49,376,008	24,326,332
1878	48,002,875	24,381,009
1879	42,170,306	25,491,356
1880	28,193,783	29,566,211
1881	36,338,701	34,038,431
1882	47,052,935	45,782,584
1883	55,147,243	39,513,225
1884	49,785,888	34,332,641
1885	45,576,510	35,566,810
1886	42,818,651	34,284,490
1887	44,795,908	35,269,922
1888	46,440,296	40,407,483
1889	50,029,419	39,519,940
1890	51,365,661	36,213,279
1891	52,033,477	37,743,430
1892	51,742,132	34,666,070
1893	52,339,796	37,296,110
1894	50,746,091	32,562,509
1895	50,179,004	35,603,863
1896	53,529,390	37,789,481
1897	57,023,342	43,664,187
1898	74,824,923	38,989,525
1899	88,506,881	39,326,485

Fiscal Years	Merchandise Imports	Merchandise Exports
1900	102,224,917	57,996,488
1901	107,377,906	67,983,673
1902	115,001,533	66,567,784
1903	129,071,197	67,766,367
1904	143,329,697	66,856,885
1905	152,778,576	70,426,765
1906	169,256,452	83,546,306
1907**	149,085,577	62,180,439
1908	205,309,803	90,814,871
1909	170,432,360	85,334,806
1910	218,004,556	104,199,675
1911	275,824,265	104,115,823
1912	331,384,657	102,041,222
1913	436,887,315	139,725,953
1914	396,302,138	163,372,825
1915	297,142,059	173,320,216
1916	370,880,549	201,106,488
1917	665,312,759	280,616,330
1918	792,894,957	417,233,287
1919	750,203,024	454,873,170
1920	801,097,318	464,028,183
1921	856,176,820	542,322,967
1922	515,958,196	292,588,643
1923	540,989,738	369,080,218
1924	601,256,447	430,707,544
1925	509,780,009	417,417,144
1926***	609,825,350	474,890,028
1927****	835,878,090	475,077,348

*   *Canada Year Book, 1926.* pp. 460–461.

**   9 months ended March 31.

***   Figures for 1926 subject to revision.

****   These figures are supplied by the Department of Commerce, Washington, and in previous years the American and Canadian figures have not coincided. This estimate must, therefore, be accepted only as approximate. *New York Times. Feb. 3, 1928.*

The World War did more than any other single factor to hasten the "Americanization" of Canadian industry. A vast increase in the demand for Canadian goods, both raw and manufactured, was united with the interruption of the flow of British exports of capital to the Dominion. During these years the total value of Canadian exports increased as follows:[120]

1912	$	314,000,000
1913		377,000,000
1914		455,000,000
1915		461,000,000
1916		779,000,000
1917		1,179,000,000
1918		1,579,000,000

As increased prices were partially responsible for this increase, it will perhaps be more accurate to show the rise in actual volume of Canadian exports. Taking 1912 as the base, the index figures of exports by volume rise as follows:

1912	100
1913	127
1914	119
1915	186
1916	242
1917	220
1918	174 [121]

Canada was forced to look to the United States for the capital which made possible this increase in productivity. As a result it is estimated that by 1920 the total of American investments in Canada was in excess of $1,300,000,000, while that of Great Britain had remained constant or slightly fallen off.[122] And this was not the end. The fact that the pound sterling was at a discount during the post-war years, while the American dollar was

[120] *Canada Year Book, 1922–1923*, Ottawa, p. 470.

[121] Taylor, "Changes in the Volume of Canadian Trade, 1890–1921," *Bankers' Journal*, April, 1923.

[122] Manchester *Guardian Commercial*, vol. VII, pp. 370 ff., quoted in Scott Nearing and J. Freeman, *Dollar Diplomacy*, New York, 1925, p. 25.

selling at a 7 to 15 per cent premium, gave a further advantage to American investors in Canada—an advantage of which they made full use. Canada, suffering from the post-war depression, was again forced to appeal for aid.[123] As early as 1918 it has been estimated that American investors owned approximately 30 per cent of all Canadian industry.[124] Since 1918 the movement of American capital across the border has continued unabated. By the end of 1924 American investments totaled, according to the American Department of Commerce, $2,538,000,000, or over $300,-000,000 more than the total of all other foreign investments. By January 1, 1928, the total American investment was slightly over $3,000,000,000 and it has been increasing at the approximate rate of $250,000,000 a year.[125] This involved an interest and dividend payment to the United States in 1926 of about $137,000,000.[126] This figure must, of course, be accepted as only approximate. An American estimate, submitted to the Pan-American Conference at Havana early in 1928, placed the total of American investments in Canada at $3,900,000,000.[127] This total is certainly too high, as it is based on a computation that makes no allowance for the maturing of bonds, refunding, or changes in ownership.

The rate of increase mentioned above may be expected to decline somewhat in the immediate future as a result of two factors. In the first place, Canadian investors are rapidly attaining a position in which they themselves can supply a larger percentage of the industrial needs of the Dominion; and Great Britain is show-

[123] G. W. Austin, "The Americanization of Canadian Industry," *American Economist,* vol. LXXI.

[124] Chalmers, "American Capital in Canada," *The Annalist,* vol. XXII, p. 208; *The Times Trade Supplement,* February, 1922; Taylor, letter in *The Canadian Historical Review,* June, 1927, p. 137, and article in *The Financial Post,* January 13, 1928.

[125] Statistics obtained from the records of the Department of Commerce up to September, 1926. The most recent authoritative study is that by Professor Taylor in *The Financial Post,* January 25, 1928; see also *Barron's,* August 9, 1926, pp. 9–12.

[126] Taylor, article in *The Financial Post,* January 25, 1928.

[127] Toronto *Star,* February 5, 1928; Hamilton, "Kanada und die Vereinigten Staaten," *Zeitschrift für Politik,* August, 1927.

ing a renewed interest in the Canadian market.[128] British investors were forced into the background during the war, and suffered severely in a number of financial catastrophes (such as the Grand Trunk Railway affair). As a result they have been slow to return, but present signs indicate a renewed interest in the Canadian field. In spite of these facts, however, the demand for American capital will continue as an important element in the relations of the two countries.

An important aspect of the American financial investments in Canada is found in the establishment in the Dominion of branch factories of American enterprises. Such a factory enjoys certain very definite advantages: it has free access to the Dominion market, it profits by the British preference, and it benefits from special trade agreements such as that between Canada and France. The automobile and similar industries find a further incentive in the fact that the Canadian tariff rate on parts is less than that on complete machines, with the result that assembling plants are economically profitable.

Estimates as to the number of such factories vary greatly. Mr. R. W. Dunn claimed in 1925 that there were 700 branch factories fully owned by parent companies in the United States, and at least 900 other establishments that were partially or completely controlled by American capital.[129] Mr. Floyd S. Chalmers, editor of the *Financial Post,* as quoted by J. S. Woodsworth, M.P., in his reply to the speech from the throne in January, 1928, placed the figure at 1400.[130]

Apart from its general high percentage of control, American capital plays an important role in many prominent branches of Canadian industry. The following table sheds an interesting light on the situation as it existed in 1920: [131]

[128] Taylor, letter in *Canadian Historical Review,* p. 138.

[129] Taylor, *op. cit.,* p. 138; R. W. Dunn, *American Foreign Investments,* New York, 1925, p. 60. A partial explanation of the discrepancies may be found in the fact that Mr. Dunn included in his 900 establishments partially or completely controlled from the United States many companies that had no American "parent."

[130] *Debates of the House of Commons,* January 31, 1928.

[131] *The Times Trade Supplement,* February, 1922.

Industry.	Percentage of capital held in		
	Canada	Great Britain	United States
Electrical apparatus	36.	12.	49.
Meat packing	57.	0.2	41.4
Rubber	40.	2.	50.
Patent medicines	12.	1.8	86.
Paint and varnish	44.	1.5	47.
Motor cars	39.	—	61.
Motor car accessories	6.5	—	93.5
Brass & copper castings	55.	—	44.9
Condensed milk	48.5	0.5	40.
Refined petroleum	46.7	0.2	53.1
Sugar	67.2	8.4	17.2
Pulp and paper	68.	4.	24.

In addition, American investors held 41 per cent of the capital invested in Canadian steel furnaces and rolling mills, and 52 per cent of that in copper smelting.[132]

American investments in Canada have been most extensive in the field of industry, but, especially of late years, the Dominion bond market has also proven attractive to American capitalists. From 1910 to 1924, inclusive, the sale of Dominion, provincial and municipal bonds has exceeded six and one-half billion dollars. These sales have been divided among Canada, the United States, and Great Britain as follows: Canada, $3,726,000,000; United States, $1,916,000,000; Great Britain, $939,000,000.[133] Earlier bond issues still outstanding reduce the American percentage, but it is, nevertheless, highly significant—and its importance becomes even more evident when viewed in conjunction with the fact that Americans control approximately one-third of Canadian industry.

[132] *Canada, Natural Resources and Commerce,* Ottawa, 1923, p. 205.

[133] "Summary of Bond Sales in all Markets, 1911–1924," *Monetary Times,* vol. LXXIV, no. 2, p. 80. During 1925, Canadian government and municipal bonds to the value of $177,167,500 were floated in the United States, and securities to the value of about $70,000,000 more were placed in the first nine months of 1926. These figures are given by the United States Department of Commerce.

The total national wealth of Canada is estimated by the Dominion Bureau of Statistics at over $25,600,000,000.[134] Granting the United States an equity of $3,000,000,000, it becomes apparent that American interests own approximately 8.5 per cent of the wealth of the Dominion.

A factor that is often overlooked is that Canadian capitalists are increasing their own foreign investments at a rather remarkable rate. Not only have Canadian banks and insurance companies invested heavily in foreign securities, but private individuals are showing an ever-widening interest in the offerings of foreign bonds and stocks. It is natural that a considerable percentage of the surplus Canadian funds should go into American industrial enterprises or governmental bonds. The following table, prepared by Prof. Taylor, gives the approximate figures for 1928, and it should be most illuminating to those who think of Canada as a debtor country:

Canadian Investments Abroad, January 1, 1928.[135]

	Total	In U. K.	In U. S.	In O. C.
Govt. loans and balances	$ 43,000,000	....	$ 7,000,000	$ 36,000,000
Balances of chartered banks	270,400,000	....	162,200,000	54,200,000
Foreign securities held by chartered banks	89,000,000	37,000,000	22,000,000	30,000,000
Insur. and trust companies	267,000,000	15,000,000	165,000,000	87,000,000
Direct R. R. and indust. invest.	268,000,000	2,000,000	151,000,000	115,000,000
Miscellaneous investments	425,000,000	10,000,000	215,000,000	200,000,000
Total	$1,362,400,000	$118,000,000	$722,200,000	$522,200,000

[134] *Report of the Dominion Bureau of Statistics,* quoted in the Toronto *Globe,* April 4, 1928.

[135] Article in *The Financial Post,* February 3, 1928; "Canadian Financial Investments Abroad," *Financial Post,* November 26, 1926. It may prove of interest that 26.2 per cent of the common stock of the Canadian Pacific Railroad is owned in the United States. *Annual Report of the Canadian Pacific Railroad,* December 31, 1927.

Thus it will be seen that the total of Canadian investments in the United States in January, 1928, was approximately $722,000,-000. The same authority estimates that Canadian investments abroad are increasing by approximately $100,000,000 a year, and that about $60,000,000 of this is invested in the United States.[136]

The situation here outlined has given rise to no little anxiety among Canadian nationalists. It is not difficult to discover, in the history of nations, examples of economic control leading directly to political sovereignty, and Canada is not lacking in prophets who point the finger of tragedy at the expanding tabulations of American financial penetration. In these figures is seen the shadow of political and social annexation. The accusation made by J. S. Woodsworth, parliamentary leader of the Canadian Labour Party, that a Dominion minister had submitted certain legislative proposals for approval to the financial interests of New York, may or may not have been justified, as reported in the Canadian press. Certainly it represents an apprehension that is widespread in the Dominion. It is, of course, perfectly logical that those who supply the money should have some voice in determining its use. If Canada were to undertake any radical measures of social reform, it is unquestionable that the United States would hesitate to underwrite Canadian loans. There is also the danger that Canadians may, through this new and intimate connection with Wall Street, lose all desire for radical social and economic reform.[137]

There are other observers, however, who refuse to be perturbed by the present situation. Among this group it is demonstrated that Canadians still own over 60 per cent of their industries; that they have purchased some 70 per cent of all Dominion, provincial and municipal bonds; that American investments in timber and mining tend to eliminate themselves as the sources are depleted; and that Canada, far from being a weak, chaotic, and divided Balkan or Caribbean state, is strong, well-governed, united, and, above all, nationally conscious. Canadians still own their land; the grain

136 *Ibid.*

137 Taylor, letter in *Can. Hist. Rev.* p. 141. It has been suggested that Wall Street has already refused to assist the Canadian government in financing an extensive policy of agriculture credits.

coöperatives, the largest organizations of their type in the world, are still in the hands of Canadians; and the railways, those vital arteries of national life, are still free from foreign influence.[138] Among those who accept this reasoning, the future of the Dominion of Canada is still in the hands of its citizens; it is to be decided by them, and by them alone.

It remains to note the recent tendencies in the trade of Canada and the United States. As shown above, the election of 1911, important as it was, did not seriously affect the commercial relations of the two countries.

The Underwood Tariff of 1913[139] marked the first definitely downward movement in American customs dues made since the Civil War. From the Canadian standpoint the most important reductions were those that placed cattle, sheep, swine, beef, veal, mutton, lamb, bacon, pork, hams, milk, cream, wool, and agricultural implements on the free list. Duties were also lowered on wheat, potatoes, horses, mules, pulpwood, and paper. As was to be expected, these reductions greatly stimulated Canadian trade. During the fiscal year 1911–1912 Canada had sent to the United States 24,090 head of cattle; 9803 sheep; and 35 hogs. In the similar period for 1913–1914 the corresponding figures were: cattle 168,731; sheep 16,244; and hogs 27,637.[140] The total value of Canadian exports of animals and animal products to the United States rose from $9,864,524 in 1912 to $24,728,798 in 1914.[141] Agricultural products exported to the United States during the same years rose in value from $11,685,611 to $32,506,548.[142] The Underwood Tariff went far to improve trade relations between the two countries, and tended to bring the American tariff level nearer to that maintained by Canada.

During the World War trade conditions were quite abnormal

[138] Canada, *Natural Resources*, p. 206; *Financial Post*, Dec. 19, 1924.

[139] The law was passed on October 3, 1913, and came into effect the following day. The New York *Times* of October 4, 1913, discusses the law at some length.

[140] These figures are from the *Canada Year Book, 1913, Published by Order of the Minister of Trade and Commerce,* Ottawa, 1914, p. 642.

[141] *Annual Report of the Trade of Canada, 1920,* p. 31, table.

[142] *Idem,* p. 32.

and a study of the figures contains little that is of value in the present discussion.[143] The situation may be summarized by stating that European demand was—in most lines—vastly increased, while goods that had heretofore been supplied by European states were now produced in Canada or the United States, or imported by one from the other.

After the war European conditions gradually returned to normal, and Canadian-American trade began a process of deflation.[144] From 1920 to 1923 this deflation, as far as Canada was concerned, was in part the result of patriotic prejudice. During, and immediately after the war the United States became increasingly unpopular in Canada,[145] while there was a great stimulus given to British imperialism. This feeling was increased by American legislative enactments, such as the Jones Shipping Bill, which have tended to hinder international commerce; the Panama Tolls Bill; the Fordney Emergency Tariff; and, finally, the Fordney-McCumber Tariff of 1922.[146] This combination of circumstances and events assisted the patriotic efforts which were being made to persuade Canadians to buy within the empire. The percentage of Canadian imports received from the United States compared with the percentage received from Great Britain, during the postwar years, is as follows:

	From United States	From Great Britain
1918	82.3	8.4
1919	81.6	8.0

[143] See page 327 for the figures of war trade.

[144] June, 1922. This does not mean that the actual total trade has decreased, but that in comparison with other countries the American trade with Canada has greatly shrunken. From supplying 82.3 per cent of the total Canadian imports in 1918, the United States had declined to 69 per cent in 1921.

[145] See Chapter X.

[146] These recent tariff enactments have been considerably influenced by the "Agricultural Bloc" in Congress, and consequently are hostile to Canada—a country of agricultural exports. See *Congressional Record,* June 29, 1922, for discussion of effects of the McCumber tariff on Canada.

	From United States	From Great Britain
1920	75.3	11.9
1921	69.0	17.3
1922	69.0	15.7
1923	67.4	17.6
1924	67.3	17.2
1925	64.0	19.0
1926	65.8	17.7 [147]

While the role of prophet is not to be undertaken with impunity, the future of United States-Canadian trade relations may be forecast with some degree of assurance. Geography has decreed that these two countries shall mutually profit from commercial intercourse, and with the increase in population and the refinement of the technique of production, so will this traffic grow. Commonsense, supposedly the crowning virtue of the Anglo-Saxon, will prohibit long-continued tariff wars, and the Dominion, having once displayed her independence, and having brought the American government to a realization of Canada's national status, will almost certainly revive the question of reciprocity.[148] This day may be far in the future, but when it comes the United States will be faced with the necessity of making greater concessions than have been offered in the past. The potential resources of Canada continually increase in importance, while the needs of American industry become more urgent every year. Canadian political leaders will not fail to capitalize this advantage. The increase of American investments in Canada, and the increase of Canadian investments in the United States (which, though small to the United States, are large to Canadians) should eventually aid in the attainment of a reasonable and mutually satisfactory control of their commercial relations.

[147] *Canada Year Book, 1926*, p. 461.

[148] This question of reciprocity was discussed by Premier King and W. S. Fielding on visits to Washington as long ago as July, 1922. Boston *Transcript*, July 6, 1922; *Canadian Annual Review for 1922*, pp. 90–91. It has more recently been suggested that Canada may try to use the St. Lawrence waterway scheme to gain tariff reductions from the United States.

CHAPTER IX

Immigration and Emigration

I. INTRODUCTION

ACCORDING to the census of 1920 there were at that time 1,117,-878 persons of Canadian birth residing in the United States, while at the same time there were in Canada some 400,000 individuals who were born in the United States.[1] Neither of these figures includes the descendants of previous immigrants; the extent to which the two peoples have mingled is suggested when it is recalled that Canadian emigration to the United States began very early in the history of the latter country, and that the migration of Americans to Canada was in progress even before the Revolutionary War. Although American immigration to Canada was important during the years following the Revolution, when the wonderfully productive lands of Upper Canada enticed many settlers across the border, this movement died down soon after the War of 1812, due to the hostility aroused in the United States by that struggle, to the opening of the regions west of the Alleghenies, and to the rapidly improving means of communication and transport to the western plains. After the American Civil War, the emigration of youthful Canadians to the rapidly expanding Union was the skeleton in the closet of Canada's national pride. Attracted by the high wages paid in the industrial centers of New England, by the greater opportunities for commercial or professional success, or by the accessibility of the excellent farm-

[1] "Composition and Characteristics of the Population," *Fourteenth Census of the United States,* Washington, 1922, p. 8; *Sixth Census of Canada, 1921,* Ottawa, 1925, vol. II, p. 238. Unfortunately, no accurate figures are available for the periods intervening between the takings of the decennial census.

ing lands of the American middle west,[2] the enterprising and ambitious youth of Canadian birth was sorely tempted to cross the
border and to seek fortune or fame in the great republic. It was
not until the opening of the twentieth century that American immigration to Canada again reached notable proportions. Between
1896 and 1914 many farmers from the central regions of the
United States, influenced by the immigration policy of the Canadian government and attracted by the extraordinary qualities
of the wheat belt of Manitoba, Saskatchewan, and Alberta, moved
to the north of the 49th parallel and took up homesteads in the
prairie provinces.

What effect this mutual exchange of citizens has had, or what
effect it may have in the future, is a matter for individual interpretation; but there can be little doubt that the influence of the
emigrants will at least tend to improve the relations of the two
countries involved. The American emigrants will interpret to the
citizens of their new homeland the ideals of the nation which they
have left, while upon the Canadians, newly arrived in the United
States, will devolve a similar duty.

Throughout the nineteenth century neither the American nor
the Canadian government was sufficiently interested in the problems of immigration to gather the accurate and detailed records
which would make the movement really intelligible to the modern
investigator. Enough has been done, however, to give some idea
of the numbers and classification of those composing the tide
of international migration on this continent, and to allow of comparatively accurate generalizations concerning it.

2. CANADIAN IMMIGRATION INTO THE UNITED STATES

Canadian immigration has been concentrated upon New England and New York, and upon the north-central states of the

[2] At this time western Canada was almost unexplored, and had little
or no connection with the centers of population. The first railroad was
opened only in the eighties; the farming land, now so extraordinarily productive, was almost inaccessible. The free land of the United States was,
on the other hand, very easily reached and was in direct communication
with the eastern markets.

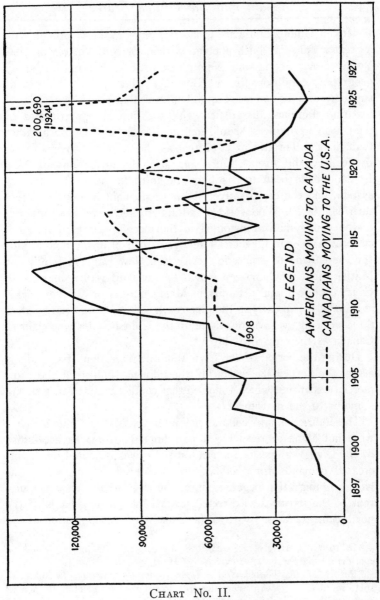

CHART No. II.

Population Movements Across the United States-Canadian Boundary

American Union. There are today few cities in the Dominion with
a greater Canadian-born population than Detroit, Boston, or New
York.[3] Nova Scotia and New Brunswick have been forced by
geographic conditions to use Boston as their principal depot of
supplies, and it has been quite natural that ambitious sons of
maritime families, dissatisfied with the limited opportunities of
their native provinces, should look to Boston or New York rather
than distant Toronto or Montreal as the scene of their life activities. To the French-Canadians also, the attractions of New
England have been irresistible. The introduction of the factory
system, and the comparatively high wages paid in textile centers
such as Lowell, Woonsocket, and Pawtucket were most inviting
to the young man accustomed to the meager salary of an agricultural laborer in Quebec. A few years of toil in the textile mills
for Pierre, and of domestic service in a New England family for
Marie, and enough money would be saved to return in state to
Canada, or to found a family in Massachusetts or Vermont. This
movement began early in the nineteenth century; and even by 1850
there were 147,711 persons living in the United States who claimed
Canada as their place of birth.[4]

During the period of the Civil War the migration of Canadians
across the border slackened, but the immense industrial and commercial expansion which followed that conflict resulted in a strong
stimulus to the movement.

The industrial and commercial interests of the United States
were not alone in receiving a new impetus from the necessities
of the Civil War period: agriculture also was benefited by the increased demands for food and raw materials. Thus, when Canadian immigration began again at the close of the war, one current of the stream was directed toward the farming lands of the
north central states. By 1870 the Canadian-born population of the

[3] In 1920 respectively 58,894, 42,008, and 50,542. The figures would be
considerably larger today. *Fourteenth Census, op. cit.,* p. 42.
[4] *Report of the United States Immigration Commission,* Washington,
1911, vol. XL, p. 35. An interesting feature of the Presidential election in
1928 was the balance of power in Massachusetts and New Hampshire held
by the French Canadian voters. See New York *World,* Oct. 30, 1928.

Union had increased to 493,464.[5] Then for thirty years the movement of Canadians into the United States reached its highest
totals, and the fact that many of these emigrants were the more
able and ambitious members of their respective Canadian communities, while advantageous to the United States, was sorely
complained of in Canada. A feeling of hopelessness seemed to
permeate the Dominion, and it was not until the opening of the
twentieth century that confidence in their national destiny was
restored to the people of Canada. The tables on page 342 make
manifest the reason for Canadian despondency.

Here it is seen that in a period of thirty years, the number
of Canadian-born residents of the United States increased by
687,791—an annual influx of approximately 23,000. When it is
realized that during this same period (1870 to 1900) the native-
born population of the Dominion itself increased only from 2,-
892,763 to 4,761,815;[6] and that the number of Canadian-born
persons residing in the United States was almost one-fourth of
the number of the same class in Canada, the serious effects which
this migration entailed upon the Dominion become apparent.

Since 1900 the southerly movement of the Canadian population
has diminished. This has been due to certain fairly obvious causes,
among which may be mentioned the great railroad expansion in
the Canadian west, the filling-up of the agricultural regions of
the United States, an increased knowledge of the potentialities of
the Canadian wheat belt, and the propagandist activities of the
Canadian government, which attracted immigrants from all parts
of the world, and which instilled in the Canadians themselves a
new enthusiasm for their northern homeland. The election of Wilfrid Laurier and the Canadian Liberal Party in 1896 struck a
note of confidence and self-reliance that soon resounded throughout the Dominion. The opening of the West and the industrial
awakening of the East offered more worthy opportunities to youthful energy and ambition. No longer were Canadians forced to
emigrate to the United States in order to find scope for their

[5] *Ninth Census of the United States,* Washington, 1871.
[6] *Report of the United States Immigration Commission,* vol. XL, p. 36.

TABLE I

NUMBER OF CANADIAN-BORN PERSONS
IN THE UNITED STATES

1870............................	493,464
1880............................	717,157
1890............................	980,938
1900............................	1,181,255
Increase, 1870–1900..........	687,791 [7]

TABLE II

GEOGRAPHICAL POSITION	1870	1880	1890	1900
North Atlantic States	250,983	343,022	490,229	650,502
South Atlantic States	2,249	3,926	5,412	6,920
North Central States	217,477	324,838	401,660	422,323
South Central States	3,880	6,180	8,153	10,262
Western States	18,875	39,191	75,484	80,800 [8]

TABLE III

COMPARATIVE GEOGRAPHICAL DISTRIBUTION
OF CANADIAN-BORN IN THE UNITED STATES

GEOGRAPHICAL DISTRIBU-TION	CANADIAN-BORN	POPULATION
	1900	1920
North Atlantic States	650,502	611,450
South Atlantic States	6,920	12,872
North Central States	422,323	331,724
South Central States	10,262	11,841
Western States	80,800	149,991 [9]

[7] Compiled from *Census Reports,* nos. 9, 10, 11, 12. The figures here and elsewhere in section I include Newfoundland as part of Canada.

[8] *Report of the United States Immigration Commission,* vol. XL, p. 36.

[9] Compiled from *Fourteenth Census, op. cit.,* p. 39, and *Twelfth Census Report.*

business or professional activities. With most of the farm lands of the United States already occupied, the prospective farmer turned more willingly to the vast regions west of Lake Superior and north of the international boundary. Industrial and commercial expansion opened new fields for the engineer, the tradesman, and the lawyer, while the growing population made increasing demands for the doctor, the clergyman, and the professor.[10] As a result of these changes, Canadian immigration into the United States was greatly diminished in volume.

The quality of the more recent immigrants has also been somewhat less satisfactory—the respectable and energetic farmers who had previously entered the central states in great numbers were now going instead to western Canada, while the numbers of unskilled immigrant laborers remained about the same. In 1910 the number of Canadian-born persons in the United States had increased to 1,196,070—an addition of only 14,815 since 1900, while by 1920 the total had actually decreased to 1,117,878.[11] Table III, moreover, clearly demonstrates that this diminution occurred principally in the agricultural communities—an effect, as has been shown, of the opening of the Canadian prairie provinces.

The really significant figures here are those for the north-central states, which show a decrease of almost 100,000 in the number of Canadian-born residents. The less important diminution in the totals for the North Atlantic states was due in some part, at least, to the American regulation against the immigration of "contract labor."[12] This prohibition undoubtedly had some effect, though it may be stated as an open fact that many industrial firms

[10] The emigration of professional men, however, continued longer than that of any class except laborers, and even today the Canadian students of law, medicine, theology, or the arts, tend to be drawn to the United States in significant numbers. Modern immigration from Canada, however, consists very largely of the poorer grades of labor—men who have been unsuccessful in the Dominion, or unskilled workers for the New England or Michigan factories.

[11] *Fourteenth Census, op. cit.,* p. 8. In 1921 there were only 8,788,483 Canadians in Canada.

[12] *Report of the Commissioner-General of Immigration,* Washington, 1920, p. 17.

in New England still import hundreds of French-Canadian laborers each year.[13]

Table IV shows the yearly immigration of Canadians into the United States for the twelve years up to 1919. It should be borne in mind, in considering these figures, that the Canadian Department of Immigration has repeatedly declared that the American figures as published are decidedly overestimated. In an investigation conducted in 1910 the Canadian department followed up 849 cases which the United States officials had listed as permanent immigrants, and discovered that 415 of those examined had entered the United States either on a visit or in search of temporary employment. Similar results were declared to have been found in a second investigation carried out in 1912.[14] Bearing this criticism in mind, the American figures given below are, nevertheless, important, and being the only authoritative statement issued by either country, they may be accepted as reasonably accurate.

TABLE IV

Date.	1908	1909	1910	1911	1912	1913	1914
Canadian Emigrants to U. S.	43,805	53,448	56,555	56,830	55,990	73,802	86,139

Date.	1915	1916	1917	1918	1919	Total.
Canadian Emigrants to U. S.	82,215	101,551	105,399	32,452	57,785	775,971 [15]

[13] In certain cases which have come to the attention of the author, the immigrant is sent for by "relatives" already in the United States and comes on a "visit," although the regulations are being more vigorously enforced each year.

[14] *Canadian Annual Review for 1920*, p. 241.

[15] *Ibid; Report of the United States Immigration Commission*, vol. XL, p. 38.

The great increase in Canadian immigration during the war years at once becomes evident, and the cause of this growth is to be found in the immense industrial "boom" which brought vast wealth to the United States, and which attracted workers from all parts of the world. Undoubtedly many of these workers did not intend to leave Canada permanently. In 1918 the Canadian Military Service Act practically stopped all male emigration.

More important to the future of the United States than the number of immigrants is the quality of those who comprise the yearly quota. An examination of the movement from this standpoint discloses many interesting facts. It reveals more clearly the reasons for Canada's discontent in reference to the vast emigration of the period from 1870–1900. Apart from the French-Canadian laborers and the fishermen and mechanics from the maritime provinces, Canada lost many of those who, by their exceptional qualifications for business or professional life, would have done much to speed the development of the Dominion. These men left Canada to seek in the United States a field where their abilities would enjoy a greater opportunity and reap a richer reward. The names of James J. Hill, Admiral Sims, Alexander Graham Bell,[16] Franklin K. Lane, Senator Couzens, and James T. Shotwell are prominent in the annals of American achievement, and they belong to men who entered the United States as emigrants from Canada. In the academic world the situation is most extraordinary. The faculties of the better American universities are honeycombed with Canadian scholars, and it is not at all unusual to find an ex-Canadian occupying the president's chair. It is probably safe to assert that no country in the world has produced, proportionately, as many men of academic distinction as has the Dominion of Canada.

The vast majority of the French-Canadians who entered the United States sought employment in the textile centers of New

[16] The inventor of the telephone was born in Edinburgh, and emigrated to Canada in 1870. Later he moved to the United States. The other names are those of men who were born in the Dominion.

England.[17] The willingness of this type of immigrant to work for lower wages than those demanded by the American workman made him particularly valuable to the employer. Table V, in comparing the average weekly wage received in the textile industry of New England by the different nationalities represented, gives an interesting sidelight on this matter.

TABLE V

NATIONALITY	WAGE
French-Canadian	$10.09
German	10.60
English	11.71
British-Canadian	11.85
Average American	11.60 [18]

Only 1.2 per cent of the French-Canadians employed in this industry received over $20.00 per week. In other words, these immigrants were willing to accept a lower standard of living than that demanded by native Americans, or other northern peoples. On that basis they cannot be accepted as an ideal addition to the population. One the other hand, however, the wages and living standards of the French-Canadians were higher than those of the Greeks, Italians, Lithuanians, Poles, Portuguese, and Armenians.[19] The Italians and Portuguese exceeded them in the percentage of married women who were engaged in factory labor.[20] The wages and standards maintained in this industry by other Canadian immigrants (chiefly from the maritime provinces) were, however, distinctly above the average.[21] Table VI, compiled from records gathered by the United States Immigration Commission, compares these types on another basis—that of literacy.

[17] 74.6 per cent of the first generation, born in Canada; 89.2 per cent of the second generation, born in the United States. Cf. *Report of the United States Immigration Commission*, vol. X, p. 79.
[18] Compiled from the figures for 1910 in *idem*, p. 83.
[19] *Ibid.*
[20] *Idem*, p. 108.
[21] *Ibid.* See Chapters IV and V for general discussion.

TABLE VI

LITERACY OF WORKERS IN THE TEXTILE INDUSTRY

NATIONALITY	MALE	FEMALE	AVERAGE
American	98.9	98.5	98.7
Canadian	97.0	98.9	97.9
French-Canadian	78.8	89.4	84.0 [22]

French-Canadian immigrants do not display any great tendency to accept the nationality of the country in which they labor. In an investigation of one of the largest French-Canadian communities in the United States it was found that only 20.3 per cent of those who had been in the United States over five years had been naturalized, and that only 5.5 per cent more had taken out their first papers.[23] A similar investigation among British-Canadian immigrants gave 34.1 and 6.6 per cent respectively. Both of these figures are below the average for foreign-born residents of the United States, and to that extent the value of Canadian immigration is to be questioned.[24] This low percentage of naturalization is probably due to the ease with which the Canadians can return to their own land. European immigrants generally come to the United States intending to stay permanently, but this is far less true of the Canadians.

Some 63 per cent of the French-Canadians engaged in the textile industry of the United States speak English.[25] Unfortunately, no studies have been made of, nor are any official data obtainable in regard to, the literacy, naturalization, and other characteristics of the Canadian (as distinct from the French-Canadian) immigrant, except with reference to the comparatively small number

[22] *Idem,* p. 143.
[23] *Idem,* p. 187.
[24] The percentage of naturalization among American-born residents of Canada was 63.6 in 1921. *Sixth Census,* p. 423.
[25] *Report of the United States Immigration Commission,* vol. X, p. 209.

who are engaged in the textile trades, and which have been treated above. Tables VII and VIII, however, do give a general idea of the type of immigrant that enters the United States from Canada. Both Canadians and French-Canadians are included in these totals—the latter comprising about 30 per cent of the whole. The figures are for the years 1908 and 1909, which may be accepted as typical.

In connection with Canadian-American migrations, mention must always be made of the "Canadian channel" through which for many years flowed into the United States a stream of European immigration. Until 1902 there was no inspection of immigrants entering the United States from Canada by land.[26] The natural result was that those Europeans who were refused admission to the United States at New York could take boat for Quebec and later cross the Canadian border. So flagrant did this abuse become that Lyman J. Gage, Secretary of the Treasury under President Roosevelt, commissioned inspectors to operate on the continental boundary, and the rules of exclusion were enforced there as at Ellis Island.[27]

As the many phases of Canadian national life develop, the tendency will be for the better and more successful classes of Canadian society to remain in the Dominion, since it will no longer be necessary to emigrate to the United States in order to discover opportunities for development. It appears that the immigrant tide of the future will be composed largely of the unsuccessful and the dissatisfied—those classes which Canada can best spare, and which the United States has least reason to desire. In the past America has welcomed and absorbed many of Canada's most promising sons; the future prospect is less bright.

3. AMERICAN IMMIGRATION INTO CANADA

The first movement of Americans into the region now known as Canada occurred in the years immediately following the cap-

[26] *Facts About Immigration*, New York, 1907, pp. 111–112.
[27] *Idem*, p. 112.

TABLE VII

1908–1909. IMMIGRANTS INTO THE UNITED STATES
FROM CANADA

YEAR	TOTAL	SEX		AGE		
		Male	Female	Under 14	14–45	Over 45
1908	43,805	35,048	8,757	4,782	36,631	2,392
1909	53,448	37,532	15,916	8,606	40,584	4,258

YEAR	LITERACY		MONEY		
	Read only	Neither Read nor Write	Number Bringing in		Total Money Brought in
			$50 or more	Under $50	
1908	131	5,435	12,534	20,736	$2,417,348
1909	138	5,991	14,850	22,513	3,464,237 [28]

TABLE VIII

1908–1909. OCCUPATIONS OF CANADIAN IMMIGRANTS
TO THE UNITED STATES

YEAR	Profession-al	Skilled Labor	Farmer	Farm Labor	Common Labor	Serv-ant	No occupa-tion	Miscel-laneous
1908	791	11,300	1,276	1,875	15,002	2,238	10,132	1,191
1909	875	11,468	1,669	1,854	16,355	2,943	16,687	1,597
TOTAL	1,666	22,768	2,945	3,729	31,357	5,181	26,819	2,788 [29]

[28] *Report of the United States Immigration Commission*, vol. X, pp. 38–39.

[29] *Ibid.*

ture of Louisburg by British and colonial troops in 1748. In an effort to assure the retention of Acadia, the British government fostered emigration to the recently acquired regions, and many settlers from Pennsylvania and New York—particularly those of Germanic stock—transferred their families and their possessions to Halifax or Port Royal.[30] There was also a considerable migration of fishermen from Massachusetts and Rhode Island to the ports of Acadia; the latter were more convenient bases for those engaged in the north Atlantic fisheries. Following the capture of Quebec by the British in 1759, and more particularly of Montreal in 1760, traders and merchants from New England and New York entered Canada in considerable numbers. A noteworthy trade was established between Montreal and Albany, and the former city was overrun with American business men.[31]

It was during the Revolutionary period, however, that the most important emigration movement took place. The Loyalists founded New Brunswick and Upper Canada; they formed the predominant group in Prince Edward Island and Nova Scotia. Thus, in a very real sense, Canada may be said to have been founded by American immigration.[32]

During the twenty-nine years between the end of the Revolutionary War and the outbreak of the second war against England, some 25,000 American farmers crossed the border into the fertile districts of Upper Canada.[33] This movement ceased at the close of the war, and thenceforward the Mississippi valley and the American west proved more attractive to the venturesome pioneers who migrated from the thirteen colonies.

For three-quarters of a century after the War of 1812 American immigration to Canada was of comparatively little importance. It was not until the Canadian Pacific Railway had opened to settlement the Northwest Territories that any considerable number of Americans emigrated to Canada, and it was not until the five years preceding the outbreak of the World War that the

[30] Bolton and Marshall, *op. cit.,* pp. 312, 322, 366.
[31] McArthur, *History of Canada,* Toronto, 1928, pp. 140–141.
[32] See above, Chapter II.
[33] See above, Chapter III.

IMMIGRATION TO CANADA

TABLE IX

Period	From United States
Calendar year 1897	2,412
" 1898	9,119
" 1899	11,945
Six months ended June 30, 1900	8,543
Fiscal year ended June 30, 1901	17,987
" " " " " 1902	26,388
" " " " " 1903	49,473
" " " " " 1904	45,171
" " " " " 1905	43,543
" " " " " 1906	57,796
Nine months ended March 31, 1907	34,659
Fiscal year ended March 31, 1908	58,312
" " " " " 1909	59,832
" " " " " 1910	103,798
" " " " " 1911	121,451
" " " " " 1912	133,710
" " " " " 1913	139,009
" " " " " 1914	107,530
" " " " " 1915	59,779
" " " " " 1916	36,937
" " " " " 1917	61,389
" " " " " 1918	71,314
" " " " " 1919	40,715
" " " " " 1920	49,656
" " " " " 1921	48,059
" " " " " 1922	29,345
" " " " " 1923	22,007
" " " " " 1924	20,521
" " " " " 1925	15,818
" " " " " 1926	18,778
Calendar year 1927	23,000 [34]

[34] Official figures for 1927, quoted in Toronto *Globe*, March 6, 1928.

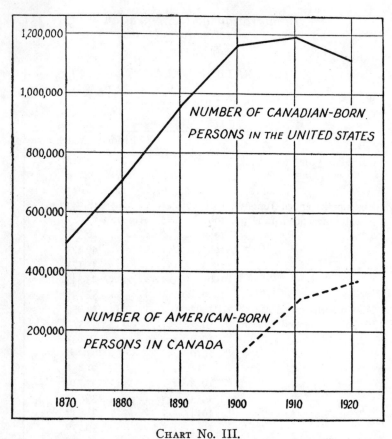

1,200,000

1,000,000

800,000

NUMBER OF CANADIAN-BORN
PERSONS IN THE UNITED STATES

600,000

400,000

NUMBER OF AMERICAN-BORN
PERSONS IN CANADA

200,000

1870   1880   1890   1900   1910   1920

CHART No. III.

Resident Aliens, 1870–1921

immigrant flood reached noteworthy dimensions. Table IX traces the course of this movement from January 1, 1897, to December 31, 1927.[35] From the figures in Table IX should be subtracted the number of Americans who annually left Canada to return to the United States. There were 8433 such removals in 1928.

The Canadian census of 1921 gave the total number of American-born persons living in Canada as 374,024.[36] Table IX shows the growth of this element of the population by decades from

[35] Table from *Report of the Department of Immigration and Colonization,* Ottawa, 1921, p. 5.

[36] *Sixth Census,* p. 238.

1871, and compares the number of those born in the United States with the number of native-born Canadians and the number of those persons residing in Canada who were born in the British Isles.[37] Here it will be seen that the number of American-born persons in Canada increased between 1901 and 1911 by some 137.4 per cent. Had the war not intervened, there can be no doubt but that the movement from the south would have continued, for some time at least, unabated.

A comparison of the number of the American-born in the three prairie provinces of Canada in the years 1901, 1911, and 1921 gives conclusive evidence that the majority of American immigrants were of the agricultural classes, and entered the Dominion to take up land in the great wheat belt of the Middle West.

TABLE X

Province	American-born 1901	American-born 1911	American-born 1921	Increase 1901–1921
Manitoba	6,922	16,326	21,644	14,722
Saskatchewan	2,758	69,628	87,617	84,859
Alberta	11,119	81,357	99,879	88,760
All Canada	127,899	303,680	374,024	246,125 [38]

It can be seen from the totals in Table X that during the decade from 1901 to 1911 the American-born population of Canada increased by 246,125, and of this total 188,341 chose the three great agricultural provinces as their destination, while only 57,-784 entered the remaining six provinces and the Yukon territory combined.

Further proof of the agrarian characteristics of the average

---

[37] *Ibid; Canada Year Books,* for 1911 and 1914.

[38] *Sixth Census,* p. 239. These figures were somewhat lowered when the 1926 census of the prairie provinces was taken. The hard years from 1922 to 1925 witnessed the removal of many Americans from Canada back to the United States. See *Census of Saskatchewan, 1926,* p. 80; *Census of Manitoba, 1926,* p. 39.

American immigrant can be found in the following classification, based on the figures for the typical years 1907–1908.

TABLE XI

Place of Birth	No. in 1871	% of total.	1881	%	1891	%
Canada	2,892,763	82.	3,715,492	85.	4,185,877	86.
British Isles	486,376	14.	470,906	10.8	477,735	9.8
United States	64,447	1.8	77,753	1.7	80,915	1.6

Place of Birth	No. in 1901	% of total.	1911	%	1921	%
Canada	4,671,815	86.9	5,619,682	78.	6,832,747	77.7
British Isles	390,019	7.2	784,526	10.8	1,025,121	11.6
United States	127,899	2.3	303,680	4.2	374,024	4.2 [39]

TABLE XII

OCCUPATION OF AMERICAN
1907–1908.   IMMIGRANTS   Number

Farmers and farm laborers	120,450
General laborers	14,606
Mechanics	8,518
Traders and clerks	4,426
Miners	2,542
Female servants	329
Unclassified	2,248 [40]

[39] *Sixth Census,* p. 38; *Canada Year Books* for 1911 and 1914.
[40] From Smith, *A Study in Canadian Immigration,* Toronto, 1920, p. 65.

The totals for the year 1926 are smaller, but the proportion remains fairly constant, as Table XIII demonstrates.

TABLE XIII

OCCUPATION OF AMERICAN
IMMIGRANTS

1926	Number
Farmers and farm laborers	7,953
General laborers	1,675
Mechanics	1,904
Traders and clerks	1,474
Miners	149
Female servants	506
Unclassified	5,117

Judged on the basis of American immigration, the immense wheatlands of the Middle West are Canada's greatest asset. And in the utilization of these areas the American immigrant has proved more valuable than any other single class. During the period from 1900 to 1909, 44 per cent of the homesteads taken up by immigrants were taken by Americans.[41] Not only did this movement increase the productivity of the prairie region and add to the total population, but in nine years (from 1912–1921) American immigrants took into Canada some $128,922,414 in stock and cash.[42]

Disregarding for the moment the natural causes (cheap land in Canada; congestion in the United States) which led to a movement of such a size as that depicted above, it is interesting to note the methods employed by the Canadian government, designed to foster immigration from the United States. Beginning its propagandist activities in North Europe and the British Isles, in 1897 the Department of Immigration and Colonization entered the American field, and here achieved its most striking successes. Advertisements were placed in thousands of farm weeklies, and pamphlets were distributed by the million. Agricultural exhibits were on display in American fairs; successful farmers from the

[41] Smith, *op. cit.*, p. 67.
[42] Figures supplied in 1921 by R. H. Coats, Dominion Statistician. See discussion of this matter in Viner, *op. cit.*, pp. 41–43.

Canadian west were sent through the United States with their glowing stories of limitless land to be had for the asking and crops that ran to unbelievable figures. Prospective settlers were taken on tours of inspection at the government expense, and agents were placed in sixteen of the largest American cities to advertise the wonderful possibilities of the Canadian prairies. Sub-agents were employed, and a bonus of $3 for a man, $2 for a woman, and $1 for a child, was paid on all immigrants whom they secured. From 1898 to 1908 the total amount spent on this propaganda in the United States was $1,936,000—or approximately $5 per immigrant.[43]

The question of the methods, costs, and numbers of immigrants procured, however, recedes before the more important problem which concerns the quality of the incoming throngs. Prior to 1908 Canada had required no inspection of persons entering the Dominion by the land frontier from the United States. The result was that European immigrants who had been rejected at Quebec took ship for New York or Boston and traveled thence by land to their Canadian destination. Realizing the inadequacy of the existing arrangements, the Canadian Department of Immigration in 1908 undertook to examine all persons entering Canada by land, as well as by sea. The immediate result was the rejection of one in every twelve immigrants who sought to cross the American border.[44] During the period from 1910 to 1918, inclusive, 151,751 such persons were refused admission into the Dominion. The majority of those barred were not American citizens, but were Europeans who feared rejection at Quebec and hoped to elude observation by entering from the United States. In contrast with this heavy percentage of rejections, the American immigrants deported from Canada after admission was less than the average of other nationalities. The average ratio of deportations to admissions for all nationalities was 1 to 235. The ratio for American citizens was 1 to 283.[45]

[43] *Report of the United States Immigration Commission,* vol. XL.
[44] The number rejected at the seaports averaged 1 in every 35. Smith, *op. cit.,* pp. 125–126.
[45] *Ibid.*

The criminal record of the American-born immigrants to Canada has not been as satisfactory as might be expected. As has been shown, the great majority of these individuals are middle-class farmers, industrious, genial, and trustworthy. They are respected and popular for their ability, their attention to business, and their democratic tendencies. There are few elements in the Canadian population less endowed with criminal proclivities.

The contiguity of the two nations has, however, facilitated the movement across the border of another and much less desirable class of immigrant. Prostitutes, vagrants, rum-smugglers and criminals of all kinds, when driven from Buffalo, Detroit, Duluth, Seattle, or other border cities by recurring periods of strict law enforcement, find little difficulty in crossing the international border. Such a migration has been made even more logical by the passage of the Eighteenth Amendment to the American Constitution—while Vancouver, Toronto, and Montreal still supply intoxicants to the thirsty visitor. The sale of intoxicants adds to the business of the allied trades. Table XIV gives some idea of this undesirable influx. It is almost impossible to apprehend such persons, and the figures here given should be multiplied many times to find the number in each class who succeed in entering the Dominion. The figures are for 1908–1920 inclusive.

TABLE XIV

REJECTIONS FOR CAUSE
AT THE CANADIAN BORDER

Cause	Number
Vagrancy	3,777
Prostitution	876
Criminality	235
Bad character	183
Procuring	144
Drunkenness	99
Service as pimps	11
TOTAL	5,325 [46]

[46] "Immigration," p. 14.

The proverbially strict enforcement of Canadian laws tends to discourage this movement, and it does undoubtedly prove effective in many cases. On the other hand, this strict enforcement results in the capture of many of those potential or actual criminals who do enter the Dominion, and thus the excellent record of the vast majority of American immigrants is tarnished. Even with these conditions working against them, however, the criminal record of those persons in Canada who claim American birth is below the general average. The following table has been compiled from figures supplied by the Dominion Statistician, Mr. R. H. Coats, for the four years immediately preceding the outbreak of the war, and for 1920.

TABLE XV

RATIO OF CONVICTIONS FOR INDICTABLE
OFFENSES TO NUMBER OF EACH NA-
TIONALITY (BY BIRTH) IN CANADA

Canadians	1 in	125.3
Other British Dominions	1 "	89.2
Scottish	1 "	65.1
English	1 "	61.0
American	1 "	57.3
Irish	1 "	45.1
Average of other Foreign-born	1 "	35.8

The situation is further clarified by a comparison of the number of convicts of each nationality, in relation to the number of adult males of that nationality in Canada. Here cognizance must be taken of certain other facts. The majority of the farmer-immigrants from the United States, intent on their home-building, and expecting to live and educate their families in Canada, become naturalized as soon as their period of probation is ended.[47] The greater number of these immigrants also are accompanied

[47] 60 % of the men and 66.2 % of the women among the American-born of the population of the agricultural provinces were, in 1916, naturalized Canadians. *Census of the Prairie Provinces, 1916.* Ottawa, 1918, p. 261.

by their wives. On the other hand, that class of immigrant destined to appear in penitentiary lists is composed in large part of men without settled domicile, and their number is not so frequently lessened by Canadian naturalization. Consequently, while on the following list the American record is not inspiring, it does not give an entirely true impression of the quality of American immigration.

TABLE XVI

NATIONAL-ITY	Chinese	British Isles	Canadian	Scandinavian	German	Russian	French	American	Italian
No. of Convicts per 10,000 adult males	5	7	7	7	9	9	21	22	38 [48]

Finally comes the question of naturalization. The value of any immigrant is based to a considerable extent upon his willingness to accept the duties of citizenship in the nation of his adoption. In this respect the American immigrant makes a better record than that achieved by the Canadian in the United States.[49]

In 1921, 63.6 per cent of the American-born residents of Canada had undertaken the duties and privileges of Canadian citizenship. Here again the explanation is to be found in the original intention of the immigrant. The average American who moves to Canada does so with the intention of remaining there permanently; the Canadian tends to go to the United States to obtain temporary employment. The percentage of naturalized Americans was much higher in 1921 than it was in 1911, having been raised from 50.1 to 63.6. This was probably due in part to the influence of war conditions, in part to the fact that 1911 was just in the middle of the great American influx, and in part to the fact that most of the newcomers had not yet had time to take out their citizenship papers.

[48] *Census Report, 1911.*
[49] See above, p. 347.

TABLE XVII

FOREIGN-BORN RESIDENTS OF CANADA, 1921

NATIONALITY	PER CENT NATURALIZED
Danish	56.3
German	61.7
French	55.1
Austro-Hungarian	59.7
American	63.6
Belgian	42.
Russian	61.4
Norwegian and Swedish	69.3
Dutch	48.3
Bulgarian and Roumanian	58.9
Average	57.7 [50]

Since touching the depths of depression in 1924, conditions in Canada have been steadily improving. In spite of the enormous burden left by the war, the country now seems to be on the verge of an era of prosperity.[51] This condition has been reflected in the increasing number of expatriate Canadians who are returning from the United States to their homes in the Dominion. During the year ending March 1st, 1925, 43,775 such migrants returned; in 1926, 47,221; and in 1927, 56,957. In the eight months to November, 1927, 31,342 recrossed the boundary.[52]

The foregoing pages give some idea of the migrations which have taken place during the past hundred and fifty years across the international frontier. The opportunities to be found in the enormous cities of the United States will continue to be attractive to ambitious young Canadians, no matter how satisfactory are

[50] From *Sixth Census*, p. 423.

[51] As the words are written, the employment figures in Canada are better than has been the case since the war, while reports of 4,000,000 unemployed in the United States are being discussed in Congress. See Toronto *Globe*, Toronto *Star*, New York *Times*, March 8, 1928.

[52] Figures supplied by Mr. R. H. Coats, Dominion Statistician.

conditions in the homeland. On the other hand, American immigration to the fertile fields of western Canada is certain to grow rather than diminish in importance, as the population pressure increases in the United States. Joined as the two countries are by geographical conditions, there will ever be a close relationship between them. That their intercourse may be harmonious and just is the hope of the vast majority of Canadians and Americans alike, and in the promotion of these ideals a most important role can be undertaken by those who leave one country to reside in the other. With every immigrant who crosses the border, mutual understanding should increase, jealousy and hostile criticism abate. The past hundred years of peace have established a worthy precedent. With the increase of intercourse and knowledge, the twentieth century should record no less worthy an achievement. In the attainment of this result the part to be played by the immigrant is significant and important.

CHAPTER X

The World War and Post-War Relations

I. THE EFFECT OF THE WORLD WAR ON THE RELATIONS OF THE UNITED STATES AND CANADA

THE World War is so recent and the emotions aroused by it so complex and so intense, that it is a very difficult subject to discuss. To view it with a right perspective, to evaluate accurately the many factors that influenced the relations of Canada and the United States, to avoid the unpardonable yet almost universal error of "judging the nation by the individual," is probably an impossible task. Yet no summary of the relations of the Dominion and the Republic would be complete which omitted the effect produced by the strain of the war.

It is probable that, in the end, the effect of wartime coöperation between the United States and Canada will be of lasting benefit in its influence on the relations of the two states. But it is beyond dispute that the immediate effect of the war was extremely detrimental; for, although Americans, in general, gained a new interest in and respect for Canada, Canadian dislike for the United States was definitely increased. This fact has been denied or ignored by Canadian politicians, by lecturers, even by the majority of Canadian newspapers, and it is probably true that the irritation and outspoken hostility of the period from 1915 to 1922 are no longer so potent as they once were. The indubitable fact remains, however, that the effect of the war on American-Canadian relations was, because of its reaction on Canada, a serious blow to the friendship of the two peoples, and that time has not yet entirely healed the wound.

The American people, as a whole, do not realize the deleterious effect that the war strain produced on the Canadian attitude toward the United States—and this is not at all surprising. Americans believe, and it is perfectly natural that they should believe, that Canada is, and of right ought to be, grateful for the assistance of the United States—assistance which made inevitable the defeat of Germany and her allies. Throughout the war, American newspapers abounded with flattering references to Canadian valor; after the United States entered the struggle the two countries coöperated at home as on the battlefield, and American soldiers gave their lives in the common cause. Why, then, should Canadians be critical toward the United States? There is, moreover, much positive evidence of Canadian good will. The newspapers of the Dominion greeted American entry into the war with enthusiastic acclaim, distinguished Canadian visitors to the United States have stressed the "cousinly" relation, and pointed with dramatic enthusiasm to three thousand miles of undefended border. American officials, visiting in Canada, have been received with uniform courtesy and cordiality.

To the American who realizes these facts, and whose knowledge of international relations is confined to the reports of the daily and weekly press, the truth about the Canadian attitude is unbelievable. Dislike of the United States would seem illogical and absurd. And yet the American who visited Canada in 1915 or 1916, or who kept in touch with Canadian opinion during 1918, 1919, and 1920, is under no illusions. To him the attitude of the majority of Canadians is provoking, painful, and quite unfair, but he does know the truth. The fact is, however, that most Americans know very little about Canadian affairs, and are not particularly interested in them.

In Canada, however, the situation is far different; Canadians cannot escape the shadow of the United States; American influence can be discerned in almost every aspect of Canadian life. Canada cannot, if she would, ignore the United States. The result has been a comparative unanimity of opinion among Canadians regarding the United States and its activities. The situation also makes it quite possible for the American people seriously to offend Canadian opinion without ever being aware of the fact.

Here, perhaps, is an explanation of the situation developed
by the World War. Of all the countries in the world, Canada
watched most closely and felt most strongly the actions and
attitudes of the United States. When these actions or attitudes
seemed to be critical of or hostile to the Allied cause, Canada
reacted more quickly and more strongly than any other country.

It may well prove that the irritation against the United States
aroused by the events of the war and post-war periods is only a
temporary condition. Certainly it is to be hoped that this is true,
and there seems to be good reason to believe that a favorable
change has already taken place—that Canadian opinion is less
hostile than it was in 1920 or 1921.

Before 1914 Canadians had been repeatedly assured, and many
of them were inclined to believe, that the United States—whatever its other faults—was somewhat more idealistic, more peace-
loving, more sympathetic in its relations with small and oppressed
states, than were the majority of strong and vigorous nations.
The policies espoused by John Hay, the arbitration treaties negotiated by William Jennings Bryan, the friendly urbanity of President Taft, the splendidly idealistic phrases of Woodrow Wilson,
and the persistently high moral purpose that marked the utterances of official America, had been leading Canadians to the belief
that the United States was, in very truth, a vital force for good
in international affairs. It is true that many citizens of the
Dominion did not love the United States—the fate of reciprocity
had proven that—but a steadily increasing number of them were
offering their respect. Having worked off a certain amount of
ill will by their votes in 1911, it is probable that Canadians as a
whole were, in 1914, more friendly to the United States than
had been the case for many years. Then came the World War, and
in the tense atmosphere of that struggle the new friendship was
sorely tested.

In order to understand the war-fostered growth of Canadian
antipathy toward the United States, it is necessary to recapture
something of the psychology—the atmosphere—of those lurid
years from 1914 to 1918. Canada entered the European conflict on

August 4th, 1914;[1] on that day Sir Robert Borden, the Canadian Prime Minister, cabled to London an offer of every assistance which the Dominion could supply.[2] The violation of Belgian neutrality was, for the majority of Canadians, the real justification for their participation in the war;[3] and the failure of the United States to protest against that breach of international law marked the first change in the Canadian attitude toward the Republic. Canadians did not expect the United States to enter the war, but they did expect a protest from the government that had so often proclaimed its allegiance to the principles of the international code. Accustomed to the tone of high morality and idealism which had characterized American public life, the people of the Dominion looked to Washington for an unequivocal denunciation of the German action. Feeling so intensely the righteousness of their cause, raised to the heights of moral integrity by a consciousness of the sacrifice soon to be demanded of them, Canadians were amazed by the inexplicable silence of the United States;[4] they felt that in its greatest test the idealism of the Republic had faltered. Of the divided opinion in the United States, of the conflicting official reports as to the actual facts of the invasion of Belgium, of the powerful influences which demanded strict impartiality on the part of the President, of the social and political consequences which might have followed a protest to Germany —of all these things Canadians knew and cared nothing; to them the issue was clearly marked.[5]

[1] Canada, of course, was in the war, as a part of the empire, without any action on her part, but the Dominion might, if it had desired, have declared its independence and its neutrality, and Britain would have been powerless, and probably unwilling, to resort to coercion.

[2] *Canadian Annual Review for 1914,* pp. 132 ff.

[3] As it was, indeed, for the English people as well. See Professor Gooch's authoritative discussion of this subject in vol. II of *The Cambridge History of British Foreign Policy;* see also *Canadian Hansard,* August 4, 1914.

[4] Victoria *Colonist,* August 6, 1914; Montreal *Star* and Toronto *Star,* August 8, 1914; Ottawa *Citizen,* August 10, 1914.

[5] It must be understood that these statements refer to the great majority —but not all—of the Canadian people. Many of the leading newspaper

Upon the outbreak of the war, the American people naturally congratulated themselves on being well out of it. Looking upon the conflict as a purely European affair, engendered by the "European system," the citizens of the United States were, being normal human beings, gratified at their isolation. But expression of this attitude—not always in a humble tone—gave rise to the second great cause of Canadian bitterness. The declaration of Newton D. Baker, Secretary of War, that the United States was "now in the dominant moral position in the world," [6] was greeted with biting sarcasm north of the international boundary, for among Canadians it was felt that they, rather than the Americans, had recognized and accepted the task of fighting to maintain the moral standards of civilization. Martin Glynn, temporary Chairman of the National Democratic Convention, declared on June 14, 1916, "Wealth has come to us, power has come to us, but better than wealth or power we have maintained for ourselves and for our children a nation dedicated to the ideals of peace, rather than to the gospel of selfishness and slaughter." [7] Nor was Mr. Glynn the only American who prided himself "on some moral quality that . . . was inherent in the attitude of neutrality." [8] Canadians resented being told that their sons were dying to uphold the "gospel of selfishness and slaughter," and refused to think of themselves as occupying a moral plane that was lower than that of American Democratic politicians. [9]

As the war progressed, a new condition developed. The United States, hitherto a borrowing country, was steadily taking rank as a powerful creditor nation. Loans to the belligerents were made in immense figures—although at first opposed by President Wilson

men and political leaders recognized the real difficulties which faced the United States—the indifferent masses in the Middle West, the vast alien population, the historic policy of non-intervention in Europe.

[6] Quoted in Beer, *The English-Speaking Peoples,* New York, 1918, p. 134.

[7] *Canadian Annual Review for 1912,* p. 209; St. Louis *Globe-Democrat,* June 14, 1916.

[8] Beer, *op. cit.,* p. 134; see also President Wilson's speech in the Springfield *Republican,* November 2, 1916.

[9] See letters in the New York *Times,* January 7, 1916.

as unneutral.[10] War orders from the Allies were creating a condition of unprecedented prosperity; high wages and enormous dividends were the commonplaces of the day; extravagance and reckless expenditure marked American society.[11] In Canada, on the other hand, although profiteers were reported to be making fortunes from paper shoes, shoddy uniforms, and decayed bacon, the people as a whole were forced to endure a period of rigid economy.[12] Comparison of the prevailing conditions in the two countries was everywhere obvious and insistent. Every month added to American wealth, to American expressions of satisfaction at being free; while every month Canada faced her growing debt, her casualty lists, her dead.[13]

Another factor influencing American-Canadian relations may at first glance seem somewhat absurd, but it was, nevertheless, of no little importance. The topical news films which were shown in Canadian theaters were of American origin and of interest chiefly to American citizens. Thus when Canadian audiences gathered for a few hours in an attempt to forget the terrible strain under which they constantly lived, they were greeted with pictures of American "preparedness" parades, of the American expedition into Mexico, of the National Guard in summer manoeuvres. The irony of such pictures to those whose sons and brothers were dying by the hundred in the war produced its inevitable and evil result.[14] Canadian newspapers, moreover, were forced to rely very

[10] *Canadian Annual Review for 1915*, p. 429.

[11] "The demand for luxuries was equalled only by the craze for entertainment—futile brains were busied with the innovation of new dancing steps rather than the issues of the European War. Cabarets were crowded —and the general atmosphere of the country was heavy with amusement and money-making." Seymour, *Woodrow Wilson and the War*, Yale, 1921, pp. 67–68.

[12] *Canadian Annual Review for 1917; idem, 1918*.

[13] A movement to boycott American goods was started early in 1915— a purely voluntary action which never amounted to very much, because Canada was forced to rely upon the United States for many articles of necessity. Toronto *Mail and Empire*, January 25, 1915; letters in New York *Times*, January 31, 1915.

[14] *Canadian Annual Review for 1919*, p. 123. On more than one occasion the American flag was hissed in Canadian theatres.

largely upon American press associations for their news. It was the dissatisfaction which this condition aroused that later resulted in the establishment of the Canadian Press.[15]

These facts did not become widely known in the United States, and Americans, in consequence, failed to understand Canadian opinion, because Canadian newspapers, political leaders and industrial spokesmen insisted on ignoring or denying the existence of an anti-American sentiment. Early in the war Canadian newspapers, were requested to tread gently when dealing with the United States,[16] and throughout the war period this suggestion was very generally observed. Public officials of the Dominion, regardless of their personal inclinations, were bound by their duty to the nation—and the nation's welfare demanded friendship with the United States.

The propaganda carried on by the Irish and German elements in the American population, while directed against England, found its most sensitive audience in Canada,[17] and Canadians, judging the nation by the individual, accepted these attacks as typical of the American attitude.[18]

The people of the Dominion knew little of the class and national cleavages of the United States. Throughout the war, in spite of the neutrality proclamation, American opinion was overwhelmingly on the side of the Allies. Millions of Americans joined with Canada in the belief that the Allied forces were contending for the more righteous cause—that German victory would result in abject surrender to militarism. As a result of this conviction,

[15] *Canadian Annual Review for 1922*, p. 71.

[16] On the authority of one of Canada's leading publicists.

[17] Owen Wister, *The Ancient Grudge*, New York, 1920, chapter 1, and elsewhere. The Hearst papers were finally barred from Canada. *Canadian Annual Review for 1918*, p. 260.

[18] Cf. New York *American*, August 7, 1914; letters in the New York *Tribune*, August 10, 1914. Any issues of *The Irish World, The Fatherland*, and the *New Yorker Staats-Zeitung* will illustrate the point. The Hearst papers, of course, were unanimous in their opposition to Great Britain. See Boston *Advertiser*, August 5, 1914; San Francisco *Examiner*, August 6, 1914.

American periodicals and political leaders, in the vast majority of cases, favored the Allied cause.

The speeches and "notes" of Woodrow Wilson and William Jennings Bryan increased the Canadian hostility. Canadians felt that the Great War was a strife of moral as well as of physical powers; yet President Wilson declared that "with its causes and objects we are not concerned." [19] In the election of 1916, Canadians were almost unanimous in their desire to see Charles E. Hughes victorious, and they were greatly disappointed when the final returns showed a reversal of the earlier reports. As most Canadians viewed it, the United States in 1916 reëlected a President who had sacrificed the national honor in order to keep his country "out of war"; [20] a man who represented the popular attitude in being unable to distinguish between the objectives of the two belligerents.[21] The demand made by President Wilson that Americans should be neutral in thought as well as deed was not the least of Canadian grievances.[22] This, however, Canadians were likely to forget in their anger at the critical, superior, or hostile

[19] From speech of President Wilson before The League to Enforce Peace, May 29, 1916; quoted in New York *Times,* May 30, 1916.

[20] Report of Wilson's reception in Canada, Boston *Transcript,* October 6, 1916.

[21] J. H. Hendricks (editor), "Life and Letters of Walter Hines Page," *World's Work,* June, 1922, p. 151.

[22] Ambassador Page, a violent Anglophile, wrote on this subject: "The President suppressed free thought and free speech when he insisted on personal neutrality. To the minds of official Washington, Germans and English are alike foreign nations who are now foolishly engaged in war." Vice-President Marshall inanely boasted that he had read no Orange Paper, Blue Paper, White Paper, or other partisan document, for fear that he would become unneutral. "The mass of American people," declared Page, "find themselves forbidden to think or talk and this has a sufficient effect to make them take refuge in indifference." *Idem,* pp. 160–163. According to Norman Angell, the American populace was "not interested in its foreign problems. It was far more interested in baseball." *Annals of the American Academy of Political and Social Science,* July, 1916. Secretary Franklin K. Lane states that the President told the Cabinet that he wished to see neither side win, "for both had been equally indifferent to the rights of neutrals." "Letters of a High-Minded Man," *World's Work,* June, 1922, p. 215.

attitude of those Americans who did not recognize the justice of the war aims of the Allies.

The *Lusitania* notes of President Wilson, and the correspondence resulting from other submarine activities, due to their length and ineffective character, gradually became subjects of sarcastic comment among Canadians. Even the newspapers went so far as to question the wisdom of the President's course. One editor declared, "We fear that the United States is not cutting a very dignified figure before the eyes of a condemning world these days." [23] Another paper in outlining the history of American protests over the *Lusitania* affair said,

> "The honor of the United States would have stood higher if, from the very commencement of the war, it had constituted itself the guardian of international law, instead of waiting until its own interests were affected." [24]

The United States, of course, was convinced that it had been the one nation in the world that *had* upheld the dictates of international law, but Canadians could not forget the violation of Belgium and America's failure to protest.

> "During the course of the war," wrote the editor of a western Canadian newspaper, "the United States government has received so many rebuffs that one finds it hard to know just what the words of national honor have come to mean." [25]

The situation was summarized by the Vancouver *World,* as follows:

> "The Republic, of course, must take its own line. The Allies can win without American assistance. But if they do so win after the *Falaba* and the *Lusitania,* we rather think that future generations of Americans will not view the prudence and discretion of the Wilson

[23] Victoria *Times,* August 24, 1915.

[24] Victoria *Colonist,* May 14, 1915.

[25] Vancouver *Sun,* May 8, 1915; see also Toronto *Globe,* May 10, 1915; Winnipeg *Free Press,* May 8, 1915; Regina *Standard,* May 10, 1915.

administration with unmoved admiration. Occasions arise in the lives of nations when it is well not to count the cost too carefully before taking action." [26]

The Canadian people naturally took the side of the British government in the argument concerning the legality of the Allied blockade, and the British definition of contraband.[27] The United States was criticized [28] for the severity of the notes written to Great Britain, notes which were couched in terms almost as vigorous as those used in the official protests to Germany for far more serious violations. (More serious because German activities endangered and destroyed American lives; whereas the British interference with American trade entailed only financial losses. There can be no doubt that Britain did extend its interpretation of the maritime rights of belligerents far beyond any previous practice, but after the United States entered the war, the regulation became still more complete and severe.)

One episode at this time was perhaps more important than any other in arousing popular feeling in Canada—the action of American destroyers in standing by, or, at the request of the German submarine U-53, changing their position,[29] while the underseas craft sank a number of British and other vessels just off the eastern coast of the United States.[30] It would, obviously, have been an unneutral action for the American war vessels to have intervened, but public opinion takes little notice of the technical demands of law in such a case. Blood, it seemed, no longer was thicker than water.

These were the outstanding causes which aroused and sus-

[26] Vancouver *World*, May 10, 1915.

[27] Garner, *International Law and the World War*, London and New York, 1920, vol. II, chaps. 32, 33, 34; Garner, *Prize Law During the World War*, New York, 1927.

[28] No distinction was made between the American government and the American people.

[29] This was denied but was believed by many. New York *Times*, October 19, 1916.

[30] *Canadian Annual Review for 1916*, p. 221; New York *Tribune*, October 16, 1916; Toronto *Globe*, October 9, 18, 1916; New York *Times*, October 9, 10, 19, 1916; Vancouver *Province*, October 18, 1916.

tained Canadian animosity toward the United States between August, 1914, and April, 1917. That this attitude was based largely on misunderstanding and on a very inadequate appreciation of the real conditions in the United States, did not lessen its potency. It was unfair, unbalanced and unjust; it took no heed of American difficulties, was critical only of failures; it did not recognize the signs of friendship, was conscious only of opposition. Yet this attitude was completely understandable—it was, indeed, inevitable—for as America waxed richer and stronger, Canada suffered, fought, and sacrificed her prosperity and her sons. America counted her profits, while Canada buried her dead.

It is, of course, now generally recognized that between 1914 and 1917 American opinion, in spite of the President's demand that the people of the Republic should be neutral in thought as well as in action, was preponderantly pro-Ally. The United States entered the war in April, 1917, and received a royal welcome from the Allied powers. Not only did the latter recognize the influence that would be exerted by America's financial, military, and naval coöperation, but they also rejoiced in the effect that America's decision would produce on neutral opinion, and on the verdict of history. A Canadian editor well expressed the feeling of all the Allied powers when he wrote,

"Canada has been waiting and watching, hoping and praying, that you would not be too proud to fight for the rights of humanity; and that you would recognize the essential difference between the German cause and ours. All Canada, all the British Empire, and all the Allies feel as if a tremendous victory had been won." [31]

The Dominion government formally welcomed the United States as a comrade-in-arms on April 19th, when Sir George Foster and Sir Wilfrid Laurier joined in hailing the era of good feeling which the American declaration of war presaged.[32] It would not be true to suggest, however, that the American declaration of war at once removed the critical irritation that had embittered

[31] Vancouver *Daily Province*, April 3, 1917.
[32] *Canadian Hansard*, April 19, 1917; *Canadian Annual Review for 1917*, p. 335.

Canadian feeling. Privately, if not in public, the view was often expressed that the United States had waited and profited during the heat of the struggle, and was now about to claim the victory as well.

As time went on, however, and as American soldiers, too, began to give their lives in the common cause, this bitterness was slowly purged away. Official coöperation between Canada and the United States—the pooling of grain, fuel, power and transportation resources, the underwriting of a Canadian loan by bankers of New York—produced a good effect upon the public mind.[33] Canadian recruiting detachments were welcomed in the United States,[34] while a reciprocal agreement was ratified to facilitate the return of draft-evaders. A Canadian War Mission was established at Washington,[35] and in every possible way the activities of the two countries were coördinated for efficiency. Immigration regulations were relaxed and thousands of American farmhands crossed the border to assist in harvesting the Canadian crops.[36] Officially and publicly, at least, the two nations were on better terms than ever before in their history, and on the American side this attitude extended through almost all classes of society. The statement of ex-President Roosevelt, on August 15, 1917, that "We have no right to consider ourselves as standing level with Canada in this fight for democracy until we have placed 5,000,000 men in the field," [37] did much to mollify Canadian sentiment. The nobly expressed idealism of President Wilson and his plans for coöperation with the war-shattered states of Europe aroused a popular response among the people of Canada. Barely

[33] The loan was floated by J. P. Morgan & Company. The pooling arrangements were made largely by Messrs. Hoover and McAdoo for the United States, and Sir George Foster, Sir Thomas White, and Mr. Hanna for Canada. *Canadian Annual Review for 1917,* pp. 353–355.

[34] Ottawa *Citizen,* July 30, 1917; Boston *Transcript,* Sept. 24, 1917; *MacLean's Magazine,* September, 1917.

[35] The Canadian Legation at Washington is a more or less direct result of this wartime arrangement. *Canadian Annual Review for 1921,* pp. 140–141.

[36] *Canadian Annual Review for 1917,* p. 357.

[37] Montreal *Star,* August 16, 1917.

had this happy result been attained, however, when all the old prejudices were revived by the end of the war and the disillusionment of the post-war years.

2. THE IMMEDIATE AFTERMATH OF THE WAR

Few periods in the history of mankind have been so prolific in the generation of international strife as the months that followed the Armistice of 1918. Scarcely had the war ended and the external pressure been removed, when centrifugal forces began to sever the bonds welded by the conflict. The scores of new problems aroused by the intrigues and mistakes of the conference at Versailles were accentuated by American repudiation of one of the few good results of the four years of devastation and suffering, and by the accentuated nationalism which was the form taken by the American reaction against the sacrifices and coöperation of the war period. But there was another and a more immediate cause for the revival of Canadian ill feeling.

It is probable that each of the Allied nations emerged from the war convinced that victory was largely due to its own efforts. This faith was expounded at various places and times by military and naval leaders of the different powers. Unfortunately, in the United States a certain section of the public undertook to proclaim the prominent part played by the American forces in a manner that was particularly provocative, and Canada, being the nearest neighbor, felt the sting most bitterly. It cannot be too strongly insisted upon that nowhere, not even in Canada itself, was the display of the "We Won the War" and "The Yanks Did It" posters more roundly condemned than among the better classes of American society. But Canada, whose half million soldiers (according to the official Canadian figures) [38] had suffered more casualties than the whole of the American army; who had taken more guns, more ground, more prisoners; and had fought for two years longer, was bitterly critical of the boasts of one class

[38] General Clark in the Canadian House of Commons gave the following

of enthusiastic American patriots.[39] Yet this was not, after all, a particularly heinous offense. The American people had not suffered enough to be chastened, and a certain exuberance was to be expected and might well have been excused. Unfortunately, it happened to be cities like Seattle, Los Angeles and Detroit—cities that were particularly well-known to Canadians—in which the most unrestrained celebrations were staged.[40] Even the sedate *Canadian Annual Review* was enticed into a discussion of "Who Won the War"—a problem "which was not initiated by Great Britain or Canada." [41]

figures for the last hundred days of the war. Quoted from *Hansard,* by the New York *World,* May 21, 1922:

	Canada	United States
Troops engaged	105,000	650,000
Days of operations	100	47
Casualties	45,830	100,000
Prisoners taken	31,537	16,000
Guns captured	623	468
Machine guns taken	2,842	2,864
Trench mortars taken	336	177
Territory freed	610 sq. miles	336 sq. m.
Villages freed	228	150
German divisions defeated	47	46
Maximum advance (miles)	86	34

[39] It might also be noted that President Wilson was the outstanding opponent of separate representation for Canada at the Peace Conference and in the League of Nations. Dafoe, "Canada and the United States," in *Great Britain and the Dominions,* Chicago, 1928, p. 245.

[40] Seattle *Post-Intelligencer,* November 12, 1918; Los Angeles *Times,* November 13, 1918. On February 9, 1919 the Detroit *Free Press* wrote: "A flood of American manhood set in the direction of the European battlefields and . . . filled and swelled until it overwhelmed the enemy that had successfully resisted the strength of half a dozen European nations."

[41] *Canadian Annual Review for 1919.* It was at this time also that the public learned for the first time of Admiral Benson's famous instructions issued to Admiral Sims during the war to the effect that the latter should not allow the British to pull the wool over his eyes as the American navy would be just as willing to fight the British as the Germans. New York *Times,* March 23, 24, 1920; Toronto *Star,* March 23, 1920.

Thus in a few short weeks was undone much of the good that had been accomplished by the months of coöperation and mutual sacrifice during the war. And this revival of Canadian ill will in an intensified form was due to nothing more serious than the exuberance and lack of taste of a small part of the American people. On such a precarious foundation does international friendship rest—when nations speak the same language and live so close together.

There were a number of other causes that contributed to the maintenance of Canadian irritation during the post-war years. Important among these were the unfavorable rate of exchange, the American tariff policy, the revival of Anglo-Irish strife and the role played therein by the Irish-Americans and their sympathizers, the problem of the Allied debts, and the attitude of the United States toward the League of Nations.

The rate of exchange was an obviously absurd basis for an edifice of international ill feeling, but unfortunately the majority of the Canadian people were not economists. Moreover, it was unpleasant—even if profitable—to hear American tourists paying their bills in Canadian shops with what some of them proudly referred to as "real" money. Even a Canadian who was not an economist could catch that inference.

As noted above,[42] the Underwood tariff of 1913 had given Canada a great many valuable concessions by opening the American market to a large number of Canadian commodities. These favors were almost all rescinded by the Fordney Emergency Tariff of 1921, and the McCumber Tariff of 1922. To Canadians this seemed like a rather gratuitous injury. The United States had, as a result of the war, become the wealthiest nation in the world, the rate of exchange was vastly in her favor, her sales in Canada far exceeded her purchases there, and yet she was not satisfied. The Toronto *Star,* Toronto *Globe,* the Montreal *Star* and other Canadian papers united in denouncing the riot of protectionism represented by these two bills,[43] while Premier Taschereau of

[42] Chapter VIII.
[43] See symposium of views in the Boston *Transcript,* May 13, 15, 1922.

Quebec threatened to retaliate by a prohibition of pulp-wood exports—an action that would stifle many American mills and newspapers.[44]

The ubiquitous Irish question has played its part in Canadian-American relations ever since the middle of the nineteenth century. The renewed discussion of this problem and its effect upon the American attitude toward Great Britain are too recent and too well recognized to necessitate recapitulation. Suffice it to say that Canada, herself a self-governing Dominion, had little sympathy for Irish republican ideals, but was an earnest advocate of the granting of "Dominion status," and Canadians looked upon any interference from the United States as unwarranted and impertinent. Canadians have never recognized the peculiar interest which America has taken—and rightly taken—in this problem, due to the presence of over five million Irish in the United States.[45]

The difficulties raised by the inter-Allied debts are among the most prominent present causes of international discord, not only on this continent but in Europe. As a debtor nation Canada is prepared to pay the sums for which she is legally responsible, but the prospect is not a pleasant one. In a long and carefully prepared article for the New York *Times,* one of Canada's leading financiers has well summarized Canadian sentiment in this matter. The statement, in part, is as follows:

"(1) That the debt is legally owing is certain.

"(2) The claim that the debts are not morally due is based on one contention only—that unless these debts be cancelled the United States will not have borne her equitable share of the burdens of the war . . . Americans will naturally resent even the suggestion that their country may not have paid her way, but this question must be quietly discussed if we are to understand the position taken by the rest of the world.

"(3) The United States had a vital stake in the war from its very beginning, though it took some time for her people to realize it . . . But it is not suggested that the American government con-

[44] *Ibid.*

[45] The American census of 1920 shows 1,037,233 Irish-born residents of the United States.

tribute anything towards expenditures made prior to the time it officially entered the struggle.

"(4) Had the United States intervened at the time of the *Lusitania* incident the war would have been shortened by two years, millions of lives and tens of billions of dollars would have been saved, the condition of Europe would not be what it is, and the problem of these debts would not have arisen.

"(5) These considerations, however, have a sentimental value only. *The case against the validity of these debts merely claims that when the United States declared war she took her place by the side of the Allies and became responsible for her reasonable share from that time on.*

"(6) The United States was unprepared and had to raise, train, equip, and transport her armies. She could, for long, render little aid except financial. The Allies had to hold the enemy back with but little assistance from her in man power. The Allies could supply the men but had already bled their people white financially. The United States could not supply men but had a plethora of wealth, much of it obtained by supplying materials to the Allies.

"(7) The services of the men placed by the Allies in the fighting line during those twelve months were given to the common cause. The hundreds of thousands of lives were given, for alas, they cannot be restored. Must the contribution of the United States be on a different basis and be considered a loan to be repaid? Are dollars more valuable than lives?

"(8) The financial assistance of the United States was of inestimable value, but if the money be repaid with interest, as demanded, do the Americans consider that the effective contribution of their country was in proportion to her population or wealth, or in harmony with her dignity? Are they content to owe their safety and victory to the sacrifices to others without bearing their fair share?" [46]

This article so well portrays the attitude of the majority of Canadians that further comment on this particular issue would be superfluous.[47] It might be recorded, however, that many citizens

[46] Statement of T. B. Macaulay, President of the Sun Life Assurance Company of Canada. New York *Times,* July 2, 1922.

[47] The Vancouver *Province* recently stated: "Payment of these billions will be a long and hard task, but it will come to an end. But will there

of the Dominion point to the action of Great Britain in cancelling the debts of her allies at the close of the Napoleonic wars, and her recent offer of a similar cancellation (in conjunction with the United States) of the present debts.[48]

Among Americans there were and are at least three typical attitudes toward this problem of the inter-Allied debts.[49] One is represented by the query that has been attributed (probably wrongly) to President Coolidge: "They hired the money, didn't they?" From this point of view the whole problem reduces itself to the simple terms of a legal and financial transaction, and failure to carry it out would weaken the whole basis upon which the economic fabric of modern society is founded. Another group favors partial or total cancellation as an aid to economic sanitation, or as a further contribution of America to the cause for which the Allies fought. A third group, revolted by the spectacle of post-war Europe, desires to use the debts as a means of keeping certain European nations in such a condition of impecuniosity that they will be unable to resort to war.[50] The problem is a good deal more involved from an American than it is from a Canadian point of view. With the best will in the world, an in-

ever be an end to the claims of certain boasters that they won the war, and would there ever be an end to the claim of the same class of people that they had rescued Britain from bankruptcy" if the debts were cancelled?

[48] New York *Times*, July 2, 1922; Toronto *Globe*, July 2, 1922. This is not really as altruistic as it seems, for Britain cannot hope (she has in fact announced that she will not try) to collect much more from her debtors than she owes to the United States. If the United States were to cancel, it would mean an absolute loss of the amount involved.

[49] The latest statement of American opinion is to be found in Dexter and Sedgwick, *The War Debts*, New York, 1928. These authors justify the American attitude on both moral and legal grounds, but nevertheless advise revision or cancellation to aid American business and to end European hostility.

[50] The terms finally proposed to France and Italy resulted in an actual scaling down of the amount to be repaid. Shortly after the treaty with Italy was signed the dictator of that state proposed an Italian air force that would "obscure the sun," and an army of five million men. Kenworthy, *Peace or War?*, London and New York, 1927, pp. 37–38.

telligent American would find his powers taxed to the utmost to discover the just and humane course to follow.

Last, and perhaps most important of all in its effect upon Canadian opinion, is the League of Nations, the attitude of America toward that body, and the international questions involved therein. The covenant of the League of Nations was prepared at Paris largely through the efforts of President Wilson and his American colleagues. This document was intended to embody the highest aspirations of a war-sick world. The covenant was ratified by all the signatory powers except the United States, where a combined drive by certain progressives and the forces favoring nationalistic isolation succeeded in defeating the efforts of President Wilson and the Democratic Party. Of course, there were many other issues involved in the election of 1920, but revival of the traditional American policy of isolation was an inevitable psychological reaction from an adventure into a European struggle. Many Americans felt that they had been cheated in the result of the war; that they had been inveigled into it by Allied (particularly British) propaganda, and that they had been used to "pull the chestnuts out of the fire" for the rapacious imperialists of Europe.[51] The vast majority of the American people went into the war in the firm belief that they were crusading, fighting in one last war which would end all wars. Yet in the ten years since the Armistice there has been no real peace. Scarcely had the war ended when the Allies fell to quarrelling over the spoils; they maintained armies on a scale far exceeding pre-war standards, and carried on sporadic operations in Russia, Asia Minor, Ireland, and the Far East. The disillusionment produced by these conditions was already well started in 1920, and in their disgust Americans returned again to their policy of isolation.[52]

[51] See Turner, *Shall It Be Again?*, New York, 1923.

[52] Commander Kenworthy has summarized this feeling: "All this is noted in America as is the persecution of racial and religious minorities and the general bestiality of European reaction. America, therefore, feels a general disgust at the welter of European nationalism, and demands repayment of the moneys lent, amongst other reasons, in order that surplus revenues shall not be spent on still more armaments." Kenworthy, *op. cit.*,

To Canadians, however, the defeat of the pro-League party in that year appeared to be due purely to selfishness—the determination of America to follow her own course, regardless of the needs, hopes, or pacific aspirations of the remainder of the world.[53] Color was given to this interpretation by the actions of the new (Republican) administration. A separate treaty was negotiated with Germany which retained to the United States all the benefits conferred by the Treaty of Versailles, and denied all obligations undertaken by signatories of the general treaty. The tripartite agreement by which Great Britain and America were to guarantee aid to France in case of an unprovoked attack was also denounced by the United States Senate. After the elevation of Senator Harding to the Presidency, the typical expression of the isolationist journals was the cryptic phrase "The League is dead." [54] Forthwith the State Department not only refused to aid the League in its many humanitarian projects, but actually failed to acknowledge receipt of letters and dispatches from the Secretariat. Later Secretary of State Charles E. Hughes did reply—*but forwarded his communications through the diplomatic agents of other countries, rather than recognize the existence of the League Secretariat.*[55] During the present administration, it should be added, the United States has coöperated much more freely.

From a Canadian viewpoint this attitude of the United States was consistent with her attitude on the debt question: America wanted all the benefits of the war with none of the obligations. The League—the one great attempt to end war—was prevented from reaching its full strength by the refusal of the United States to do her part. Whether or not this criticism is justified is quite be-

p. 111. It should perhaps be added that the United States has not been inconspicuous in post-war imperialism. Her recent extensions of control in the Caribbean are not the product of altruism.

[53] For the Canadian attitude toward the League see the manifesto signed by Premier Mackenzie-King and by former Premiers Borden and Meighen and others in *The Canadian Press* for May 19, 1922.

[54] Boston *Transcript,* November 7, 1920.

[55] See the Holt-Fosdick-Hughes correspondence in the New York *Times* during the week of July 17, 1922.

side the point. The important fact is simply that this is the Canadian opinion, and that it explains in some measure the sceptisism with which Canadians now view all American professions of international good will and pacific intentions.

The difficulty which the American faces in his attempt to understand the Canadian attitude is enhanced by his own usually very sincere liking for the Dominion and its people. During the war American papers and officials were not backward in expressing their admiration for the great efforts put forth by the northern nation. Even "the man in the street" was more conscious of the existence of Canada and more impressed with Canadian accomplishments than ever before. Since the months of coöperation during the last year of the war the American people as a whole have been decidedly friendly; they believed that common sacrifices had drawn the nations together, that mutual respect and mutual sympathy had resulted from the struggle.[56] As far as the United States was concerned this was, indeed, the result. Why it was not true in Canada has been suggested above. If the future relations of the two countries are to be on a high plane of respect and friendship, it behooves both Canadians and Americans to make some effort to understand the point of view of those who dwell on the other side of the line that marks the Dominion from the Republic.

3. RECENT DEVELOPMENTS

A. The Annexation Question.—Were this book written for Canadians alone it would be quite unnecessary to include in this chapter a discussion of annexation. As far as the people of the Dominion are concerned, this issue is absolutely dead.

It is conceivable, although from present indications unlikely, that with the lapse of time Canada may break the strong bonds of affection that unite the Dominion with the remainder of the British Empire; it is inconceivable, if history has any meaning whatever, that Canada should unite, politically, with the American Republic.

[56] Pepper, *American Foreign Trade,* New York, 1919, p. 264.

The justification of this statement is to be found not so much in Canada's love for the empire as in the growth of Canadian nationalism. If the bonds of empire alone kept Canada from joining the Union, the prospects of America's "Manifest Destiny" being fulfilled would be very much brighter than they actually are. But it is Canadian nationalism, rather than Canadian imperialism, that will preserve the independence of the Dominion.[57]

So strong has been the growth of national feeling in Canada that the government at Ottawa is now, to all intents and purposes, as "free" as any government in the world. The bonds that still unite Canadians to the empire are bonds of love and admiration [58]—any attempt on the part of Britain to coerce the Dominion almost certainly would result in an immediate declaration of formal independence. Such a possibility is not contemplated by any sane person on either side of the Atlantic. Even a Tory government in Britain would as soon think of issuing orders to Paris or Washington as to Ottawa.

If Canadian nationalism, then, has been strong enough to bring about this change in imperial relations in less than one hundred years, it is certainly strong enough to guarantee the Dominion against any peaceful attempts on the part of American individuals or American officials to bring about annexation to the United States. What might happen in the event of war between Great Britain and the United States is a question that cannot be answered here.[59]

[57] It has long been argued by imperialistic Canadians that independence from Great Britain would be but the first of two steps to annexation to the United States. This, in the opinion of the author, is a misreading of history. There was a time, undoubtedly, when Canada was so weak and divided internally that annexation *would* probably have followed the severance of the imperial bonds. But that condition no longer exists, and cannot (as far as it is humanly possible to forecast the future) exist again.

[58] The writer is, of course, aware that certain technical conditions still exist that place Canada in a position of inferiority. Since the Imperial Conference of 1926, however, the Dominion government has the legal right to end this situation whenever it wishes to do so. The necessary steps are gradually being taken. See the Prime Minister's speech in *The Canadian Hansard,* January 30, 1928.

[59] For an excellent discussion of this subject see Kenworthy, *op. cit.*

No discussion of annexation that omitted reference to the French-Canadian attitude would be complete. The people of Quebec know that if Canada were to join the American Union they would lose most, if not all, of the special privileges they enjoy at present. No American Congress would look favorably upon the religious and linguistic situation that exists in Canada. The French-Canadians form 28 per cent. of the Canadian population; of the United States and Canada together they would form only 2 per cent.[60] Now their numbers make them powerful; if annexed, "Americanization" would immediately be undertaken by the many agencies in the United States that exist for such a purpose.

As a final proof that annexation is no longer a real issue, it should be necessary only to point to the fact that it failed to win the support of the Canadian people when it would obviously have resulted in comparative economic prosperity. If annexation did not appeal to Canadians during the dreary and desolate years between 1870 and 1895, it is not likely to be more successful at a time when Canada's *per capita* foreign trade is the highest in the world and her wealth is steadily increasing.

In spite of these facts, however, there is still a considerable body of American opinion that believes in the inevitability of ultimate annexation. This was shown most clearly in 1911,[61] but that it has not since died out can be testified by the reading of American newspapers or listening to private discussions on the subject. The number of Americans who understand the real situation is constantly increasing, but it is probably safe to suggest that well over half the people of the United States, if closely questioned, would confess to a belief in the ultimate triumph of annexation.[62] Even newspapers that are generally as well informed

[60] *Canada Year Book, 1926,* p. 106.
[61] See above, Chapter VIII.
[62] The author has himself carried out a number of experiments with university students on the subject. In every case over 90 per cent of the students favored, and over 80 per cent prophesied, annexation. There is no reason to believe that the opinion of other groups would show any smaller percentages.

as the New York *World* and the New York *Times* have made serious mistakes in their appraisal of Canadian opinion in this matter.[63] Another type of American newspaper misleads its public by constant references to the Canadian "desire" or "struggle" for freedom.[64] It was this same misapprehension of Canadian feeling that led to the many post-war proposals that Britain should sell Canada in settlement of her war debt to the United States.[65]

The truth, however, seems gradually to be gaining ground, and the issue will almost certainly drop into the background as time goes on. There is no disposition on the part of any considerable group in the United States to force Canada into the union, and there is no good reason why the future relations of the two states should not be thoroughly satisfactory without political union.

B. The Canadian Legation at Washington.—One factor that should go far toward improving the relations of Canada and the United States is the establishment of a Canadian legation at Washington, and the sending of an American minister to Ottawa. Not only is this development of direct intercourse likely to prove successful from the point of view of international understanding and good will,—it is also a unique departure in the realm of international law and practice. It is an excellent example of the triumph of commonsense and economic necessity over the technicalities of legal science.

On May 5th, 1919 Mr. Newton W. Rowell, President of the Canadian Privy Council, announced in Parliament:

"While the several British Ambassadors at Washington have rendered admirable service to Canada, our business with the United

[63] On January 12, 1918 the New York *Times* editorially forecast the political union of the two countries. The editor later admitted that he had probably been misled. New York *Times*, February 5, 1918.

[64] This is especially true of the Boston *American* and other Hearst journals.

[65] This question was argued several times in Congress. *Canadian Annual Review for 1922*, pp. 81–82.

States is now on so large a scale that the government is convinced that our interests can be adequately protected only by a Canadian representative resident in Washington." [66]

On May 10th of the following year the British and Canadian governments simultaneously announced that a Canadian minister to Washington would be appointed. It is generally believed that Mr. Rowell himself might have had the position if he had been willing to take it, but he refused the opportunity. After a great deal of delay, the explanation of which has never been fully disclosed, the Canadian Minister was actually appointed in 1927, and at the same time an American representative was sent to Ottawa.

The position occupied by Mr. Massey at Washington and Mr. Phillips at Ottawa is a peculiar one, but no more peculiar than that occupied by Canada herself among the states of the world. That a colony should be given separate representation in a foreign state, and should herself receive such representation, would have been considered quite impossible even in 1900. Yet today it is an established fact, and a fact that is a real tribute to the commonsense and good will of Great Britain and the United States, as well as to the growing importance of the Dominion of Canada. It is not, perhaps, too much to hope that these appointments will, in addition to facilitating commercial intercourse, result in an increased knowledge, sympathy, and good will.

C. The Ownership of Hudson Bay.—One of the problems that Mr. Massey and Mr. Phillips (or their successors) will have sooner or later to solve is that connected with the status of Hudson Bay. The Canadian government is now completing a railway from Winnipeg to Fort Churchill on the shores of the Bay. It is intended to use the new line to facilitate the movement of Canadian wheat to European markets, and it may be considered part of the general movement which seeks to divert this traffic from American to Canadian ports. Heretofore, a large share of Canada's wheat has been shipped through American ports—par-

[66] *Canadian Annual Review for 1921*, pp. 140-141.

ticularly Buffalo and New York. Recently attempts have been made to guide this flow to Montreal, Halifax, Prince Rupert, and Vancouver. Fort Churchill will speed this movement, by providing a new Canadian outlet.

With the development of a well-equipped harbor on the shores of this northern sea, however, a new question will be brought into prominence. Has Canada the right to treat Hudson Bay as a territorial sea? In the past this question has not been considered sufficiently important to warrant international discussions: except for an occasional whaler or supply ship, the waters of the bay have seldom been disturbed. This is easily understood for, although the bay is reputed to be teeming with fish, there has been no ready means of conveying a catch to market. The fishermen of the maritime provinces and New England could fill their holds on the banks of Newfoundland, and did not need to make the long and dangerous passage to the distant waters of Hudson Bay. Now, however, a readily accessible market will be provided for those who pursue their occupation in the northern sea, and it is altogether probable that every season will see an increasing number of ships entering the bay to partake of the harvest to be reaped from its virgin waters. It is probable that many of these newcomers will be American vessels. Will Canada allow them to fish in the bay; or has she the right to exclude them or to make rules for their governance?

When this question was unofficially presented to the United States government in 1920, the Department of State went on record as being of the opinion that Canada did not claim Hudson Bay as territorial water. This statement, however, was quite inaccurate, for Canada had declared in an Act of 1906 that "Hudson Bay is wholly territorial water of Canada," [67] and the statement was reiterated in 1920. When this fact was brought to the attention of the Department of State, it was given "attentive consideration," [68] and there, apparently, the matter rests.

[67] "Fisheries Act," *Revised Statutes of Canada,* 1906, chapter 45, sec. 9, sub-section 12.

[68] According to a letter in the possession of the author from Mr. A. A. Adee, Second Assistant Secretary of State.

In 1920, however, this problem was of no immediate importance, but with the building of the Hudson Bay Railway the situation is entirely changed.

By a strict interpretation of international law, Canada has no right to claim Hudson Bay as territorial water. This is not the place for a technical discussion of the legal aspects of the matter; suffice it to say that for some two hundred years it has been generally recognized that the three-mile limit marks the extent of territorial waters.[69] Thus, if the mouth of a bay is more than six miles across, it has usually been recognized as part of the "free" sea. In certain instances this rule has been modified, as in the famous *Alleghenian* case, when, by a decision of the United States Supreme Court, Chesapeake Bay was declared to be territorial water of the United States, although something more than ten miles wide at the mouth.[70] There have been, moreover, a number of attempts made to have the limit extended, and if the original principle upon which it was based has any real validity, it should obviously be very much increased.[71] But the channel leading out of Hudson Bay is *sixty* miles across at the narrowest spot. Nevertheless, Canada can make out a reasonably good case for her claims. In the first place, the bay is completely surrounded by Canadian territory, and such conditions have been accepted as giving title in more than one case in the past. The United States has claimed the whole of Chesapeake and Delaware Bays;[72] Great Britain holds Conception Bay in Newfoundland, which has an entrance twenty miles wide and is forty miles deep; Russia even asserts jurisdiction over the White Sea.[73]

[69] This recognition arose originally from the fact that the state was felt to have special rights over such waters as it could defend properly; eighteenth century cannon had a range of some three miles, and the area of control was adopted from this distance. Hershey, *Essentials of International Public Law and Organization*, New York, 1927, pp. 295 ff.

[70] *Ibid.*

[71] *Idem*, p. 296, notes.

[72] Russia, and later the United States, once even went so far as to claim Bering Sea which, strictly speaking, is not a bay at all. See above, Chapter VI.

[73] Hershey, *op. cit.*, p. 302, notes.

A second, and perhaps more effective, justification of the Canadian case is to be found in the fact that for more than twenty years the claim has been uncontested. If objection was to be taken to this claim on the part of the Dominion, it should have been taken at the time the claim was first advanced. Failure to do so has given Canada a right to presume that other nations have agreed to her assertion of ownership. The lapse of such a period would seem to give the Dominion some right to claim that "a continuous and secular usage has sanctioned" her control.[74]

Nevertheless, the problem will probably be raised, and in all likelihood by the United States. It is certain to come up if Canada attempts to legislate for American fishermen who use the bay, and this the Dominion government will undoubtedly do. There is no reason to suppose, however, that the disagreement will at all seriously mar the good official relations that now exist between the two countries. But it would be well to have it settled during days of peace and before a crisis arises to clothe the issue in the lurid garments of a newspaper controversy. Now it can be decided in cool deliberation, and if necessary the result can be reached as a compromise. But once let the national passions be aroused by some dramatic development (the seizure of an American fishing vessel by a Canadian cutter, for example) and the whole issue will be inflamed by appeals to "national honor," "freedom of the seas," and similar catchwords. Then compromise will be impossible and a serious situation might well develop. The time to settle such difficulties is before they arise. It might well be submitted to the adjudication of the International Joint Commission.

D. The International Joint Commission.—One of the most important, most satisfactory, and most unique developments in the history of American-Canadian relations is the organization and successful operation of the International Joint Commission.

[74] See Scott, *Resolutions of the Institute of International Law, 1916;* quoted in Hershey, *op. cit.,* p. 302, note. On the whole question of Canada's claims see Balch, in *American Journal of International Law,* vol. VI (1912); pp. 409 ff.

It is unfortunate that the existence and labors of this commission are not better known. It is quite probable that the vast majority of the people of Canada and of the United States have never heard it mentioned, and yet it is one of the most interesting developments in the international relations of the twentieth century. It is an entirely unique organization, and one which deserves far more recognition than it has ever received.[75]

The International Joint Commission originated in an effort to develop a satisfactory method of dealing with the innumerable problems that were constantly arising as a result of the geographic and political relationships of the two countries. It was particularly designed "to prevent disputes regarding the use of boundary waters" but the terms of its creation also included the statement that it was intended "to settle all questions that are now (1909) pending between the United States and the Dominion of Canada involving the rights, obligations, or interests of either in relation to the other or the inhabitants of the other; along their common frontier, *and to make provision for the adjustment and settlement of all such questions as may hereafter arise."* [76] The tenth article of the treaty provides [77] specifically that "The Senate of the United States and His Majesty's Government with the consent

[75] This lack of publicity is, in one respect at least, a good thing: it goes far toward keeping the national and chauvinistic spirit from exercising a baneful influence on the work of the commission. During its 17 years of existence this commission has dealt with 23 cases and with only two exceptions the decisions have been rendered unanimously—an example of sanity and coöperation almost unheard of in international affairs. See the account of Dr. W. A. Riddell's address before the Security Committee of the League of Nations on February 22, 1928 in the Montreal *Star,* February 22, 1928. See also MacKay, "The International Trust Commission between the United States and Canada," *American Journal of International Law,* April, 1928, p. 292.

[76] Preamble to the Treaty of 1909, quoted in *Canada Year Book, 1926,* p. 971. Mr. Root, then Secretary of State, may well be considered the founder of the commission; he desired to establish "a judicial board, as distinguished from a diplomatic or partisan agency." Statement of L. J. Burpee, quoted in Falconer, *The United States as a Neighbour,* Cambridge, 1925, p. 78.

[77] *Treaties between Canada and the United States 1814–1925,* Ottawa, 1927, p. 312.

of the Governor-General-in-Council may by joint consent refer to the Commission any question or matter of difference that may arise between them or the inhabitants of the two countries." Thus the Commission is, in actual fact, a permanent tribunal for the settlement of whatever problems may arise between Canada and the United States. The only limit to its power is to be found in the possible unwillingness of the Senate or the Canadian Cabinet to submit to it problems of the most vital importance. Nevertheless, it is hardly an exaggeration to call it "a League of Nations for the particular benefit of Canada and the United States." [78]

The most important factor in the original creation of the Commission was the necessity of having some joint authority to settle problems that were annoyingly frequent along the international boundary. At a number of points along the frontier rivers cross from one country to the other; [79] elsewhere rivers and lakes form the boundary and islands were subjects of dispute; along the St. Lawrence difficulties were very frequent; while problems of water power and water supply were constantly arising.

The genesis of the Commission may be found in the International Waterways Commission established in 1902. The duties of this body were very limited, being restricted to the investigation of the lake and river waters along the border. They were expected to report on lake levels, condition of the water, the reasons for and effect of diversions, and similar subjects. [80] This Commission did excellent work, but its powers were too limited and by the Treaty of 1909 it was agreed to create the present International Joint Commission. [81] This treaty, in addition to the organization of the Commission, provided for free navigation of all boundary waters, including Lake Michigan and all canals uniting boundary waters, [82] provided for the protection of those who were injured

---

[78] *Canada Year Book, 1926*, p. 972.

[79] The most important of these are the Kootenay, Columbia, Saskatchewan, Red, and Richelieu.

[80] Falconer, *op. cit.*, p. 78.

[81] The text of this treaty, which was confirmed by the Canadian Parliament in 1911, is to be found in Statutes of 1911, 1–2, *George* V, c. 28.

[82] This had particular reference to the Welland Canal.

by diversion of these waters, and gave the commission mandatory power to legislate in regard to levels, obstructions, diversions, or pollution.

During the seventeen years of its existence the Commission has disposed of a large number of problems, any one of which, under the old system of diplomatic intercourse, might have dragged along indefinitely, and which would certainly have been attended with possibilities of serious friction. Among the more important problems undertaken have been the Sault Ste. Marie water power cases, which involved the levels of Lake Superior and consequently the interests of the cities on its shores, the Lake of the Woods investigation, the St. Lawrence River navigation and power investigation, and the diversion of the waters of the St. Mary and Milk Rivers for purposes of irrigation in Montana and Alberta.[83]

The commission as now organized consists of six members, three appointed by the President, three by the King.[84] They meet as a single body with an American chairman presiding when the meeting is in the United States; a Canadian is in the chair when the session is in Canada. There are two fixed meetings annually: in Washington in April, in Ottawa in October, but other meetings are held at frequent intervals.[85]

Up to the present there have been no cases submitted to the commission which involve its general powers. It is to be hoped that a precedent of this sort will be established in the near future. But whether employed or not, the power is there, and it is quite conceivable that it may yet prove of real importance in the history of American-Canadian relations. This will be the more likely if an intelligent and informed public opinion can be developed in the two countries to understand, to strengthen, and to support

[83] *Canada Year Book, 1926*, p. 972.

[84] The Canadian members are appointed, on the recommendation of the Canadian Prime Minister and his Cabinet.

[85] *Canada Year Book, 1926*, p. 972. The present members of the commission are: For the United States, Clarence D. Clark, Chairman; Fred T. Dubois; P. J. McCumber; William H. Smith, Secretary. For Canada, Charles A. Magrath, Chairman; Sir William H. Hearst; George W. Kyte; Lawrence J. Burpee, Secretary.

the work of this unique organization in the realm of international affairs.

E. Canada and the Monroe Doctrine.—It is impossible to conclude the discussion of American-Canadian relations without some mention of the Monroe Doctrine, and Canada's position with reference thereto. The suggestion that the Dominion should join the Pan-American Union has been given an added impetus as the result of the recent recognition of Dominion autonomy and the constantly growing importance of Canadian commercial relations with the United States and Hispanic America. It is quite clear that Canada will never formally recognize the present theory upon which the Monroe Doctrine is predicated—the theory, as Secretary Olney expressed it, that "the United States is practically sovereign upon this continent and its fiat is law upon the subjects to which it confines its interposition" [86]—but if the doctrine should evolve into a mutual agreement among the sovereign states of the western hemisphere, the possibility of Canadian participation will be tremendously enhanced.

The position of Canada at the present time is most anomalous. There can be little doubt that if the Dominion were attacked in a war of conquest by a European or an Asiatic power, the United States would intervene and prevent the establishment in the Dominion of a transoceanic sovereignty. Had Germany, for example, been successful in 1914 and undertaken to organize a colonial administration in Canada, it is quite certain that the United States would have intervened to prevent it. The mere suggestion of the possibility of a Japanese conquest of the Dominion would produce vigorous action on the part of the American government. In taking this action the United States would certainly invoke the authority of the Monroe Doctrine. Yet at the present time

[86] *United States Foreign Relations, 1895.* This statement is often referred to as being an extreme extension of the Monroe Doctrine. To candid observers, however, it must be clear that it is extreme only in its direct and forcible phrasing; the implications of the doctrine remain the same even when phrased in the mellifluous eloquence of a William Jennings Bryan.

Canada boasts of loyalty to a European King, and neither officially nor unofficially acknowledges the Monroe Doctrine as applicable to herself.[87] Yet if threatened with extreme and immediate danger, the Dominion would almost certainly invoke its protection. The contingency is, of course, remote, but nothing in the history of nations is impossible.

This situation is far from being satisfactory. The time seems to be rapidly approaching, if it has not already arrived, when the Monroe Doctrine should be revised in the light of modern conditions. A definite statement of policy prepared and endorsed by all the sovereign states of this hemisphere, conferring special favor upon none and common obligations upon all, with a specific recognition of equality in rights under a revised and strengthened code of international law, may be too much to expect as an immediate development, but it is the only basis upon which can be evolved a satisfactory solution of the present situation—a situation marked by dissatisfaction in Latin America, a refusal to face realities in Canada, and an inevitable, enforced, and somewhat domineering imperialism in the United States. The internationalization of the Monroe Doctrine would go far toward curbing the activities of the professional chauvinists of Latin America, and it would greatly strengthen the hands of those forces in the United States that are opposed to the policy of exploitation in the Caribbean and Central America. Finally, it would awaken Canada to a realization of her obligations as a member of the community of American states.

4. THE FUTURE RELATIONS OF THE TWO STATES

Canada and the United States have lived as neighbors for over one hundred years without resort to war. During that time problems have arisen that were not easy to remove, and yet the good sense of the two peoples has triumphed and the fragile bonds of peace have not been broken. The difficulties have not all been ended,

[87] The Monroe Doctrine itself is of course recognized by Canada and all other signatories of the covenant of the League of Nations.

but there is today less reason to contemplate strife between the Republic and the Dominion than at any time in their mutual history. If there were no other reason, the fact that Canada is too strong to be bullied, yet too weak to be a serious rival, would make war most improbable.

Among the immediate problems facing the governments at Ottawa and Washington are the perennial fisheries dispute, the Chicago water diversion which has affected the levels of the Great Lakes, and the power development on, and the canalization of, the St. Lawrence River. In the case of the St. Lawrence project—a development which would turn Toronto, Toledo, Fort William, and Chicago into ocean ports—there is an excellent illustration of how geographic and economic matters can at times cut across political boundaries. For here the provinces and states which border the Great Lakes are united in opposition to the states and provinces which oppose the opening of a deep passage to the sea: New York and Quebec are aligned against Ontario, Ohio, and Illinois.[88] None of these problems, obviously, is likely to result in a very serious disagreement.

There is only one real cloud on the horizon of American-Canadian relations, and even its existence is usually denied. It is probable that nothing but war between Great Britain and the United States can seriously affect the pacific intercourse of Canadians and Americans. The fact that such a war appears to be improbable does not justify the contention that it is impossible. Neither does the fact that it would, in all likelihood, result in the complete overthrow of our form of civilization.[89] In the prevention of such a calamity it may well be that Canada will play the part of mediator and interpreter. Of all countries in the world the Dominion has the most to lose by such a conflict.

Apart from this one contingency, the future relations of Canada and the United States should be characterized by a growing in-

---

[88] See *St. Lawrence Navigation and Power Project*, New York, Institute of Economics, 1928; see also the series of articles appearing in the Toronto *Star* during January and February, 1928.

[89] On the causes making for such a war and the probable role of Canada should it occur see Kenworthy, *op. cit.*

timacy and understanding, an increased coöperation, and a mutual respect. A vast development of trade and a greater ease and frequency of personal intercourse are inevitable in view of the growth of population and the rapid improvement in means of transportation. It is not unreasonable to believe that these changes will make for a more soundly based friendship. Unless some totally unforeseen catastrophe intervenes, the peaceful record of the past hundred years should be maintained on an even higher plane during the century to come. In a war-wracked world Canada and the United States must continue to prove that peace is not an impossible ideal, that states can best maintain their national honor not by resorting to the law of the jungle, but by reasoned and constructive friendship, conditioned by understanding, governed by justice, and founded on peace.

INDEX

INDEX

Aberdeen, Lord, appointed successor to Palmerston, 181; as appointing Lord Ashburton to settle Northeastern boundary dispute, 181; as praising Webster-Ashburton Treaty, 185; as offering compromise on Oregon question, 209 f.; Pakenham on poor geographical knowledge of, 237; as corresponding with Everett on *Washington* incident, 264

Abolition, See AMERICAN CIVIL WAR; BEECHER; SLAVERY

Acadia, British desire to retain, 350; as recipient of emigration from United States, 350

Act of Union of 1840, as result of Lord Durham's recommendations, 117

Adams, William, as poor representative of Great Britain at Ghent in 1814, 97

Adams, Charles Francis, on abrogation of Elgin-Marcy Treaty, 299

Adams, John, as American Peace Commissioner at Paris in 1783, 33; as advocating the hanging of all Loyalists, 42; on nature of Whig mobs, 45; on right of access to Newfoundland "banks" of United States citizens, 257; on Treaty of Paris, 258

Adams, John Quincy, as diplomatic representative of the United States at Ghent in 1814, 97; as protesting Russian claim to sovereignty over Bering Sea, 242

Adams, Samuel, letter of, to merchants of Montreal, 16

Aguilar, as sailing as far north as Oregon Territory in 1602, 189

Alabama, The, as allowed to escape, 138

Alabama claims, British Columbia considered as possible payment for, 160

Alaska, Russia as selling, to United States, 214; Canada as possible purchaser of, 229

Alaska boundary, 210 ff.; map of, 213; articles on which dispute over, was founded, 212 ff.; United States as refusing British offer of commission to settle, 215; various proposals for settlement of, 216; appointment of commissioners to settle, 217 ff.; Canadian opinion of delegates appointed by the United States to settle, 219 f.; problems involved in settlement of, 221 ff.; decisions of tribunal appointed to settle, 224 ff.; Canadian reception of decision on, 227 ff.; McKinley's attempt to settle, 306

Alaska Commercial Company, as leasing Pribiloff rookeries, 244

Alaska Fur Company, 245

Alberta, American-born population of, 325, 353; American immigration to, 338

Alexander I, Emperor, as asserting Russian jurisdiction over Bering Sea, 242, 248

Alexander VI, Pope, bull of, partitioning the New World, 200; see BUCHANAN

Alexander Archipelago, Treaty of 1824 as guaranteeing the United States the use of, 211 f.

Alleghenian case, 388

Alverstone, Lord, appointed to commission to settle Alaskan bound-

iii

The Church (Toronto), as opposed to annexation, 130
Church of England, as benefiting by Constitutional Act of 1791, 104; see WORSHIP
Church of Scotland, Constitutional Act of 1791 extended to, 105; see WORSHIP
Cincinnati (O.), Fenian activity in, 147
Citizen, The (Ottawa), on award of Bering Sea tribunal, 253
Civil War, see AMERICAN CIVIL WAR
Clark, see LEWIS AND CLARK
Clark, Hon. Champ, on annexation as result of reciprocity, 317
Clay, Henry, on Canadian desire for annexation, 64; territorial ambitions of, denounced in maritime provinces, 66; as diplomatic representative of United States at Ghent in 1814, 97; on proposed terms for settlement of Oregon boundary controversy, 196
Clergy, status óf, in New France, 8; influence of, in New France, 9; as displeased by abolition of compulsory tithing, 11; as regaining power in Canada after American attacks in 1778, 33; see ROMAN CATHOLIC CHURCH; CHURCH OF ENGLAND; CHURCH OF SCOTLAND; TITHES; WORSHIP
Cleveland, President Grover, as favoring reciprocity agreement with Canada, 304
Cobden, Richard, Great Britain as dominated by philosophy of, 124; hold on British Columbia as endangered by Great Britain's acceptance of doctrines of, 159; see BRIGHT
Cochrane, Admiral, as capturing city of Washington, 95; letter from, to Monroe on burning of Washington, 95
Cockburn, Sir George, as capturing city of Washington, 95
Colfax, as sympathizing with Fenian activities, 152

Colonies, Great Britain as willing to dispense with, in 1848, 124; see SPANISH COLONIES; BRITISH COLONIES; THIRTEEN COLONIES
Colonist, The (Victoria), on annexation of British Columbia, 163; on decision of Alaska boundary tribunal, 227; on American aggression in Bering Sea, 245; on award of Bering Sea tribunal, 253
Columbia River, discovered by Captain Robert Gray, 190, 200; as suggested boundary for Oregon Territory, 195; provision for free navigation of, included in treaty settling Oregon boundary dispute, 210
Commercial interests, War of 1812 not caused by, 62
Commercial union, Canadian movement for, 304 ff.; see RECIPROCITY
Conception Bay, held by Great Britain as territorial water, 388
Confederacy, Great Britain as subject of hatred in the, 138; British neutrality as making impossible a victory for the, 139; raids on northern states initiated from Canadian base by, 142 f.; see AMERICAN CIVIL WAR
Confederate Council on Commercial Treaties, as visiting Washington in 1866, 300
Confederation, see FEDERATION
Confederation League, organized in 1868, 164
Congress of the United States, see UNITED STATES CONGRESS, CONTINENTAL CONGRESS
Congress of Vienna, importance of, as distracting attention from Treaty of Ghent, 96
Connecticut, as refusing to supply militia in 1812, 78
Constitution, The, victories of, in War of 1812, 88
Constitutional Act of 1791, as creating Upper Canada, 49; as creating land endowment for Protestant